## ALSO BY SAMUEL M. KATZ

*No Shadows in the Desert: Murder, Vengeance,*
*and Espionage in the War Against ISIS*

*Beirut Rules: The Murder of a CIA Station Chief*
*and Hezbollah's War Against America* (with Fred Burton)

*Harpoon: Inside the Covert War Against International*
*Terrorism's Money Masters* (with Nitsana Darshan-Leither)

*The Ghost Warriors: Inside Israel's*
*Undercover War on Suicide Terror*

*Under Fire: The Untold Story of the Attack in Benghazi*
(with Fred Burton)

*Jihad in Brooklyn: The NYPD Raid*
*That Stopped America's First Suicide Bombers*

*Relentless Pursuit: The DSS and the Hunt for the al-Qaeda Terrorists*

*The Hunt for the Engineer: How Israeli Agents*
*Tracked the Hamas Master Bomber*

*The Night Raiders: Israel's Naval Commandos at War*

*Fire and Steel: Israel's 7th Armored Brigade*

*Anytime, Anywhere: On Patrol with the NYPD's Emergency Service Unit*

*Israel Versus Jibril: The Thirty-Year War Against a Master Terrorist*

*The Elite: The True Story of Israel's Secret Counterterrorist Unit*

*Soldier Spies: Israeli Military Intelligence*

# THE ARCHITECT
# OF ESPIONAGE

## THE MAN WHO BUILT ISRAEL'S MOSSAD INTO THE WORLD'S BOLDEST INTELLIGENCE FORCE

# SAMUEL M. KATZ

SCRIBNER

NEW YORK   AMSTERDAM/ANTWERP   LONDON   TORONTO   SYDNEY/MELBOURNE   NEW DELHI

Scribner
An Imprint of Simon & Schuster, LLC
1230 Avenue of the Americas
New York, NY 10020

First Scribner hardcover edition November 2025

SCRIBNER and design are trademarks of Simon & Schuster, LLC

Simon & Schuster strongly believes in freedom of expression and stands against censorship
in all its forms. For more information, visit BooksBelong.com.

For information about special discounts for bulk purchases, please contact
Simon & Schuster Special Sales at 1-866-506-1949 or business@simonandschuster.com.

The Simon & Schuster Speakers Bureau can bring authors to your live event.
For more information or to book an event, contact the Simon & Schuster Speakers Bureau
at 1-866-248-3049 or visit our website at www.simonspeakers.com.

Manufactured in the United States of America

1   3   5   7   9   10   8   6   4   2

Library of Congress Cataloging-in-Publication Data has been applied for.

ISBN 978-1-6680-5974-6
ISBN 978-1-6680-5976-0 (ebook)

*To the victims of October 7, 2023.*
*May all their memories be a blessing.*

# Contents

# Meir Dagan's Timeline

| | |
|---|---|
| 1945 | Born, Kherson, Ukraine |
| 1950 | Made aliyah (emigrated) to Israel with his parents and older brother |
| 1963 | Conscripted into the Israel Defense Forces (IDF) |
| 1967 | Fought as an officer in the Sinai Desert during the 1967 Six-Day War |
| 1970–72 | Created and commanded the Grenade Reconnaissance Unit, an undercover special operations counterterrorist unit in the Gaza Strip |
| 1973 | Fought in the 1973 Yom Kippur War as part of a special operations task force for the reserve division that crossed the Suez Canal into Egypt |

| 1974 | Transferred to the Armored Corps as a company and then battalion commander |
| 1980 | Named commander of the South Lebanon Region unit |
| 1982 | Promoted to the rank of colonel and given command of the 188th "Barak" Armored Brigade and fought in Lebanon during the 1982 Operation Peace for Galilee war |
| 1982 | Promoted to the rank of brigadier general and served as commander for the newly formed Lebanon Liaison Unit, which ran special forces and intelligence operations against Palestinian and Iranian-backed terrorist groups |
| 1985 | Named commander of the 36th Armored Division |
| 1987 | Appointed the chief of staff's advisor for terrorism affairs |
| 1991 | Appointed the head of the Operations Brigade in the IDF General Staff |
| 1993 | Appointed the assistant head of Operations IDF |
| 1995 | Retired from active military duty |
| 1996 | Appointed the head of the Prime Minister's Counterterrorism Bureau |

| | |
|---|---|
| 1996–99 | In the reserves, commanding officer of the Northern Corps |
| 2001 | Served as chief pollster for Ariel Sharon's election campaign |
| 2002 | Appointed as the head of the Mossad |
| 2011 | Ended his two terms as Mossad director |
| 2015 | Delivered the "We Deserve Better Speech" in Tel Aviv |
| 2016 | Succumbed to liver cancer at the age of seventy-one |

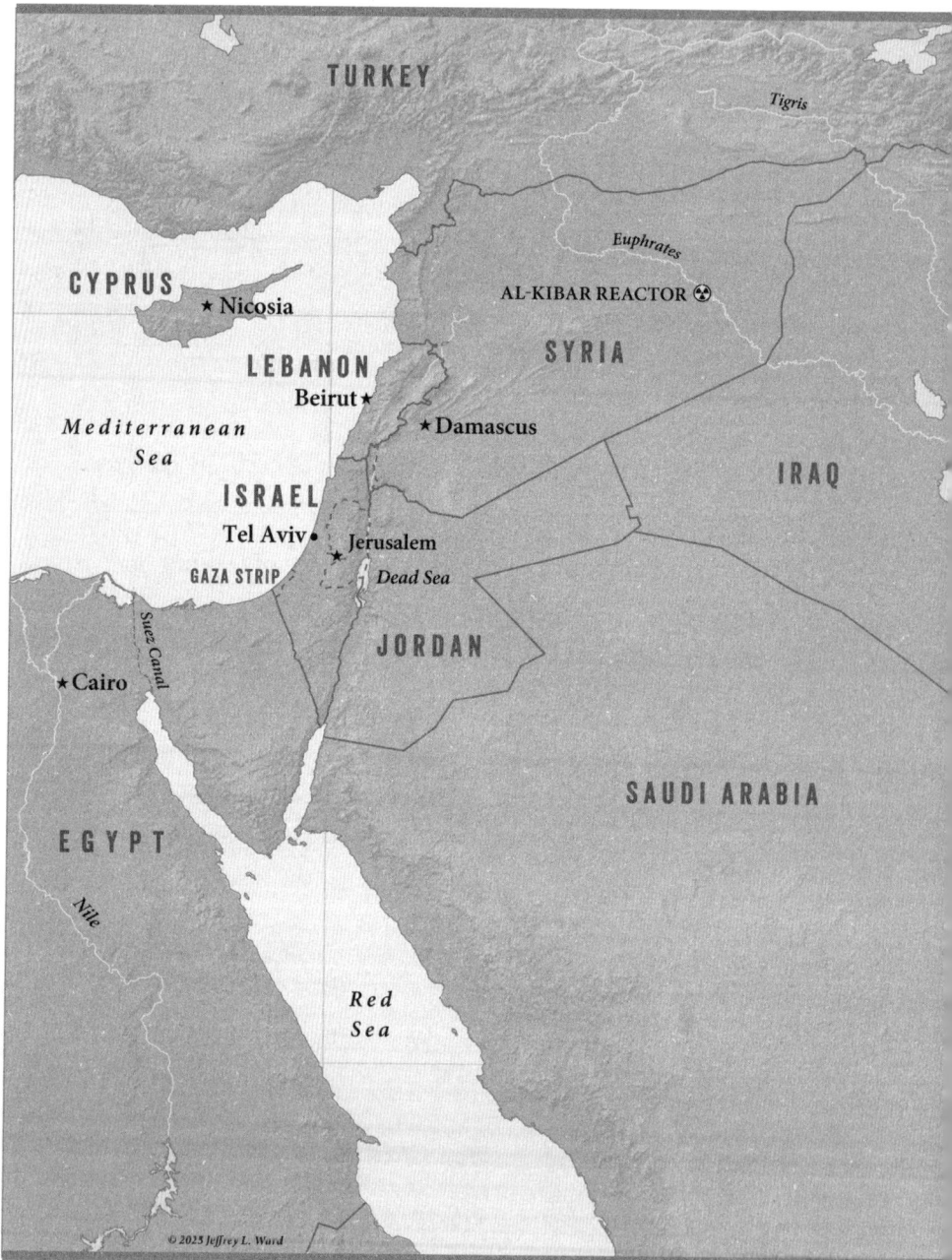

TURKEY

*Tigris*

*Euphrates*

CYPRUS

★ Nicosia

AL-KIBAR REACTOR ☢

SYRIA

LEBANON

Beirut ★

★ Damascus

*Mediterranean*
*Sea*

IRAQ

ISRAEL

Tel Aviv •

★ Jerusalem

GAZA STRIP

*Dead Sea*

JORDAN

★ Cairo

*Suez Canal*

SAUDI ARABIA

EGYPT

*Nile*

*Red*
*Sea*

© 2025 Jeffrey L. Ward

# MEIR DAGAN'S MIDDLE EAST

Caspian
Sea

Tehran ★

IRAN

FORDOW NUCLEAR FACILITY ☢

☢ NATANZ NUCLEAR FACILITY

★ Baghdad

N

*Tigris*

*Euphrates*

0 Miles        100        200        300

0 Kilometers    200    300

KUWAIT

Persian
Gulf

Manama ★

BAHRAIN

QATAR

Dubai •

★ Doha

★ Riyadh

Abu Dhabi ★

U. A. E.

# A Note to the Reader

L ike many non-native-born Israelis, Meir Dagan adopted a Hebrew
surname, changing it from Huberman to Dagan while he was a captain in the army and determined to make a career in the military. When
the Jewish state was born in 1948, many newcomers opted to Hebraicize
their names to fit in, appear more Israeli, and shed any connection to the
lands where their families had perished in the gas chambers of Eastern
Europe or fled the pogroms of the Arab Diaspora in Damascus, Tripoli,
Aden, and Baghdad. Forging a new identity was both psychologically
refreshing and an act of defiance that the new Jewish spirit would not
be broken.

Mostly, though, the new immigrants wanted to emulate the Sabra,
the name adopted by native-born Israelis who worked the land and built
the foundation of the new country. The Sabras were named after the
edible desert cactus growing in Israel that had a hard and prickly exterior but was sweet on the inside. The Sabra was unapologetic—strong,
unflinching, and stubbornly determined. The Sabras were in control,
and for those who had survived the camps or the long trek across the
Middle East, assimilating with a Hebrew last name was a career booster.

To avoid confusion, I will limit the use of the surname Huberman
as much as possible and refer to the tenth head of the Mossad simply
as Meir or his Hebraicized name Dagan in the post-1973 chapters.

In the world that existed before the Hamas invasion of southern Israel on October 7, 2023, news of this book was greeted with great excitement inside some of the capitals of the Arab nations. Throughout his career, Meir Dagan had been an honored guest inside the intelligence headquarters and palaces of the Middle East. Those who had worked with him and those who knew him as a trusted friend wanted to go on the record and share their views about this remarkable soldier, spy chief, and statesman. But the Hamas attack against Israel changed everything. Although these spies and royals privately wished that Israel would teach Hamas a lesson and wipe it off the face of the earth, publicly the message had to be one of solidarity with the Palestinian people. Relations between Israel and the Arab world—on every level—became frosty. Many officials who worked with Dagan and admired his capabilities could no longer have their quotes about an Israeli spy chief featured in a book. To protect the anonymity of those who still wanted their reflections of Dagan known, I have used pseudonyms when and where applicable.

This same format has been applied to certain retired members of Israel's intelligence community who wanted to be quoted on the record. After lifetimes of working in the shadows, these veterans headed for careers in the private sector after retiring from active duty. However, some, especially those who consulted throughout the Middle East, returned to the shadows following October 7. Others, wary of the coordinated campaign in the international courts, the media, and social media platforms targeting Israeli officials past and present as "war criminals" for the conflict to eradicate Hamas in Gaza, preferred not to be named, even though they are years out of the game. As a result, and to protect their identities, when applicable, quotes will be attributed to pseudonyms or used anonymously. A lot of information about the Mossad was made public after October 7 and especially following the assassination of Hamas leader Ismail Haniyeh on July 31, 2024, and the exploding beepers and walkie-talkies in the hands—and on the chests—of Hezbollah operatives on September 17 and 18, 2024. But a lot still must stay in the vault, even details about events that transpired decades earlier.

Although Meir Dagan died in 2016, subsequent events have underscored his dedication to the preservation of the Jewish state and confirmed his prescience in matters of intelligence and special operations as a measure to safeguard Israel from the permanent threats the country faces.

# The World View from the Head of Mossad's Office

*Leadership is the ability to move people above and beyond normal
circumstances, especially in those cases where people are afraid or
unsure of themselves*

—Meir Dagan, April 2009, from a speech to graduates
of a command course at Mossad headquarters

When a newly appointed Mossad director enters headquarters on
his first day at work, he gazes out of his office window and tries to
figure out how to steer a safe course for Israel through the crosshairs
of a dangerous world. Being the head of the Mossad demands making
daily life-and-death command decisions. Israel's very security hangs in
the balance of actions taken or not, intelligence assessed correctly, and
the collateral damage of information processed errantly. The pressures
of the job are unfathomable.

The head of the Mossad must balance the operational necessity of
decisive action with the tempered mandates of patience and restraint.
He is an administrator who manages a large and often bureaucratic
organization. The director must also be a general who navigates a
treacherous battlefield with a secret army posted to locations—many
fraught with danger—around the world. The Mossad chief represents
Israel to other members of the global intelligence fraternity so that he

can address critical issues of tactical and strategic interests that are of common concern in friendly and not-so-friendly capitals around the world. The Mossad director is Israel's national emissary in talks about war, peace, and all the dangerous gray areas in between.

The most sensitive topics, urgent matters of national security and strategic requirements, are discussed at Mossad headquarters near Tel Aviv, but any plans must be authorized inside the prime minister's office in Jerusalem. The director must know how to sell complex missions to the prime minister, often those involving significant risk and potential fallout that are critical to the safeguarding of the nation, and he must argue against politically motivated plans that place Israel's national security at risk. The position of Mossad director is a balancing act of imperatives and opportunities. It has been called the most difficult job in all of Israel.

Meir Dagan dreamed his entire life of sitting in the director's chair. Few men in Israel's history were more suited for the position. He was born in the ashes of the Holocaust, in what is today Ukraine. His parents were burdened by the loss of suffering in the Second World War, and it instilled in their youngest son the importance of strength and survival, and the need for a Jewish homeland as an insurance policy against any other attempts to exterminate his people. Dagan became a career soldier and was known as a special operations and counterterrorism specialist.

Throughout his thirty-two years in uniform, he fought in three conventional wars and countless counterterrorist campaigns. The scars on his body were landmarks of the battles he fought. His mind always thought twelve steps forward. For a man who fought the enemy at point-blank range, he possessed an unrivaled comprehension of the global strategic reality. His boundless imagination created new tactics and strategies in the fight against terrorism and Israel's enemies who sought nuclear weapons.

On the conventional battlefield, Dagan was blessed with an extra helping of natural daring and courage. Leadership was in his DNA, and he developed a distinctive brand of command that would carry him up the ranks and eventually earn him the rank of general. Dagan viewed his rank as a great responsibility and an honor. He was not just a soldier.

He possessed an insatiable fascination with the world around him that he satisfied through painting and sculpting, listening to classical music, and travel. Dagan had a voracious appetite for constant adventure and learning, and he believed that he could learn from everyone—from the president of the United States to the workers who cooked and cleaned at Mossad headquarters.

Dagan entered office as Israel's spy chief a year after the 9/11 attacks and two years into the second intifada, a Palestinian suicide bombing war against Israel's cities that would leave over one thousand dead. The world changed in 2001, following the al-Qaeda attacks against the United States, and the Mossad would have to change with it. He was the perfect choice to lead Israel's foreign espionage at this dangerous crossroads of history.

The new world order demanded that the Mossad no longer rest on the laurels of its past exploits. It had to be more dynamic, intuitive, and devious than its enemies. Its actions needed to be decisive. Dagan reinvigorated the service with a newfound appreciation of the pricelessness of intelligence as an *actionable* commodity, and he instilled a decisive way of thinking so that Israel's spies did not react to disaster, but rather did everything in their power and their bag of dirty tricks to preempt, forewarn, and punish before the fact. Under Dagan's leadership, the Mossad would no longer be a service provider to A'man, the Israeli military intelligence directorate and the nation's largest espionage force. The Mossad would become *the* service. After he took the elevator to his new office at Mossad HQ, Dagan's first order of the day was that the agency would not only gather intelligence on the threats facing Israel but would also act *decisively* to stop them. He used a lifetime of lessons learned as a warrior and special operator to turn the Mossad into an instrument of power and a weapon of strategic diplomacy.

Under Dagan, new tactics, like covert financial warfare, became part of the Mossad's arsenal. Old tactics, such as targeted killings, became new core strategies. Enemies of Israel who posed a threat to the country and the Jewish people were justifiable targets. Although Israel was a high-tech country, called Startup Nation, and enjoyed a First World standard of living and liberal beliefs, the country was a part of the world that had the explosive potential for savage retribution, where

vengeance was always preemptive, even if it sometimes gave the outward appearance of being purely punitive, and violence was always a
measure of last resort.

Israel spoke to its friends—and especially its rivals and enemies—
through its spymasters. Jordan's King Hussein called the practice "clandestine diplomacy,"[1] and Dagan, like his predecessors and successors,
placed enormous emphasis on developing nurturing friendships across
the Arab and Islamic worlds. These nations—those that had diplomatic
ties to Israel, like Egypt and Jordan, and those that did not at the time,
like Morocco and the Kingdom of Saudi Arabia—welcomed the Mossad
director inside their palaces and headquarters to talk of peace and to
prevent war.[2] Dagan was not only respected in these circles, but he was
also revered. *Al-Ahram*, the influential Egyptian newspaper founded in
1876, called him "Superman." In other circles, he was known as the "King
of the Shadows." His behind-the-scenes work in the Arab world laid the
foundation for the peace treaties that would ultimately be known as the
Abraham Accords. The spy chiefs from these nations understood that
the Middle East was best served by forming a common barrier against
the nefarious aspirations that emanated from Iran and its proxies.

The Iranians created Hezbollah shortly after the Khomeini-led revolution and Israel's 1982 military adventure in Lebanon, as an expan-
sionist extension of the Islamic Republic's war against the West, which
serendipitously produced a Shiite Crescent across from the Persian
Gulf to the Mediterranean. Hamas, an offshoot of Egypt's Sunni Muslim Brotherhood, and the Islamic Jihad were opportunistic pawns that
Tehran could use to attack Israel—a relatively inexpensive and risk-free
way for Tehran to fight the Jewish state to the last dying Palestinian.
Dagan understood that Hamas and Hezbollah did not pose existential
threats to the Jewish state. But an Iran on the march, especially one
equipped with nuclear weapons, did.

Prime ministers lost sleep worrying about yesterday's polls and
tomorrow's primaries. Generals and spy chiefs lay awake at night
worrying about long-term threats. During his time in office, and until
his death, Dagan was outspoken in his belief that Israel did not have the
means to unilaterally and permanently destroy Iran's nuclear aspirations.

He understood military overreach and the disastrous implications that a foolhardy gesture of first-strike bravado would entail for Israel. Dagan also knew that Israel had a trump card in stopping Iran: its ultra-strategic relationship with the United States. Solidifying the intelligence ties between the CIA and Mossad was a strategic goal for all heads of Israel's intelligence agency, but it was imperative for Dagan. Years of cooperation and mutual interests had forged a de facto operational alliance between the two nations, where the two services worked together to settle old scores and prevent nuclear thresholds from being crossed, but Dagan used his years in office to nurture, strengthen, and expand them beyond what had been thought possible. The bonds were too important to be left solely in the hands of elected officials.

Four CIA directors viewed Dagan as a respected military man, a wise counsel, and a full-fledged partner. He was but one of a handful of foreign intelligence chiefs to be an honored guest inside the White House. President George W. Bush considered him a trusted friend and wrote that he was the most impressive world leader he had ever met face-to-face.[3]

Dagan would have been relieved that the pillars of the countries' relationship stood unflinching and strong the day after what transpired on October 7, when the United States provided Israel with a needed military buffer against Iran and its surrogates. But he would have been shattered by the fact that both the Shin Bet, Israel's internal security agency, and A'man, the IDF's Military Intelligence Branch, had received the Hamas playbook for invading Israel, code-named Jericho Wall, two years before the October 7 attack and done nothing with the information.[4] Operational intelligence, according to Dagan, was a precious commodity that cost lives and national resources to acquire and was never to be wasted. That responsibility came with the burden of accountability. Israel's intelligence services, Dagan believed and preached to anyone who would listen, were the guardrails of Israel's democracy and the country's very survival. They could never be caught by surprise, by what the 9/11 Commission called a "failure of imagination."[5]

It was easy, perhaps, for modern and democratic Israel, one protected by the IDF and its intelligence services, and bolstered by a European standard of living and high-tech innovations, to forget that it was situated in a Middle East populated by the likes of al-Qaeda, Hamas, ISIS, and Hezbollah. But that memory lapse was one of the factors that had allowed the horrible day of October 7 to transpire—a day that shattered one of the foundations that made Israel an exceptional nation, a nation that existed to protect Jewish lives—those who were third-generation Israeli, those whose parents came from Arab and European lands, and those who still lived in the Diaspora—from the savagery that had befallen the Jewish people for centuries. Protecting Israel's citizens from harm was the most important mission of the country's elected leaders and its security heads.

*           *           *

The man who leads the Mossad must be laser-focused on the present with one eye always looking ahead at what the future could bring. But Dagan's vision was directed by somewhere in the past, and to him, his mandate and the responsibilities it carried were very personal. Every morning when he entered his office and at night before he went home, Dagan looked at a black-and-white photograph of SS officers laughing at his maternal grandfather moments before he was executed in Nazi-occupied Poland. Every visiting head of a service, including those from Arab nations, along with Mossad officers and agents about to be sent overseas on missions vital to the safeguarding of the Jewish state, looked at that photograph as well, as a narrative tool that Dagan used to speak of the importance of the possible sacrifice that Israel's warriors in the shadows would have to make to ensure that Jews would never again be systematically targeted for annihilation. That was his sworn life's calling. Meir Dagan wore that responsibility as a badge of honor. It is what defined his life as a soldier and a spy chief. He realized the inescapable symbolism of being the first and last head of Israeli intelligence who had been born inside the ashes of Hitler's Europe.

John Le Carré once wrote that the intelligence services are the only real expression of a nation's character. Le Carré was Meir Dagan's favorite novelist,[6] and he believed that these sentiments held enormous importance. The character of Israel's espionage services—and Dagan himself—were defined by the Jewish history and the battles Israel has been forced to fight to not only survive but also thrive in the face of relentless threat and adversity. The ethos of this responsibility required that Israel's foreign intelligence agency be more innovative, daring, and audacious than its enemies, in defense of the Jewish state and the Jewish people around the world. Every chief of Israel's national intelligence service has shared that daunting responsibility.

Thirteen men have led *Ha'Mossad Le'Modi'in U-La-Tafkidim Meyuchadim*, the Institute for Intelligence and Special Tasks, between the spy agency's creation in 1949 and the Hamas terror attack of October 7. Meir Dagan, who led the organization from 2002 to 2011, was the most remarkable and impactful. His actions, leadership, and special brand of defiant chutzpah left a mark on the service he led, and the Middle East in which it operated, that would last for years to come.

# Away from the Office
# One Sunny Fall Day

Under normal circumstances during the early-morning hours of an autumn weekday, the twelve-mile drive from the luxurious apartments in northern Tel Aviv to Ben Gurion International Airport should take less than a half hour. But nothing was normal when the armored blue BMW sedan ferrying Mossad director Meir Dagan raced toward the VIP terminal in the darkness before the first light of that warm autumn dawn. Dagan, a career soldier, was used to starting the day hours before sunrise. An aide and a bodyguard held on for dear life while R.,* his trusted driver, displayed his Le Mans skills as the vehicle maneuvered across the highway at top speed. Dagan caressed his pipe as he read some files in the backseat, unfazed by the acceleration. The car reached the tarmac in only ten minutes. Dagan nodded a glance of approval at his driver and then checked his watch to await the motorcade of his travel partner. The Mossad director religiously believed that twenty minutes early was on time. It had been drilled into him during thirty-two years of military service. He never kept others waiting and detested when others did it to him, especially the prime minister. Benjamin Netanyahu was always late.

---

* Identity withheld for security reasons.

It was routine for the head of the Mossad to travel overseas in secret, incognito, or even in disguise. But the prime minister's schedule was a matter of public record, and whenever and wherever the prime minister went, he was accompanied by a phalanx of reporters. But not this morning. The press had been given a cover story that Netanyahu was visiting a secret army unit in the south, to throw them off his trail, and he left the official residence on Balfour Street traveling incognito with a smaller-than-usual security package of armed agents from Unit 730, the Shin Bet's dignitary protection force. The prime minister made it to the tarmac with no fanfare. Both Dagan and Netanyahu boarded a private jet—a loaner from a well-to-do-Israeli businessman—with a small contingent of armed men. This trip was not on the official schedule. It was a mission of high-stakes covert diplomacy.

The Mossad director traveled with an aide. Netanyahu brought Uzi Arad, a former high-ranking Mossad official and his trusted national security advisor, and Major General Meir Kalifi, his military secretary.[1] Only a handful of security men were on board the flight. The aircraft had been swept for listening devices or anything else that could be used to compromise the passengers. For security reasons, the pilot was only told of the flight path—one cleared with the intelligence services of several friendly nations—shortly before the flight was cleared for takeoff. The day's new sun had risen when the jet raced into the sky. There were plenty of water bottles and snacks stashed on board. It would take approximately three hours for the plane to reach Russia and make its final approach to a military airfield near the Black Sea port city of Sochi. Russian president Vladimir Putin was waiting in Bocharov Ruchey, his palatial summer residence, along with representatives from his intelligence services. Officers from Russia's SVR, the country's foreign intelligence service, monitored the flight's progression.

Shortly after being elected to office in February 2009, Netanyahu had taken several day trips with his security inner circle. Most were to nearby destinations—Amman, Cairo, or elsewhere in the Arab world—and undertaken far from the prying eyes of the media.[2] But the meeting with Putin was different. It was a high-stakes huddle concerning an Israeli national security imperative: controlling Iran's aggressive nuclear ambitions. Dagan and Netanyahu wanted to keep the meeting secret. Still, they also knew that America's intelligence agencies monitored Putin's whereabouts around the clock and that news of the secret trip would reach Barack Obama in the PDB, the President's Daily Briefing. That was intentional, as well.

Dagan had spent seven years working closely with President George W. Bush, his National Security Council, and the CIA. The American president adored the scrappy Israeli spy chief. Dagan enjoyed an unprecedented relationship with Bush. "How many heads of a foreign espionage service that is not part of the Five Eyes* are invited to the White House?" a former Mossad division chief would reflect.[3] Israel had known what to expect from its growing operational and intelligence-sharing alliance with the United States during the Bush years, but Obama was an unknown equation who had given signals that America would not be an unconditional strategic friend to the Jewish state.

Netanyahu's first meeting with Obama, in May 2009, when both were just elected as heads of state, was a disaster. Obama disciplined the Israeli prime minister about settlements and the stalled peace treaty. A month later, the American president selected Egypt as the first destination of his global travels and the launch of his foreign policy agenda. The opening sentence of Obama's speech at Cairo University was "I've come here to Cairo to seek a new beginning between the United States and Muslims around the world."[4] "Muslims around the world" covered the Palestinian issue. It meant an American attempt at a reproachment with the Islamic Republic of Iran. Containing—if not deterring—Iran from its nuclear ambitions through covert actions and economic isolation had been the primary objective of Dagan's Mossad.

Putin's summer palace was straight out of the luxurious holdings of Peter the Great, or the lair belonging to a James Bond villain. The grounds were meticulously maintained, and flora was common in the

---

* The Five Eyes is an Anglosphere espionage service alliance formed between the United States and Great Britain following the end of the Second World War but later expanded to include Canada, Australia, and New Zealand. The arrangement was top secret for years (only officially acknowledged in 2005) and remains the world's most important—and effective—intelligence-sharing arrangement.

warm weather of Sochi. A brownish-gray clay roof complemented the building's pale stone exterior. The Black Sea could be seen from the main entrance. Marble buffed to a mirror shine guided visitors into the main parlor and off to rooms decorated with light blue carpets and chandeliers adorned with prisms made of the finest Czech crystals. Paintings depicting Russian military glory hung on the walls. This was not the home of a former KGB agent who'd spent his formative years in Eastern Europe. It was the residence of a czar.

A motorcade from Putin's FSB security detail rushed the Israelis toward the residence. The convoy was low-key by Russian standards; the secret police had hours earlier, for precaution, cleared the route of any traffic. Under normal circumstances, a platoon of the Russian Presidential Regiment would have been standing at attention in their dress uniforms, polished SKS assault rifles and sabers at the ready. Photographers would have been on alert to document the arrival. But this meeting never happened. There would be no official mention of it anywhere.

The Russian president, who waited for no one, looked forward to seeing Dagan. He respected world leaders, but it was understood that he admired the Israeli spy chief. The Mossad director in Putin's eyes was a warrior and a no-nonsense shadow warfare professional. Netanyahu did not share the Russian president's sentiments. The prime minister had inherited a Mossad director who had served two previous Israeli leaders and was nearing the end of his second term. Netanyahu did not like anyone who had previously worked for someone else.[5] He, as it has been said, viewed Dagan as boorish. But Dagan always chuckled when he was looked upon that way based on his outward appearance and mannerisms, joking that "he only looked simple."

Yet Dagan had an infectious personality with a strong sense of humor. Part of his charm was that he projected a sense of being someone who had emerged from a hardscrabble existence out of defiant dedication, as an act of spite and mission; someone who confidently thrived for all the right reasons. Dagan tethered his everyman first impression to the computer-like analytical mind of an unrivaled strategic savant.

Putin, the politician, understood the lies that world leaders were compelled to tell their public and foreign counterparts at clandestine summits such as this one in Sochi that fall day in 2009. The former intelligence officer knew all too well about the strategic implication that those lies could conceal or create, enhancing his appreciation of Dagan's position and presence. Netanyahu would never admit it, but he was jealous that being the gatekeeper of vital aspects of Israel's national security made Dagan in many ways the most important man in Israel. Netanyahu hated walking in anyone's shadow. Dagan understood the military chain of command and the respect that came with protocol and higher office and realized that he was in Sochi to support his prime minister and advance the security needs of the State of Israel. But Putin understood Dagan's world better than Netanyahu's, and the two men, one a former KGB spy and the other a spymaster, had a natural rapport. "Putin trusted Dagan," one of the Israeli spy chief's deputies explained. "Politicians could lie, it was part of their game, but those in the intelligence business knew who could be counted on. Dagan's word was good as gold. And the Russian president knew it."[6]

Nurturing diplomatic relations with Putin was an Israeli national necessity—for mutual interests, but also because of conflicting regional objectives. In fighting the Chechen offshoots of al-Qaeda, Russia was a frontline state in the war against Islamic fundamentalism, but Moscow was also the primary patron and protector of Syria, a narco-terrorist police state that had tried two years earlier to go hot with a North Korean nuclear reactor that the Mossad and the Israeli Air Force took out. Syria was also a gateway for Iranian intelligence and proxy operations against Israel in Lebanon and around the world. Putin's espionage services knew all the actors in the Middle East, and they exerted influence on everyone—Hezbollah, Hamas, the Islamic Jihad—the good, the bad, and the ugly. It was in Israel's strategic interest to keep Putin as a sometimes friend and an acknowledged adversary. The spies were the ones who maintained the communications.

Russia was a major arms supplier to Iran and, more importantly, the principal source of reliable military spare parts that the Islamic Republic needed to maintain aging Soviet-era missile systems Tehran had purchased from North Korea, Libya, and just about any black-market source eager to skirt Western sanctions and Israeli and American intelligence.

Putin's spies knew a lot of what was going on inside the Islamic Revolutionary Guard Corps and the nuclear facilities conducting the research and development needed to turn Iran into a nuclear power.

The Israeli mission to Sochi was an effort for the two most important men in Israel to explain to Putin that Jerusalem's position on Iran acquiring nuclear capabilities would not change because of the new American administration. Netanyahu and Dagan wanted to hear if Putin could provide any new insight into what was happening; the two were certain that the Russian president and his security advisors at the meeting wanted a glimmer of any tidbits of intelligence that the Israelis thought it wise to share. Such meetings were always exercises of give and take, a "you show me yours and I'll show you mine" of carefully chosen diplo-speak and high-stakes brinksmanship. The Israelis respected Putin but knew he would probably be unhelpful and possibly even duplicitous.

Details of what was discussed behind closed doors inside the eavesdropping-proof presidential study in Bocharov Ruchey, like the meeting itself, have never been made public, but Iran was the primary topic on the prime minister's agenda.[7] It is believed that the meeting, an exchange of positions and intelligence, lasted over two hours—a long time for a conference between two heads of state and their intelligence chiefs. Trusted interpreters made sure that nothing was lost in translation.

The meeting ended with handshakes. An honor guard escorted the Israeli contingent to their awaiting armored vehicles and the quick race back to the tarmac. The private jet was cleared for immediate takeoff. The Israelis did not utter a word until Russian airspace was far behind them.

The aircraft touched down at Ben Gurion International Airport as the day's sunlight headed west over the Mediterranean Sea. Netanyahu was reunited with his protective package and driven to the Aquarium, as the glass-enclosed prime minister's office in Jerusalem was known. A news reporter had gotten wind of the secret trip to Sochi, and staffers would need to quash the story on national security grounds. Israel had a vibrant free press, but reports were subject to military censorship.

The Mossad director got into his awaiting armored car, lit his pipe, and ordered his driver to take him back to headquarters. His deputies and division heads waited in the conference room. They knew it would be a long night at the office and had instructed the kitchen that they could expect to work well into the evening. What had been discussed in Sochi mattered.

Dagan demanded that any sit-down with him, whether in his office on a Friday morning to talk about personal matters or around a conference table with the heads of all the operational branches, be predicated on the concept of an open forum of ideas. Dagan hated people who went along for the sake of going along. He despised yes-men. When he briefed his deputies about what had been discussed with Putin, he demanded a plan of action.

The pillar of Dagan's espionage doctrine during his time at the Mossad was simple: not a shekel would be spent on air travel, no expenditure of manpower and resources would be invested, and no lives would be risked in the tradecraft of operations in targeted countries unless it would produce actionable intelligence. If the by-product of covert action was not likely to lead to something tangible that advanced Israel's national security and the Mossad's role in achieving that goal, he would not authorize the effort. Meir Dagan's clandestine universe centered around the endgame.

The meetings at headquarters often lasted well past midnight. Plans were discussed. The merits and risks of possible action were debated. Some of the most fantastic and awe-inspiring operations in the history of the Mossad were conceived in Dagan's office late at night while he smoked one of the endless number of pipes on his desk and drank a cup of dark tea talking to a deputy who sat across from him exploring the envelope of what was operationally feasible, in a room engulfed by the fragrance and cloud of pipe smoke. Wild ideas were tossed back and forth between Dagan and those he admired and trusted most. The building was often empty, just two men talking when both were too tired to head home. "This was when we were most creative, and the boldest in our thoughts, in figuring out ways to deal with the people and the powers that threatened Israel," a former branch chief remembered with a smile, "this was when history was made, the kind that in most cases can never be published."[8]

Some of the ideas tossed around as dawn's first sunlight neared would play out weeks or months later. Others, the nucleus of outside-the-box fantastic notions, would play out in Beirut, Damascus, and Tehran many years later.

The shadow war to stop Israel's enemies from posing an existential threat to the Jewish state was an around-the-clock effort, but the meetings were also forums for an open and sometimes painfully frank sharing of ideas. There were enormous risks—to lives and national interests—in every operational blueprint and mission conceived in that room, and Dagan wanted everyone's thoughts and apprehensions vocalized—especially his own. As he often said, "Anyone who doesn't cast doubt is not suited to be in the intelligence profession."[9]

# BOOK ONE

# SOLDIER

# CHAPTER 1

# Proof of Life

On the morning of January 30, 1945, a twenty-five-year-old Polish woman named Mina Huberman was admitted to the maternity ward of a hospital in the Ukrainian city of Kherson, a major port on the Dnieper River liberated months earlier by the Red Army. She was malnourished and in labor. Hours later, a nurse emerged to deliver the good news to her husband Shmuel that a large and healthy son had been born into the world. The proud parents named their child Meir, Hebrew for "one who shines." Contrary to the story either mistakenly repeated or conveniently manufactured, the young baby who would come to be known as Meir Dagan was not born on a train in the smoldering ruins of eastern Ukraine in the closing days of the Second World War.[1]

Meir's birth—and the fact that Shmuel and Mina were even alive— was a true miracle considering that they had escaped Hitler's Final Solution after five years of hard labor in a desolate Soviet work camp. Shmuel and Mina were Polish Jews from Łuków, located sixty miles southwest of Warsaw and north of Lublin. Łuków was nothing more than a shtetl, a small island of Jewish faith, life, and cohesive community. At one point in the early twentieth century, three-quarters of the Jews on the Continent lived in a shtetl, often at the mercy of Czarist pogroms and greedy Polish landlords.

Life inside the shtetl was simple and poor. It was centered around the dream of family success and community survival and anchored by the spiritual bonds of the Jewish faith. The synagogue was the foundation of the community, and the rabbis were their pillars. Prayers—and any official acts of worship—were always conducted in Hebrew, as were religious studies, the anchor of the shtetl. Young boys were schooled in a *cheder*, the Hebrew word for room, where a primary curriculum of religious studies was often taught in the rabbi's home or an extension of the synagogue. Girls were educated at home by their mothers. Yiddish, a German amalgamation of Hebrew, Aramaic, and Slavic languages, was the glue that connected most Jews throughout Europe. It was spoken, read, and used in literature and comedy, by peasants in the shtetl, as well as among the more assimilated Jews of Eastern Europe who lived in cities like Warsaw and Krakow, and those who managed to escape the misery and poverty and seek freedom from persecution in the United States.

The Jews of Poland, even those who could trace their family trees hundreds of years ago, were outsiders, unwelcome and despised. Antisemitism was the currency of day-to-day life in the postwar remnants of the Czarist Russian empire, and Zionism, the yearning for a Jewish homeland, had become a twentieth-century hope against the hatred and violence that those in Łuków and hundreds of similar communities had endured for centuries. The return to Zion, the reunification of the Jewish people and their ancestral home, and the creation of a paradise mosaic of redemption, return, and faith, became a small glimmer of hope for some who no longer wanted to be targeted as second-class citizens in the land of their birth. *Der Judenstaat*, Theodor Herzl's manifesto and the blueprint for modern Zionism, was a bestseller in Yiddish. It was the book of choice for young and rebellious men and women who demanded a better—and safer—future.

Nineteen-year-old Shmuel Huberman was one of those rebels. The young man was short and stocky, handsome with dark eyes and an ample supply of charisma. He was a community leader of the local chapter of the *Hashomer Ha'Tzair*, or the Young Guard, a socialist-Zionist organization, and he dreamed of one day building a new secular nation in the ancient homeland of the Jewish people in what was British

Mandate Palestine. He was also madly in love with sixteen-year-old Mina Slushni, a pretty and petite girl with raven-colored hair, who was known for her contagious smile. Her parents were merchants and very observant; an uncle was a noble rabbi, and the family was highly revered for their strict adherence to the Torah. Mina's parents objected strongly to Shmuel, only strengthening the young people's attraction.

The two teenagers defied their parents and committed an unthinkable crime in the close-minded world of the Łuków shtetel—they traveled to a nearby town, found a rabbi, and eloped.[2] They were outcasts for three years, until the birth of their son Eliezer led the families to reconcile. And then the Germans invaded Poland.

The Wehrmacht, with the SS in tow, seized Łuków on September 19, 1939—eighteen days after invading Poland and launching the Second World War. There were no legitimate targets near the town, but the Luftwaffe had bombed it around the clock. Jewish homes and businesses were set ablaze from the moment the Germans marched in. Men were beaten; some were placed against a wall and shot. German forces rounded up hundreds of Jewish women, imprisoned them inside a synagogue, and locked the doors. Mina Huberman was one of the women inside, hearing machine gun fire in the distance, clutching her young son and fearing that the Germans would set the building on fire. The rumors of atrocities against Jewish women spread quickly during the first few weeks of the war. The Germans eventually unshackled the doors to the synagogue and allowed the terrified captives to flee. The soldiers laughed as the women and their children escaped, but they ran into a Łuków that was engulfed in flames. Thick, black, acrid smoke filled the town's air as the wooden buildings burned.

There was one glimmer of hope, though. The Soviet Union had invaded Poland on September 17, a by-product of the secret Molotov-Ribbentrop Pact that dictated the German-Soviet split of Eastern Europe. In some Polish towns, the Wehrmacht and the Red Army paraded together to celebrate their victorious conquest, and in early October, the Germans in Łuków were temporarily replaced by a contingent from the Red Army. The Soviet soldiers who marched into the town found a smoldering ruin.

The Russians were no strangers to the Poles. Many Jews feared the Russians even more than the Wehrmacht—sentiments reinforced by years of pogroms, rapes, and murder under the czars. The panic was exacerbated the day after the Soviets entered Łuków when a young officer let it be known that he wanted all the Jews in town to gather in the main synagogue. A captain from the NKVD, the Soviet secret police, addressed them. He banged on the *bimah*, the wooden stand from which the rabbi gave his sermons on Saturday mornings, trying to get everyone's attention. To everyone's surprise, the Soviet officer introduced himself as a Jew and addressed the gathered in flawless Yiddish.[3] "Listen, people," he shouted. "If you want to save yourselves and your families, leave Łuków and come with us. We offer you hard work and difficult conditions, but you will live. You must all listen to me. I am offering you salvation."[4]

Virtually all of Mina's family opted to remain in Poland. But she and Shmuel, along with Shmuel's sister Lola, their mother, her second husband Leib Shulstein, and two of their children were more pragmatic and accepted the Soviet's offer. Shmuel and Mina went home and crammed what would fit into a leather suitcase; most of the space was reserved for Eli's clothes, for hot and cold weather. Shmuel left with just the clothes on his back and one prized possession: a tattered copy of Theodor Herzl's book.[5]

At just after dawn the following morning, under the watchful eyes of a Red Army battalion, eight members of the Huberman family, along with a few hundred other Jewish men, women, and children from Łuków, boarded a Soviet troop train that would take them east. The journey covered over fifteen hundred miles and took several days to complete. They crossed endless plains and railroad towns toward Moscow, before diverting northward toward the Ural Mountains and the Komi Republic. Conditions on the transport were Spartan. Sanitation was abysmal, and the food was sparse. What would await them at their final destination—a labor camp in the middle of an endless forest—was much worse. The Russian winter was approaching.

For the next five indescribable years, the Huberman family endured the backbreaking work of cutting down trees, clearing land, and paving roads in Soviet labor camps, and the anguish of trying to stay alive. The Russians did not exterminate the Jews they rescued from the Nazis; they did not discriminate against anyone in the camp because all were viewed with contempt and suspected of being criminals trying to sabotage the war effort. The NKVD were cruel slave masters, and anyone caught not working or fulfilling their assignment often paid with their lives. They did not tolerate disobedience, complaining, or any individuality that interfered with the twelve daily hours of hard labor. Work was life. It meant food and shelter.

Everyone capable of labor worked, no exceptions. The elderly and sick worked in the bakery or some administrative capacity. The children in the camp were looked after by the old and the young alike. Eli Huberman's babysitter was herself a child. The Soviets also allowed families to remain together. Dozens shared a crowded hut. In the cold of winter, everyone huddled around a wood-burning brick and mortar stove in the center of the hut. In the summer, the heat was suffocating. Great effort was made to celebrate the Jewish festivals, despite the NKVD's attempts to dissuade the sentimentality of religion and promote communist ideology.

Life was frighteningly uncertain in the camps. Following Hitler's invasion of the Soviet Union in June 1941, the Jews in the labor camps feared that the Nazis would make it to the Urals. They feared for their lives.

Somehow, remarkably, the workers at the camp managed to keep an approximation of normalcy throughout the day-long work in the forests and mills. Romances flourished. Shmuel's sister Lola met Izak, a young medical professional, and the two fell in love and wed. Babies were even born in the captivity of the forced labor camp, but women and newborns often died, succumbing to the lack of medical care, hygiene, and nutrition. The elderly also became statistics, markers in a prison camp graveyard.

In October 1944, five years into their seemingly endless exile, Mina learned she was five months pregnant. She had thought that her swollen stomach was the result of malnutrition. Half-starved on rations, her body decimated by hard work in the water with logs, and sharing what food she had with her growing son had altered her menstrual cycle[6] and sense of what was happening with her body. She feared having to give birth in the Urals, but the Soviets, wanting their forced labor force to keep up with the Red Army's advances, loaded the two hundred fifty inmates of the work camp onto a train and transported them sixteen hundred miles south toward Kherson. Eight members of the Huberman family moved from a desolate barracks into a two-bedroom apartment. The apartment even came with an icebox, indoor plumbing, and a radiator for heating; it was like having a suite at the Ritz.[7] For the first time in what seemed like forever, the family believed they would survive the ordeal. They intended to return to Poland.

*          *          *

In August 1945, in an agreement between Stalin and the newly installed Communist government in Warsaw, people who were forced to flee in 1939 and after would be allowed to return to their homes. The Huberman family trekked back to Łuków hoping to find anyone who might still be alive. News of what the Nazis had done to the Jews of Europe became horrifyingly real when the family reached Kherson. For the first two years of the war, the arrest and murder of Jews were haphazard—random shootings, sexual assaults and rapes, and other acts of utter inhumanity. In May 1941, twelve thousand Jews were herded into the Łuków Ghetto. Virtually all were sent to Treblinka, northeast of Warsaw, where close to a million Jews were slaughtered in industrialized extermination. The ghetto was dismantled later that year. Shmuel and Mina learned that they were two of only one hundred fifty Jews from Łuków to survive the Holocaust.

Well over three hundred members of the combined Huberman, Slushni, and Shulstein family would perish in the Holocaust. Mina's father, Ber, who had been convinced that the Germans were too sophisticated and too cultured to wish the Jews of Europe harm, was beaten and mocked by the SS before being murdered in a purge of one of the many ghettos the Nazis established in Poland to implement their Final Solution. A German propaganda photographer captured the moment, shortly before he was executed, when SS troopers made Ber sit on top of another Jewish prisoner as if he were straddling a horse, seconds before he was shot and killed. That image, published later in a historical account of the elimination of European Jewry, would have an enormous impact on Meir in his later life.

The Polish government allowed the Huberman family back into Poland but only if they moved to Dzierżoniów, formerly Reichenbach, in Lower Silesia, five hundred fifty miles from the shtetl.[8] Ostensibly, the move was to repopulate former areas of Germany now ceded to Warsaw. Still, the Communist government feared that the return of the surviving Jews, eager to reclaim properties that had been stolen from them by Catholic neighbors and party bosses, would result in violence. Right-wing nationalist anticommunists targeted the Jews as agents of the Bolsheviks. The Communists mistrusted the Jews as agents of capitalism. What happened to the Jews of Poland during and after the Second World War was one of the most blatantly orchestrated mass property thefts in history. It is said that the Holocaust ended in Europe in 1945 but ended in Poland in 1948. Years after the end of the Second World War, Jews stuck in transit in their former homes were victims of pogroms, murder, and theft.

Shmuel went back to work at *Hashomer Ha'Tzair*, organizing survivors so that they could begin their journey to the Middle East and work for the creation of a Jewish state in British Mandate Palestine. He also worked for the American Jewish Joint Distribution Committee. Formed in 1914, the JDC was created to help Jews starving in the no-man's-land of the First World War Eastern European battlefields. The organization tried to rescue Jews from Hitler's Europe before and during the Second World War as well; it is believed that from 1939 to 1944, the JDC brought over eighty thousand Jews from Nazi-occupied Europe to safety.

Following the establishment of the State of Israel on May 15, 1948, the Huberman family realized that their time in Poland was fleeting. The Communist government in Warsaw was firmly in the Soviet bloc, and the Soviets, Shmuel learned, would soon close Poland's borders to Jewish migration.

*                    *                    *

Italian ports did a brisk business handling maritime traffic, registered and the other kind, that smuggled Jews into Palestine before the Second World War and immediately after that. Although Mussolini's regime was aligned in lockstep with Hitler, the Italian fascists had a more transactional view of the plight of German and Austrian Jews seeking refuge from the oncoming storm. The Haganah, Israel's pre-independence army, hired vessels to breach the British blockade and rescue as many Jews as possible. Those networks were reestablished following the end of the war in Europe when the dire need to ferry the survivors of the Holocaust to the future Jewish homeland became a political matter in the international discussions over Palestine. Following the establishment of the State of Israel, the clandestine traffic became legitimate and commercial. The brisk business continued, though the emergence of El Al, the Israeli national airline, provided the quicker, though far more expensive, form of travel.

The SS *Caserta* was one of the mainstays of the route. The twenty-year-old converted freighter and now passenger steamer hit ports across the seas and sailed Jews from Europe and Arab lands to a new home in Israel. The journey between Italy and Israel took between five and seven days, though the travel time was often longer, when the ship called on ports in Arab North Africa where Jews were waiting. In April 1949, with three hundred Czech survivors, the *Caserta* traveled from Naples to Tripoli, to collect another four hundred Libyan Jews.[9] In January 1950, Shmuel and his family boarded the SS *Caserta* in Brindisi after a long trek through Central Europe. They carried only a few belongings and the harsh memories they were determined to leave behind.

The SS *Caserta* was barely seaworthy. The ship smelled of an overheated engine. It almost capsized once in tumultuous seas.[10]

The coast of Israel came into view on a windswept winter morning five days after the *Caserta* set sail. The outline of Mount Carmel jutted up into the gray sky, as did the cranes and freighters clustered in the Haifa port. The ship's passengers crowded the main deck to see for themselves. The pious removed prayer books from their coat pockets and prayed.

Not Mina. Although she came from religious stock, the horrors of the Holocaust had knocked all the faith out of her tiny frame. "How could God, if there is a God, allow one million children to be murdered?" she told her boys repeatedly as they grew up, Eli Huberman would later reflect; the boys never prepared for or celebrated their bar mitzvahs.[11]

Prayer could no longer be an excuse used as armor to protect the Jewish people, Mina would instruct her sons. It was a lesson Eli would always remember and one that Meir would never forget.

CHAPTER 2

# Newcomers

The new Jewish state was a far cry from the land of milk and honey following independence. The country was a chaotic mess undergoing the painful transformation from concept to new nation; recovering from a war of independence, in which 10 percent of the population had been killed in the fighting, while at the same time building a new nation that was to be populated by a sea of incoming Jews from all over the world. An astounding 638,597 new immigrants flooded the country after the last British soldiers left and the new nation of Israel was declared.[1] In the thirty-six months that followed the establishment of the country, Israel's population doubled.

The newcomers arrived from all over the world. Displaced persons who had survived the death camps, Jews from the Arab Diaspora who had been forced to uproot centuries of coexistence with their Muslim neighbors to start fresh in the new nation, as well as freed prisoners who had been held in British internment facilities for trying to break through the Royal Navy's blockade. Jews who spoke a Tower of Babel of languages multiplied by more dialects than could be counted soon had to learn modern Hebrew and become full-fledged citizens of the new nation. They were light-skinned and dark-skinned. Some were highly educated, graduates of the finest universities of prewar Europe, and others were being introduced to the twentieth century for the first time, leaving an untouched existence in countries like Libya and Yemen for what was a new world. There were children born on their way to Israel, and octogenarians whose last wish on earth was to set foot in the ancient Jewish homeland turned modern sanctuary before they died. It was a true *Kibbutz Galuyot*, the gathering of exiles that Moses had promised the Israelites in Deuteronomy 30:1–5: "Even if you are exiled to the ends of the world, from there the Lord your God will gather you, and from there he will bring you back."

The undertaking was Herculean in scope and biblical in symbolism, and seemingly beyond the capabilities of the new nation. Israel, barely able to feed itself, let alone care for the immigrants who continued to flood the nation's harbors and airports, was impoverished and over-whelmed by reconstructing roads and infrastructure that had to be built, repaired, or rerouted.

New immigrants who had the necessary means could rent apart-ments or buy land, but few emerged from Europe or the Arab world with money. The agricultural settlements, the collective farms, offered a home and a job for some, but working the harsh land, often along the frontier where Arab terrorists frequently carried out cross-border raids, was not suitable for everyone.

The Israeli government's solution was the construction of temporary housing camps throughout the country known as *Ma'abarot*, the Hebrew word for transition camp. The temporary cities were bare and often dismal. Housing consisted of tents, sometimes wooden barracks, shared restrooms and showers. They were muddy, desolate, and designed to be a first step in building a nation of immigrants, refugees, and sur-vivors, who could assume a national identity, gain fluency in a shared language, and become solid citizens who could contribute to the birth and growth of a nation.

\*     \*     \*

Shmuel, Mina, and their two boys were first sent to an absorption camp near the Crusader port city of Atlit, just south of Haifa, and then to a transitional camp near Sarafand, an abandoned British military base near Lod, a primarily Arab city and home to the country's main international airport. The family was assigned an elongated abandoned brick British barracks with a corrugated tin roof that they shared with other families. A dozen languages were spoken inside the rickety building. Married couples argued, babies cried, and the elderly cursed and complained. Families had no privacy. Towels and bedsheets hung on rope lines created the illusion of being separated from the other families occupying the barracks. Still, it was hard to achieve any sense of escape when snoring, farting, and belching created a nightly soundtrack to the squalid conditions.

Shmuel had been certain that his work on behalf of the Zionist youth both before and after the war would warrant special treatment upon his arrival in Israel. But there were no marching bands to greet him in Haifa when the SS *Caserta* docked, and he was not rewarded with accommodations more suitable for a man of his prominence in the ma'abara. He felt betrayed and abandoned. The fledgling state, like all new countries with waves of immigration, was a nation of *protektzia*—where who you knew was rewarded with a special sort of status that should have been a dividend for hard work, courage, and accomplishment. It was bad to be the perennial outsider, the last newcomer in a land of newcomers, and forced to work twice as hard for half the credit and the chance to fit in. This anger would sour Shmuel's outlook on the world; the indignation would follow him for the rest of his life.[2] He would impart this lesson of embitterment on his sons—Meir, then six years old, took it to heart.

Shmuel and Mina slept on army cots that the British Army had left behind. The boys had to share one bed. Eli and Meir occupied themselves with the other children, though both shared a voracious appetite for reading. The older brother loved the sciences, and Meir enjoyed books about history and adventure. Eli was more cautious and reserved in personality, and Meir was the adventurer who showed few signs of fear, often wandering off to explore the far reaches of the camp. But the two boys were inseparable, with Eli tagging along to wherever his brother ventured. Meir was heartbroken when Eli was sent to live with his uncle and grandparents in a suburb of Tel Aviv so that he could attend a proper elementary school.

But the ma'abara was temporary. With government subsidies eliminating the need for a sizeable down payment, Shmuel and Mina bought a small one-bedroom apartment in Bat Yam, a hardscrabble suburb that hugged the Mediterranean shoreline directly south of Tel Aviv. The ground-floor apartment was barely big enough for two people, let alone a family of four. The parents slept in the bedroom and the boys shared a small sofa. Somehow, everyone managed. Everyone in Bat Yam got by. No one traveled abroad on holiday. People did not own cars. The homes were not wired for telephone service; the wait for a private line could extend for decades. Children played in the street, turning empty lots of sand and debris into soccer pitches. Neighbors came over to share a coffee without knocking. Everyone was in the same boat. It created a sense of camaraderie among the neighbors.

Shmuel eventually opened a laundromat. Mina worked there as well; Eli would help out after school. Later, Mina worked as a cashier in a supermarket chain. The salaries were meager but just enough to get by, and in 1954 they upgraded to a larger home—a one-bedroom third-floor apartment at 38 Independence* Boulevard in the center of Bat Yam. The building was on a wide, tree-lined avenue less than half a mile from the Mediterranean shoreline, but the apartment was far from spacious. The kitchen was minuscule, and the apartment had only one shower and toilet. The boys did not have rooms of their own and did their schoolwork in the living room. They would also sleep on the same L-shaped sofa well into their twenties when both were soldiers.

No one in the neighborhood had much money. When a child had a few spare coins in their pocket, perhaps a small gift from grandparents, and went to the corner kiosk for a cold grapefruit drink, the other kids followed jealously. Most of the children in the Amidar neighborhood in Bat Yam were immigrants or the children of immigrants; most of the kids in the neighborhood were either born in the remnants of Hitler's Europe, or their parents had somehow survived the Holocaust. Meir

---

* The Hebrew name for the boulevard is *Ha'Atzma'ut*. The neighborhood is now populated with immigrants from the former Soviet Union and Ethiopia, and the building where the Huberman family lived still stands.

was dark complexioned and was often mistaken for a newcomer from Morocco or Iraq.

Amidar was a place where learning how to fight earned social status. The children took after their parents; the kids fought in the street. Meir learned he could take on someone twice his size. His nickname in the neighborhood was Pancho, after the famed Mexican bandit. He was fearless and always willing to take risks, someone who learned to cut corners and throw a punch when needed.

More wary Eli looked out for his younger sibling. They got into trouble together, sometimes sneaking into a Tel Aviv cinema to watch the film of the day—often a Hollywood retread screened years after it had been shown in the United States or Europe. Few kids in the Bat Yam neighborhood had the money to see a movie, so sneaking in was a common practice and an escape from the entertainment-light existence. The boys liked cowboy films, and Meir liked thrilling movies about war and intrigue,[3] but their favorite movie was *Johnny Belinda*, the acclaimed 1948 film starring Jane Wyman as a deaf-mute and Lew Ayres as the doctor who tries to teach her.

Eli was studious with an aptitude for the sciences. He was disciplined and organized. Meir was rambunctious and an explorer prone to disappearing—sometimes on expeditions around the neighborhood and then other times on treks across the country. His rambunctious spirit was fueled by a children's book series called *Hasamba* by Yigal Mossinson. *Hasamba*, the Hebrew acronym for *Havurat Sod Muhlat Be'Hehlet*, or The Absolutely Absolute Secret Group followed the heroic adventures of a group of Tel Aviv children who helped the underground Haganah fight the British. Other books in the series had storylines involving the Israeli military and its security services. "Meir tried to organize his friends to emulate the *Hasamba* gang in the dunes around Bat Yam," Eli remembered.[4] He envisioned himself going out on secret missions even at a very young age.

Meir had a devilish sense of humor that sometimes exceeded his young age, and unlike his older brother, he absorbed knowledge at his own pace and found school boring. He was a *shovav*, the Hebrew word for one who is perpetually naughty, and could not help but get into trouble. He was often ordered to go to the principal's office because of his behavior and then sent home. He was so disruptive, legend had it, that teachers entered the classroom, yelled at Huberman to leave the room, and then only started teaching once he was out the door. Still, his parents made him take accordion lessons, and he practiced at home. If he liked to do something, he did it faithfully. He could not tolerate being bored. Meir loved to read, just like his brother. His reading level surpassed his age, and the small Bat Yam apartment was always full of books borrowed from the nearby library, taken from school, or used paperbacks purchased for a few agorot, the Israeli version of the penny. There were books beneath his pillow and under the couch. Even books that he had read before were cherished and read once again. Meir liberated magazines from the trash and tried to read newspaper headlines from newsstands rather than in the afternoon edition. Television was a decade away, so most Israelis—including preteen Meir—received the news from the radio. At the top of every hour, a national news broadcast interrupted all programming with updated headlines about the precarious security situation along Israel's frontiers.

In 1954 and 1955, new stories of Arab guerrillas crossing the frontiers to attack the kibbutzim and moshavim* around the Egyptian-occupied Gaza Strip and near the border with Jordan were always the lead headlines in the country's newspapers, followed by accounts of Israeli retaliatory commando raids. The accounts of daring nighttime action by Israel's brave soldiers captivated ten-year-old Meir's imagination. Although the Israel Defense Forces were tight-lipped about their military exploits, the name of one man somehow always made it into the broadcast: Major Ariel "Arik" Sharon.

Meir grew up in awe of the Palmach, Israel's pre-independence commandos, and he read tales of their battlefield exploits and dreamed of being a hero like them. In his eyes, Ariel Sharon was the personification

---

* A kibbutz and a moshav are both types of agricultural settlements that emphasize collective labor. A kibbutz is based on socialist principles, rigidly organized, and highly bureaucratic. A moshav is, for the most part, a collective community that promotes private and individual ownership of land and property. In the early days of Israeli independence, the citizen farmers—tough, physically fit, and regimented to be unemotional in their thinking—took a leading role in the ranks of the IDF.

of this new breed of warrior. He was a Sabra, and embodied a fearless arrogance that the immigrants admired—a new breed of Jew. In August 1953, after a bloody summer of terrorist attacks, Lieutenant General Moshe Dayan, the Israel Defense Forces chief of staff, ordered Sharon to assemble a special operations retaliatory unit that could use daring and decisive strikes deep behind enemy lines to persuade Arab guerrillas, known as the fedayeen, to stop launching raids against Israeli border settlements. The force, known as Unit 101, was made up of men who had reputations of being rogues and adventurers—textbook cases of square pegs in round holes whose imaginations and capabilities exceeded the norms of conventional military thinking. Unit 101 was a closed club: acceptance was by invitation only, and only fifty men made the cut. They were allowed to wear unofficial uniforms; they carried weapons, such as German MP40s and American Thompson submachine guns, that were untraceable. The unit was meant to be completely deniable.

But Unit 101 made headlines. Their punitive raids were designed to be preemptive—to instill such destruction in areas that the fedayeen used to launch attacks that the villages that provided the guerrillas a haven would think twice before letting them use the areas as a base of operations from which to attack Israel. The unit's first operation was a retaliatory strike against a fedayeen base in the Gaza Strip that resulted in fifty dead. A raid against the West Bank village of Qibya in response to the murder of an Israeli woman and her two children resulted in sixty-nine Jordanian guardsmen and civilians killed. There was an international outcry. U.S. secretary of state John Foster Dulles halted aid because of the severity of the Israeli commando operation and voted to censure Israel in the United Nations.[5]

Israeli prime minister David Ben-Gurion disbanded Unit 101 because of the international backlash. But Sharon was news—he was on the front page of the newspapers and featured on the radio, and Meir, determined never to be bullied, was fascinated by him, wanted to emulate him.

Israel became stronger as Meir grew up. The Jewish state developed into a military power to be reckoned with. Colonel Arik Sharon's paratroopers captured the Mitla Pass in the Sinai Desert in the 1956 war against Egypt, a conflict that Israel fought alongside Great Britain and France. Boys schooled in the horrors of the Holocaust were determined to be the type of Jews that could not be led to extermination. They were tough and determined. This distinction became of great importance to young Meir. At about this time, the eleven-year-old took stock of the fact that the circle around him of uncles, aunts, cousins, and even people he thought of as grandparents had different last names than his. They were not blood relatives; they were all incomplete pieces from a generation that was damaged by devastating loss. These survivors grasped what they could and whom they could. They were psychologically scarred, and many—including Shmuel and Mina—made a point never to discuss with their children the war years and what they endured. There was an emptiness among these walking wounded and a fear that they might one day have to endure the horrors again. In a televised interview with noted psychologist Yoram Yovell, on Israel's education channel, Dagan would later say that his parents never threw food away.[6] Even moldy bread and other things that would not be eaten were kept because their mindset was that the crusty remains of week-old bread could one day save their lives.

In 1957, Eli was conscripted into the ranks of the IDF. Watching his older brother return home from the army in uniform, carrying a weapon, having become a defender of the country, impacted twelve-year-old Meir. Thoughts of military glory became far more important to him than studying for his bar mitzvah or school. His mind wandered in class; he seemed bored by the mental confines of a desk, a notebook, and rigid authorities.

At home, Shmuel was dismissive and distant to his two sons. Bitter that his efforts in Poland on behalf of *Hashomer Ha'Tzair* were never appreciated or rewarded upon his arrival in Israel, with a position in government or at an agency that had prominence and brought financial reward to him, Shmuel Huberman carried that slight with him for the rest of his life. "He was a good father," Eli Huberman would recall, "but not a warm and loving one."[7] Even years later when Meir was a general, Shmuel would say, "I have one son who's a scientist and another who's in the army."

The responsibility of nurturing the two boys fell on Mina's shoulders. She encouraged her sons, overlooking their shortcomings and bolstering their dreams. In May 1960, Meir's head filled with a new source of pride and inspiration.

For years, Israel did all it could to keep its foreign espionage service, the Mossad, *le'Modi'in U'le Tafkidim Meyuhadim* (the Institute for Intelligence and Special Operations), out of the public eye. Better known simply as the Mossad, the service dated back to the Haganah, the army of pre-independence Israel, and the ability to recruit Jews from across the Diaspora for missions of vital national importance—often behind enemy lines in Arab states. Few in the country knew the name of its espionage agency or Isser Harel, its enigmatic director. Beyond spying on the country's enemies, one of the Mossad's tasks was hunting Nazi war criminals who had escaped Allied hangmen after the war's end and the Nuremberg trials. Adolf Eichmann, the SS bureaucrat who helped to blueprint and implement Hitler's Final Solution, topped the Mossad's most wanted list. In March 1960 he was found in Buenos Aires, the capital of Argentina, living under an assumed identity. Two months later, he was in Israel—kidnapped by a team of Mossad and Shin Bet agents. Israel did not want the daring operation to be a secret, nor could it be: Eichmann was to be tried in an Israeli court for genocide.

The Mossad suddenly became the focus of international curiosity and a massive media frenzy in a day and age when such commotion was still done courtesy of newsreels, radio flashes, and newspaper headlines. Isser Harel, never one to shy away from the tabloids, made sure that the world knew who he was even though his identity was supposed to be a closely guarded state secret.

Nazi-hunting men in the shadows bringing Hitler's henchmen to justice was a source of great pride for a nation populated by hundreds of thousands of Holocaust survivors. It was also the source of enormous fascination for a fifteen-year-old teenager in Bat Yam whose realization that he was a survivor of sorts had become a rite of passage that would define much of his future life.

Meir immersed himself in the newspaper accounts of Eichmann's capture and he imagined himself one day carrying out covert missions on Israel's behalf.

CHAPTER 3

# Soldier

Upon reaching their eighteenth birthday, Israeli teenagers receive a conscription notice informing them of the date on which they are to report for military duty. Mandatory military service is the great equalizer and unifier of Israeli society. The army is where the sons of fifth-generation native-born Sabras and immigrants to the Jewish state who do not speak Hebrew and struggle to find their place in a strange new home both become full-fledged members of the Israeli experience by wearing the uniform and defending their country. The journey from high school student to soldier begins at *Ba'ku'm*—the Hebrew acronym for the IDF's Absorption and Selection Base in Tel Hashomer, an eastern suburb of Tel Aviv.

On a hot summer morning in August 1963, Meir Huberman answered the induction call he had received after turning eighteen. It was a Sunday, the start of the workweek in Israel, and Meir Huberman wanted to reach the conscription base early—before everyone. He had wanted to be a soldier for as long as he could remember, even though many of his high school classmates dreaded the day they would have to report for national service. Mina stood in the small kitchenette and prepared a sandwich and some fruit for the bus journey to the base. Shmuel read the paper and listened to the news on a transistor radio. Meir wore a white short-sleeved shirt and a pair of dark shorts. He was

21

sturdy and confident, like the native-born Israelis he tried so hard to emulate, and scrappy. He did not fear a thing, not even leaving home for the first time. Mina put some money in Meir's pocket before he left—not a lot, but enough to hopefully buy a snack in the base's canteen. He promised to write home the first chance he got. He could not call—the apartment did not have a phone line installed.

Few Israeli families—especially in Bat Yam—owned a car, so Meir took a bus to the army. The housewives who looked at their world from their windowsills yelled at him and wished him the best of luck in the army. There were few secrets in the Bat Yam apartment building and the women told him to be careful. Mina Huberman would have wanted to hold her son's hand as she walked with him to the bus stop, but, as his brother Eli remembered, "Meir's rebellious and proud nature would never agree to such a gesture."[1]

It took over an hour for the intercity bus to traverse a circuitous route from the Tel Aviv working towns toward Tel Hashomer. The base was at the end of a cul-de-sac covered by eucalyptus trees that offered shade to a few kiosks selling soft drinks and sandwiches to the recruits who wanted one last taste of civilian life before settling for army food. A reservist wearing the khaki fatigues from one uniform and the olive shirt from another stood guard over an iron gate, a Czech-made Mauser rifle, a relic from the Second World War and Israel's fight for independence, slung over his shoulder. Meir handed the sentry his notice and was directed to a long line of eighteen-year-olds from across Israel waiting to be processed.

Meir was issued the serial number of 499165. An identification mugshot was taken for his identification book. The young recruit scowled defiantly for the image, rather than smile as the photographer had demanded. A female soldier serving at a metal press created his dog tags: two to be worn around his neck. A team of medical officers inoculated each new soldier with two shots in the arm and the dreaded tetanus injection in the fleshy part of the backside. Soldiers who served three years and those who spent thirty years in uniform always remembered the intense pain and tennis ball lump that every soldier knows lingers unforgivingly for days.

Meir and a hundred other nameless and faceless young men were taken to a long room with supply stations where his gear would be issued. He received a khaki canvas kit bag, two medium towels, three pairs of underwear, three white undershirts, five pairs of heavy gray socks, two pairs of black leather combat boots, a sweater, a winter parka, some hygiene equipment, and a few items such as shoe polish and a brush. The soldiers also received a small stipend to buy food or cigarettes at the canteen. For some soldiers, the advance pay, to be taken out of their next month's salary, was more money than they had ever held.

The master sergeant was an intimidating figure by design. His mission was to demoralize and frighten the new class of soldiers out of their last grasp on civilian life. He barked orders and hurried his men, usually giving them no more than thirty seconds to get from station to station. He divided the soldiers into platoons and had each assembly march to a row of tents where they would stow their gear. When the sergeant yelled the name Huberman, expecting someone with a European appearance to respond to the name, the drill sergeant scolded Meir every time he stood up and said, "I am here, sir." Huberman liked the stir the mix-up caused. He had grown up around kids whose parents came from Arab countries. They were proud, and resilient, and, most importantly, they did not take abuse from anyone.

That night, a few conscripts cried in their bunks, frightened to be away from home for the first time. The cockier ones, or those who could bombastically camouflage their raw recruit trepidation, boasted about their plans to volunteer with the paratroopers and wanted to know when they would be issued with an Uzi submachine gun. Meir mostly kept to himself and avoided the false displays of bravado his platoon mates were acting out. There was no need. He removed a razor-sharp commando dagger from his rucksack and quietly slipped it into his kit bag so the others would not see and report him to the drill sergeant. Personal weapons were not allowed at the induction base.

*     *     *

Every IDF conscript undergoes a series of medical and psycho-technical examinations in the months before their call-up. Their stamina, intellectual, and psychological profiles are measured and then recorded into an assessment formula that decides which young soldiers are suitable for combat duty and which ones are not; which ones have the aptitude, confidence, and charisma for command, and which ones do not. The parameters are assigned a profile number, a score of sorts, which dictates a soldier's military career from conscription until they are too old to be called up for the reserves. Meir Huberman's numbers were off the charts—indicating that he was made of the right stuff to serve in one of the IDF's elite units and to lead men into battle.

The most secretive commando force in the IDF's Order of Battle was Sayeret Mat'kal—or the General Staff Reconnaissance Unit.* Based on the model of Great Britain's 22nd Special Air Service Regiment and the motto of Who Dares Wins, Mat'kal was formed in 1957 as a covert intelligence-gathering force to carry out long-range reconnaissance missions far from Israel's frontiers. The unit was created because of the failures of Operation Cricket, when three Israeli paratroopers and two infantrymen ventured behind Syrian lines in the winter of 1954 dressed in civilian clothes, to plant a series of listening devices to tap into military lines of communication. A Syrian army patrol ambushed the team. They were taken to Damascus, where they were tortured in captivity. One of the soldiers, Corporal Uri Ilan, committed suicide rather than disclose classified information and inserted a small note into his clothes that he scribbled with the words "I did not betray."[2] The debacle in Syria convinced many officers who worked in the intelligence and covert battlespace, especially a major named Avraham Arnan, that the IDF needed a force of special men who could carry out the most complex and dangerous assignments and not get caught.

Arnan was the new unit's first commander. He had recruited former fighters in the Palmach, the Haganah's elite Strike Companies who fought the British and then battles against the Arabs for Israel's independence; veterans of Unit 101; and rogues and outside-the-box

---

* The unit remains one of the Israeli military's three tier-one special operations units, the other two being Flotilla 13, the naval commandos, and Shaldag, the Israel Air Force's elite long-range penetration and irregular warfare force. *Shaldag* is the Hebrew word for the kingfisher bird.

thinkers who were daring, physically fit, and who displayed a cunning, above-average intelligence.

Sayeret Mat'kal was so top secret that its name would not be mentioned in the Israeli press until twenty years later. It was rumored that the chief of staff kept the list of the names of the unit's operators in his desk drawer. Being part of this unit was considered as prestigious, if not more, than being a fighter pilot—especially since the unit was so hush-hush, only adding to its aura of exclusivity and mystery. The unit's first known operation was in Lebanon in 1962. The action was not mentioned in the Israeli press, and it remains classified over sixty years after it was carried out. Meir wanted to be a member of this exclusive club more than anything in the world.

Most of Sayeret Mat'kal's personnel came from the kibbutzim and moshavim—native-born, tough, and entrenched, from birth, with a work ethic connected to the land. Others came from prominent families. They were the elite in a young nation that strived to be egalitarian. One such officer was a twenty-one-year-old named Ehud Brog, a native of Kibbutz Mishmar HaSharon—a young commander of extraordinary leadership and irregular warfare skills who would command the unit, change his surname to Barak, Hebrew for lightning, and one day lead the IDF and the country as its prime minister. Hebraizing one's name was considered a strategic move for those wishing to advance their military and—possibly—political aspirations.

To be allowed to even volunteer for a unit like Mat'kal, a conscript had to survive a grueling week-long audition known as a *Gibush*, Hebrew for formation. It was like Hell Week for the U.S. Navy SEALs— recruits were subjected to harsh physical and psychological challenges and exams to determine what each candidate's breaking point was. Those administrating the arduous series of seemingly pointless drills and obstacle courses cared less about how fast a hopeful could run or negotiate climbing a rope, and more about how that person overcame pain, fear, cold, and exhaustion. Human mettle and psychological elasticity were more important than natural-born abilities. Those hoping to earn a spot on the unit's opening day basic training roster were also subjected to exercises where teamwork was stressed.

Danny Yatom was one of a hundred conscript hopefuls vying for the handful of spots being offered to Mat'kal candidates—the unit only held open auditions once a year. Yatom, a native of Netanya, was shy and skinny. Unsure of himself and inherently reserved, he scanned the other conscripts in the pool of wannabes until he saw one soldier who was a magnet of attention. It was Meir. He was telling jokes and laughing. "He was also hurling his commando dagger at a target he had carved into a tree," Yatom remembered. "I do not belong here," Yatom thought, "I don't know how to do these things."[3]

Meir did not want to be one of a crowd—he wanted to be *the* center of attention. Ultimately, both Meir Huberman and Danny Yatom would be picked. It was the start of an intensive basic training program of advanced combat skills, irregular warfare, and pseudo-shadow warfare that the unit was perfecting. Yatom would continue his path in the Mat'kal, participating in some of the unit's most spectacular operations and eventually reaching the rank of deputy commander.* Meir would not make it through the eighteen-month course; he washed out before completing the lengthy training regimen.[4]

No reason was given for his ouster—Mat'kal commanders did not oblige those who did not make the grade with explanations concerning their dismissal. Deep down, Meir never forgave the slight. He blamed the elitists for keeping him out, men like Ehud Barak—and two brothers named Netanyahu who made names for themselves as one of the Chief of Staff's Boys: one, Yoni, immortalized for leading the hostage-rescue operation in Entebbe in July 1976, and Benjamin, known to the world as Bibi, who would become Israel's longest-serving prime minister.

Meir was sent to the 202nd Paratroop Brigade, the IDF's elite infantry force and its sole airborne unit. The paratroopers were heroes in Israel—having performed a combat jump in 1956 to seize the Mitla Pass in the Sinai Desert. Their uniforms depicted elite status that made them stand out: crimson red berets, olive Class A smocks, and brown leather

---

* The two men would remain friends; their careers would cross paths for the next forty years on battlefields across the Middle East—in the Armored Corps, in Lebanon, in IDF HQ, and in the elite club of men who would go on to serve as directors of the Mossad.

jump boots. Paratroopers wore silver metal jump wings—the reward of four static line day jumps and one at night from a World War Two–era C-47 Dakota or a French-built Nord Noratlas N-2501IS—above the left breast pocket of their dress uniform. They carried indigenously produced Uzi 9mm submachine guns. When Meir walked down the main street in Bat Yam wearing his uniform, a folded red beret fitted snuggly into the left epaulet of his tunic, the neighbors who had watched him march off to the army stared in absolute admiration.

Meir was a squad leader in the brigade's *sayeret*, or reconnaissance force. His unit operated on forays behind enemy lines gathering intelligence, sabotaging enemy installations, and lying in ambush for marauding fedayeen bands that crossed the 1949 armistice lines with Jordan and Syria and the 1950 armistice frontiers with Egypt, to attack border agricultural communities. They trained to coordinate strikes with other units and to operate as a cohesive long-range tip of the spear for the brigade. Meir's reconnaissance force trained with American-made Sikorsky S-58 helicopters to deploy on lightning strikes against fortified targets far from friendly lines. The brigade saw it fit to send him to Officer Candidate School at the Sirkin Army Base near Petach Tikvah. When he returned to the brigade months later, it was as a second lieutenant: a platoon commander.

Like many soldiers of his generation, Meir saw combat before his twenty-first birthday. The engagements were small at first, but the firefights against guerrillas escalated into major battles and geopolitical incidents. Sometimes mortar and armor support had to be summoned. The reconnaissance force carried out dozens of cross-border raids between 1965 and 1966. The largest operation that Lieutenant Huberman participated in was Operation Shredder, in November 1966.

The Arab states used the Palestinian issue as a tactical spark to employ guerrillas in attacks against Israel. Fatah, led by an Egyptian-born engineer named Yasir Arafat, was the largest Palestinian force. Financed and armed by Syrian and Egyptian intelligence, and supported by the Soviets, fedayeen squads crossed into Israel's vulnerable border settlements and killed civilians; they mined roads and planted improvised explosive devices near water and power stations. Each fedayeen attack and Israeli response risked bringing the region closer to war.

On the night of November 11, 1966, three Israeli border patrolmen were killed by a land mine planted by the fedayeen near the Hebron Hills on the West Bank. The IDF General Staff determined that nearby residents—and Jordanian troops stationed there—were assisting the guerrillas and providing them shelter and protection.* The Israelis responded forty-eight hours later. It was an all-hands-on-deck gesture of military deterrence. In the retaliatory operation, code-named Shredder, the paratroop brigade attacked the village of Samu. According to estimates, over four hundred soldiers took part in the raid.

The Jordanian garrison fought back, though. Resistance was fierce and a pitched battle ensued. Royal Jordanian Air Force Hawker Hunter jets scrambled to repel the paratroopers, and a flight of French-built Israel Air Force Mirage IIIC fighters raced to the skies to intercept. The fighting in and around Samu lasted hours, and when the smoke cleared, sixteen Jordanian soldiers were dead, as well as three villagers. Lieutenant Colonel Yoav Shaham, commander of the 202nd Battalion, was the lone IDF fatality.

Following the attack, IDF chief of staff Lieutenant General Yitzhak Rabin was quoted as saying that had Israel not responded to the fedayeen sabotage, it would have been as if "the blood of Israel is wasted!"[5] The fighting would be the harbinger of much worse to come.

*          *          *

Meir Huberman was discharged from military duty weeks after Operation Shredder. He had completed his three years of mandatory service, plus a few extra months to compensate for the officer's instruction. His commanders noted that Lieutenant Huberman displayed coolness in the field and courage under fire and had the makings of a superior combat leader. Meir enjoyed his time in uniform, though somehow the disappointment of not continuing in Sayeret Mat'kal dampened his

---

* King Hussein of Jordan, who had held secret talks with Israeli leaders—political, military, and intelligence—tried to stop the Palestinian attacks from the West Bank, then under Jordanian rule, but was unsuccessful.

thoughts of making a career in the army. He was almost twenty-two years old, a combat veteran, and still sleeping on the same L-shaped sofa with his brother. Eli was in graduate school studying clinical micro-biology at Tel Aviv University."[6]

The Beatles' "We Can Work It Out" was played regularly on Israeli radio, as Meir pondered his options: School perhaps? Maybe travel? But, in truth, his military service had barely begun.

# CHAPTER 4

# Combat Leader

econd Lieutenant Meir Huberman was discharged in December 1966. His three-plus years as a reconnaissance paratrooper, squad leader, and finally junior officer were over. He could have stayed in the army. The pay for professional soldiers was good, especially compared to what people earned in the regular job market. There were perks to being a member of the professional officer corps, and there was social prestige for a platoon leader with combat experience.

He also loved art. Although he never received any specialized training, he had an amazingly natural ability to draw, paint, and mold creations from clay, stone, and metal. Meir could spend hours with watercolors or oils, imagining Middle Eastern vistas from memory or from photos he had seen in library books. He especially loved to sketch the faces of Arabs and Jews. He was fascinated by the textures, complexions, and dramatic features of the people he saw on the street, and their languages. He embraced the diversity of the country that he lived in and wanted to use his artistic ability to illustrate his nation, one he realized was a stew of mesmerizing religions, cultures, and people.

But as much as he loved his art, and as much as he enjoyed his time in the military, Meir was also pragmatic. His parents, even his permanently supportive mother, would have scoffed at the notion of him wasting his years of higher education to study art. The country needed engineers, builders, and farmers; Eli was studying biochemistry with hopes of becoming a physician. Meir would have to do something to earn him a living—anything that could secure a future outside the one-bedroom apartment in Bat Yam. He became a member of the reservist army, where he would serve in one capacity or another until his fifty-fifth birthday.

The IDF tried to keep conscript units together in new reservist formations to sustain friendship and maintain force cohesion. Meir was assigned to the 80th Paratroop (Reserve) Brigade; it was convenient since the unit was headquartered in Ramle, a forty-minute bus ride from Bat Yam. The battalions of the reserve force trained together to be ready at a moment's notice to deploy in war. Many homes in Israel did not have telephones, so the army kept records of neighbors lucky enough to have an indoor line. Code words were assigned to each brigade. In times of crisis, these names or phrases would be repeatedly read on the radio so that soldiers would know who was being mobilized and when to report.

By the spring of 1967, it became apparent to many in the reserves that they needed to stay close to their radios. The Middle East was heading toward a full-scale war.

*　　　　*　　　　*

The emergence of the fedayeen as a deniable force of violence that the Arab states bordering Israel could use as a proxy to stretch Israel's defenses backfired. Every terror attack warranted harsh retaliation. Every raid and punitive response inched the region closer to a full-scale conflagration. The tit-for-tat was combustible—ripe for miscalculations and chest-beating maneuvers.

On April 4, 1967, a dogfight erupted over the northern Israeli skies between a flight of IAF Mirage IIIC fighters and Syrian Air Force MiG-21s.* Syrian artillery positions atop the Golan Heights lobbed shells

---

* The IAF had the upper hand when it came to the MiG. A year earlier, in Operation Diamond, the Mossad had convinced an Iraqi Air Force MiG-21 pilot to defect his combat aircraft to Israel. At the time, the MiG-21 (NATO code name Fishbed) was a frontline fighter in the Soviet bloc; American pilots had come up against it in the skies

at Israeli farmers, prompting the IAF to launch retaliation; the Syrians launched interceptors of their own. Ultimately, the IAF and the Syrian Air Force would order over one hundred combat sorties. The French-built Mirage jets were superior to their Soviet-built adversaries; Israeli pilots were better trained than their Syrian counterparts. The supersonic aircraft maneuvered in pursuit of one another; 30mm cannons were fired, and air-to-air missiles were launched. Six of the Syrian MiGs were blown out of the sky. All the Mirages returned to base safely.

The Soviets falsely informed Egypt's President Nasser that Israel was mobilizing its military and sending troops to the frontier with the Golan Heights, a basaltic plateau at the southwest edge of Syria east of the Sea of Galilee.[1] Egypt and Syria mobilized their armed forces; Jordan declared that its forces were ready for war. A United Nations Emergency Force, the UNEF, a multinational assembly of peacekeepers flying the blue-and-white UN flag, had helped police the demilitarization of the Sinai Peninsula since the last Middle East war, in 1956.

On May 18, President Nasser kicked the UNEF out of the Gaza Strip and the Sinai Desert altogether and deployed divisions of Egyptian armor and infantry into position for a confrontation with Israel;[2] Egyptian forces took over vacated UN positions in Sharm es-Sheikh overlooking the Straits of Tiran, a strategic waterway at the Red Sea entrance to the Gulf of Aqaba that was vital to Israeli maritime traffic and controlled access to the port of Eilat. Israeli prime minister Levi Eshkol had warned that closing the Straits of Tiran would be viewed as an act of war. On May 22, Nasser ordered them closed. Israel formed a national unity government and prepared for the inevitable.

Following the war, President Lyndon Johnson commented, "If a single act of folly was more responsible for this explosion than any other, it was the arbitrary and dangerous announced decision that the Straits

---

over North Vietnam. Israel shared the secrets of the aircraft with Western intelligence agencies, solidifying a growing alliance between the Mossad, the CIA, and sister services across the world. According to the book *Israel's Secret Wars: A History of Israel's Intelligence Services* by Ian Black and Benny Morris, CIA director Richard Helms was quoted as saying that Israel made good use of the intelligence it gleaned from the defected MiG in the dogfight of April 4, 1967.

of Tiran would be closed. The right of innocent, maritime passage must be preserved for all nations."[3] It was a Guns of August moment of epic proportions—in which miscalculation resulted in a historic chain of events that would change the Middle East forever.

*     *     *

Second Lieutenant Meir Huberman was one of the hundred thousand reservists summoned to duty in late May. He received his emergency call-up orders; his unit's code name was mentioned on the radio, summoning him to duty. He donned his fatigues, grabbed his kit bag, and headed to his mobilization base, where he would be issued his combat gear and Uzi 9mm submachine gun. It appeared as if every able-bodied man had been mobilized for frontline service.

Leaving Bat Yam and heading toward the central bus station in Tel Aviv was surreal. Defensive ditches were being dug along the main thoroughfares of Israel's largest city. Air raid shelters were prepared with emergency rations. There was even talk that mass graves would be prepared—all in anticipation of an expected Egyptian invasion. The Israeli public had no way of knowing that the IDF was confident that it could win a war against Egypt—and possibly Jordan, Syria, and the other Arab states—in a matter of days.[4] The CIA and Britain's MI6 assessed that it would take Israel approximately a week and a half to crush the Arab armies.[5]

The 80th Paratroop Brigade was led by Colonel Danny Matt, a 1948 War of Independence veteran and one of the founders of Israel's airborne capabilities. The division commander was Major General Ariel Sharon, who had become a rising military star, and was determined to become the IDF's chief of staff one day, but his aspirations were higher. He wanted to be prime minister.

Sharon's ego was impossible to contain, but his bravado was based on undeniable military and leadership capabilities. What Sharon lacked in humility, he more than made up in charisma. Blond and built like a buoy, he looked like a husky General George S. Patton, and he would have considered the comparison pure flattery. His military presence was larger than life, and he instilled enormous confidence in the men he led that he would guide them directly through whatever the enemy could throw at them and race them to victory. There was no such order as "forward" in an Israeli officer's lexicon, Sharon imparted to his combat leaders, only "follow me!"[6]

The young soldiers, even those in the reserves, were perplexed by the impenetrable confidence displayed by their senior commanders. The newspapers warned that the Jewish state faced unimaginable peril; *The New York Times* reported that the small IDF was no match for President Nasser's well-trained and highly disciplined army.[7] The brigade commanders seemed impervious to the propaganda beaming from Radio Cairo about President Nasser promising to push the Jews into the sea. Jordan had placed its British-trained army under Egyptian command and there was no doubt that Syria and the other Arab states would join in once the artillery barrages began.

But beyond the fear that *all* soldiers feel before battle, there was a sense that this was their generation's time to fight a war even though the Egyptian Army outnumbered them by a margin of ten-to-one. The paratroopers wondered what the Egyptian attack would look like. It was Israel, though, that would strike first.

*          *          *

At 07:45 on the morning of June 5, the Israel Air Force spearheaded a preemptive strike aimed at destroying the Egyptian Air Force and guaranteeing Israeli air superiority in the conflict. The Mossad and A'man had spent years and great resources gathering intelligence on the habits of Egypt's pilots and the daily routines at air bases across the country; the surprise attack was targeted to strike just as airmen and their crews were sitting down to breakfast. By noon, over two hundred top-flight Soviet-built bombers and fighters had been destroyed, twisted hulks of smoldering metal on runways cratered and rendered inoperable. The war against Egypt was decided before the first Israeli tanks entered Sinai. The Jordanian Air Force responded by attacking cities in Israel, and the IAF took care of King Hussein's air arm in hours. Israeli aircraft also took out the Iraqi and Syrian Air Forces. The skies belonged to Israel. The outcome of the ground war was already decided. Sinai came first.

Because of the topography of the Sinai Desert—jagged cliffs, valleys, and areas of flat sand—there were only three ways an army could move tanks into Sinai: the coastal plain through Gaza, the eastern approach along the Gulf of Aqaba, and the central axis that ran through the critical junction at Abu-Ageila in northwestern Sinai approximately fifteen miles from the Israeli line. The Egyptians defended the crossroads with a sizeable artillery force protected by a series of trenches.

On the first day of the fighting, as the first wave of Israeli aircraft returned from their strike, the 84th Division under General Yisrael Tal moved forces into the Gaza Strip, as Sharon's 38th Division moved toward Abu-Ageila. The key to Sharon's strategy was to have the paratroopers outflank the sizeable Egyptian defenses. As the sun began to set on the first day of fighting, elements of the 80th Brigade would board a squadron of S-58 and Aérospatiale SA 321 Super Frelon transport helicopters for the dunes south of Um-Katef. The junior officers, like Meir Huberman, were impressed with the audacious creativity of the plan.

There was a quick meal before the mission, time for a last smoke, and then onto buses and the awaiting helicopters. The reservists had been milling about at a forward operating base for over ten days anticipating action, and they resembled a rogue force wearing mismatched gear: French lizard-pattern smocks and British World War Two surplus airborne combat helmets—the same ones the 6th Airborne Brigade, the legendary Red Devils, had used when they jumped into Arnhem twenty-three years earlier. The paratroopers did not shave, and the ruffian appearance personified the gritty egalitarian structure of the Israeli military. Few—if any—saluted, and the standard military protocol had the soldiers calling their officers by their first names. But what Lieutenant Huberman and the paratroopers in his brigade lacked in accepted military appearance and discipline they made up for in combat ability and leadership.

The French-built fighters and attack craft of the IAF roared through the skies, the sounds of explosions in the distance becoming the soundtrack of that first morning of war. And as the choppers touched down on the dunes, the paratroopers attempted to march hurriedly for Um-Katef. The dunes were far steeper than the intelligence estimates; many were impassable, with some being forty feet high. The paratroopers, especially those carrying the French-built LRAC de 73mm Mle 1950 antitank bazookas that weighed fifteen pounds, sank quickly with each step.

The nighttime assault on Um-Katef was a real war—it was not a retaliatory raid, and the enemy manning RPK machine guns were well-trained soldiers and not the ragtag fedayeen. This was for real. The platoon and squad leaders realized that this was their moment of truth. When the first flares were fired into the cold desert night sky, their men would have blood on their boots.

The battle for Um-Katef took only several hours. The paratroopers fought fiercely, and the Egyptians resisted. But by dawn, Lieutenant Huberman and his men watched as hundreds of prisoners of war were marched off toward Israeli lines. As the paratroopers rested, and restocked their ammunition, army radio reported heavy fighting in the West Bank and around Jerusalem. The Jordanian Army had attacked first and had been repelled. The following morning, on the third day of the war, Colonel Mordechai Gur, commander of the 55th Reserve Paratroop Brigade, announced that the Temple Mount was in Israeli hands and the Old City of Jerusalem captured. King Hussein's army, along with tens of thousands of West Bank refugees, streamed across the Jordan River.

On June 9, Israeli armor and infantry units climbed the volcanic plateau of the Golan Heights and attacked the Syrian fortifications. A detailed map of the Syrian defensive positions had been obtained by Eli Cohen, an Egyptian-born Jew and Mossad master spy who had infiltrated the upper echelons of the ruling Baath Party and was almost appointed defense minister. Soviet military intelligence specialists helped the Syrians capture him, and he was hanged in Marjeh Square in Damascus on May 18, 1965.* On June 10, the last day of the war,

---

* Cohen's body has never been returned to Israel. Years later, as head of the Mossad, Meir Dagan would spend countless hours in his office—and with his intelligence officers—thinking of ways to return Cohen and all of Israel's unaccounted-for soldiers and spies buried in enemy lands, back to Israel.

Meir Huberman and the 80th Brigade were flown by helicopter into the southeast Golan Heights.[8]

By nightfall, the war was over.

*               *               *

Israel's victory in the 1967 Six-Day War was epic and improbable. It embodied the biblical story of David vs. Goliath. The upstart Jewish nation had slain the giant. The face of Moshe Dayan, the Israeli defense minister who wore a patch over the left eye, became a symbol for the new Israeli superpower. For young officers like Huberman, the events were exhilarating. The victory was infectious. He had fought in his first war and realized he was good in combat.

While stationed on the newly established front lines in the north, Lieutenant Huberman walked into the brigade's administrative office and requested to return to the regular army.

# BOOK TWO
# COMMANDO

# CHAPTER 5

# The New World Order

In December 1969, an IDF singing troupe released a song to define the tumultuously violent times Israel was experiencing in the years following the Six-Day War. It was called *"Shir La'Shalom"* ("A Song for Peace"), and its opening lyrics were "Let the sun come in beyond the flowers, do not look back let them go. Eyes open in hope, not through gunsights, sing a song of love, and not for wars."

There was hope in Israel that the six days in June 1967 had been the Jewish state's war to end all wars. In the euphoric days that followed the capture of the Sinai Desert, the Golan Heights, and the West Bank, along with the reunification of Jerusalem, the dream was that the Arab nations would respect the fact that Israel was an irremovable reality in the Middle East and that the Jews would not and could not be pushed into the sea. The men who fought in that war did not want their sons to have to follow in their footsteps. But optimism was always a fool's currency in a region where hatred takes centuries to be extinguished. When the "Song for Peace" made it to number one on the charts, Israel was nearly three years into a bloody war of incessant casualties, bloodshed, and horror. The last day of the Six-Day War never came.

Although the Arab states were stunned by the unexpected Israeli victory and daunted by the Jewish state's undeniable military superiority, they were determined to show the world that although humbled, they were far from being destroyed. On August 28, 1967, the Middle East's kings, princes, and presidents met in Khartoum, Sudan, for an emergency meeting of the Arab League. At the conference, one of anger and shame, a usually disjointed organization issued a unanimous decree: no negotiations with Israel, no recognition of Israel, and no peace with Israel. Arabs and Jews are still suffering from the ramifications of the infamous "Three No's" pledge.

The Egyptians also landed helicopters full of special operations companies behind Israeli lines. Huberman worked alongside Unit 424, Southern Command's reconnaissance commando force better known as *Shaked*, the Hebrew word for almond.* Almond Recon's specialty was patrolling large swaths of the southern border on jeeps and by foot, and chasing down infiltrators, Egyptian commandos, and terrorists. The unit's commander was Lieutenant Colonel Danny Wolf (Rahav), a veteran paratroop officer whose military vision was shaped by David Stirling, the "Phantom Major" who founded Britain's Special Air Service: "Who Dares Won."

*     *     *

First Lieutenant Meir Huberman listened to the "Song for Peace" and news of terror attacks around the Middle East from his office in El Arish, the beachfront capital of the Sinai Desert and home to over a hundred thousand people and his division headquarters. He was a junior operations officer covering a sector that stretched from the Gaza Strip to the Suez Canal for the military administration that ran the captured territory. The canal, closed to commercial shipping since 1967, was the no-man's-land separating Israeli and Egyptian forces and the fault line during what became known as the War of Attrition. Israeli lines along the waterway were subjected to relentless Egyptian artillery fire, which prompted Israeli retaliation. Meir's primary mission focus was

---

* The IDF had three regional commands—Northern, Central, and Southern—each with a reconnaissance unit named after beans or nuts. Northern Command's commando section was named *Egoz*, or Walnut; Central Command's reconnaissance force was named *Haruv*, or Carob; and Southern Command was *Shaked*, or Almond.

the city of El Arish and missions to stem Egyptian special operations and intelligence forces.

Huberman liked working with the division's intelligence and commando units—especially Almond Recon—to formulate operations to hunt Egyptian special forces teams in the dunes of Sinai. Like the Almond Recon commander, he developed a reputation as being slightly eccentric. He brought a small sample of his art supplies with him to headquarters in the provincial town, and in the rare moments of spare time, he would paint portraits of the locals and vistas of the windswept desert plains by the waves of the Mediterranean. Tall palm trees jutted out from the beach where Huberman found a niche in blueprinting the details of complex and dangerous cat-and-mouse operations hunting Egyptian commandos. The operations officer had to think like the enemy in guessing where they would land and what targets they would go after; he also had to have a devious tactical imagination to plot out areas where the Egyptian forces could be ambushed. The work required an officer with a sly sense of creativity who was also a hunter and had no reservations about going for his prey's jugular. So, too, did counterinsurgency.

*         *         *

The War of Attrition was a tit-for-tat low-intensity conflict characterized by artillery exchanges and commando raids that had the potential of escalating into a full-fledged war. Washington and Moscow tested their latest weapon systems in the skies over Egypt and Syria, lessons learned that were proving invaluable to assist American air assets that struggled against the Soviet-made surface-to-air missiles in the skies over Vietnam.* The battles had become an extension of the Cold War:

---

* On the night of December 26–27, 1969, Israeli reconnaissance paratroopers launched a daring raid against an Egyptian antiaircraft radar installation on Ra's Ghareb, on the African side of the Gulf of Suez. Rather than blow up the facility, the commandos stole an advanced Soviet-supplied P-12 ground-to-air radar. The seven-ton system was loaded onto an Israel Air Force helicopter and flown back to Israel, where it was dissected and analyzed. The CIA and American Department of Defense were afforded an early yet significant example of strategic intelligence sharing between Israel and the United States.

the United States had become Israel's principal arms supplier, and the Soviet Union supplied Egypt and Syria.

There was another front in the War of Attrition that would erupt into a never-ending conflict—international terrorism. Palestinian national liberation groups, with the help of the KGB and the other Warsaw Pact intelligence arms, along with the People's Republic of China and North Korea, had become useful pawns in the new theater of the Cold War and turned Israel's new borders and frontiers across the world into their new battlefield. Fedayeen officers now based in Jordan, Syria, and Lebanon were sent to advanced espionage and command courses throughout the Eastern Bloc.

The Popular Front for the Liberation of Palestine was one of the most capable and far-reaching of the terror factions to emerge from the Six-Day War. The PFLP was the creation of Dr. George Habash, a Christian-Palestinian physician from Lod* who was schooled in medicine and radical politics at the American University of Beirut; Wadi Haddad, known by his nom de guerre Abu Hani, also a Greek-Orthodox Christian, was Habash's operational mastermind.

The PFLP pushed a Pan-Arab agenda, wanting to rid the Middle East of Israel and all Western imperialist vestiges. Its declared politics were Marxist-Leninist, making it an enemy of the monarchies in the region. The Syrian government supported the PFLP with weapons and diplomatic cover. The vast deserts of Jordan were used to establish terror training camps. But the Lebanese capital—and its banks, casinos, beachfront cafés, expensive prostitutes, and factional chaos—attracted Saudi princes, Hollywood film stars, and radicals of every political persuasion. The Soviet Embassy in Beirut was a convenient conduit for KGB support; the money flowed in, as did the small arms, explosives, and an army of advisors. Beirut International Airport was the PFLP's frequent flyer launching pad for a new offensive.

On July 28, 1968, El Al Flight 426, on a scheduled route between London and Lod Airport (later Ben Gurion Airport) with a stop in Rome, was hijacked by three Palestinian men shortly after taking off from the

---

* Lydda in Arabic.

Italian capital. The aircraft, a Boeing 707, was diverted to Algiers, the capital of Algeria. Women and children, along with non-Israelis, were released. The terrorists held twelve Israeli passengers and the ten-man El Al crew captive for forty days, until Israel released sixteen Palestinian prisoners.

The success of the El Al hijacking* emboldened the PFLP. When attempts to hijack El Al airliners failed due to increased security at airports in Europe and on board the Israeli flag carrier, they resorted to machine-gunning Israeli aircraft on the tarmac in Zurich and Athens. On August 29, 1969, a PFLP team led by a female terrorist, Leila Khaled, hijacked TWA Flight 840 flying between Rome and Tel Aviv with a stopover in Athens; it was diverted to Syria, where hostages were held for a month.

The largest PFLP operation of the period was Skyjack Sunday—the September 6, 1970, hijacking of three aircraft from Pan Am, TWA, and Swissair. An attempted hijacking of a fourth, an El Al flight, was thwarted by sky marshals; one hijacker was killed, and a second, Leila Khaled, was overpowered and handed to British authorities in London. The TWA flight was flown to Cairo, and the other three jets were taken to Dawson's Field outside Amman, the Jordanian capital. Once television news crews arrived at the desert landing strip, the hijackers released their hostages and then blew up the airliners. The audacious act, and the images of the cockpits erupting in a flash of smoke, fire, and debris, was the trip wire that ignited a civil war in Jordan, as King Hussein felt he was losing his kingdom to the upstart Palestinian factions who had turned the country into a state within a state.

---

* The hijacking resulted in massive and revolutionary security overhauls for El Al. The airline initiated a structural upgrade of its fleet of aircraft so that the main cabin and cargo holds were reinforced to withstand bomb blasts and gunfire. Ground security teams interrogated passengers about who packed their luggage, asking if they had received anything from anyone to bring in their bags. Most importantly, every El Al flight carried armed sky marshals, veterans of Israel's special operations units and Shin Bet, who were trained to shoot it out at thirty thousand feet rather than allow the aircraft to be hijacked. As a result of the security program—considered years ahead of its time—El Al was considered the safest airline in the world, prompting terrorist groups to target other flag carrier airlines during what became known as the age of air piracy.

*              *              *

In the summer of 1970, U.S. secretary of state William Rogers helped to negotiate a gradual ceasefire to end the War of Attrition. The guns fell silent after the Jordanian Civil War and Egyptian president Nasser's fatal heart attack, suffered while negotiating terms between King Hussein and Yasir Arafat. The civil war, known as Black September, ended with the Palestinian groups being kicked out of Jordan and forced into Lebanon and Syria in search of new bases of operation against Israel. The PFLP saw the Gaza Strip as the perfect blank canvas ripe for a revolution.

When Israel captured the Gaza Strip from the Egyptian Army in June 1967, it also assumed control of the almost four hundred thousand Palestinians who lived there. Unlike Jordan, which bestowed citizenship on the Palestinians living in the West Bank between 1949 and 1967, Egypt never recognized the inhabitants of Gaza as anything more than refugees—a weapon of misery that could be used against Israel across the armistice lines. The Egyptians kept the Gazans impoverished, and with the help—and money—of the United Nations—settled tens of thousands inside eight official refugee camps. The United Nations Relief Works Agency, UNRWA, administered the refugee camps and provided food, services, and a stipend to those who lived there. Although Gazans were allowed to work and some even to study in Egypt, 60 percent of the population of Gaza were registered as refugees.[1] Living under Egyptian military control was harsh and hopeless.

Initially, the new Israeli rulers were treated with the benefit of the doubt. The IDF provided basic services—food, electricity, sanitation—to the population, and Gazans were issued work permits to earn salaries inside Israel. The Jewish state in 1967 was a far cry from the powerhouse it would become years later, but Israeli wages were greater than what a Gazan could earn under Egyptian rule; the Israeli lira was much stronger than the Egyptian pound. However, economic realities were often outdone by nationalistic aspirations. The fedayeen was still a powerful force inside Gaza—especially inside the refugee camps, where UNRWA allowed Fatah to be the true administrator of day-to-day life.

But after the creation of the PFLP, and their international exploits in air piracy, Arafat's men had rivals in Gaza. A sizeable percentage of Gaza's population considered themselves Egyptian, not Palestinian, and the PFLP ideology of a Pan-Arab revolution and anticolonialist Marxism appealed to the young who, following the student riots in Paris and the antiwar movement in the United States, wanted to join in on the global revolutionary movement. The socialist messages emanating from PFLP literature was liberating to many Gazans who were not religious and felt threatened by the rigid fundamentalist preaching of the Muslim Brotherhood.

There was no shortage of men willing to take up arms against the Israelis in Gaza. According to some estimates, the Egyptians had a standing army of five thousand Palestinian soldiers in Gaza, men trained for operations against Israel. After the IDF conquered Gaza and Sinai, the brigades simply burned their uniforms and hid their weapons and equipment in caves and bunkers. The IDF captured warehouses full of weapons abandoned by Egyptian forces, including thousands of assault rifles and submachine guns, hand grenades, and hundreds of thousands of rounds of ammunition, but there were still ample supplies of weapons for anyone wanting one.

The other Palestinian factions in Gaza operated from smaller arsenals. The PFLP had to build a complete weapons armaments acquisition supply chain. Some weapons were purchased from Bedouins in the Sinai Desert who rummaged the battlefield of 1967 in search of whatever would fetch a top price, but Israeli intelligence manipulated many of these Soviet-made grenades to explode the moment the pin was pulled rather than after the prescribed four seconds. Dozens of terrorists were killed as a result.

The PFLP turned to the sea—small ships sailing from Lebanon and Syria that could evade Israeli naval patrols and unload tons of arms and ammunition along the beaches of Gaza. Senior PFLP operatives also used this route to bring in commanders and vital communications.

According to the IDF, between 1969 and 1970, Palestinian terror groups perpetrated over one thousand attacks of varying kinds against Israeli military targets and civilians who ventured into Gaza. Graffiti was painted on building walls throughout the strip quoting Dr. Habash's opening manifesto when he created the PFLP: "The only language the enemy understands is that of revolutionary violence. The historic task of the hour was to open a fierce struggle against it, turning the occupied territories into an inferno whose fires consume the usurpers."[2]

By the end of 1970, the terror groups had killed 128 fellow Palestinians and 15 Israelis.[3] Groups like Fatah and the PFLP focused much of their violence on suspected collaborators, men and women whom the Israelis referred to as "Returners to Zion."[4] Some provided the Israelis with information for profit; others used revenge as a motive. Rumors alone were enough to have someone sentenced to death. Everyone had an agenda. Members of the Muslim Brotherhood accused individuals who sold drugs and alcohol of working with the Israelis, guaranteeing that they would be lined up against the wall. Fatah members accused rivals. Prostitutes, who served all sides, were specifically targeted. No one was spared—not children, the elderly, and not even pregnant women.[5]

Sharon was furious about the PFLP's audacity and its growing military prowess. So, too, was chief of staff Lieutenant General Haim Bar-Lev. According to reports, Avraham Arnan, the founder of Sayeret Mat'kal and the head of the Military Intelligence Collections Department, presented General Sharon with the idea of the unit creating an Arabic-speaking undercover force.[6] Several soldiers were interviewed for the new unit, all with a passing knowledge of Arabic. The unit had little direction; their initial training, all live-fire, was designed as wild and dangerous.[7] Enormous resources were invested in this Sayeret Mat'kal initiative—weapons, training courses, and intelligence instruction about the human and topographical makeup of the Gaza Strip. They bought Arab costumes and even ventured deep inside Gaza for training exercises. The new force was small and experimental

Sharon seemed disinterested in having units outside his direct control—and outside his sphere of allegiance—handle a potential make-or-break career challenge. He searched for an officer who mirrored his thought process and personality. He had heard accounts of a young paratroop officer of boundless courage and wanted to meet him. In February 1970, Meir suffered a debilitating wound that should have ended his military career. His jeep struck a land mine[8] planted on a sandy stretch of road near El Arish by Egyptian commandos. Meir had ventured into the minefield because a series of Katyusha rocket launchers had been positioned at his base and were timed to launch the 122mm projectiles. Disregarding his own safety, he rendered the devices safe and hit a mine on his way out of the explosive-laden ambush. Chunks of shrapnel, jeep chassis, and bone tore through Meir's calves and thighs. He was flown by helicopter to Sheba Hospital in Beersheba, where doctors saved his legs and his life.

Meir's friends and fellow soldiers urged him to leave the army with a medical disability. A sane individual would have accepted a pension and created a new life. He was never able to shake the pain, no matter how many surgeries he would endure.

Meir did not want his parents to worry about the severity of his wounds. He did not want them to see him bandaged up.[9] He used the time convalescing to teach himself English and master speaking it with the fluency of someone who'd spent his entire life in the United States or England. He listened to the BBC World Service on a battered AM transistor radio.

Lieutenant Huberman returned to base with a walking cane and a Doberman named Pako. He smoked a pipe like a learned professor—no one in their twenties smoked a pipe in Israel and certainly not in the IDF. "He was determined to be unique," Sami Mutzafi Barak, a junior military intelligence officer in Southern Command who first met Meir after his injuries and would become a lifelong comrade and friend, remembered, "and he wanted to stand out. The pipe, the cane, and the classical music that he listened to on a battered transistor radio were Meir's props. He fought his entire life to shed the new-immigrant insignificance that was often thrust upon the non-native-born soldiers."[10]

Returning to active duty and being eccentric were Meir's way of letting the army know he would not be overlooked the way Sayeret Mat'kal had deemed him unsuitable material six years earlier. Yossi Ben Hanan, a veteran tank officer and later general made famous for a 1967 *Life* magazine cover photo showing him triumphantly clutching a captured Egyptian Army AK-47 while cooling off in the Suez Canal, who would later become Meir's closest friend in the world, summed it up best: "Wherever he was, he was never just another one. He was always *the* one!"[11]

Huberman's unmatched courage was known throughout the command. Accounts of what happened in the minefield had become legendary. Sharon liked talking to men of all ranks, especially those with reputations for arrogance and courage. He summoned the young officer to his office for a behind-closed-door meeting.

Most twenty-five-year-old lieutenants would be apprehensive about meeting a general, but Meir welcomed the chance. Known as someone who spoke the truth no matter who he was before and the ramifications, Lieutenant Huberman relished the opportunity. This was his chance to impress. He polished his brown leather boots and folded his red beret sharply into the left epaulet of his Class A olive tunic before hitching a ride to Southern Command HQ in the Negev Desert town of Beersheba.

Generals could keep the lower ranks waiting hours before seeing them in their office. Huberman despised tardiness, and Sharon relished punctuality. An orderly ushered the young lieutenant in right on time. Huberman saluted his commanding officer, and Sharon offered Meir coffee and cake. They sat on an old sofa that, three years earlier, had belonged to an Egyptian general. The two shared a passion for reading and studying military history; they had rambunctious senses of humor and a penchant for telling dirty jokes. They were kindred spirits. The meeting in Beersheba was the start of a lifelong friendship. Sharon was the first person in Meir's life who genuinely appreciated his potential.

The general and the lieutenant sat for over an hour—an unheard-of allocation of time for a man of Sharon's rank. Sharon turned to Meir and asked how he would handle rounding up the terrorists on the wanted list. Huberman did not stammer for a second. "The best way is to move around Gaza in civilian clothes, like the locals, so that we can get close to them."[12] Sharon was impressed. The Mat'kal experiment was top secret, as only a handful of officers knew of its existence, and the fact that a young lieutenant would have the creativity to come up with an idea like that on his own impressed Sharon greatly.

Ariel Sharon wanted Meir to handle the challenge that Southern Command faced in Gaza, and he gave him command of a small new unit: *Sayeret Ha'Hofim*, or the Coastal Reconnaissance Unit.[13] Fatah and the PFLP were armed with weapons brought into Gaza via the sea. The boats ferrying arms sailed from Alexandria, Beirut, and Latakia. They were met at night and in international waters by Palestinian fishing boats that dodged Israeli naval patrols to reach prepared beachheads where the weapons could be unloaded and transported for safekeeping. Huberman's men worked the Almond Recon commandos to locate smuggling points where fishermen and small craft assembled to ambush the smugglers and their customers on the shoreline spots concealed by palm trees and dunes and off the beaten path of regular IDF patrols.

Promoted to captain, Meir made the most of his new command. He dressed his men like Gazans to gather intelligence and patrol the coast as if they were local fishermen. He also had his men patrol the beaches of Gaza before dawn sitting atop camels while dressed as Bedouins. He sat with local Palestinians and enjoyed a shared breakfast of fava beans and eggs to establish an ad hoc network of sympathetic friends and informants.

Meir requisitioned a seaside villa in the northwestern stretch of the Gaza Strip that had belonged to Ahmad Shukeiri, one of the founders of the Palestine Liberation Organization (PLO), who had commanded the five thousand Palestinians serving in the Egyptian military. His home became Meir's headquarters. It even boasted a basketball court.

*       *       *

On Saturday, January 2, 1971, Robert Aroyo, an Israeli resident from the Tel Aviv suburb of Kiryat Ono, spent the day touring the Gaza Strip with his family. Gaza was not a closed military zone, and Israelis regularly traveled through the strip to visit Sinai. Gazans embraced the vehicular traffic; the tourists boosted the local economy. The main east-west and north-south arteries were packed with Israeli cars—especially on weekends. But at a junction heading home, the Aroyo family turned left instead of making a right and ended up in the Jabaliya refugee camp.

Two Palestinian teenagers working for the PFLP were lying atop a rooftop waiting for an IDF patrol to pass when they saw the family's car with its yellow-and-black Israeli license plates. Thinking that civilians were a better target than soldiers, one of the teenagers tossed a Soviet-made F-1 fragmentation grenade through the window of the slow-moving car. It landed in the backseat, where Robert's wife Preeti and his two children—four-year-old Abigail and seven-year-old Marc-Daniel—sat. The blast killed the two children instantly; Preeti was critically wounded.

Israelis were horrified to learn of the murders of the two children. Defense Minister Moshe Dayan blamed Southern Command for not containing the outbreak of terror in Gaza. General Sharon blamed Dayan for grandstanding when he should have cautioned citizens to stay clear.

The murder of two Jewish children ignited Meir, lighting a sense of urgent action. He remembered sitting in the kitchen in Bat Yam and listening to Mina's soft-spoken anger at God for not protecting the one million children killed in Hitler's Final Solution. Meir understood this now to be a full-scale insurgency. He wanted to play a more central role in fighting the terrorists.

Shortly after the Aroyo murders, the men of the small Mat'kal-led counterinsurgency experiment were told to pack their gear, load it onto trucks, and head across the Gaza Strip to the Coastal Recon's villa. Sharon had decided to unify the two units into a single force. The dozen or so men were met at their new home by a dark-complexioned man in civilian clothes wearing black canvas sneakers and carrying a World War Two–era Thompson submachine. "I'm Captain Huberman," the man said and smiled. "Call me Meir."

Meir was determined to turn his new unit, called *Sayeret Rimon*, or the Grenade Recon, into the IDF's first operational—proactive—undercover force. He even contracted an insignia company to create a unit badge, a hand grenade as the handle for a winged dagger, to accentuate the unit's combat prowess. He imagined that Grenade would be just as much a psychological force as a tactical one. Meir understood that the new unit needed to get under the skin of the men they pursued; to be successful, the unit had to haunt the minds of the men who perpetrated acts of terror and make men who perpetrated violence afraid of the surroundings they felt safe in. It was a perfect incubator for a later career in establishing intelligence protocols and defining the operational needs of dirty trick expediency. A report on Israel's Kan 11 television network would even categorize the unit as a "bunch of bastards."[14]

Sharon let his young officer use his imagination and courage as he saw fit. Meir shifted the unit's primary focus from intelligence gathering to gathering intelligence for proactive tactical counterterrorism.[15] He was only twenty-six years old and, as it would soon become apparent, had become the most important man in the Gaza Strip.

# CHAPTER 6

# Chameleons and Trigger Pullers

eutralizing the emergence of the Fatah and PFLP terror hub in Gaza demanded proactive intelligence gathering and quick turnaround analysis. The General Security Service, or *Sherut Ha'Bitachon Ha'Klali*, Israel's domestic counterespionage and counterterrorist service, better known by its Hebrew acronyms Shin Bet or Shabak, was the lead agency involved in fighting terror. The Shin Bet shared responsibility for Gaza with A'man, the IDF's Military Intelligence Branch. A small army of Shabak and Military Intelligence case officers was rushed to Gaza in late 1970 to manage the enormous workload. It was an all-hands-on-deck effort. The territorial conquests of the 1967 War overwhelmed both intelligence services.

Before 1967, the Shin Bet's primary mission had been to hunt enemy agents—Arab and Eastern European. Because the service focused primarily on the KGB and the other Warsaw Pact espionage services, the Shin Bet had a vast network of agents and sources behind the Iron Curtain, which led to some monumental Cold War victories. It was the Shin Bet, not the Mossad, that got its hands on the text of a secret speech made by Nikita Khrushchev in 1956 where he denounced Joseph Stalin—according to reports, a copy was handed to the Shin Bet liaison officer at the Israeli Embassy in Warsaw and shared with the CIA, in one of the first-ever joint efforts by the intelligence services of the United States and Israel.[1] The

Shin Bet director in 1970 was Yossef Harmelin, a Vienna-born counter-intelligence specialist. He spoke German and Hebrew. Not Arabic. He understood double agents and hunting spies more than battling terrorists.

A'man, the Hebrew acronym for *Agaf Ha'Modi'in*, shared the counter-terrorism responsibility for the Gaza Strip—and the West Bank—with the Shin Bet. A'man was Israel's largest intelligence-gathering service and, considering that the greatest threat to the Jewish state's survival came from the combined conventional Arab armies, it was the country's most important, the umbrella force for numerous intelligence units at the command and corps level and featuring an all-important research division that assessed threats and the location of both military and unconventional targets. The whole thing was led by Major General Aharon Yariv, a veteran of the British Army in the Second World War who was a master strategist and credited for much of the behind-the-scenes intelligence successes that enabled Israel to be victorious against such overwhelming odds in six days in June 1967.

The Shin Bet and A'man ran a comprehensive campaign inside Gaza relying on HUMINT—the human intelligence gathered by running agents, establishing sources, and using bribery, coercion, and rewards for information. Intelligence officers from the Shin Bet's Arab Desk ran assets and sources inside Gaza. Unit 504, the HUMINT force inside Military Intelligence, was responsible for recruiting and handling agents, assets, and sources. It was a hands-on and in-your-face undertaking, with the Israeli intelligence officers against hundreds of hardcore, heavily armed operatives and thousands of accomplices and sympathizers. This was not a conflict where winning hearts and minds was applicable.

Intelligence was the currency of Israel's day-to-day counterterrorism effort in Gaza. But Arabic capabilities—language skills and successfully masquerading as the local Gazans—were the key to victory.

Israel's armies had disguised special operations personnel as Arabs before, pre- and post-independence. In 1938, during the height of the Arab Revolt, an eccentric, creative-minded no-nonsense British Army intelligence officer stationed in Palestine named Captain Orde Wingate put together a mixed hundred-man counterinsurgency to kill saboteurs and guerrillas in the villages where they lived. Wingate, a Christian

Zionist, a mad eccentric, and someone who fashioned himself an inventor of innovative tactics, knew that the British Army in the Northwest Frontier force in India and the Royal Irish Constabulary had used similar tactics battling guerrillas. Wingate's creation, known as the Special Night Squads, was made up of British soldiers and Haganah operatives, mainly men from the Jewish Supernumerary Police, who forged innovative tactics, including inserting teams dressed as locals into Galilee Arab villages to hunt down terror suspects.

The Special Night Squads were effective, perhaps because their tactics were accentuated by reprisals and violence. They did not shy away from beating prisoners, and they showed little mercy to anyone who resisted. Force, guile, and fearlessness were tangible currencies in Britain's counterinsurgency campaign—tools that Wingate would use during the Second World War when he created what was known as the Gideon Force, a sabotage unit that targeted Italian positions in Sudan and Ethiopia. Later, as a brigadier, Wingate led the legendary Long Range Penetration Groups, better known as the Chindits, fighting the Japanese deep behind enemy lines in Burma.

Years later, the Palmach, the Haganah's elite Strike Companies, created a force of Arabic-speaking operatives for espionage and sabotage missions. Known as the Arab Platoon,* the unit fought with the British in Lebanon and Syria in 1941 during the campaign against Vichy French forces. Moshe Dayan, a Special Night Squad veteran, lost his eye in Lebanon fighting with the platoon.

During Israel's War of Independence and the years that followed, the *Mista'arvim*, Hebrew for those who dress and act like Arabs to

---

* The Yishuv, the Jewish population of pre-independence Israel, was made up of people from the four corners of the world and spoke hundreds of languages and dialects. Before the Second World War broke out, tens of thousands of refugees from Germany and Austria reached the shores of British Mandate Palestine wanting to fight against Hitler. The Palmach recruited some of them into an undercover unit called the German Platoon, which was to function as a fifth column if Field Marshal Rommel's Afrika Korps smashed through Allied defenses in Egypt and made it to Palestine. When the Germans were stopped at El Alamein and the tide of the conflict shifted, members of the German Platoon were sent by the British Special Operations Executive into POW camps to gather intelligence by posing as members of the Wehrmacht and Luftwaffe.

conduct military operations or gather intelligence, were the first espionage agents for the nascent Israeli espionage community. Drawn from Jews who came from Syria, Egypt, and Iraq, these men were able to blend in seamlessly inside the capital cities of Damascus, Cairo, and Baghdad, and dispatch detailed reports back to Mossad and Military Intelligence headquarters. Sayeret Mat'kal, it is reported, had experience masquerading as Arabs, but that was for long-range penetration missions across the Middle East,[2] and not for a long-term deployment to a place like Gaza.

When the Sayeret Mat'kal advisors built the cadre of what was to be the undercover intelligence-gathering unit for Gaza, they sought the advice of veterans of the Haganah's Arab Platoon, most retired from the military or security services, who happily lent their expertise.[3] Meir inherited these men when they assumed command of the overall undercover special operations unit for Gaza. They were known as the Chameleons, the name of the wily reptile that can change color and appearance, because that would become their primary mission: disguise themselves into a myriad of appearances to blend into particular settings for intelligence-gathering missions. The Chameleons were predominately Jewish, Israelis of the Middle Eastern Diaspora. Meir realized that for long-term and deep penetration, Grenade would need the genuine article and not merely Jewish Israelis from Middle Eastern families who had dark complexions and could muster a few phrases in their parents' native tongue. He blueprinted the Chameleons—and much of the unit—around Bedouin and Druze NCOs and officers: members of the Arabic-speaking minorities who served in the ranks of the IDF with great distinction and courage.

The Bedouins, fierce and stoic warriors, were used primarily as trackers. They worked alongside frontline IDF units to scan the sandy roads near frontier fences to identify footprints and marks that signaled a hostile infiltration. The Druze were conscripted into IDF service. An ethnoreligious minority in Israel that developed out of Ismailism, a branch of Shiite Islam, the Druze are native Arabic speakers and maintain Arab culture as an integral component of their identity. They do not consider themselves Muslims; they swear allegiance to the nation where they reside, and most live in Israel, Lebanon, and Syria. Meir had come across the Bedouin and Druze trackers while serving in Sinai chasing Egyptian commandos. They were cool under fire and had a penchant for adventure—precisely the type of soldier he was looking to lead operations in Grenade.

The Druze and Bedouin Chameleons had to work at their craft. The Arabic spoken by the Bedouins in villages of the Negev Desert and the Druze villages in Galilee was distinctively different than the cadence, accent, and slang of the Arabic spoken in Gaza. Mastering Gazan Arabic and learning the proper banter and a lexicon of words and phrases that did not exist outside the strip required hours of endless instruction.

Inside the unit, the Bedouins and Druze were known as the Speakers since they were the only members of the unit who were supposed to talk to the locals in Arabic. But if Meir saw something special in one of the men in his command, he was allowed to don a costume, even though he did not know a word of Arabic. As much as he was fascinated by Arabic art and culture, Meir himself did not speak the language. He could tell a joke or two in Arabic, especially the dirty ones, and he knew a few Koranic blessings and niceties to honor his hosts before a meal or a get-together.[4] He could not hide his Israeli accent laced with the hint of a Polish timbre, though. He viewed this colloquial illiteracy as a challenge and not a handicap. He donned local costumes on all undercover assignments. Israeli officers led from the front. Meir would not sit in a command post monitoring an operation on a radio while his men were in danger, alone, and surrounded by the enemy.

Members of the unit recall that Meir liked the theatrics of dressing up. It built the esprit de corps of an elite fighting force that was both unconventional and delightfully eccentric. Meir had discretionary funds at his disposal, as all elite unit commanders did, and he spent significant resources shopping for clothes in the markets of Gaza. Store owners were shocked that an Israeli officer would be so enthusiastic to purchase fashion items popular with the men—and women—of Gaza.

The Chameleons had to be convincing—their disguise had to be foolproof down to the smallest detail. They could not have any military identification on them, and nothing that linked them to Israel. Their sandals had to be the kind found in the markets of Gaza. They used the local soap brand and brushed their teeth with Egyptian paste so that they would not stand out. They smoked Cleopatra cigarettes made by the Eastern Tobacco Company in Cairo. Cleopatras were harsh but they were cheap, and even the most suspicious members of a Palestinian terror group knew that no Israeli in his right mind would dare smoke them.

When the Chameleons went shopping, they always bought clothes that were seemingly too large. Shopkeepers, especially those who sold them female garments, used to wink at the Israelis, thinking that these were for wives who were of a hefty size, something considered very sexy in Egyptian cinema at the time. But not only were they meant to fit men, they also had to conceal holsters, ammunition magazines, grenades, radio equipment, and commando daggers. The Chameleons would be close-quarter combat specialists, designed to engage their targets at point-blank range, and their primary weapon of choice was the pistol: British and Soviet-made handguns that were easy to find in Gaza. Meir's sidearm of choice was a 9mm German-made Luger pistol that he had procured out of an arms cache captured from Lebanese gun runners. Years later Dagan would reflect, "There was training in rapid shooting with pistols and the development of an instinct to respond to [enemy] fire. We went through all the skills [required] to use a weapon in any situation."[5]

The Chameleons had to know how to use the Port Said, the Egyptian-manufactured version of the Swedish Carl Gustav submachine gun that had a folding stock and could fit under clothes. Meir requisitioned plenty of Soviet-made AK-47s and SKS assault rifles when his men masqueraded as terrorists. They wore special jackets with hand-sewn pockets to conceal their weapons and magazines.[6]

Grenade Recon never fielded more than thirty or forty Chameleons.[7] It was a small group: tight-knit and mission-focused.

The unit's quick reaction force was the largest contingent inside Meir's commando army. They were responsible for manning observation posts, rear security, and roadblocks, and consisted of approximately eighty combat-proven reconnaissance soldiers. Meir preferred squad leaders and operators from Almond Recon—special operations–capable soldiers who could work in small independent formations in dangerous terrain.

Meir handpicked every member of the unit—conducting all entry interviews himself. He sought men with exceptional weapons skills who had a little bit of cowboy and crazy intertwined. They also needed an endless supply of patience because they would have to lie in ambush for long periods when and where the Chameleons planned to engage their targets. Most importantly, they had to be disciplined and relied upon not to shoot the disguised operators during a firefight. The unit trained incessantly in live-fire friend-or-foe identification drills. One of the officers earmarked for the unit was a young Almond Recon lieutenant named Shmuel Paz. Meir believed in the click of a personal connection; he either liked you or did not, and a bond developed between the two. Paz became the operations officer and later the unit's second in command.[8]

Meir's new unit worked closely with Almond Recon. Southern Command's reconnaissance force was the parent unit of Meir's smaller outfit, and the two forces operated alongside one another. When Wolf fell ill, his deputy battalion commander, Major Amatzia Chen, took over.

An agronomist by profession, Amatzia, known by his nickname Patzi, was another one of the square pegs in a round hole attracted to the small unit world that Sharon collected in his command. Meir viewed the Almond Recon commander as a special operations warfare role model—an officer and a gentleman of unrivaled imagination. He had led spellbinding raids deep behind the Suez Canal and into Jordan—some that he assessed might never be declassified. He had the reputation as someone who had killed more enemy soldiers than anyone else in the IDF: Egyptians, Arab Legionnaires in Jordan, Syrian commandos, and Saudi mercenaries.[9] Chen had also established a special unit within Almond Recon—a cross-border raiding team known as the Vipers that survived countless engagements with the enemy and saved the lives of his men under hellacious fire. Meir found a kindred spirit in Patzi. But both men took an instant liking to one another and became lifelong friends.

\*　　　　\*　　　　\*

Grenade Recon was supported by an administrative cadre of communications specialists, intelligence officers, secretaries, cooks, and mechanics who kept the unit operational. Most of the support staff were women completing their mandatory two years of military service. Grenade never had more than 150 soldiers on its log, and Meir maintained a dossier on each one of them. He wanted to know which ones came from poor homes and had to work on furloughs to help the family survive, and which families had ill parents and siblings. He felt responsible for them, like a father, and helped whom he could however he could—a remarkable display of leadership and maturity for an officer who was still only twenty-six years old. The paternal bond Meir practiced with those under his command would be a practice he followed religiously with every unit, battalion, brigade, and division he led. This was the foundation of leadership he instilled years later at the Mossad.

\*　　　　\*　　　　\*

Meir never received special operations or espionage instruction to prepare him for creating a clandestine unit like Grenade Recon. He possessed an inherently wily tactical understanding of complex strategic challenges. "It was something," a former combat officer who served with Meir years later would comment, "that commanders had or did not have. It was not something that could be bought or learned. It was an indefinable gift, a form of genius, and early on in his career, Meir showed everyone that he was blessed with extra helpings of it."[10] The unit was a perfect incubator for a later career in establishing intelligence protocols and defining the operational needs of dirty trick expediency.

Sharon gave Meir a blank check to create the counterterrorist unit he wanted to build. Theirs was a relationship of pride and kinship. The affection and, most importantly, the trust, were unconditional. Sharon would authorize whatever resources and requests, no matter how bizarre, that Meir asked for, including exotic weapons, ammunition that was nearly impossible to find in Israel, and civilian and military vehicles of all makes.

Grenade Recon had a free hand in poaching other units for operators, intelligence officers, and support staffers. As head of Southern Command, Sharon promised to run interference if Meir's special operations unit caused havoc among the conventional forces deployed to Gaza and the civil administration that ran day-to-day life. All that General Sharon demanded was results. He did not doubt that Meir would deliver.

Life at the unit's villa was a nonstop orchestra of vehicles coming and going that was conducted to a soundtrack of constant gunfire. Impromptu pistol ranges were set up and used around the clock so the Chameleons and the tactical force could hone their handgun skills. Tins of inedible *Luf*, the IDF version of preserved bully beef, were improvised targets for close-range live-fire drills. The beef cans were part of the IDF soldier's combat rations, but many thought they were nothing more than a prescription for guaranteed dysentery, so the soldiers liked shooting them up, though cleaning up the post-training mess was always a hated chore. According to published accounts, and urban legend, Meir would wake up in the morning, relieve himself with one hand, and shoot at empty soda cans and bottles with the other.[11]

Meir was the ringmaster of an enclosed universe. The soldiers invited to live inside this special world felt privileged to be part of an unscripted adventure. There were men dressed in Arab garb sitting in the mess hall next to soldiers in their olive fatigues. Heartrending melodies from Umm Kulthum, the songstress dubbed the Voice of Egypt, played on transistor radios as the Bedouin soldiers prepared coffee laced with cardamom over a fire. There were always barbecues on the base, and the men ate a lot of fish caught daily in the Mediterranean. And always, Pako, Meir's beloved Doberman, along with other dogs he adopted, barked when the sounds of gunfire were heard in the distance.

*          *          *

Mohammed Yassin was the deputy PFLP commander for the entire Gaza Strip and was considered one of the most important targets on the Shin Bet's most wanted list. He had a talent for secrecy and a gift for ruthlessness; he hunted collaborators and traitors and made examples of those he suspected. Yassin's nom de guerre was *Abu Nimer*, the "Father of the Tiger," but he was more like a ghost. He was always one step ahead of the Israelis. On numerous occasions, after weeks of surveillance and countless human hours of stakeouts, Grenade operators would storm a building certain to encounter Abu Nimer only to find an empty room, but the coffeepot was still on the stove and lit cigarettes were still burning in the ashtray. There were always rumors of the elusive terror commander, but never the man in the flesh.

The only image of Abu Nimer that the Shin Bet and A'man possessed was a fuzzy photograph from an old Jordanian mug shot. The image, though, was enough for the intelligence officers to get a fix on his eyes and his high cheekbones. Meir kept a copy of the photo on his desk and one in his canvas rucksack.

On January 29, 1971, Meir took a squad of men out for an early-morning motorized patrol of an internal road connecting the Jabaliya Refugee Camp and Gaza City. The unit was relatively new, and Meir wanted his men to become familiar with the local landscape, especially hiding places and caves near the patches of agricultural land and citrus groves. The patrol consisted of two World War Two–era jeeps armed with passenger-mounted .30-caliber machine guns. Meir rode in the first jeep. He wore a field jacket and smoked his pipe as his driver maneuvered at top speed along the muddy road. A Palestinian taxi, a white Mercedes, passed the reconnaissance troopers. The cab was packed with passengers, but Meir caught a glimpse of a face he had studied for weeks. It was Abu Nimer.

Meir signaled the jeeps to block the taxi and ordered his men to surround the Mercedes. The operators aimed their AK-47s at the vehicle. Meir approached cautiously with his sidearm, but Abu Nimer, sitting next to the driver, opened the front passenger door and produced an F-1 fragmentation hand grenade. He pulled the pin and said, "We will all die here." Meir shouted "*Rimon!* (Grenade!)" and lunged at Abu Nimer, making a go for the terrorist's hands. Meir wrestled him to the ground, clutching the hand holding the grenade to make sure the safety lever was still held down tightly and the striker did not hit the primer activating the device. Meir was not one to lose a wrestling match. He overpowered Abu Nimer and carefully inserted the safety pin back in its place, saving the lives of the Palestinian cab passengers and those of his men.* "The arrest of Abu Nimer would define the unit and its commander," Shmuel Paz later remembered.[12]

---

* In April 1973, IDF chief of staff David Elazar awarded Captain Meir Huberman the *Itur Ha'Oz*, the Medal of Courage, for the act of gallantry and the risk of life. It is the IDF's second-highest medal of valor.

# CHAPTER 7

# The Director and His Theater of Dirty Tricks

.

The Hostile Terrorist Activity Most Wanted Notebook was a collection of the men—and a few women—wanted by the Shin Bet and Military Intelligence for their involvement in hostile terror activity. The publication—classified as only "Guarded" and not "Top Secret"—had a limited release and was issued to the commanders of various unit heads and their operations officers who worked in the Gaza Strip. Each page consisted of a mug shot or a physical description, a name, known aliases, addresses, last location seen, and details of why the man or woman was wanted. The book was designed like a looseleaf binder where pages could be easily removed or added, and it was organized alphabetically and constantly updated. The Most Wanted Notebook featured terror suspects who were at the top level of an operational command or led a terror network or cell, and had blood on their hands. At its peak, the book listed close to one thousand names.[1]

Many of the wanted terrorists hid out in the eight United Nations–run refugee camps throughout the Gaza Strip.* The camps were established in 1948 and 1949 after Israel's War of Independence. Egypt was

---

* The camps are Rafah, Jabaliya, Khan Younis, Al-Shati, Nuseirat, Bureij, Maghazi, and Deir el-Balach.

determined to manipulate the Palestinian refugee issue for its own political and military advantage in its fight against Israel. Palestinians who fled to Gaza were not offered Egyptian citizenship, often forbidden from working or buying land, and faced a harsh existence at the hands of the Mukhabarat, the secret police, which was under strict orders from Cairo to use the poverty and suffering as a launching pad for resentment and guerrilla activity against Israel.

The refugees lived in tents and shantytowns of hovels funded by the UNRWA, which ran camps throughout the Middle East, in Jordan, Syria, and Lebanon. UNRWA paid the refugees a stipend, delivered food and other necessities, and ran schools. The tent cities and shantytowns soon became permanent overly congested places of squalor. Raw sewage ran through the narrow streets and up and down alleyways, and the stench, especially in the summer, was overwhelming. The Egyptians did nothing to improve the quality of life; crime was rampant. There were six homicides a month in the camp when Egypt ruled the Strip. That number increased exponentially when Israel took over. Unlike the Egyptians, the Israelis did not execute murderers.

Fighting crime inside the camps had collapsed by 1970. Defense Minister Dayan believed in an "Enlightened Conquest," one where political freedom and economic opportunity would convince the Palestinians in the West Bank and Gaza Strip that their lot in life was improved under Israeli rule. He removed Israeli police stations from the camps so that the population would feel autonomous and not under occupation.[2] He repositioned the police along the major thoroughfares, and inside civilian administration buildings, basically letting the Palestinians handle things on their own.

Once the Israelis left the camps, the terrorists took over and they used UNRWA to radicalize the young generation in classrooms that became small-scale guerrilla indoctrination universities. Peace with Israel and coexistence were not included in the curriculum. The education was all about resistance. UNRWA personnel earned two paychecks: one from the United Nations headquarters in New York City and another from the local terror commander in the camp. Fatah and the PFLP were completely in charge of security and day-to-day life.

Lookouts were everywhere. Outsiders were not welcome. Those who were foolish or unlucky enough to enter one of the camps—like the Aroyo family—risked death. But the camps were precisely where Meir and his men had to work. It was where weapons were stored, hunted operatives sought haven, and future attacks were planned.

*        *        *

Grenade Recon operated in small independent teams, though every operation required hundreds of man-hours of planning and preparation. Meir and Shmuel Paz had to travel back and forth to the Shin Bet's Gaza HQ for endless meetings to coordinate missions. The Chameleons had to be briefed to prepare the proper costumes and requisition vehicles for the undercover infiltration. Observation posts had to be established on rooftops surrounding a targeted location where a suspect was believed to be holed up.

The backup force had to be looped in to know which nearby access and escape points needed to be blocked off. The cavalry, usually commandos from Almond Recon, had to be placed on standby to react in force should the Chameleons require tactical assistance. Nearby units had to be notified that a particular sector would be active so that a patrol would not come to a controlled situation with guns ablaze. The biggest risk the Chameleons faced was a blue-on-blue shooting—being hit accidentally by friendly fire because the responding soldiers—nervous conscripts or tired and frightened reservists—thought the armed Arabs they were engaging were terrorists.[3]

Because the refugee camps were so hard to penetrate, the unit used creative thinking to blend in. They dressed as women in Islamic robes; the younger Chameleons rented donkeys—or sometimes borrowed them without the owner's consent—to impersonate Bedouin black marketers selling cigarettes and alcohol. Battered white Mercedes taxis were the most convenient form of infiltration—the cabs were considered public transportation and innocuous.

Any military operation in the camp was risky—but the undercover work was truly hazardous. If the intelligence was off, or the raiding team was unlucky, the hunters could easily become the prey of an over-whelming number of guns. The fear was what the terrorists would do if they abducted one of Grenade Recon's operators. From the onset of the PFLP's air piracy campaign, hostages were taken to yield a hefty return of imprisoned comrades. It was the cruel reality of a bazaar that peddled innocent human life that a captured operator, even his corpse, could fetch a hefty ransom. The terrorists, primarily the PFLP, wanted to capture one of Meir's men.

The terrorists also had a most wanted notebook, and when Grenade's operations began and word of the men in the shadows started to per-colate throughout Gaza, Palestinian commanders offered thousands of Israeli liras, the currency used in the strip, for one of the undercover operatives—dead or alive. Meir's men knew of the bounty. But they also knew that their unit commander and General Sharon would do everything in their power, including turning Gaza upside down and inside out, to secure their release. Perhaps one of the reasons why no member of the unit was ever seized was because the Palestinians also knew what the Israelis would do as a response.

Grenade Recon operated outside the refugee camps as well, in Gaza City, and the nearby towns. The countless olive and citrus groves were the easiest. The terrorists liked to meet in the late hours of the night in the fertile fields to prepare a strike against an Israeli target. It was cooler at night; for the married cell commanders, an excuse to meet with comrades in arms also provided a convenient way to step out. The Chameleons, often reinforced by the Shin Bet and military intelligence officers, followed their behavior patterns closely.

The Chameleons began to appear in shops, on street corners, inside teahouses, and in the homes of wanted suspects. They watched; they listened. They identified shops run by an owner with PFLP sympathies by the banners displayed behind the counter, and which ones sported a photo of Yasir Arafat. Photos of Leila Khaled, the notorious PFLP skyjacker and pinup of the terror group, were hung on walls through-out Gaza.

The Chameleons looked for weaknesses in the men they hunted and surveilled: which one cheated on his wife; which one was gay.

Blackmail and shame were potent weapons in turning a suspect into an invaluable source of information once sent back into his element. Meir authorized the use of collaborators; he saw them as force multipliers and even permitted some who had earned his trust to ride along with the Chameleons and help ferry a force to their target. There was nothing clean about counterinsurgency.

Suspects who did not resist arrest were taken to Shin Bet head-quarters for processing and questioning. Those who fought back and threatened the lives of the unit's men were shot and killed. Meir would later reiterate that he had never killed anyone who was not carrying a weapon. There was no middle ground. Comply or die.

Meir invented tactics unique to the unit and specific to the surroundings. One of the most notable was what became known as the Straw Widow.[4] The tactic involved taking over a home and staking it out until the targeted individual walked through the door and realized he was trapped. The operators usually confined the residents in a room where they could not communicate with anyone or warn the men that the Israelis were lying in wait. Most of the terrorists featured in the Most Wanted Notebook knew that they were marked for arrest. They tried to stay one step ahead of the Shin Bet and Meir's squads by spending each night in a different bed. Meir devised a plan where the terrorists' sexual patterns were analyzed. "Even the terrorists had physical, natural, needs," Shmuel Paz would remember, "and it would prompt men with a price on their head to risk it all for a few hours of intimacy with either their wives, mistresses, or even boyfriends."[5] And that's where Meir and his men would be waiting. There were three possible outcomes: surrender, surrender and collaborate, or resist and be terminated. Many thought that they could outfight Meir's men. The battles were usually one-sided.

Meir and his NCOs devised notoriously devious methods of making the terrorists fear the ground where they felt safest. In one operation in the Jabaliya refugee camp, Shmuel Paz remembered, the IDF publicized that it was abandoning a structure it had used as a temporary headquarters, but not before Meir's men burrowed out deep pits in the cellar where they could lie in ambush. When, at night, squads of armed Palestinians entered, the Israelis made sure they did not exit. Grenade Recon operators used this tactic repeatedly until the terrorists stayed clear of the building. Dozens were arrested and killed in these operations.

The intelligence commanders were in awe of how Meir and his men worked, but not everyone was happy. Meir and his men caught the ire of the military governor, Brigadier General Yitzhak Pundak, who was responsible for the Gaza Strip and northern Sinai. Every time there was a shooting incident, and a terrorist was killed or wounded, Pundak would arrive at the scene and demand an investigation. Pundak wanted to win the hearts and minds of Gazans as an alternative to resistance, and he viewed Meir and his men, an extension of Ariel Sharon, as wild men and even went as far as to court-martial Grenade personnel—including Paz—charging them as being nothing more than a hit squad. In many ways Pundak was right. The unit killed anyone who posed a threat to Israeli personnel and anyone with blood on their hands.

Pundak brought fourteen charges of murder against Grenade operators, usually if terrorists were shot while fleeing.[6] None of the accusations resulted in convictions; they were impossible to prove and always dismissed.* It is suspected that Dayan appointed Pundak so that he could keep an eye on Sharon, whom the defense minister viewed as a future political rival.[7]

Dayan was right.

*          *          *

Major General Sharon, beyond his military accomplishments, was a shameless showman and a master manipulator. He was always on

---

* Before he died in 2017, Pundak published a book about the military mistakes made by General Sharon and his undercover commandos in Gaza. In an article for the weekend supplement for Israel's largest newspaper, *Yediot Aharonot*, on May 4, 2017, titled "*Ha'Zikiyot Shel Meir*" ("Meir's Chameleons"), noted journalist Ronen Bergman wrote that Pundak claimed that Sharon, Almond Recon, and Grenade were responsible for the radical indoctrination of an entire generation. He claimed, "The terrorist leaders in the late 1980s and early 1990s were children when their parents and relatives were killed."

television—Israel only had one station—and he choreographed impressive feats of power and style, such as racing through the desert in his
black Dodge Dart staff car surrounded by sword-wielding Bedouin
chiefs on horseback.[8] Sharon made a point of providing select journalists with exclusive access and occasional scoops to ensure positive
press. He even allowed Ron Ben-Yishai, the defense correspondent for
Channel One, to get an up close and personal look at Meir and his men
in action on an actual mission in the orchids of Gaza. His reporting at
the time, under the strict restrictions of the IDF Military Censor, could
not reveal any of the details of the undercover work, or anything about
the force commander. It did not matter. Sharon liked to dangle scoops
to reporters as a long-term publicity investment—capital that could
yield dividends when needed.

General Sharon was a frequent guest at the villa. He was there at
least twice a week, usually to authorize some of Meir's grandiose operations, and he made sure that the men had a barbecue when he was at
their base. He even brought supplies of meat and hot dogs: anything
to spoil *his* men.

Generals led armies on conventional battlefields in head-on con-
frontations. Intelligence chiefs led spies into a shadowy no-man's-land
of deception and manipulative tradecraft in engagements that took
months—sometimes even years—to yield an outcome. Meir wanted
to create a paradigm somewhere in the middle. He reviewed Shin Bet
reports, read A'man translations of terror statements from Beirut that
were written about in the Arab press, and began to craft meaningful
dirty tricks.

Because of the need for secrecy, the leaders of the terror groups in
Beirut and Damascus were known by noms de guerre, usually beginning with the word *Abu*, or "Father of." But they were faceless code
words on handwritten notes. The PFLP commanders in Gaza could
not know who the men who sent them weapons and instructions
were. It inspired Meir to conceive a daring plan to upend Dr. Habash's
entire PFLP network of compartmentalized and interconnected cells in
Gaza. He would let collaborators and informants know that the PFLP
headquarters in Beirut was sending senior officers and a shipment

of weapons and explosives by sea, and they expected local cell leaders to meet them at a predesignated fishing pier. The terrorists used
mother ships, usually Algerian freighters that crisscrossed the Mediterranean to unload smaller wooden vessels in international waters.
The deception had to be spot-on for the operation to work, and a
seaworthy vessel was acquired and brought to a remote pier in the
port of Ashdod, where Grenade Recon operators had to paint it in
colors and markings that would not arouse suspicion.[9] The operation
was code-named Industry.

Six men made shore in Gaza: Meir, two Grenade recon troopers, a
Bedouin Chameleon, and two trusted collaborators.[10] They wore clothing purchased in an Arab land and weapons that were untraceable to
the IDF. They were met at a pier by a force of Chameleons and made
a point to be loud so the locals would see what had happened. In the
days before social media, the rumor mill was an immediate means of
spreading information. To enhance the deception, soldiers arrived to
intercept the visitors from Lebanon. A faux firefight was even staged.
To simulate that one of the visitors from Lebanon was hit by Israeli
fire, the group killed a chicken and spread its blood on the ground.[11]
The theatrics were convincing. Meir and his men disappeared into the
Gaza night.

Word spread in the towns and in the refugee camps that PFLP operatives from Lebanon were on the run, hunted. They hid out in orchids
and behind buildings. The children even brought them tea and snacks.
When Meir's team established contact with someone representing a
PFLP cell who could arrange a meeting, a Grenade Recon fire team
was waiting at the rendezvous. Anyone armed was killed; scores were
taken prisoner.

Operation Industry was such a rousing success that it was repeated
several times, each variation differing slightly from its previous edition.
Meir enjoyed the tradecraft. He had a knack for it.

Night after night, disguised operators emerged from the darkness,
supported by heavily armed backup, and hunted the names of the terrorists. The legwork and preparation were done in the early evening, the
silent deployments after midnight, and the engagements in the hours

before dawn's first light. It was one of the reasons why Meir developed a reputation as someone "who ate Arabs for breakfast."[12] The force wrote the counterterrorist manual on the fly, utilizing brute force and boundless guile. The number of names on the Wanted List shrunk every week, as did incidents of terrorist violence.

# CHAPTER 8

# Curtain Call

Gaza was not Israel's sole terror front. Lebanon had become a trip wire for a protracted and prolonged war when the Palestinian groups banished from Jordan in September 1970 set up headquarters in Beirut, and training camps throughout the country. Residents of Israel's northern communities became the targets of cross-border raids, massacres, and artillery fire. What has become perpetual carnage began on May 22, 1970, when pro-Syrian Palestinian terrorists rocketed a school bus near Moshav Avivim along the Lebanese border and killed twelve—including nine Israeli children. Israel retaliated with air strikes. The back-and-forth of attack and retaliation continued. It has never stopped. Terrorist armies doomed Lebanon to the fate of being an endless battlefield.

Palestinian groups also accelerated their efforts overseas. Under fire in Gaza, the PFLP stepped up its war against civil aviation. The tactics of air piracy changed into attacks designed to be heinously catastrophic. The strikes also involved international partners. On May 30, 1972, three Japanese Red Army gunmen, acting on behalf of the PFLP, opened fire at the baggage claim area of Lod Airport, and killed twenty-six travelers including seventeen American pilgrims to the Holy Land from Puerto Rico. PFLP offshoot groups also emerged. One such faction, the Popular Front for the Liberation of Palestine—General Command, planted barometric bombs on aircraft flying to Israel to try to blow airplanes out of the sky—a harbinger of attacks like Pan Am 103 sixteen years later. Letter bombs were sent to Israeli embassies and notable Jewish figures around the world.

The Black September Organization, a deniable special operations force within Fatah that was named after and created to avenge the Jordanian Civil War seized a Belgian Sabena Airlines jet in May 1972 and forced it to land in Israel, but a force from Sayeret Mat'kal, masqueraded as airport maintenance workers, stormed the aircraft, rescuing the hostages on board. Five months later, Black September terrorists seized members of the Israeli Olympic team in Munich, West Germany, and killed eleven athletes live on television to an audience of a billion people who watched the horror interrupt the Summer Games of Peace. A Fatah spokesman would describe the Munich Olympic Massacre ominously: "A bomb in the White House, a mine in the Vatican, the death of Mao Tse-Tung, an earthquake in Paris could not have echoed through the consciousness of every man in the world like the operation at Munich. . . . It was like painting the name of Palestine on the top of a mountain [that can] be seen from the four corners of the world."[1]

Gaza became a sideshow: a distant war far from the public eye. But it was a remarkably successful counterinsurgency campaign. It pitted terrorists against soldiers who adopted the dress, mindset, and tactics of the men they hunted. Grenade Recon was the IDF's first operational undercover counterterrorist unit—one that would serve as the template for numerous units that would play a pivotal role in fighting the first and second intifadas, as well as the Swords of Iron War that followed the Hamas invasion of southern Israel on October 7, 2023.

Grenade Recon eviscerated a generation of terror leaders and sent those who remained into hiding, wary of reentering the fray. The names of over five hundred men filled the Most Wanted Notebook when Meir's unit commenced operations. By the end of 1972, only ten names remained.[2] Grenade and the supporting Israeli units had not only cut the grass, as the removal of mid-level terror operatives was known in IDF circles, but they had also pulled up many roots.

With the level of violence subdued, the Israelis bulldozed obstacles and paved roads throughout the Gaza Strip. Ostensibly it was to improve the quality of life for the local population, but it also allowed Israeli military and police forces to respond everywhere in Gaza. The civil government authorized tens of thousands of permits for Palestinians to find work in Israel. The national liberation the terrorists advertised could not compete with a quiet and prosperous way of life. General Sharon's plan, executed by Meir and his men, had been successful. Gaza would remain relatively quiet for fifteen years, but Israel's victory was temporary and deceiving.

The clandestine counterterrorist campaign waged by Meir was the ugliest point-blank form of warfare imaginable. The killing of armed men, even those who were responsible for the deaths of innocents and Israeli soldiers, required the operator to ignore personal and political beliefs and be singularly mission-focused. The unit developed a reputation as being nothing more than a hit squad—efforts by Brigadier General Pundak did little to dilute the moniker. "I am not responsible for myths," Meir would later comment. "The unit acted according to the rules of engagement and legal definitions that all Israeli soldiers operate under."[3]

The tactics, though, warranted measures that were unsavory and opened the debate about how and to what lengths combating terrorism pushed men over the edge. The up-close-and-personal engagements in homes, alleys, and refugee camps required men with skill sets that were dangerous when not contained, and that also took a psychological toll on those asked to venture into danger night after night. Some would claim, years later, that the experiences had left them with PTSD.[4]

In numerous interviews, Meir remained unapologetic. During the year-and-a-half Grenade was operational, he said, they operated in a kill-or-be-killed reality. There were no philosophical debates of morality and proportionality of counterinsurgency warfare or intelligence tradecraft when whoever had the faster pull of a trigger, and the better plan, lived to fight another day. None of Meir's men were killed in the point-blank battles they fought and the dangerous pursuits into the darkness his men conducted. That was all that mattered. That was the true burden of leadership.

＊　　　　＊　　　　＊

Major General Ariel Sharon's ambition had long been to be the IDF chief of staff. He viewed the position as a stepping stone to a political future and, ultimately, being elected prime minister. In January 1972, though, Defense Minister Moshe Dayan appointed David Elazar as Israel's top soldier. Elazar was a veteran tank officer—more of an Eisenhower than a spotlight-grabbing Patton—and Dayan wanted the rambunctious, larger-than-life general out of the spotlight.

Dayan also transferred responsibility for the Gaza Strip to Central Command—a petty attempt to remove the counterinsurgency success story in Gaza from Sharon's legacy. Grenade Recon was immediately disbanded. Meir and his men were dispersed among numerous commands throughout the army. The men were resigned to their fate. The unit had achieved its objective. Many left the regular army. Others returned to Almon Recon.

Meir married Bina Palgi, his longtime girlfriend, in 1972. The twenty-six-year-old had been born in Israel—a Sabra whose parents made aliyah from Turkey. Meir met Bina in El Arish after the Six-Day War; she was an army nurse and was sent to Sinai along with a group of doctors to rebuild the local hospital. The medical emissaries lived in the old Egyptian police barracks, but they ate their meals in the IDF base, and the officers were happy to charm the pretty nurses around the mess hall table. The two dated throughout Meir's time in El Arish and Gaza, sneaking dates while he was on leave and not visiting his parents and brother in Bat Yam. Meir might have been ferocious in battle, but he was "charmingly quiet," Bina remembered, "reserved but interesting."

Known among his friends and comrades as having a very off-color sense of humor, Meir did not use his best material on Bina while they were dating. He was sensitive and gentle, even though the image of a slave to emotion and sensitivity is hard to equate with the man who led the undercover unit in Gaza. He also appeared to be frightened of commitment.[5] After four years of courtship, Bina gave him the ultimatum he feared, even though she knew he was the one and that the two of them would not break up. After she gave him the now-or-never warning, Meir, a man intimidated by nothing that could be thrown his way, bought a ring, an apartment in Bat Yam, and a suit for the wedding.

The rumor was that he purchased his outfit in the best haberdashery in Gaza. A military rabbi officiated the ceremony in a Bat Yam wedding hall with a jazz band playing at the reception, where Ariel Sharon was the guest of honor. The couple had no money. They used the cash and checks in the envelopes they received to pay for the ceremony.[6]

Meir and Bina Huberman lived in a small apartment in Bat Yam near his parents and began a life together. With a wife to look after, Meir wondered what he would do with himself. He thought about going to school; he was thinking of going to an advanced IDF command school to see if he would become a professional soldier. He continued to paint and read. The newlyweds planned to raise a family. Noa, the couple's oldest, was born later that year.

*         *         *

Ariel Sharon retired from active duty in April 1973 and entered politics. His beliefs were right of center, and he joined the Liberal Party, one of the groups in opposition to the ruling Labor government led by Prime Minister Golda Meir and Defense Minister Dayan. By July, Sharon helped spearhead the consolidation of several right-wing parties, including Herut, led by Menachem Begin. Sharon was forceful and demonstratively outspoken—a human steamroller who used the controversies and victories of his military service as badges of honor. Elections were scheduled for November.

Old soldiers do not fade away in Israel. Sharon was still a general even though he had thrown his hand into the tumultuous world of Israeli politics; he was a flag officer and given command of a reserve armored division, the 143rd. War was not expected in the fall of 1973—at least that was the assessment of A'man and the Mossad. Just in case, Sharon, like all senior officers in charge of large forces, kept close contact with his favorite officers, especially those from the Almond and Grenade Recon units. If there was going to be a fourth Arab-Israeli war, he wanted to fight alongside officers he knew, whose leadership abilities under fire were tested, and whose courage and loyalty were unquestioned.

Meir's time in Gaza would define him for the remainder of his life. Enemies viewed him as a cold-blooded killer who would stop at nothing to achieve his objectives, and his admirers—even rivals—looked at his courage and creativity with awe. The experience made his career. But he was proud always to remind his critics and rivals that his unit never killed a civilian or someone who was not involved in terror activity.

# CHAPTER 9

# Behind Enemy Lines

Tasa was a lonely Israeli military outpost in the middle of the Sinai Desert. The base sat at a junction on two intersecting crossroads, controlling east-west and north-south movement for heavy vehicles and equipment, especially tanks. The base was a Spartan depot that ensured the harshest conditions: it baked under the day's desert sun and froze under the chandelier-like candescence of the Sinai night stars. The soldiers stationed there were far from anything other than mountains or scorpions. Tasa felt as if it were light-years from the beaches of Tel Aviv or the stone streets of Jerusalem. Colonel Amnon Reshef's 14th Armored Brigade was headquartered in Tasa. It fielded 110 modified American-made M48A3 main battle tanks spread out along the Artillery Road, a strategic thoroughfare behind the Suez Canal. On the other side of the waterway was an army of over half a million Egyptian soldiers.

Israel's defense doctrine in Sinai was dependent on the overconfident understanding that A'man would have at least a forty-eight-hour advance notice of any Egyptian plans to cross the canal. This would give the IAF time to preemptively strike Egyptian air defenses and duplicate the 1967 attack plan of hitting air bases across the country and winning the war on the ground by dominating the skies above.[1]

*     *     *

War was not expected in 1973. The assessment of A'man, the fatal conception handed to the prime minister and the army, was that the Arab states dared not risk the battlefield humiliation suffered six years earlier in the Six-Day War.

At 13:55 on the afternoon of Saturday, October 6, 1973, a swarm of Egyptian Air Force MiGs and Sukhoi fighters and bombers struck IDF positions throughout Sinai. Hundreds of Egyptian artillery batteries bombarded Israeli positions along the front in a devastating blitz. Complete divisions of Egyptian infantry and armor units crossed the canal into Sinai. In some cases, Israeli forces manning isolated fortifications along the Suez Canal were besieged and outnumbered five hundred to one. Some held out, but most of the positions of what was known as the Bar Lev Line were overrun. Colonel Reshef's tank brigade tried to hold back an onslaught of eighty thousand Egyptian infantrymen and eight hundred tanks until Israeli leadership could recover from the earth-shattering shock of being caught by surprise and rush the reserves into the fire. The 14th Brigade lost ninety-four men in the opening hours of the war.

The attack broke the solemn prayers of the Day of Atonement. It was Yom Kippur, the holiest day in Judaism, and only a skeleton contingent of soldiers was on duty along Israeli lines opposite the canal and up north atop the Golan Heights, where the Syrians struck in a simultaneous and highly coordinated attack. The air strikes and artillery bombardment, and the thumping sounds of helicopter rotor blades ferrying commandos behind Israeli lines, caught many soldiers on the line deep in prayer in forward synagogues. The Arab surprise had been absolute.

Jordan's King Hussein had warned Israel that Egypt and Syria were plotting a surprise attack, but Prime Minister Meir did not act.[2] The Mossad learned of the impending simultaneous strike hours before the Egyptian aircraft took off on their missions. The prime minister decided against launching a preemptive strike out of fear that Israel would be labeled the aggressor. Across Israel, reservists left synagogues and their homes to race to their collection points and race toward their units. Men grabbed whatever gear they had at home and kissed their parents, wives, and children goodbye. Many soldiers were still fasting as they raced to find a ride to the front. Mothers and wives wondered when they would see their sons and husbands again. There were almost no telephones, and the usual means of communication was postcards sent via army mail.

Meir was at home in Bat Yam when he heard the coded words that summoned Israel's citizen army to war. He was not religious, and he was not in the local synagogue when news of the Arab attack came. All Meir had to do was grab his uniform and some gear and head to the front. He kissed Bina goodbye and bid farewell to his parents. Mina and Bina then began praying that they would not receive the dreaded knock on the door and see two army officers and a rabbi.

Meir was in between commands, not assigned to a specific unit, but he was determined to be in the thick of the Israeli effort to hold off the invading armies. He hooked up with Ariel Sharon, commander of the 143rd Reserve Armored Division based at Tasa, and joined the tens of thousands of reservists rushing to their forward mobilization points. He hitched point-to-point rides down south. Traffic jams of tank transporters, fuel trucks, commandeered civilian buses, and civilian vehicles littered the narrow roadways. This was not how Israel had marched to war in 1967—confident in a decisive victory.

There was great trepidation along the southern front. Israel Air Force Mirage and Phantom combat aircraft battled Egyptian MiGs in dogfights, the thunder of artillery exchanges growing louder as the Israeli soldiers, primarily reservists, neared the canal. Meir arrived at nightfall along with other past and present members of Almond Recon looking to fight a war alongside the general they knew and admired. Ariel Sharon was already in the underground command bunker at Tasa managing a dozen radio frequencies and scanning maps of the battlefield.

Hours after the war began, three battalions of Egyptian commandos were transported behind Israeli lines on forty-six Soviet-built Mi-8 transport helicopters. Many of the commandos failed to locate targets and abandoned their missions. Others, though, were determined to conduct their missions. In one lethal encounter, Egyptian special forces located a convoy of Israeli reservists and slaughtered over thirty of them. Hunting—and killing—the commandos became a priority for Sharon.

Colonel Wolf, the former commander of Almond Recon, had been an instructor at the IDF Staff College and rushed to the division's staging area in Beersheba to take command of Sharon's divisional reconnaissance force. Sharon had enormous respect and personal admiration* for the special operations commander.³

The 143rd Armored Division consisted of three tank brigades, the 247th Paratroop Brigade, and assorted combat engineering units. It also fielded a special divisional reconnaissance unit. But Sharon wanted more. He augmented his force with a special operations-capable team of irregular warfare specialists who could be trusted with sensitive missions deep in the enemy's rear and with experience in counterinsurgency. Amatzia Chen, who had taken over Almond Recon when Wolf fell ill, was studying at the Interservice Command and Staff College when the war broke out. A man without a unit, he asked Sharon to join his command and was placed in charge of the ad hoc commando-hunting unit designed to be a fast-moving mobile force that could travel far across the sands and gather intelligence as well as deliver lethal firepower to targets far from friendly lines. Observe and obliterate: their mission was to be invisible. The unit became known as "Force Patzi." Only a few senior officers knew of their existence.

Patzi and Meir "borrowed" a couple of jeeps and two American-made M113 APCs. The officers grabbed a few FN MAG 7.62mm light machine guns and as much ammunition and explosives as they could steal without the division supply officer noticing. There was no advanced equipment in the division armory—only just enough Uzi submachine guns, grenades, and winter parkas to carry out brief engagements with the Egyptians. They gathered provisions. Out in the desert, the unit was on its own.

There were never more than twelve men in the unit. They were all stragglers, primarily veterans from Almond Recon who, for one reason or another, had found themselves without a unit when the war broke

* Like many kibbutzniks and men who served in the top-tier and elite units of the IDF, Wolf's politics were left of center. He believed in coexistence with the Palestinians and that ultimately ruined his friendship with Sharon.

out and became impatient with army bureaucracy when it took too long to find a battle to join. All traffic was heading south. It was not hard to find a ride to the front.

On the third day of the war, as the sun set, two jeeps and an M113 left Tasa to break through the Egyptian lines. The men had a pot and some Bedouin coffee grounds in their kit. And they had to be careful when brewing the cardamom-laced beverage in the desert—smoke or a flame could give away their positions.[4] Patzi and his men drank the rocket fuel with their weapons always in hand. The sounds of jets twisting and turning in the skies above evading cannon fire and barrages of lethal Soviet-made surface-to-air missiles created a soundtrack of total war.

\*          \*          \*

The operators were summoned from location to location—like ambulance drivers responding to calls of service. Whenever there was an Egyptian Air Force MiG pilot shot down or there were reports of commandos operating behind Israeli lines, Force Patzi was called into action. Desert combat was usually carried out at great distances across the open sands. Most of the men had AK-47s—a throwback to the days in Gaza when they carried the same weapons used by the enemy. Patzi's men armed with Uzi submachine guns had to engage the enemy at closer ranges. Sometimes the fighting was hand-to-hand, where rifle stocks and even helmets were used as blunt-force weapons.

One such encounter happened on October 8—the first of Israel's counterattacks to push the Egyptians back across the canal. Egyptian artillery spotters had been flown in behind Israeli lines, and Sharon ordered Force Patzi to locate and terminate them because Israeli forces along the line of containment were subjected to pinpoint barrages.

Patzi's men searched the dunes carefully, wary of tank-hunting commandos that roamed Israeli lines. The sand whipped in the harsh desert winds and got into everything: engines, nostrils, gun barrels, and mouths. The elements presented a significant challenge to the reconnaissance troopers, especially when driving. Protective goggles helped, but only slightly. It was often difficult to see ten meters ahead.

The Egyptians used the soft sand to dig deep, and foxholes made it virtually impossible to see them from a distance.

One of the FN MAG gunners on the lead jeep noticed what he thought was a trash bag fifty meters ahead of their path, but as the vehicles neared the object, they saw it was a camouflage tarp covering a large foxhole where three men in khaki fatigues were hiding. The Egyptians fired first, though Patzi and his team ended the engagement in minutes. The Israelis had three light machine guns at their disposal that raked the sands with unrelenting fire. When Patzi, Meir, and the other reconnaissance troopers inspected the bodies of the men they had killed, they noticed that they were artillery officers with maps of Israeli positions, and a Soviet-made radio used to call in strikes.

*      *      *

The Syrian and Egyptian armies made significant advances in the first ninety-six hours of the war. On the Golan Heights, only a handful of Israeli tanks making a desperate last stand—sometimes outnumbered one hundred to one—stood between the Syrian army and Galilee. An impossible last stand and some strategic gaffs by Syrian generals snatched defeat from victory, allowing the IDF to regroup and go on the counteroffensive, retaking territory lost in the first few days and ultimately pushing toward Damascus. The Syrians—and their Soviet patrons—pushed the Egyptians to take the pressure off the northern front by mounting an offensive in Sinai before their protective mobile surface-to-air missile and gun batteries could neutralize Israeli air superiority. The Egyptians acquiesced, but the Israelis were not only waiting for them but also preparing a bold move to win the war. At a depot near Tasa, General Sharon assembled bridge-laying and amphibious equipment to be used in a counterattack across the canal, into Africa, and in the process, encircle the Third Army and 250,000 men—trapping them for the kill.

On the night between October 13 and 14, twenty-four hours before Egypt was to mount its large-scale offensive, a hundred and fifty commandos from the 183rd Battalion based in Ismailia were flown to a desert landing in four Mi-8 helicopters and positioned themselves ten kilometers from Tasa.⁵ They dug in atop a towering mountain-like dune and readied their RPGs and wire-guided AT-3 Sagger antitank missiles at the roadways Israeli armor would use to race into battle; they also fielded 122mm recoilless antitank rifles and SA-7 Strella shoulder-fired antiaircraft missiles. The landing zone was within walking distance of Sharon's canal-crossing assembly point, posing a great security threat to the top-secret Israeli plans. Force Patzi was assigned the task of destroying the Egyptian force.

The twelve-man force headed into the black night, carefully maneuvering the two jeeps and M113 across the dunes, racing from peak to peak to try to locate any sign of the heliborne force. Two tanks from the 600th Armored Brigade accompanied the recon troopers.

At dawn's first light, Patzi's men stumbled into the center of their dug-in positions. "I ordered the driver to go fast in reverse," Chen recalled, "and not a U-turn. The music [gunfire] had already begun."⁶ The battle began at 0630 hours.

A hellacious firefight erupted. The Egyptians hit the Force's M113, killing the driver and another soldier; a third was critically wounded. The small force did not have a medic in its ranks, and Patzi and Meir raced to the aid of the mortally wounded men to try to stop their bleeding. "Everyone was covered in blood," Chen remembered, "we weren't doctors."⁷ One of the men who had been ripped apart by the machine gun and RPG fire was close to death and reciting prayers and psalms. Patzi radioed divisional headquarters demanding a helicopter medevac for the wounded man, but the air force refused, citing the battle's proximity to the Suez Canal and the Egyptian surface-to-air missile umbrella. Five minutes later, Sharon radioed back. "The chopper will be there in five minutes." The wounded soldier's life was saved.⁸

The Egyptian fire intensified as the rescue chopper neared. The Israelis closed ranks and raced toward the Egyptian emplacements to engage the enemy at close range—a special forces tactic of pure dare. The Egyptian commandos fought from their foxholes, and the Israelis used speed and cover to advance. Nine men remained. Patzi, Meir, and the rest of the force outflanked the Egyptian positions and hit the dug-in commandos from three sides. The battle lasted less than an hour.

As the smoke from the destroyed M113 and the countless RPGs fired and grenades tossed billowed into the day's rising sun, Force Patzi counted one hundred dead Egyptian commandos.[9] About twenty had managed to flee into the desert.

Meir never forgot the lesson of command and the importance of being larger than life when in command of forces under fire. Sharon was more than a rambunctiously arrogant general—he was a star. Other generals, even the defense minister, came to see *him*—he did not tolerate sitting in waiting rooms, biding his time until he could be seen. He also attracted great attention to reinforce his reputation. When world-renowned Canadian folk singer Leonard Cohen came to Israel to aid in boosting morale after the outbreak of the war, the singer and poet gave a field performance to Sharon's 143rd Division, with the men from the 143rd Divisional recon force and Force Patzi right up front next to him.[10]

*          *          *

On October 14 Egyptian and Israeli armor fought the largest tank battle since Kursk during the Second World War. The offensive that the Egyptian military did not want to launch ended up as a turning point in the war—a decisive defeat that would allow Israel to strike back and force Cairo to ask for a ceasefire. The Egyptians had moved beyond the range of their SAM umbrella and were vulnerable to Israeli tanks and aircraft. The Egyptian attack began at 0630, and by sunset they had lost two hundred and fifty tanks and a thousand dead. The stage was set for Sharon's ambitious plan—the crossing of the canal—to bring the war home for the Egyptians. It was code-named Operation Gazelle.*

For several nights, using darkness as cover, small teams made up of Sayeret Mat'kal operators and Wolf's and Patzi's reconnaissance troopers crossed the canal to search for an ideal location for an IDF bridgehead. They used inflatable boats to paddle across, wary of sentries and mines.

---

* It has also been referred to as Operation Knights of Heart and Operation Valiant.

The missions were dangerous; some veterans have referred to them as suicidal. It was Meir's first time in Africa.

At night, as General Sharon's staff prepared their plan and the reconnaissance troopers rested, Meir reviewed maps and intelligence briefs instead of sleeping. Like all of the soldiers in the reconnaissance unit, he was tired, hungry, and had been wearing the same fatigues for over a week, but he worked into the early-morning hours smoking his pipe as he wrote down notes and sketched a few diagrams, then raced into General Sharon's command post with an idea to precede the canal crossing: kidnap or assassinate General Abdel Munaim Wasel, commander of the Third Army and its quarter of a million soldiers. The operation was a throwback to Gaza: Meir's force would go undercover, donning Egyptian army uniforms, and slipping through enemy lines to General Wasel's field headquarters. Chameleons who could mimic an Egyptian dialect were recruited to be the speakers. "Every detail of the operation was broken down in finite detail with nothing left to chance," Shmuel Paz would remember, "typical Meir."[11]

Sharon approved the plan immediately. But he had to get the operation authorized by his commanders—Chief of Staff David Elazar and Defense Minister Dayan—and they refused it outright. Meir was shattered, but he learned an invaluable command lesson, Amatzia Chen remembered. "Meir created something out of nothing, and people like that who are creative know that receiving approval is like a transfer of responsibility. So [he learned] do the thing because if you request authorization you pass on accountability. And Meir never [again] handed off responsibility."[12]

The crossing would take place without Meir's plan.

For Operation Gazelle to succeed, Sharon's armor punch had to drive a wedge between the Egyptian Second and Third Armies, isolating both forces, before additional armor could flow across the canal and cut off one of them. The audacious move has been described as one of the most brilliant maneuvers in modern military history.[13] To reach the waterway, though, Egyptian positions in an agricultural settlement known as the Chinese Farm north of the Great Bitter Lake and east of the canal had to be wiped out. The job fell to the paratroopers, but Israeli intelligence had miscalculated the strength of the Egyptian garrison and the number of tanks they fielded. In some of the heaviest fighting of the war, the Egyptians waged a ferocious defense of their positions, chewing up company after company of Israeli paratroopers, killing over seventy of them. The battle lasted for two days. Meir, working with Wolf and Patzi, led search parties under fire to retrieve the wounded. There were hundreds of wounded lying in the sand; dozens of Israeli tanks and armored vehicles had been destroyed. Meir and the reconnaissance forces faced hellacious fire as they ran through the gauntlet to reach the dead and the dying. The lessons from the battle of the Chinese Farm—and the war—would stay with Meir for the remainder of his years serving Israel—those who assembled intelligence assessments and those who interpreted them did not have the luxury of poor judgment or overconfidence.

On the night between October 15 and 16, Sharon's tanks crossed the Suez Canal. A radio code word—Acapulco—indicated that the Israelis were in Africa. The Israeli counterattack broke the back of the Egyptians. Israeli armor and infantry flooded across the first bridgeheads and then others. The Israel Air Force neutralized Egyptian air defenses.

General Sharon's move to trap the Third Army succeeded: nearly a quarter of the Egyptian Army was surrounded and helpless, dangerously short of drinking water and food. The plight of the Egyptians created a superpower showdown. The Soviets could not allow their most important ally in the Arab world to face a second humiliating defeat in six years, and they placed eleven airborne divisions on high alert. Soviet premier Leonid Brezhnev was going to impose a Moscow-controlled cessation of hostilities. The Nixon administration, beset by the Watergate scandal, placed U.S. forces worldwide on DEFCON 3, the highest state of peacetime readiness.[14] When the shooting stopped on October 24 following a United Nations–imposed ceasefire, Israeli armor was sixty miles from Cairo.

*    *    *

The 1973 Yom Kippur War officially ended on October 25 when the UN ceasefire took effect. Israeli armor was only twenty-five miles from Damascus when the ceasefire was called. General Sharon's tanks and a force of armor and infantry were positioned along the road to Cairo.

The fighting might have been over—and Israeli and Egyptian mediators may have met in the sands of the African desert on the road to the pyramids to hammer out the details of an amicable cessation of hostilities—but it would be months until the troops were demobilized. On January 20, 1974, Major General Sharon issued a Special Order of the Day in which he wrote, "I want you to know that I have never served alongside warriors like you. You were the greatest of all! I have never felt the brotherhood of warriors and friendly relations as they were in our division. It was a warm home that always gave me confidence in our strength and ability."

There was no euphoria to accompany the Israeli victory. It was impossible to define any conflict as victorious when 2,521 Israeli soldiers were killed in battle and another 7,500 wounded. The war was the deadliest conflict that Israel had fought since the 1948 War of Independence. The fact that the country's intelligence services had been caught by surprise revealed a state of unreadiness, and confusion shocked the country to its core—especially its fighting men. Everyone came back from the front lines a different person.[15]

*             *             *

Following the Yom Kippur War, the IDF faced an enormous manpower shortage of junior officers. An entire generation had been killed or critically wounded. The army's greatest shortage was in the Armored Corps. The IDF lost over one thousand tanks during the conflict, and with them, it lost battalion and company commanders—men vital to leading the World War Two–size armor conflagrations that were fought atop the Golan Heights and in the Sinai Desert in 1973. For a captain with a wife and hopes of raising a family eager to reach a high rank and make the army a career, transferring to tanks was a pragmatic and possibly rewarding move. Even though Meir Huberman was at heart an infantry officer, a commando, and the leader of men who operated clandestinely, he changed the badge in his beret, donned a Nomex coverall, and entered tank commander's school.

At one point during his instruction, he felt that it was time to hang up the uniform. He felt uncertain and insecure and confided in Patzi that he did not know if he had the right stuff to become a battalion or brigade commander. Patzi told his old protégé to think it over again. And look at the men around him and realize that he was braver and more creative than them all.[16] Meir listened and decided to make the army his life.

There was a small glitch, though. Virtually all the senior officers in the IDF had foregone their names from the European and Middle East Jewish Diaspora and taken Israeli Hebrew surnames: Patzi Chen was born Amatzia Haimovitch, Danny Wolf later changed his name to Rahav, and even Ehud Barak, whom Meir fought alongside in Sinai and especially at the Chinese Farm, was born Ehud Brog. If Meir had any chance of becoming a colonel or even a general, he would need to Hebraicize his name.

So, with a few signatures on mimeographed legal forms and without much other fuss, Meir Huberman became Meir Dagan, the Hebrew word for grain.

A new man, a new Israeli, and a professional soldier had been created.

# BOOK THREE

# COMMANDER

# CHAPTER 10

# Northern Armor

There was a solemn beauty to the hills of Galilee that it was impossible not to fall in love with. In the winter, the area looked like Switzerland sans the snow and skiers. The cedar trees towered high into the sky; rows of olive trees and lush fields were visible as far as the eye could see. In the summer, when Tel Aviv and Israel's other cities baked in the harsh Middle Eastern sun, Galilee received a refreshing mountain breeze that made the hottest days of July and August comfortable, and the nighttime downright chilly. To many in Israel, the area of the country's north was simply a paradise. Guesthouses and small family-run hotels dotted the towns and agricultural communities.

But across the frontier, past the barbed wire border fence, minefields, and army patrols that separated paradise from the realities of Lebanon, were men with hellish intentions. Beirut, once called the Paris and French Riviera of the Middle East rolled into one, had been turned into a transit hub and corporate headquarters for over a dozen Palestinian groups that swore to annihilate Israel and used terror to achieve their goals. International terror groups seeking the unification of Ireland, independence for Armenia, control of South Africa, and a new violently produced communist social restructuring in West Germany, France, and Italy, flocked to the training camps set up around the country; irregular warfare centers of excellence paid for by the Warsaw Pact intelligence services. Southern Lebanon became a jumping-off point for Palestinian attacks across the frontier into Israel. The year 1974 saw some of the bloodiest attacks ever.

On April 11, three terrorists from the Syrian-controlled Popular Front for the Liberation of Palestine—General Command crossed the frontier into Israel and attacked the border town of Kiryat Shmona. The target was an elementary school, but it was Passover, and the building was closed for the holidays. The terrorists then moved to an apartment building and embarked on a killing spree. Armed with AK-47s and RPGs, they barricaded themselves on the top floor and engaged responding soldiers and police; according to Associated Press reports, the terrorists threw several children out the window to the street below.[1] Eighteen people, including two soldiers, were killed in the attack.

A month later, in nearby Maalot, the bloodshed continued. On May 14, three terrorists from the Maoist North Korean–supported Democratic Front for the Liberation of Palestine crossed the Israeli border from Lebanon and, after killing five people, including a four-year-old boy, took 115 children hostage at an elementary school. A standoff ensued; the terrorists demanded the release of jailed comrades and placed their captives in the windows of the two-story building to deter any rescue attempt. But a team from Sayeret Mat'kal stormed the school. The rescue bid failed.* Instead of fighting the Israeli commandos, the terrorists turned their guns on the children, killing twenty-two.[2] At the time, it was the worst terrorist attack in Israel's history.

Israel's response was always immediate—air strikes, naval and artillery shelling, and commando raids against terror targets throughout Lebanon. The former French mandate, a conglomerate of Christians,

---

* Two years after the Munich Olympic Massacre, when countries across the world created full-time dedicated hostage-rescue teams, Sayeret Mat'kal's unsuccessful rescue operation prompted the Israeli government to create a nationwide law enforcement counterterrorist and hostage-rescue force that could be summoned at a moment's notice to respond to any large-scale terror event. The new force was placed under the command of the Israel National Police Border Guard and was called the Ya'ma'm: the Hebrew acronym for Special Police Unit. The Ya'ma'm would become the world's most experienced intervention unit: after October 7, 2023, it executed several dazzling rescue operations inside Gaza, pulling Israeli hostages from heavily fortified Hamas positions.

Sunnis, Shias, and Druze, was fractured even before the arrival of the Palestinian groups from Jordan in the aftermath of Black September. In 1975 the country erupted into full-scale religious civil war. Israel sided with the Christians and the Shias who, populating south Lebanon, had suffered the wrath of Palestinian guerrillas who stole land, abused the local women, and initiated Israeli retaliatory strikes every time they used the area to launch an attack.

The Lebanese Army dissolved when the civil war began. Soldiers—especially the officer corps—joined existing militias or started their own. Major Saad Haddad, a Greek Catholic from the southern village of Marjayoun, created the anti-PLO and pro-Israel "Army of Free Lebanon." Marjayoun was known as an upstart town and was the sight of hand-to-hand combat between Vichy French and Australian troops during Operation Exporter, the British-led invasion of Lebanon in 1941 that involved the Haganah's strike companies.

Haddad's new army consisted of five hundred men and was one of the few militias in the country to include fighters of all faiths. Haddad's men were trained and equipped by the Israelis. Access between the two warring nations was facilitated by an area of the eighty-mile border with Lebanon known as the Good Fence. The Fatima Crossing in Metula allowed people and goods to cross. It was a lifeline for the Maronites and Catholics up north who, with social and medical services in Lebanon destroyed by civil war, were able to receive emergency medical care in Israeli hospitals and preventative care in nearby clinics. Lebanese farmers sold their crops in Israel.

In March 1978, after Palestinian terrorists in Lebanon landed on the Israeli coast and killed thirty-five people in an attack aimed at derailing the Camp David peace talks with Egypt, Prime Minister Begin authorized a large-scale ground incursion into southern Lebanon that reinforced the military ties between Major Haddad and the IDF. The Israeli military created a command, known as the South Lebanon Region, to manage the strategic cooperation with Major Haddad's militia.

In 1980, Major Haddad drove to the unit's headquarters in Metula to meet the newly appointed Israeli commander for the South Lebanon Region. His name was Lieutenant Colonel Meir Dagan.

*          *          *

Some special operations officers found the transition to tanks to be difficult. But Dagan found the world of armored warfare fascinating and was even ashamed about his trepidation in joining the Armored Corps. His instructors noted that he was an excellent student and a quick learner. Leading columns of Israeli-modified British-built Centurion tanks, known in the IDF as the Sho't, was a different universe than heading into the Jabaliya refugee camp in disguise carrying a suppressed 9mm pistol. He adapted and embraced the technical knowledge to operate a tank, keep it running and supplied, and maneuver on expansive and fast-moving battlefields. Armor commanders had to know how to coordinate various aspects of a mobile attack together with supporting infantry and artillery. If in Gaza or Sinai Dagan was a director writing a creative script, here he was a conductor of a large orchestra. In the shadows, an operator survived on his wits and ability to improvise. A tank lived and died by the ability of its crew to work together as a well-oiled machine. As a battalion commander, Dagan had to lead and coordinate dozens of tanks as a singular force. He had a knack for maneuvering multiple pieces on a chessboard, even if those rooks and knights weighed over fifty tons. Unlike special operations, where killing is often done with a blade strike across the throat or with a pistol shot at point-blank range, tank combat is distant, fought at ranges of a thousand yards or more.

Armored warfare was a grimy, dusty, and greasy world. The fluids and lubricants to keep engines and main armament cannons clean and operational left tank crewmen filthy. In combat, when leaving the vehicle was not an option, crews had to use a bucket for a bathroom. The smoke and debris were suffocating, but Meir loved the noise of the Continental AVDS1790-2AG engine being revved up and, as commander, firing the Browning M2 .50-caliber heavy machine gun from his turret's cupola.

Yossi Ben Hanan, was Meir's tank commander instructor after the 1973 war—and the two would become best friends. Meir was a company commander in the famed 7th Armored Brigade, the same armored force that saved northern Israel during the 1973 war and fought a desperate battle to stop a Syrian tank onslaught, where they were outnumbered by over one hundred to one. Dagan rose up the ranks quickly. As a battalion commander responsible for over five hundred soldiers, his path to advancement was set.

Dagan moved Bina and, by 1980, two children—Noa and Dan—from Bat Yam to northern Israel. The family lived in a comfortable house in Kibbutz Mahanayim, north of Rosh Pina, a small hillside hamlet of three thousand people in Upper Galilee. Rosh Pina was located less than ten miles from the Lebanese frontier and only a forty-minute drive from the Syrian border. The homes had lovingly manicured gardens and cobblestone driveways. Life there could be tranquil, even though the melodies of chirping birds were sometimes interrupted by the roar of combat aircraft flying patrols near the border.

Most battalion commander–level officers believed in distancing themselves from the lower ranks. Even in an egalitarian army like the IDF, there were trappings and privileges of command. But Meir viewed command differently. He participated in everything his men did—cleaning the bore of the tank's 105mm cannon, changing a tread, and loading ammunition.[3] He ate with his men. He viewed each of them as part of a larger family unit—members of an armored force that could only thrive together.

But Dagan's special operations background followed him to Northern Command where he was known was a man with great knowledge and experience in dealing with Arabs. Brigadier General Avigdor Kahalani, recipient of Israel's highest award for valor for leading the 7th Armored Brigade's 77th Battalion in its epic defense of the Golan Heights and the legendary battle for the Valley of Tears, and Dagan's future division commander, commented, "I saw [him] in the field a lot and he had an immense understanding for the Arab mentality and its way of doing things that made him stand out." When it came time for the IDF to serve as the dirty jobs coordinator in the security zone of South Lebanon, Dagan got the job.

The man responsible for Dagan's unit was Major General Avigdor Ben-Gal, the OC Northern Command. The two men came from similar backgrounds and understood one another's life story. The lanky general, a Holocaust survivor born in Łódź with the name Janusz, would be known in Israel simply as "Yanush" throughout his life and military service. During the 1973 war, Ben-Gal commanded the 7th Armored Brigade that saved most of the Golan Heights from being overrun by Syrian armor and infantry—his decisive leadership under enormous pressure and overwhelming firepower saved the front and the war. He was a hero of Israel, a stern commander, though a nonconformist who preferred to seek forgiveness rather than ask permission.

Ben-Gal's direct boss was IDF chief of staff Lieutenant General Rafael Eitan. Known simply by the nickname "Raful," Eitan was a veteran of the 1948 war battles of Jerusalem and a tough-as-nails, highly decorated paratroop officer who had been Ben-Gal's division commander in 1973.

Both generals knew that Dagan was something of a *Mamzer*, the Hebrew word for bastard. In the vernacular of irregular warfare trade-craft, the word meant "brilliantly devious." Dagan's Gaza reputation preceded him—it was one that a defense correspondent for *Haaretz*, a left-of-center newspaper often dubbed the *New York Times* of Israel, said consisted of "his specialty being separating an Arab from his body."[4] Dagan enjoyed the celebrity aspect of it all, regardless of its accuracy.

Dagan was a natural to serve as the commander of what became known as the South Lebanon Region unit. His counterparts in the IDF thought he was a little crazy, and the Christians and Shiites were told to fear him, which in southern Lebanon meant respect. Notoriety served him well throughout his career.

*       *       *

The job of South Lebanon Region commander was more than a military posting—the position was highly political. The work involved sensitive issues connected to covert operations, ties to militia groups across Lebanon, as well as administering aid and economic support to the local population who was under the protection of Major Haddad and who held an affectionate opinion of Israel. The IDF and Saad Haddad's army worked clandestinely on operations of sabotage, skullduggery, and intelligence gathering against the Palestinian—and international—terrorist groups that were based in the south and beyond. Dagan was driven around southern Lebanon in a black Mercedes together with a protective detail of Israeli and Christian personnel.

Dagan liked to travel into Lebanon with Lieutenant Colonel Amiram Levin,* a veteran of Sayeret Mat'kal whom Meir knew from the Egyptian front in the 1973 war when he participated in operations deep behind Egyptian lines. Before the war, Levin had participated in the April 1973 Mossad-initiated commando raid on Beirut that targeted Black September's top leadership; after the war, he led the assault team that tried to rescue the schoolchildren in Maalot. Levin was a textbook operator and a solid field commander. Like Meir, he had switched from special operations to the Armored Corps in 1978, after ending a tour as Sayeret Mat'kal's commanding officer. He was the commander of the 188th Armored Brigade's 74th Battalion that served in the north, and someone Meir trusted for sensitive operations in southern Lebanon. "We were alike," Levin would tell Israeli television once, "we stole a few horses together."[5]

Being South Lebanon Region commander required Dagan to be part George Smiley, John Le Carré's legendary master spy, and part James Bond—an intelligence officer who ran agents, recruited sources, and led direct action operations against heavily armed and dangerous individuals. Southern Lebanon was a landscape of treachery and assassinations; Dagan became a target for killers and was betrayed by those he sent out to spy for him, sold out to a higher bidder or a larger cause.

He never flinched at the dangers—even when gunmen stormed the safe house where he was meeting with Major Haddad and additional sources. "Everyone in the room hit the floor," a junior officer remembered one such instance, "but Meir pulled his pistol out and fought back."[6] Two of the gunmen were killed. "As the saying goes in Arabic," a former colleague of Meir's in the intelligence business commented, "they ended up meeting their virgins. Dagan and his men simply made

---

* In later years, Levin would serve as commander of the 188th Armored Brigade, Northern Command, and, following his retirement from the IDF, deputy head of the Mossad under Meir Dagan's predecessor, Ephraim Halevy.

for them."[7] Dagan was not going to let an attempt on

for them."[7] Dagan was not going to let an attempt on
his life interfere with a meeting that had taken weeks to plan and where
refreshments had already been ordered.

One aspect of Dagan's work at the unit that he enjoyed most was
being the ruler of a small kingdom. Multiple headquarters—Northern
Command, Military Intelligence, and even the Defense Ministry—left
Dagan to his own devices. Anyway, what he felt the higher ranks would
object to was omitted from his status reports—what happened in South
Lebanon stayed in South Lebanon. One example was an operation called
"New York, New York." Expanding on his false flag mission in Gaza
when Grenade Recon personnel posed as Popular Front officials, Dagan
and his men posed as Fatah security officials. They rounded up Arafat's
men and accused them of being traitors; the suspects were taken to a
faux detention facility where they were questioned by Dagan's men, as
well as by Lebanese militiamen, into revealing detailed secrets about
the Palestinian terror network in the south.[8]

Face-to-face contact defined the cooperation between Israel and
Haddad's Army of Free Lebanon. Dagan and Haddad met frequently
on both sides of the fence. The weekly strategy sessions in Israel were
routine—without much fanfare or added layers of security and secrecy.
Haddad and his security and intelligence chiefs would sit around a battered wooden conference table and review names, events, and threats
both sides faced that required special handling. Generous supplies of fresh
fruit and snacks were always on the table. The ashtrays needed constant
cleaning. The smoke and smell from so many Israeli-made cigarettes,
Time or Broadway 80s, was stifling; the Lebanese preferred American
cigarettes along with Cuban cigars. Dagan drank tea from a glass cup in
pure *kommissar* fashion. He would light his pipe, listening intently, as the
men around him spoke. He always sat at the head of the table.

Dagan and his entourage—the security detail and added experts
from the intelligence and special operations community—traveled to
Marjayoun and other points around southern Lebanon when needed.
According to accounts, Dagan also traveled to locations beyond the protection of the Christian-controlled south. He visited Beirut and places in
the Beqaa Valley near the Syrian border. He traveled incognito and with

the express consent of local warlords and militia chiefs who all shared a common hatred of the Palestinians and wanted them out of Lebanon. Dagan met frequently with Bashir Gemayel, the Maronite head of the Lebanese force, also known as the Phalangists, the country's largest Christian army. Israeli intelligence divided Lebanon between A'man and Mossad. There were gray areas, of course, and Dagan's semi-private enterprise crisscrossed between them all.

The South Lebanon Region command established a satellite office in Haddad's headquarters fortress, but strict security protocols were in place every time Dagan and his staffers traveled there. Sometimes Dagan traveled in disguise. As a dark-complexioned man, he liked masquerading as a local guerrilla commander or a village elder. The espionage game was theater—a universe of scripted, improvised, and creative movements. South Lebanon reminded Dagan of what Gaza was like a decade earlier, though the terrain was much bigger and the stakes far larger.

Dagan's visits to the south required intensive advance work and highly detailed security precautions. The twisting mountain roads were ideal ambush points, and threats were everywhere. Helicopters were visible and noisy, not a practical mode of transportation when stealthy arrivals and departures were required.

The Christians entertained their guests in lavish Lebanese style. Dagan and his men were recipients of enormous feasts with an endless meze and meats of multiple varieties. Meir loved falafel and hummus; numerous interpretations of each dish filled the overflowing tables. Militiamen doubling as waiters brought mountain-high plates with different types of flat bread out of the oven. Welcoming visitors to one's fortress was an honor—even if the guest of honor was from across the frontier and from an enemy state. No matter how many pounds of meat, fava beans, and bread were consumed, the festivities ended with the obligatory coffee and tea and a table full of honey-draped desserts.

The rooms were always filled with a blinding cloud of cigarette smoke and the ubiquitous bouquet emanating from Dagan's pipe. The meals lasted for hours—as did the discussions. Somehow, Meir's reputation from Gaza preceded him. His hosts asked questions about the counterterrorist campaign and the stories of late-night operations against the PFLP. There was always a point in the evening when one of the hosts would ask to see Meir's weapon—and this always made his security detail anxious. The Lebanese loved the Israeli-made Uzi 9mm submachine gun.

The networking, the effort to establish human contact—telling dirty jokes and discussing Middle East intricacies and rumors about terror chieftains and princes—built trust and loyalty among his Christian partners and their Shiite allies. The spy game was all about one man's belief that the other could be relied upon not to betray him. But sometimes the hunter was also the hunted. Dozens of local militiamen—sometimes hundreds—would stand guard outside the homes, restaurants, and fortresses where these meals were held. The local Palestinian warlords would have paid a king's ransom for the chance to kidnap or kill Israeli intelligence officers. Dagan used several unmarked Mercedes when venturing in and out of southern Lebanon. He did not follow a routine, alternating his routes and travel times, to shake off surveillance and any attempts at an ambush.

Much of what Dagan did in his office nurturing ties with the Lebanese Christians and waging a campaign against Palestinian terror targets was kept from Prime Minister Menachem Begin and Defense Minister Ezer Weizman.[9] It was certainly kept out of sight and out of mind from Major General Yehoshua Saguy, the A'man chief, and a cautious man of deliberate long-term thinking who was opposed to rogue enterprises across the border that had the potential of enveloping the region in full-scale war. But Raful and Ben-Gal wanted A'man out of the loop, and both men usually got what they wanted. Secure telephone and radio lines—outside the network of A'man eavesdropping capabilities—serviced communications between Ben-Gal, Raful, and Dagan.

Most of the operations that emanated out of Dagan's office were small in scale, selective strikes, the kind that were known in the IDF vernacular as "tweezer operations." Many focused on selective small-scale assassination strikes of lower-ranking Palestinian terror commanders. The favorite tactic used was fitting cans of food or even a donkey with an improvised explosive payload; many of the devices were built by Dagan himself, in remote locations of nearby border agricultural settlements.[10]

Meir loved to tinker, a friend and comrade who worked with him during this period commented; he was an artist, who always thought of a creative way to do something, especially if it was underhanded and sent a loud and clear message to Israel's enemies.

Operation Olympia would be different. There was no way to execute a region-changing clandestine strike without the prime minister's knowledge and authorization.

*       *       *

The three-story apartment building at 61 Jabotinsky Street in the northern Israeli town of Nahariya was only five-and-a-half miles from the Lebanese border and 675 feet from the Mediterranean shoreline. The concrete façade was eroded by the salt air and the winds that hit the windows looking out on the beach. The Haran family—Danny and Smadar, and their two daughters Einat and Yael—were asleep on the night of April 22, 1979, when the shooting started. A three-man terrorist team from the Palestine Liberation Front,* a pro-Iraqi faction within the PLO, landed on a Nahariya beach and, after killing a police officer, attacked the block

---

* The PLF, headed by Muhammed Zaidan, aka Abu Abbas, launched the hijacking of the MS *Achille Lauro*, an Italian-registered liner, on October 7, 1985. The *Achille Lauro* was on an eleven-day cruise of the Mediterranean with 785 passengers—including a group of American Jewish senior citizens from New York and New Jersey. When the ship was seized, the terrorists shot and killed sixty-nine-year-old Leon Klinghoffer and threw his body and his wheelchair overboard. The objective of the PLF act of sea piracy was to land the terrorists in Ashdod, one of the ship's ports of call, and then seize the disembarkation point to secure the release of Samir Kuntar. When the attack failed, the Egyptian government intervened to help negotiate an escape for the terror cell. The Egyptians even furnished an airliner and a ten-man man security detail from the country's counterterrorist unit, Force 777, to protect the escape. Abu Abbas was given a seat on the aircraft. But when the Reagan administration learned that an American citizen had been killed, it worked alongside Israeli military intelligence to intercept the Egyptian aircraft. F-14 Tomcats from the aircraft carrier USS *Saratoga* were scrambled and the EgyptAir 737 was diverted to an Italian-run NATO airfield in Sicily. A task force from SEAL Team 6 and the army's 1st Special Operations Forces Detachment—Delta was waiting. The Americans had orders to storm the aircraft, though the Italians intervened, allowing Abu Abbas to escape. U.S. Special Forces captured him eighteen years later near Baghdad during the American invasion in 2003. He died of "natural" causes the following year.

of apartments searching for victims. They broke into the Haran apartment and dragged Danny and Einat away; Smadar managed to hide in a crawl space above their bedroom with two-year-old Yael and a neighbor.

The terrorists rushed Danny and Einat to the beach, where their Zodiac inflatable craft was waiting, but a team from the 1st Golani Infantry Brigade's reconnaissance force responded. A standoff ensued at the beach and then a shoot-out. Samir Kuntar, a sixteen-year-old member of the terror trio, shot Danny Haran in front of four-year-old Einat and then drowned him for good measure. Kuntar then took his AK-47 and smashed it over Einat's head, killing the young girl. Kuntar was the only survivor of the raiders. He would spend the next twenty-nine years in prison. Smadar Haran, desperate to shield her daughter in the crawl space, inadvertently suffocated Yael.

The murder of the Haran family horrified Israel. There were calls for the Israeli judiciary to instate the death penalty for terrorists. The terror attack outraged senior officers in the IDF's Northern Command responsible for Nahariya, especially Ben-Gal. He raced to Nahariya and saw the bodies of Danny and Einat. He heard the cries of Smadar. The scene left him shaking. Raful demanded a harsh and meaningful response, and was even quoted as saying, "Kill them all!"[11] However, the two officers did not expect much from Defense Minister Weizman, a British-trained combat pilot who helped build the Israeli Air Force and led its decisive victory in 1967. Pilots did not like to get their hands dirty—to them, war was fought antiseptically and gentlemanly in the blue skies of battle. Weizman wanted to be a diplomat, the one to authorize large-scale vengeance.

Ben-Gal and Eitan turned to Dagan for a solution. The South Lebanon Region commander sequestered himself inside his headquarters, locked in his office with maps and intelligence binders and working through the night.

This operation had been code-named Olympia in honor apparently of a popular Tel Aviv eatery where high-ranking military officers liked to eat.[12] Others would claim that the name was chosen because of the impact the operation would have on destroying the world's top terror chieftains, who were responsible for the 1972 Munich Olympic Massacre.

Olympia was audacious, an idea of pure game-changing chutzpah, and had the potential to change the Middle East forever. At its core was the assassination of PLO chairman Yasir Arafat and his minister of defense Khalil al-Wazir, better known by his nom de guerre of Abu Jihad—an attempt to decapitate the Palestinian leadership in one explosive flash. The grandiose scheme required the support of Shiite agents who Dagan recruited to deliver the hundreds of kilograms of high explosives that would kill scores—including innocents—but eradicate the symbols of Palestinian terror. The agents were recruited from the predominantly Shiite section of south Beirut known as the Dahiya, a lower-income area near the airport where the Palestinians were despised. The Palestinians were Sunni; when they arrived in 1948, and especially in 1970 from Jordan, they upset the delicate balance of social order that had existed in the country for centuries—during the times of the Ottomans, during the French mandate, and especially after independence.

One plan was to target a theater where the terror leadership would hold a rally. In the end, though, it was decided to target the annual military parade celebrating the creation of the PLO on January 1, in Beirut's main sports stadium. The endless array of speeches from the various leaders of the different groups inside the PLO, promising that the destruction of the "Zionist Entity," were recycled every year.

An undertaking of such magnitude and intricacy as the targeting of the parade required months of intensive planning; a healthy supply of money, equipment, vehicles; and a slew of other components of trade-craft infrastructure needed in covert operations. Such an effort would also need political support.

*     *     *

Menachem Begin made it his life's mission to show the world he was one Jew who was no longer willing to be a victim. Born in Brest-Litovsk in Czarist Russia, he was a graduate of Warsaw University, held prisoner in Vilnius by the Soviet NKVD following the Nazi invasion of Poland, and ultimately was an officer cadet in the Free Polish Anders' Army that was sent to British Mandate Palestine in 1942. He joined the Irgun, a right-wing nationalistic underground group that split from the mainstream Haganah and openly attacked British forces. He was responsible for the bombing of British military headquarters in the King David Hotel in Jerusalem; the group kidnapped British sergeants and hanged them after the British hanged Irgun prisoners. British authorities labeled him a Jewish terrorist.

Bespectacled and small-framed, Begin looked meek, but he harbored a fiery rage of determined survival. In 1977 the Likud Party he led defeated the long-ruling Labor Party to control the Knesset. He brought that resolve to the negotiating table when he signed the Camp David Peace Treaty with Egypt in 1979. And, on a sunny afternoon in June 1981, he sat at a table flanked by IDF chief of staff Rafael Eitan and Israel Air Force commander Major General David Ivry to tell the world that Israeli F-16s had bombed Saddam Hussein's nuclear reactor at Osirak near Baghdad. Saddam Hussein had threatened to wipe out the Jewish state with nuclear weapons. To the men who survived Hitler, Never Again truly meant Never Again.

The Israeli raid, code-named Operation Opera, captured the world's attention and admiration. Israelis were in awe of the country's airpower and the courage of its pilots. Begin decided to maximize the wave of nationalism and admiration and called snap elections for August. The Likud won, and as a reward for his political support, the prime minister appointed Ariel Sharon as his defense minister. The dream team for rogue action was now in charge. Work on Operation Olympia intensified.

The ambitious once-and-for-all eradication of the Palestinian terror leadership—the men responsible for hijackings, massacres, and hostage-taking, the men responsible for the murder of the Haran family—centered on a scorched-earth plan of mass destruction—one where scores of innocent people would be killed, as well. Shiite operatives would plant large amounts of explosives underneath the reviewing stands where the terror chieftains and their key lieutenants would be sitting. The first blast would kill many, but in case the explosion failed to take out the intended targets, two radio signal–controlled car bombs positioned at the stadium's exit would take out any of the VIPs rushing to flee.[13]

"The operation was pure Meir," Ephraim Sneh reflected. He was a close friend of Dagan's who'd been a combat surgeon during the bitter battle for the Chinese Farm and one of the medical officers for the Entebbe rescue, and who would succeed Dagan as South Lebanon Region commander. Sneh commented "that the skullduggery of the South Lebanon Region command was the perfect place for a man like Meir to learn the spy business and develop ideas about what the profession entails. No one could compete with his operational creativity. No one before and certainly not since."[14]

As the cold winter winds blew across southern Lebanon and northern Israel, and the time until the scheduled PLO event went from months to weeks to days, everything for Operation Olympia went according to plan. The Shiite operatives planted the explosives in the stadium and prepared three vehicles with their payloads. Dagan and Ben-Gal felt that the operation could not come back to hurt Israel—after all, the men who planted the bombs were Lebanese, Shiites no less, and not Israelis.

The Mossad and A'man, at first, were unaware of the plan, but Major General Saguy was suspicious that something major and nefarious was underway. He tried to tap Dagan's telephone lines.[15] Eventually, morsels about Dagan's plan spread among a small group of senior intelligence officers. Their universal response was one of horror and outrage. Women and children would attend the event. The civilian death toll could be in the thousands. Foreign diplomats sat in the VIP section at the annual PLO celebration—including ambassadors from the Warsaw Pact nations and the People's Republic of China, representing significant world powers that supported the Palestinian groups.

Days before the intended strike, word of the plan reached Prime Minister Begin. Sharon, Eitan, Ben-Gal, and Dagan were summoned to the Ministry of Defense, where the prime minister conducted weekly national security business from a small satellite office in the main chancery. A'man chief Saguy was there, as well. Begin listened to his generals and officers attentively, like a judge in family court as parents fight over the custody of a child during a bitter divorce. He absorbed the points of the arguments and thought quietly about the merits of the case presented to him, sipping a glass of tea and rubbing his chin as he pondered his decision. He looked at the men in the room, all in their Class A uniforms, with a stern remoteness, and ordered the operation aborted. The prime minister did not have to give any explanation for his decision. He was no longer an underground leader. He was a head of state and recipient of a Nobel Peace Prize for making peace with Egypt, and maintaining regional quiet and a strategic relationship with the United States—even if it allowed Arafat to live another day—was more important than a golden opportunity to decapitate a generation of fiendish killers.

For the next few days, the Mossad, now recruited into the fold, worked hard to dismantle the devices so that no unauthorized explosions would happen.

*          *          *

Was Operation Olympia a failed opportunity to eradicate some of the world's most dangerous terrorists with one flip of the switch, or was it an example of reckless overreach that could have ignited a cyclone of regional horror thwarted in the nick of time? Killing men like Arafat and his lieutenants would have killed thousands of innocent civilians. Letting them live ultimately costs thousands of lives as well.

When Prime Minister Begin assembled his defense minister and top generals inside the cramped confines of his Tel Aviv office to review the pluses and minuses, Meir Dagan had kept quiet, even though he was the architect of the operation and had blueprinted it from being nothing more than a figment of his imagination to the last details—including the types of vehicles the Shiites would use for vehicle-borne improvised explosives. But he was the junior rank in the room. He stood silently and listened.

Watching the prime minister weigh the risks of Olympia versus its rewards was a master class for Dagan in the burden of leadership and strategic thinking. Begin viewed Arafat as a clear and present danger to the Jewish people. But he worried about the body count among noncombatants and what the American response would be. President Ronald Reagan and his national security staff had been caught off guard by the Israeli raid on the Iraqi nuclear reactor, and to dilute Arab anger, the Pentagon had suspended the delivery of six F-16 fighter bombers to Israel and voted in favor of a United Nations Security Council resolution condemning the raid.[16] Begin believed that the potential blowback from Operation Olympia trumped the tactical gains. Although Dagan and his team had spent countless man-hours, untold amounts of cash, and other resources preparing Operation Olympia, the final decision was with the country's elected leaders. The buck stopped at the prime minister's desk. Dagan's imagination might have been boundless, but the power of devious planning and covert warfare was limited.

The chaos and internal infighting around Operation Olympia could have ended Meir Dagan's career. Semiprivate endeavors were anathema to the rigid command structure of the IDF. As far as A'man was concerned, Dagan had gone rogue—a dangerous precedent for an officer with the rank of lieutenant colonel. But Dagan had a powerful benefactor. Sharon appreciated his protégé's special brand of genius. Still, someone had to pay the price for the debacle. Sharon fired Ben-Gal—a highly controversial move considering his war record, particularly in the 1973 war.

Weeks before his thirty-seventh birthday, Dagan learned he was being promoted. Now a full colonel, Meir Dagan was given command of the 188th Armored Brigade. Over the previous few years, Dagan had fallen in love with tanks and armored warfare and wanted to be back in the turret of his Centurion tank.

Ariel Sharon was planning a military operation against the Palestinian domination of Lebanon and the threat the guerrillas posed to northern Israel. The Israeli defense minister wanted *his* man to lead the main armored thrust across the frontier.

# CHAPTER 11

# Lightning

Bina Dagan was three months pregnant with the couple's third child when her husband sequestered himself at his headquarters in Metula planning Operation Olympia. Meir rarely made it home during those early months. There was no time. There were not enough hours in the day to combine a normal family life with the demands of leading a covert cross-border campaign.

His home in Rosh Pina was a forty-minute drive south down Highway 90 from the headquarters. He had a driver and a staff car, but his work on both sides of the Good Fence started long before the emergence of the new day's sun and ended well past midnight. If he tried to make it home to sleep in his bed beside his wife, he would have to leave minutes after arriving. Dagan slept on an army cot in a small room behind the office.

Military wives like Bina accepted their fate. They had to share their husbands with the army, and the higher the rank, the less time they would have with their spouses. "Meir was never nervous or angry when he came home," she would remember. "He believed in the people of Israel and the Jewish state. No one was more patriotic. Israel always came first; family second."[1]

Countless households in Israel were run by married women who became single moms six days a week. Bina was stoic. She was the CEO and warden of the family home. She was a nurturer and disciplinarian. The reality was not easy, but it was accepted. As difficult as it was for Meir and Bina to cope, they were living proof of the vow of Never Again. They had built a family unit with grandparents and cousins that extended across the country and beyond; Eli, who had become a world-renowned biochemist, had left Israel to study and work in the United States.

Meir battled the exhaustion of leading a covert campaign as much as he fought to ignore the pains of his injuries. He never let either get in the way of him being a devoted husband and a doting father. He refused to be the sheriff at home and did not attempt to instill military-like discipline in the household. He tried as best he could to be nurturing and supportive of his children, like their grandmother Mina and never be dismissive like his father. He always smiled even when he did not feel like it, wanting Bina and the kids to enjoy him coming home and not dread his return because he was too exhausted or irritable to make the most of the limited time he had to spend with them. The kids adored their father who on his one day off woke up early to take the family on day trips across northern Israel.

Meir came home every two or three weeks. He never wanted to let Noa and her brother Dan, named after a friend who was killed in the Yom Kippur War, know how tired he was when they jumped on his bed on Saturday morning wanting to know what adventures he had planned for them. Northern Israel was beautiful all year round, but especially picturesque in the winter months when everything was green from the ample rains and the snowcapped Mount Hermon on the Golan Heights provided an Alps-like backdrop. There was the beauty of the rolling hills near Safed and Mount Meron; Banias, a natural waterfall at the tributary of Mount Hermon, was a refreshingly beautiful must on Saturday-morning nature treks for the family. Sometimes, Meir took the kids to the brigade's base for weekend target practice to compensate for the long stretches away from home. The children loved firing the machine guns.

If he found the time at home, Meir painted and sculpted. The areas around the kibbutz, especially Rosh Pina, gave him majestic vistas to paint, and there was an abundance of interesting faces, Jew and Arab, to paint in the villages of Galilee. The family home always had a welcoming aroma of pipe tobacco and oil-based paints. Meir's artwork, framed and on tables, filled the house. Brushes were everywhere. Classical music filled the background of his studio.

But Meir had another family: his soldiers. When Dagan was promoted and given command of the 188th Armored Brigade, he became the adopted father of a large fighting force of all ranks as members of his extended clan. Meir's son Dan remembers that the house was always full of soldiers and military vehicles parked in the driveway. The kitchen was a mini war room where captains and majors sat down and had coffee and cake while managing brigade business. Noa Dagan, Meir's firstborn, recounted in an interview that she does not remember Passover seders at home that did not have several of his soldiers sitting around the holiday table.

The 188th, known as the *Barak* (Hebrew for Lightning) Brigade, fielded three tank battalions—the 53rd, commanded by Lieutenant Colonel Haim Mor; the 74th commanded by Lieutenant Colonel Amiram Levin; and the 71st commanded by Major Eyal Ben-Reuven. These officers were his sons, the head branches of his armored force, but the battalion company commanders were like his grandsons, a future generation he could guide to higher ranks. His favorite was Captain Tuval Gvirtzman, commander of M Company in Ben-Reuven's 71st Battalion. The twenty-two-year-old officer was known by all ranks simply as "Tuli." He was an exceptional tank officer with an irremovable smile and a fascination with armored warfare. He was also a celebrity in Israel—a popular children's song had been written years earlier about him when he was seen frolicking around the beach. Dagan always allowed Tuli's tank to lead all exercises. The young officer was supposed to leave the army in July of 1982.[2]

Wanting his brigade ready for action, Dagan put the 188th on a war footing. The brigade trained constantly and conducted exercises to integrate operations alongside engineer and infantry units. "Meir took nothing for granted. He wanted his men ready for any scenario. After spending two years in Lebanon, he knew that Israel's next war would be up north, against terrorists fighting a guerrilla war, the Syrian Army, or both," Lieutenant Colonel Baruch Spiegel, the commander of the 1st Golani Infantry Brigade's 12th Battalion and an officer who would work with Dagan, remembered. "Meir could always see the chessboard and insist on knowing what will happen five moves forward."[3]

On March 31, 1982, less than three months after assuming command of the 188th Brigade, Dagan issued a directive to all his company and battalion commanders titled "Subject: The State of Israel is Facing War." The one-page document opened with the sentence "The State of Israel is facing immediate war, and in my estimation, it will happen in the next few months." His opinion, he wrote, was based on the geopolitical realities of four zones of strategic interest, primarily Syria, Lebanon, and Palestinian terrorists. It addressed military and political updates of these regions and closed with the challenge to his men: "I find it appropriate to present this assessment to you for us all together in a joint effort to organize and plan to prepare strength in all areas on the assumption that the war is at the gate and we must enter it prepared in the best possible way and all your actions and labors will be the question you ask yourself what else should I do to be more prepared."

Dagan put the brigade through an intense training cycle. He was determined to have his force ready for any contingency they might encounter.

*     *     *

Four Arab nations share a direct land border with Israel. In the spring of 1982, two frontiers were peaceful—Egypt, by treaty, and Jordan, by tacit agreement. A permanent state of war existed atop the Golan Heights along the no-man's-land of antitank mines and demarcation with Syria, though a mutual adherence to a ceasefire held a quiet status quo. Only Lebanon—and the jagged forty-eight-mile-long frontier it shared with Israel—was dangerously hot. Despite the best efforts of Israel's intelligence agencies—and the dark art operations waged by Meir Dagan and his office—Palestinian terror groups were entrenched in positions and forward operating bases throughout southern Lebanon. On the night between April 7 and 8, 1981, five terrorists from the pro-Iraqi Arab Liberation Front had crossed the barbed wire fence near the south Lebanese town of Odaisseh into Israel and cut their way into Kibbutz Misgav Am. The terrorists killed two, including a four-month-old infant, and then barricaded themselves inside the kibbutz nursery. The first rescue bid by an IDF unit failed; the second, by a team from Sayeret Mat'kal, succeeded, and the terrorists were killed.

The United Nations, as well as U.S. special envoy Philip Habib, force-fed numerous ceasefire agreements to Israel and the various forces that occupied Lebanon. The violence was tit-for-tat, and each side tested the tolerance of the other. There were close to twenty-five thousand Palestinians under arms in Lebanon in the spring of 1982. They belonged to over a dozen factions and splinter groups allied with capitals around the Middle East and beyond. Fatah was the largest but not the most significant; there were anti-Arafat elements inside this hodgepodge army, mainly extremist forces supported by Iraq's Saddam Hussein and Libyan strongman Muammar Gaddafi. The Palestinian base of power was inside twelve refugee camps throughout Lebanon. UNRWA administered the camps and the terror factions ran them.*

Beirut was the center of the Palestinian seat of power. It was where Arafat's headquarters was and where most of his army was based. It was the capital of Palestine, a fractured city run by the most powerful and heavily armed gang in its confines.

Lebanon had another component to it, though. By 1982, both A'man and the Mossad had forged a military and political alliance with the Lebanese Forces commanded by Bashir Gemayel. The Phalangists, as they were also known, were the largest Christian militia in the fractured country, and the strongest politically, as well. Their seat of power was Christian East Beirut and its northern suburbs. Gemayel allowed the

---

* Before, but especially following the October 7, 2023, Hamas invasion of southern Israel, the Israeli and American governments contended that UNRWA educated and indoctrinated generations of Palestinian civilians to wage a terror war against Israel. The United States, as well as governments in Europe, cut off funding to UNRWA as a result of the organization's support for Hamas and the other factions that perpetrated October 7 and kidnapped civilians (including the bodies of those who had been murdered).

Mossad to establish a satellite station near Jounieh, a coastal city ten miles north of Beirut, its shores protected by Lebanese Forces gunboats supplied by the Israeli Navy. The ties between Israel and Lebanon's Christians had been ongoing for almost twenty-five years, ever since 1958 when Lebanese president Camille Chamoun reached out to the Jewish state for assistance during a crisis in the country.[4]

The Christians in Lebanon were far from a homogenous bunch. They were often fighting with one another, committing gory massacres to prove a point or take out a rival in the same way that crime families did in Sicily, leaving dead wives, daughters, and sons in the aftermath of every vendetta. Clan-run, the militias had varied motives, ranging from political survival to black market control and narcotics trafficking.

The Christian warlords also trafficked in intelligence. Beirut had always been an espionage epicenter, dating back to the days of Kim Philby—the Americans, British, French, Soviets, as well as the Egyptians and Syrians maintained extensive espionage networks inside the country. There were double, triple, and quadruple agents everywhere working for several agencies and then selling secrets on the open market. Bashir Gemayel himself was on the payroll of the Central Intelligence Agency for years.[5] In early 1982 alone, President Ronald Reagan signed a top-secret memorandum authorizing the CIA to dish out ten million dollars to Gemayel and the Lebanese Forces in addition to the large sums of cash the Christian warlord received annually from Langley; according to reports, the request for the CIA money came directly from Ariel Sharon.[6]

During the civil war, the Lebanese Forces showed a penchant for brutality. Ever fashionable, female Christian soldiers wearing tightly tailored uniforms were rumored to slice off the ears of the Palestinians they killed and keep them in their Chanel purses. A former Mossad official who visited Beirut in 1981 remembered asking his Lebanese Forces guide about what was cheap in the country, hoping to come home with a souvenir. His escort responded, "Human life. That's the cheapest."[7]

The Mossad took the lead in dealing with the Lebanese Christians. But A'man and the IDF maintained their ties, as well, even though the assessment at headquarters was that the Christians were fractured and unreliable allies. There were secret rendezvous on Israeli naval missile boats; Gemayel was hosted at border kibbutzim and elsewhere in Israel. One thing united the dominant Christian militias—their hatred for Saad Haddad, Dagan's man in the south, whom the other warlords viewed as a sellout to Israel.

Israel's relationship with the Christians motivated Ariel Sharon to devise a military plan to rid Lebanon of Palestinian terrorists and install an ally of the Jewish state in the presidential palace—an ambitious military move to create a Judeo-Christian bloc in the Muslim Middle East. A cornerstone of Israel's national security doctrine dating back to Prime Minister Ben-Gurion was what was referred to as the Triangle Theory, developing regional non-Arab allies (to the north the Turks, the Kurds, and the Iranians, and in the south the Ethiopians and the Sudanese) to help offset the enemies the Jewish state had to deal with directly on its borders.[8] This doctrine expanded by establishing intelligence and security service ties with developing countries beyond these triangles—in Africa, Asia, and as far afield as South America—where Israel's shadowy and tactical know-how could be used to forge diplomatic ties. Coups and revolutions—in Sudan and Iran—offset this pillar of Israel's shadow diplomacy. Still, in Lebanon, Israel had its first-ever opportunity to exercise this strategy with a border state.

The plans, called Little Pines, Big Pines, and Rolling Pines, envisioned an Israeli push into Lebanon, eradicating the Palestinian terror presence and redefining the ethnic balance to make the Christians assume control of the country. As usual with any scheme to change the Middle East, the best-laid plans ended up in carnage.

On June 3, 1982, Shlomo Argov, Israel's ambassador to Great Britain, was shot in the head as he entered his car following a reception at London's Dorchester Hotel by three members of the Abu Nidal Organization firing Polish PM-63 submachine guns. The Israeli ambassador was critically injured in the attack but survived. The orders for the attack had come from Baghdad, as Iraq's intelligence service, at odds with Yasir Arafat, wanted to use the attempted assassination to discredit the PLO chairman and give the Israelis the provocation needed to take him out. Arafat took the bait and ordered his forces to unleash Katyusha rocket barrages against the towns of northern Israel. Tens of thousands of civilians hunkered down in their bomb shelters. Sharon had his casus belli. The IDF was ordered into Lebanon.

At 04:00 hours on the morning of Sunday, June 6, the tanks of Colonel Meir Dagan's 188th Armored Brigade left their forward pens near Kibbutz Kfar Giladi and headed toward Metula. At exactly 11:00 a.m., Meir Dagan received the order to attack. Scanning the road before him from the commander's cupola, he was the first Israeli soldier into Lebanon, launching what the Israelis referred to as Operation Peace for Galilee.

Standing before the Knesset, Prime Minister Begin vowed that when the IDF reached the Awali River forty kilometers from the Israeli border, the combat would end. Battalion and brigade commanders knew that was false. They had prepared for this war and a push to the Lebanese capital. The IDF was going all the way to Beirut.

# CHAPTER 12

# Bloody Beirut

D o not shoot at civilians!
Do not shoot at white flags!

Only shoot at the terrorists and Syrians who shoot at you first![1]

Lebanon might not have been the graveyard of empires like Afghanistan, but it was a lethal trap that lured its victims deeper and deeper into an inescapable vortex of slow death. Colonel Dagan's orders to his brigade were clear and precise, but wars were never orderly, especially those fought against an enemy that used civilians as cover. His armored column moved fast into Lebanon that sunny Sunday noon. The long line of Sho't main battle tanks and support M113 APCs kicked up a cloud of dust as the landscape of Metula and northern Israel grew farther into the rearview mirror with each meter they traversed.

The men who stood upright in their turrets, manning their cupola-mounted .50-caliber heavy machine guns, scanned the terrain searching for threats: snipers, improvised explosive devices meant to ignite an ambush, or teams of RPG-wielding Palestinians in their lizard-pattern camouflage fatigues trying to take out the lead Israeli tank in the column. "The spring was coiled tightly," the soldiers ready for immediate action, one of Dagan's men commented for the news cameras.[2] Everyone in those first hours was tense. The enemy held the high ground.

But the company commanders encountered showers of sweets. Men and women thanked the tank soldiers for rescuing them. In the hillside villages of south Lebanon, old women threw rice and rose petals at the Israeli armor. They waved Lebanese flags and greeted the Israeli soldiers as saviors, unshackling them from the hell of Palestinian occupation. Arafat's men had not been kind to the local Shiite and Christian inhabitants: men were murdered, women and girls were raped, and homes and fields were burned if tribute was not paid to the nearby terror commander.

The 188th Armored Brigade was part of the 36th Armored Division, which was the IDF's regular force stationed in Israel's north. It was commanded by Brigadier General Avigdor Kahalani, one of the IDF's most capable and decorated tank officers. The 36th Division's mission was to slice up through the center part of the south and then swing west toward the Mediterranean where the force would connect with the 91st Division at Sidon and then push toward the Lebanese capital where, according to the plan, the combined force would cut the main Beirut-Damascus Highway and connect with Gemayel's Lebanese Forces.

The brigade bypassed positions held by the peacekeepers from UNI-FIL, the United Nations Interim Force in Lebanon, sent to serve as a deterrent to Palestinian attacks against northern Israel. The force, made up of contingents from nations such as Fiji and Ireland, was ineffective in the best cases; they often aided and abetted the Palestinian terror squads, who made their way to Israel via the UN checkpoints. The blue-helmeted soldiers stood silently as columns consisting of hundreds of Israeli tanks rolled past their positions. Dagan knew the battlespace from his time as regional commander; he had passed many UNIFIL checkpoints in disguise in the car of a warlord going to his late-night meetings. Dagan did not require maps to know where he was: he had a photographic memory for the topography. When the brigade moved forward, Captain Tuli Gvirtzman led the charge.

The terrain was tailor-made for tank-killing teams—narrow, constricting roadways and surrounding hills made maneuvering difficult for the hulking armored vehicles. Palestinian squads equipped with RPGs and recoilless antitank rifles could stall an entire advance by simply taking out the lead vehicle and then bottlenecking a convoy in a preset kill zone. Dagan had prepared his commanders for such eventualities, teaching them to respond quickly with their cupola-mounted heavy machine guns and to hit moving targets on the first shot with the tank's 105mm main armament gun. Israeli tank commanders—especially those under Dagan's command—moved upright in their turrets, exposing them to the risk of enemy fire. "We felt the whoosh of rockets fired at us that barely missed our heads," Eyal Ben-Reuven remembered. "Meir was undaunted by the enemy fire. He directed his force and moved forward."[3]

Some of the conscripts he commanded were fresh out of high school, barely past their eighteenth birthday. This was their first war—it was his fourth.

The horror of conflict and the exhaustion and burden of command were hard to mask. The men under his command were fighting and dying. His anguish was palpable; the responsibility was overwhelming no matter how hard he tried to mask it with a smile and the outward reassurance of calm. Senior officers in the brigade knew that the loss of every man killed or seriously wounded impacted him. One of his favorite young officers, Lieutenant Uzi Arad from the 71st Battalion, was shot in the head by a Palestinian sniper as he searched for an enemy mortar position. Arad had lost a brother in a previous war, and Dagan debated whether he should recommend that the young officer continue as a professional soldier, not wanting his family to risk another son. Dagan put on the persona that he was a warrior with ice water running through his veins, but he was an emotional man, and even many years later, thinking of the men he led who never made it home got to him.

There was no time to think of the personal pain and the heartbreak that the families of the fallen would undergo when parents and wives received the dreaded knock on the door. Dagan still had a mission to accomplish, and a brigade of men whose lives were in his hands. The push into Lebanon continued.

The fighting intensified once the brigade crossed the Akia Bridge over the Litani River and then moved on toward Nabatiyeh, before moving west and then up north toward Beirut, attacking Sidon and the Ein el-Hilweh refugee camp, southeast of the sprawling port city. In Sidon, Dagan wanted to take the city without a shot being fired. He dismounted his tank, walked into the central police fort, and told the local commander that he should call all the local Palestinian commanders and other armed elements in the city to surrender and assemble their weapons in the town square. Units of the Lebanese Army, which by 1982 had been rendered to a do-nothing force no longer interested or capable of defending the fractured nation, complied. The Palestinians, loosely organized in pseudo-military formations, were waiting. It was the night of June 7 into the early morning-hours of the following day. The Palestinians were dug in. Firing positions were embedded inside people's homes.

Fighting in the densely populated confines of Sidon and the Ein el-Hilweh refugee camp was challenging for armored formations. The IDF doctrine of *Tohar Ha'Neshek*, Purity of Arms, dictates how and when deadly force can be used, and soldiers had to exercise maximum restraint and a moral compass to protect innocent civilians from becoming casualties. "The terrorists were our enemy, not the Lebanese," Dagan would later reflect, "and I gave specific orders not to open fire on positions where we might hit civilians, some of them I knew from the security zone [in southern Lebanon]. It was one of the reasons why we didn't capture Nabatiyeh at first but bypassed it."[4] But Palestinian forces, and later Syrian commandos that joined in the conflict, used the local population as human shields, hiding behind groups of people trying to seek shelter from the furious combat only to be placed in between the Palestinians and the Israeli guns.

*          *          *

The Israeli invasion went beyond engaging Palestinian terror factions. When the IDF entered Lebanon, it sent an armored division east to neutralize the massive Syrian presence in the country, primarily in the Beqaa Valley. Damascus had always viewed Lebanon as a province, part of Greater Syria, and was determined to bolster the Palestinian entities in the country as a proxy front against Israel. Syria had twenty-five thousand troops in Lebanon; a daunting ring of the latest Soviet-produced surface-to-air missile batteries was meant to deter the IAF. In a series of dramatic preemptive moves, including the use of unmanned aerial vehicles, or drones, for the first time in combat, Israeli aircraft destroyed the Syrian SAM batteries; in air-to-air combat, the IAF shot down ninety Syrian MiGs and Sukhoi combat aircraft without suffering a single loss.

Israel had two objectives in the war—make it to Beirut and oust the Palestinian terror factions from the country, and see Bashir Gemayel take the reins as the new Lebanese president, ushering in a changed Middle East. In meetings between Defense Minister Sharon and Lebanese Forces commander Gemayel, the understanding had been that once the Israelis reached the road to Beirut, the Christians would join the fight. But early in the war, it was clear that they had no intention of joining the Israeli effort. They preferred to sit on the sidelines and watch.

For the push to the Lebanese capital, Meir Dagan's tank brigade was transferred to Brigadier General Amos Yaron's 96th Division—that force had landed on the Lebanese coast at the Awali River north of Sion courtesy of the Israeli Navy landing craft. From there, they would push on to Beirut. The suburb of Kfar Sil was in their way.

Kfar Sil, located in the southwestern approach of Beirut International Airport at Khalde, was not the type of small village that the IDF rolled through in south Lebanon. It was affluent and modern. Apartment buildings were five and six stories high; the private homes looked like villas, and some had swimming pools. The suburb sat below a hill where the Lebanese Army had an army fortress. Kfar Sil was also a line in the sand for the Syrian 85th Brigade—complete with three mechanized battalions, a tank battalion, and an artillery battalion, as well as a battalion of well-trained commandos and other special operations elements. Kfar Sil was Syria's last line of defense around Beirut. If it fell, overall Syrian control over the Lebanese capital would collapse.

The initial Israeli attack, assigned to the 211th Armored Brigade, met with stiff resistance. Casualties mounted. Meir Dagan's tanks were summoned to the rescue. Together with the Golani infantrymen under his command and a battalion of paratroopers, the battle for Kfar Sil was hard fought; engagements were waged at what is known as "zero-range": point-blank tank-versus-tank encounters at twenty and fifty meters. Dagan supervised the movements across the town and up its main street, where Syrian tanks and commandos waged a determined defense. Hand-to-hand battles were common; the 188th Brigade tanks and their Syrian counterparts hit one another in nonstop combat. The Syrian commandos were equipped with the Soviet-made AT-3 Sagger wire-guided antitank missiles that had exacted such a heavy toll on Israeli armor during the Yom Kippur War. The Syrians set up sniper positions from terraces and rooftops; they deployed the French-manufactured MILAN wire-guided antitank missiles with great effectiveness at night, since they were equipped with thermal sights.

Amid the battle, 74th Battalion commander Levin notified Dagan that several senior Syrian officers were holed up in the basement of the Kfar Sil school, using the cellar as a staging area to regroup. Rather than call them out to surrender or summon tanks to surround the building, Dagan ordered Levin to grab his assault rifle, and some grenades, and follow him. Brigade commanders were not supposed to suit up and fight like infantrymen—they had strategic responsibilities along with the lives of their men to consider. Although Dagan was never impulsive when it came to tactical decisions, he felt as if there was no time to lose. Within minutes, and a brief firefight, the Syrian officers were dead.[5]

It took a combined force of Dagan's brigade and battalions of infantrymen and paratroopers nineteen hours to neutralize Kfar Sil's main street. A tank commander in Major Ben-Reuven's 71st Battalion called the fighting pure hell; wherever an Israeli tank appeared in the open, whenever a Golani infantryman raised his head, the Syrians unleashed terrible fire, Ben-Reuven would recall.[6] Dagan summoned several Caterpillar D-9 bulldozers to clear the debris of destroyed armor and allow the Israelis to push through. Dagan offered the Syrians two options in Kfar Sil: flee or die.[7]

IDF chief of staff Lieutenant General Rafael Eitan called the battle the toughest of the entire war.[8] Dagan's brigade lost ten killed in the action and many more wounded. Once the shooting stopped in Kfar Sil and Dagan's tank led his columns toward the approaches of Beirut, the suburb was an apocalyptic hell. Charred Syrian tanks littered the main road and the alleys in between homes; some had had their turrets blown completely off their chassis. Thousands of shell casings of all calibers littered the main road. The temperatures hovered in the high nineties; the remains of the dead swelled in the brutal heat. Israeli and Syrian forces paid a dear price in blood for every inch of the cursed town in the Lebanon quagmire. It would be a harbinger of much worse to come.

*          *          *

Numerous high-ranking officers and intelligence types toured the battlefield during the first week of the fighting as Dagan's brigade moved on to Beirut. Dagan remembered that one of the senior men gazing at the terrain was Major General Yekutiel "Kuti" Adam, the deputy chief of staff. Prime Minister Begin appointed Adam as the next head of the Mossad, and even though the general was still in uniform and the posting was not official, he had already led Tzomet, the Mossad branch responsible for HUMINT as a good way to learn about the organization from within. On the fourth day of the war, Adam found Meir's tank just outside the Christian coastal town of Damur and climbed aboard. They spoke about the bitter fighting and the challenges that lay ahead, and before they parted, Adam said that when he was formally in the position of Mossad director, he'd reach out to Meir.[9] Dagan had always dreamed about working at the Mossad, and thoughts of a new and challenging opportunity entered his mind. The two men embraced, and Adam continued his tour of the front with his aide Colonel Haim Erez. The next day, both Adam and Erez were dead. Caught in a Syrian artillery barrage, they sought shelter in the basement of a building where, unbeknownst to them, Palestinian guerrillas had been hiding. Adam was the highest-ranking Israeli officer killed in Operation Peace for Galilee.

The front in the Beirut sector stabilized as the war continued. Israel laid siege to Beirut to force Yasir Arafat and his legion of Palestinian fighters to leave and to push Bashir Gemayel toward becoming an active player in the conflict. The IDF—and Israel's intelligence services that operated in the shadows—summoned Dagan for special tasks in the middle of the fight. "He knew the landscape, he knew the players, he knew what needed to be done, and how it needed to be handled," a former officer in the 1st Golani Brigade commented. "There were times when he'd take me in his jeep to a hill overlooking a location in Beirut," Eyal Ben-Reuven recalled, "and he'd say start counting backward: ten, nine, eight. . . . When it got to one and then zero, there'd be a huge explosion."[10]

Defense Minister Sharon never relinquished his desire to eliminate Arafat—an event he was certain would be a home-improvement project for the Middle East. A special team, code-named Herring (*Dag Maluach* in Hebrew) was tasked with killing the PLO leader; his code name was Fish Head.[11] Dagan, along with operatives from the Mossad, A'man's Unit 504, and Sayeret Mat'kal, hunted Arafat, calling in air strikes and trying to pinpoint the wily Palestinian leader's location and summon on-call flights of F-4E Phantom fighter bombers when the intelligence was accurate. On numerous occasions, the aircraft were racing toward Beirut, their pylons packed with bombs, only to have the mission aborted because of fears that the collateral damage of innocent lives would be unacceptable.

\*            \*            \*

During a respite in the fighting, at a command post on the outskirts of Beirut, an exhausted Brigadier General Yaron, Dagan's new division commander, summed up the first month of combat with a perspective that only a tired soldier could articulate: "In his chaos, the one who can reorganize better will be the one who wins."[12]

From the hilly ridges of Kfar Sil, Dagan and his battalion commanders scanned the southern approaches to Beirut and the international airport. There were ceasefires throughout the war, temporary lulls that allowed the combatants and civilians to recover and reassess. The decision-makers also needed time to reevaluate their options. Israel had gone all the way to create a new Lebanon, a new Middle East reality, and its military achievements were downgraded by an unreliable ally in the Christians and a nervous ally in the United States eager to contain and end the hostilities. President Ronald Reagan dispatched his special envoy to the Middle East, Undersecretary of State Philip Habib, to try to sort through the mess. Israel was closing its ring around Yasir Arafat and his PLO bastion in Beirut and utilizing air and artillery forces to attack terrorist positions. Beirut was a city of over two million inhabitants, and images of it being relentlessly bombed on television newscasts around the world were damning for Israel and its American superpower ally. Prime Minister Begin and Defense Minister Sharon believed that military pressure on Arafat's legions trapped in the city was the only way they would surrender and leave. The Israeli move on West Beirut was known as Operation Cousins, named so, it is suggested, as a "dig" at the unraveling relations between the United States and Israel over the war in Lebanon.[13]

By early August, after engaging the Syrian 85th Brigade along the ultra-strategic Beirut-Damascus Highway connecting the Lebanese and Syrian capitals, the 188th Armored Brigade moved into southwest Beirut. Destroying the PLO in Lebanon, and buying peace for Galilee, was still the war's primary publicly stated objective. On the night between August 2 and 3, Meir Dagan received instructions to move against terrorist and Syrian emplacements in Bourj el-Barajneh, its adjacent refugee camp, and the areas around the airport.

The shantytowns and slums in southwest Beirut were accidentally perfect for urban warfare. Israeli forces moved cautiously and slowly through the densely populated terrain. The Palestinians fired mortars from courtyards near apartment complexes, challenging Israeli commanders to maneuver in a way to avoid unnecessary casualties to their men and the local civilians.

Dagan scanned the horizon from his tank, gazing at Beirut through his field glasses while monitoring a dozen radio frequencies and examining twice as many maps. The landscape he saw was surreal. The area in front of him was a hellacious battlefield of urban destruction. To the north, he saw tall buildings and life—the skyline of a city that had once been the Middle East's capital of decadence and indulgence. He knew the city well from his earlier covert assignments. He hoped to return as a visitor and enjoy the meze feasts in the city's legendary restaurants. But dreaming was a dangerous commodity in Lebanon.

Before dawn on August 4, Dagan received orders to take Beirut International Airport. He summoned his battalion commanders and the officers in charge of artillery and air cover to meet in the command post behind a M113 APC. The men were exhausted; two months of war had taken its toll. It was still dark as the officers huddled. Someone had prepared a pot of powdered coffee. Everyone smoked cigarettes. The humid air was stifling, laced with the smell of diesel fuel and nicotine. The sounds of odd angry gunfire in the distance provided an inescapable soundtrack to the hell they were in and the gauntlet they were about to enter. The fear was that the terrorists had fortified the airport in the hope of making a symbolic last stand.

The airport and its surrounding area were a staging area for what was referred to as the chaotic fruit salad of Lebanon—men of different camouflage fatigues, berets, and other assorted garments who controlled small swaths of gangland terrain. Palestinian guerrillas, Syrian commandos, Al-Mourabitoun* militiamen, and other armed Sunnis all staked a presence at the airport because of its strategic importance. There were civilians outside the terminal, carrying with them suitcases and their belongings wrapped in blankets, hoping to flee the fighting in and around the Lebanese capital. The fear was that a battle would break out with the civilians caught in the crossfire.

Dagan peered through his field glasses, looking to avoid unnecessary collateral damage, and spotted a remote building used by the airport's fire brigade. He summoned Lieutenant Colonel Spiegel and Captain Amir Meital, junior Golani officer,† and the three drove there together;

---

* Known in English as the "Sentinels," this West Beirut force consisted of two thousand fighters who followed a Nasserite ideology. Primarily Sunni in makeup, they were allied with Palestinian forces in Beirut and were trained and equipped by the PFLP and DFLP.

† On the night of December 8–9, 1988, Lieutenant Colonel Amir Meital, commander of the 12th Battalion, would be killed in a daring commando operation against an underground fortress south of Beirut belonging to Ahmed Jibril's PFLP-GC. The amphibious and heliborne raid, code-named Blue and Brown, used Rottweilers fitted with explosive packs to destroy the terror tunnels. It has been speculated that the raid was meant to preemptively deter Jibril from participating in a terror-for-hire plot hatched in Tehran to destroy an American airliner in retaliation for the accidental shooting down of an Iran Air jet over the Persian Gulf by a U.S. Navy vessel in July 1988. Jibril survived the raid. Thirteen days later, Pan Am 103 was destroyed over Lockerbie, Scotland, killing 259 on board and 11 on the ground.

tanks covered their progression onto the tarmac. The fire brigade building was already abandoned, the firemen and rescue personnel long
gone. The dinner from the night before was still on the table and the
ashtrays were crammed with cigarette butts. Black fireman helmets and
yellow reflective bunker gear hung unused on coat hooks. Dagan put
on a helmet, found a jacket that fit his frame, and intended to explore
the airfield in disguise. He loved to masquerade. He had handed helmets and jackets to Spiegel and Meital when the telephone rang. It was
the airport manager watching everything from the control tower. He
sounded nervous.

Dagan sensed the airport manager's trepidation. He always addressed
people with the respect due, and he tried to reassure the man in a
mixture of Arabic and English, but his tone was stern. "You have thirty
minutes to start displaying white flags and surrender and no harm will
come to you or anyone here. But if you resist and fire upon us, we will
fire back." The three Israelis returned to the forward command post to
plan their assault. They kept the fire gear as souvenirs.

Twenty minutes later white flags began to appear across the airport.
Levin's 74th Armored Battalion and Lieutenant Colonel Baruch Spiegel's
12th Battalion moved cautiously across the perimeter fence and toward
the tarmac and terminals. After seizing the areas around the airport,
Spiegel's forces attacked from the north, moving south. The runway was
littered with destroyed aircraft from Middle East Airlines, the Lebanese
flag carrier. The Israeli tanks and infantrymen moved out before the
sun's first light. They captured the airport shortly after daybreak without
a shot fired in anger.

Dagan established a command post in the control tower that overlooked the airfield and much of the city. He found a kettle and made
some tea for his officers. He lit his pipe while looking at the Lebanese
capital below him. The moment of achievement was interrupted by the
swoosh of Sagger missiles being launched from a distance. And then
came the explosions and the sounds of gunfire and men screaming in
pain.

Dozens of Syrian commando tank-killing teams emerged from the
buildings around the airport and launched a lethal strike of Sagger

antitank missiles at the Israeli armored formations. Lieutenant Colonel Levin's Centurion was hit, blowing the 74th Battalion commander completely out of his turret and onto the ground below. Chaos ensued, as the barrage of Saggers expanded to include commando tank-killer teams, some dressed as civilians, firing RPGs. Dagan ordered the 74th Battalion to the sidelines and the 71st into the fight. And then the skies opened with a tremendous artillery barrage. Syrian batteries miles away had zeroed in on the tarmac and unleashed a relentless assault on the advancing Israeli tanks. The Israelis took casualties. The battalion's lead tank, Tuli's, suffered a direct hit. He was killed instantly.

Dagan went on the brigade's radio frequency and summoned Major Ben-Reuven, ordering him to the control tower. News delivered in person was always bad. As Ben-Reuven reached the brigade's command post overlooking the tarmac, the Mediterranean, and much of Beirut, Dagan turned to him with a sunken face and said Tuli was dead. There was a pause, and then Dagan's knees buckled; his large form slumped forward. Tuli's death broke him. He collapsed in a burst of tears that was very uncharacteristic of him. Ben-Reuven consoled Dagan, hugging him awkwardly as they embraced, trying to hug one another over their cumbersome Kevlar body armor. It took a few moments until Dagan could pull himself together, and then he continued to direct the battle and the counterattack.

News of Dagan's breakdown spread quickly down the chain of command. It could have caused trepidation among the ranks that their brigade commander had suffered a crippling psychological blow, but it had the opposite effect, earning him endless affection and permanent respect. The soldiers in his brigade felt honored to serve under a man who showed emotion for them. He always spoke about the fighting force being a family unit. That emboldened men to fight and even sacrifice themselves in combat. "If a brigade commander can be tearful over *my* company commander," Ben-Reuven remembered, "then I love him even more."[14]

August 4 was a costly day for Dagan's brigade. It lost thirteen men at the airport, but there would be little time to mourn and reflect. The war continued.

*               *               *

Israel's stranglehold around West Beirut, the Muslim half of the city, was strengthened once the airport was captured. The Palestinian and Syrian predicaments inside their shrinking fortress grew more hopeless. A determined effort was made to avert the nightmare scenario of full-scale warfare inside the heavily populated confines of the Lebanese capital. The city was already decimated by years of civil war and now the Israeli invasion. Philip Habib's shuttle diplomacy between Beirut, Damascus, and Jerusalem intensified. On August 13, an agreement was reached to oversee the evacuation of Syrian and Palestinian forces from Beirut. Peacekeepers—French paratroopers, American Marines, and Italian amphibious troops—would supervise the evacuation and protect the residents of the Muslim half of the Lebanese capital. Between August 21 and 31, six thousand Syrian troops would retreat on land and the eighty-five hundred Palestinian guerrillas, including Arafat, would depart by sea. The Palestinian fighters fired their AK-47s into the air as they were loaded onto passenger liners for new exiles in Algeria, Tunisia, and Yemen, their determination to fight Israel and avenge the creation of the Jewish state unchanged by another battlefield humiliation. Yasir Arafat raised the V-sign hand gesture in defiance as he boarded his ship to Tunis while Israeli snipers awaited the order to kill him—a command that never came.[15]

The multinational force was in Lebanon for only fifteen days.

Bashir Gemayel was elected president of Lebanon on August 23. He was to be sworn into the office thirty days later. There were hopes in Jerusalem that Gemayel's first act as Lebanon's new leader would be to sign a peace accord with Israel. But Gemayel refused. He was adamant about not being seen as an Israeli puppet.

The best-laid plans of spies and statesmen can unravel in the flash of hundreds of kilograms of high explosives. In the afternoon of September 14, Bashir Gemayel was assassinated when a powerful bomb planted by Syrian agents detonated in his political headquarters. His body was identified by a Mossad agent in Beirut who recognized the ring and watch he was wearing. Everyone braced for the carnage to follow.

The IDF had a plan of action, code-named Iron Brain, should an incident unravel the country. The Lebanese Army was supposed to assume control of the capital, but hours after Gemayel's murder, the troopers remained in their barracks. Israeli forces moved into West Beirut but refrained from entering the refugee camps in the capital, particularly Sabra and Shatila, even though it was believed that some two thousand Palestinian guerrillas who had refused exile were sheltered there. The Lebanese Forces, eager for payback, vowed to search the camps for terrorists. Inexcusably, the Israelis let them do it. The Maronite forces assembled at Beirut International Airport. Meir Dagan, and the men of the 188th Armored Brigade stationed there, looked on curiously, though fearing what was to come.

The killings began on the night of September 16. For the next two days, the Lebanese Forces and Christian militiamen perpetrated a horrific massacre inside the Sabra and Shatila camps, killing men, women, and children. Similar crimes were committed in the Fakhani neighborhood nearby. Israeli forces entered the camp on September 19 to render medical aid to the wounded, restore a sense of order, and protect the Palestinian population from future acts of retribution. To this day, the *official* death toll from the massacre is 328 killed and 991 missing.[16] Some accounts claim that as many as 3,500 people were killed.

The international peacekeepers returned to Beirut shortly to protect the Lebanese from one another. On September 29, Israeli forces were withdrawn from the city to defensive lines to the south. The Iranians, and their bloody revolution, had arrived. Lebanon was doomed to suffer.

*　　　　*　　　　*

The Sabra and Shatila Massacres were the final unraveling of Israel's grand scheme to rid itself of a lethal terror presence on its northern border and bring about a new reality of peace and cooperation with a Lebanese state free of Palestinian guerrillas.

Some say that the three months in Lebanon during the summer of 1982 changed Meir Dagan forever. The brigade he commanded lost twenty-five soldiers and officers during the combat—twenty-five sets of families to visit and console. Dagan felt responsible for each young man who did not return to his home. He carried that burden for the remainder of his life, his emotions showing at the annual memorial services held in their honor. Even when he was the head of the Mossad, spearheading covert actions that could never be publicized, he did not mind crying at these events to show how much the loss of these men, his men, meant to him. Dagan, a former subordinate would reflect, was a man of war who hated wars.

Meir Dagan was never on record blaming Ariel Sharon, his mentor, for the 1982 invasion and the eventual debacle of Israel's involvement in Lebanon. The two men shared a rich past and a fruitful future. Dagan would later comment that Israel should have hit the Palestinians harder, rendering the PLO completely ineffective, and the retreat of its forces to the Israeli side of the border, as a deterrent to any terror army that dared threaten northern Israel.[17]

Lebanon became a stark lesson to Dagan about the limitations—and dangers—of military power and the aspiration to set events in motion that could spiral dangerously out of control. Meir Dagan realized that Israel's military might was critical to the survival of the Jewish state, but it needed to be used wisely and strategically. Overreach was always a dangerous possibility—even in campaigns rooted in the best of intentions.

# CHAPTER 13

# The Land of Martyrs and Spies

D ir Qanoun an-Nahr was typical of the many small villages that dotted the hills of southern Lebanon. There was one road in and out. The small shops selling the basics—meat, spices, kitchenware, and clothing— of day-to-day life lined both sides of the narrow thoroughfare. Other than the cars in the driveways, Dir Qanoun an-Nahr had not changed much over the centuries. A thousand or so residents lived in homes that were large and spacious. Construction was always vertical, as parents and their married children, and their children, lived under one always-growing roof. Dir Qanoun an-Nahr was Shiite, and religious enough that the men flagellated themselves with chains and cut their scalps to bleed for the holy day of Ashura, but the melodies offered by Shiite songstresses, belting out erotic tunes of love and desire, could also be heard throughout the village. When the Iranians arrived, always visiting at night, posters of scantily clad female singers were replaced by paintings of Ayatollah Khomeini next to slogans extolling martyrdom.[1] The village elders came to hear the emissaries from Iran preach at the local mosque. The visitors spoke perfect, though heavily accented, Arabic. The young men also came. One teenager was particularly impressed by what the Iranians had to say about the rewards of paradise. His name was Ahmed Qasir.

The young man had left school in the fifth grade to work at his father's vegetable stall on the main road. He enjoyed soccer and music.

According to some accounts the family had lived in Saudi Arabia and Libya; his parents were deeply religious. The seventeen-year-old Qasir was chubby and sported a pubescent mustache. He was shy and had never slept away from home before, but on the night between November 10 and 11, he slipped out a bedroom window. A black Mercedes sedan, driven by an Iranian intelligence officer, picked him up a few hundred yards away down the darkened road; three men from Beirut were also in the vehicle. The young man had never driven a car before, and he was given a few final pointers about how to shift gears while negotiating the climbs and descents of the mountain roads. He had memorized his route before being handed the keys to a white Peugeot 504 sedan. At the first rays of light early on November 11, the teenager put the keys in the ignition and drove out of an indoor garage near the village. He headed west. The Peugeot 504 weighed 2,646 pounds out of the factory. The car that Qasir drove was significantly heavier. The vehicle was laden with 440 pounds of high explosives and multiple land mines.

Only the farmers were on the road that foggy Thursday dawn. It took Qasir less than a half hour of grinding his gears to reach the outskirts of Tyre, the fourth largest city in Lebanon, and one that jutted into the Mediterranean, toward the Israeli military headquarters—a seven-story complex housing army, Border Guard policemen, and intelligence units, including the Shin Bet and Military Intelligence's Unit 504 HUMINT force.

A military policeman standing guard duty next to a wall of sandbags outside saw a white Peugeot 504 speeding in from the west. At 7:15, the Israeli headquarters in Tyre collapsed in a blinding flash of light, the seven stories reduced to rubble beneath a rising plume of black smoke.[2] By the time rescue squads were summoned to pick apart the pancaked rubble of the building, sixty-seven soldiers and policemen were dead, along with nine Shin Bet agents and fifteen local detainees. Lebanese and Palestinian terror suspects were housed in holding cells in the building's basement. They were killed in the suffocating fireball of the blast.

The blast was heard in Dir Qanoun an-Nahr. It was raining that morning, but the mushroom cloud was seen by all villagers alarmed by the distant thud. By the time the first Israeli helicopters landed nearby to evacuate the dead and wounded, the men had set up a mourner's tent and the women cooked a festive feast to celebrate Qasir's actions. The bombing of the Israeli HQ became known as the Day of Martyrs.[3]

The assassination of Bashir Gemayel, combined with the departure of Palestinian guerrillas, had created a malignant power vacuum inside the country that the Syrians and Iranians were eager to exploit. The Shiites of the southern Beirut slums were emboldened by Tehran's efforts to mobilize them into a lethal force of resistance. The Ayatollah Khomeini's portrait adorned buildings that somehow managed to remain standing after the Israeli siege. Emissaries from the Islamic Revolutionary Guard Corps and the Ministry of Intelligence and Security traveled from Damascus to Beirut with truckloads of weapons and cash. In the south, the Shiite villagers who had seen Dagan's tanks and soldiers as liberators soon viewed the IDF as just another occupier. From their base of operations in the ancient Roman town of Baalbek in the Beqaa Valley, the Iranians sent instructors to the south to train a generation of disenfranchised youth that martyrdom operations could secure their rightful place in paradise against the Israelis and Americans.

The bombing caught the Israeli government completely by surprise. Prime Minister Begin was in New York City, on the opening leg of a lengthy visit to the United States. The Israeli defense establishment was not prepared to inform its soldiers—or its citizens—that the war known as Operation Peace for Galilee had unleashed a new terrorist enemy that threatened to bring the Iranian brand of suicide operations to Israel's northern frontier. Although investigators who responded to the blast examined the bits and pieces of Qasir's Peugeot and tested the twisted frame of the sedan for explosive residue, the military censor's office forbade any inference that the headquarters was hit by terrorists and peddled a story that propane tanks used for cooking had accidentally blown up. The lie would be the official government stance for forty-two years.[4]

Israel had built its geopolitical strategy and long-term regional aspirations around Bashir Gemayel. But Lebanon had changed since the switch was triggered on the 180 kilograms of military-grade explosives that afternoon in Beirut when the Lebanese president-elect and many of his key commanders evaporated into a blinding flash. The assassination paralyzed Israel's intelligence capabilities inside the country. "Israel was rendered blind," Reuven Ehrlich, Dagan's chief intelligence officer, would comment. "IDF commanders knew nothing of the interwoven complexities of the Lebanese landscape."⁵ The reality of the fractured nation became even more puzzling after the suicide bombing of the headquarters in Tyre.

Brigade commanders usually remained at their positions for three-year terms. Colonel Meir Dagan had led the 188th for less than a year when he was summoned to the Kirya, the Department of Defense campus housing IDF headquarters in the heart of Tel Aviv. Northern Command needed an officer with the necessary experience and the devious ruthlessness to handle the emerging threats. Israel needed eyes and ears in Lebanon. Dagan enthusiastically accepted the challenge.

On November 22, Dagan was promoted to brigadier general in a small ceremony for family and army brass at IDF headquarters in Tel Aviv. As is customary at such presentations, the wife of the officer being promoted helps place the new ranks on her husband's shoulder epaulets. Meir wore his Class A uniform, ironed, with his jump wings, armored corps pin, campaign ribbons, and bravery medal above his left breast pocket. Compliments were shared and refreshments were served.

A week later, Brigadier General Dagan was driven across the Israeli border into Lebanon. His personal effects and gear were in a khaki canvas kit bag; he also brought boxes of his painting materials and books. He lit his pipe as the staff car moved north up the narrow roads that twisted around hills plush with green. Shepherds tending to their sheep looked curiously at the vehicles racing around treacherous bends that many had trouble negotiating at slow speeds. Farmers tended to their olive trees using the same techniques and tools their ancestors had used during the French Mandate and the Ottoman Empire. Marjayoun, Dagan's new home—until further notice—was only six miles from Metula, but it was centuries apart.

The command given to Dagan was called Ya'ka'l—the Hebrew acronym for Lebanon Liaison Unit. His Marjayoun headquarters was an imposing fortress. It had been a French citadel during the mandate and an Ottoman palace before that. A French general and a Turkish pasha had sat in the same office Dagan now called his own. The office view they shared of majestic cedars and the snowcapped Hermon mountain range to the east had not changed over time. Neither had the ethnic mess and religious hatred that the previous rulers had also administered over.

The compound was a two-story-high square of sandstone. The roof boasted a skyline of radio antennas and satellite dishes. A large Israeli flag flew atop the main building and at the center of a parade ground. Major Haddad's militiamen were everywhere. Empty fuel drums, filled with cement and rocks, as well as concrete barriers, were placed in a zigzag formation to force drivers to slow down before reaching the main gate—an effort to mitigate the risk of vehicle-borne suicide bombers smashing into the compound. Machine gun posts and barbed wire concertina ringed the perimeter.

It was winter in Lebanon, the rainy season. Sometimes it even snowed. Conditions were harsh for fighting a counterinsurgency campaign in the hills with mud everywhere.

*     *     *

The Lebanon that Dagan assumed responsibility for was a much different country than he had encountered when in charge of the South Lebanon Region unit. The Palestinians were gone, routed, but alliances had shifted. The Christian Lebanon that the Israelis had hoped for was an obliterated dream. The Phalangists never recovered from Gemayel's assassination. The Palestinians were sent into exile across the Middle East. And, the United States, who, along with French and Italian peacekeepers, had secured Beirut and protected the Palestinian refugee camps, tried to restore a semblance of stability inside the country. But the fractured ethnic and religious puzzle that was Lebanon once again came apart at the seams, helped by the Syrians, who proved themselves to be the puppet masters dictating the country's future, and the Iranians, who weaponized the Shiite population of the capital, the Beqaa Valley, and the south to fulfill Khomeini's calls of "Death to America" and "Death to Israel." Dagan's onetime Shiite allies had splintered into new causes and affiliations: some moderate and nationalistic, while others had regrouped—and rearmed—with a new agenda and a lethal strategy.

The new unit's primary mission was to build Major Haddad's militia into a conventional fighting force that could secure the southern half of the country and serve as a protective buffer between the chaos of Lebanon and the communities of northern Israel. Haddad's men were cleared of participating in the Sabra and Shatila Massacres, but they were an undisciplined and unproven fighting force. Dagan acted as a paramilitary officer, training the militia to be more professional and combat-proficient; the force was renamed the South Lebanon Army. Haddad's new army received surplus World War Two–era M51 Sherman tanks and M3 half-tracks to increase its mobility and firepower. Container loads of AK-47 assault rifles—captured from the Egyptians, Syrians, and Palestinians, and made in the Soviet Union, East Germany, Romania, and North Korea—were issued to SLA fighters. Every soldier in Major Haddad's army received a salary of approximately three hundred dollars a month—a significant stipend for a militiaman in Lebanon. SLA fighters were sent to Israel for tactical instruction and leadership courses.

The Lebanon Liaison Unit was, on paper at least, an administrative command that connected the civilian populations and interacted as a link to communities needing basic services, humanitarian relief, and even the settling of disputes involving clans, businesses, and municipalities. Dagan was, in essence, the Israeli governor for most of the areas of Lebanon that the IDF controlled, and most of his schedule involved holding court and utilizing the army's reach and Solomon-like negotiating skills to keep the peace. But behind closed doors, when religious leaders and civil servants came seeking his aid, he could gather invaluable intelligence on what was happening inside the villages and towns of the area.

That mission statement, as said, was on paper. The Lebanon Liaison Unit was also an umbrella command for counterinsurgency, special operations, and espionage against the terror targets emerging in the Israeli-held south. Dagan became one of Israel's spymasters in south Lebanon.[6]

Although the lines were murky, and there were a lot of gray areas and overlaps, the Mossad and Military Intelligence shared Lebanon. Operations north of the Awali River were the responsibility of the Mossad, and areas south of the tributary, twenty-five miles from the Israeli frontier, belonged to the military. The Mossad maintained a station north of Beirut, in a fortified villa along the shores of Jounieh, the Phalangist seat of power north of the Lebanese capital. The perimeter was secured by operators from Flotilla 13, Israel's naval commandos.[7] The station chief in 1983 was Eliezer "Gaizi" Tzafrir, who had extensive experience in the Arab world, most notably in Kurdistan, assisting the Peshmerga in their fight against the Iraqis. He also understood the Shiites—he was the last Mossad station chief in Tehran and organized the evacuation of Israel's embassy—and intelligence presence—after the Shah fell and the mullahs took over.

A necessary firewall existed between Tzafrir, Dagan, and other arms of A'man and the General Staff operations directorate that handled clandestine work in Lebanon. But their paths crossed occasionally, though only in Israel. Covert action in the areas that Israel controlled remained Dagan's domain. He led many operations personally, contrary to the risks a man of his rank needed to take. When he traveled the country in uniform, Dagan moved around in a convoy of military vehicles. He carried a sidearm and a Mini-Uzi submachine gun or an AK-47. On secret assignments, when he met with local mayors or top-level sources, the favored mode of transportation was two undercover BMW sedans parked on the Israeli side of the fence. When his driver, A.,* crossed the border, he would change the license plates from Israeli to Lebanese.[8] Dagan liked to wear a black leather jacket when going undercover. He always showed up to meetings sporting Ray-Ban aviator sunglasses. He had gained weight and looked more like a local crime boss than an Israeli brigadier.

Dagan's appearance, the weapons he carried, and the heavily armed entourage that followed him wherever he went were the props of a shadow theater for projecting power and earning respect. The men he met with—Sunnis, Christians, Shiites, and Druze—revered him. "Arabs

* Identity withheld for security reasons.

don't hide their respect," Amiram Levin remembered. "They never made him wait. They shared their problems with him because they knew he could be relied upon to bring solutions. He treated everyone like human beings. Everyone was a possible partner."[9]

*          *          *

The emissaries from Iran's Islamic Revolutionary Guard Corps (IRGC) dispatched to Lebanon met regularly with individuals who were faceless and nameless to the Western intelligence services, to prepare and plan what would be a game-changing terror offensive in the region. There were no dossiers on the religious clerics who had studied in Iraq and were now recruiting men who were pious or who wanted to fight the Israelis and the Americans.

The most important of these representatives was Ali Akbar Mohtashamipour, the Iranian ambassador to Damascus. Although only thirty-six years old, Mohtashamipour was one of the most powerful men in the revolution, having been a favorite student of Ayatollah Khomeini and then one of his most trusted advisors when the cleric was exiled to Iraq and later France. Beyond his religious acumen, Mohtashamipour was a master manipulator in forging strategic alliances; he established operational ties with Yasir Arafat and the Palestine Liberation Organization.[10] Soon, young and zealous Iranians were sent to Lebanon to undergo counterintelligence, demolitions, and special operations training. Mohtashamipour was obsessed with spreading Khomeini's revolution to Lebanon and establishing a base of operations for the fight against Israel. The cleric was one of the founders of the Islamic Revolutionary Guard Corps.

Mohtashamipour convinced Khomeini to appoint him Iran's ambassador to Syria. Amicable but determined, Mohtashamipour convinced Syrian president Hafez al-Assad to let his men travel into Lebanon to establish a cadre of operatives and the mechanism to support an anti-Israel front. Assad agreed and allowed the IRGC to establish a base of operations in an old fortress in Baalbek and plant the seeds of a Shiite resistance force. Mohtashamipour invited Shiite clerics and like-minded triggermen from across Lebanon to visit him in the Beqaa. The men he met all knew one another from religious studies in the Shiite holy city of Najaf, Iraq. To Western intelligence—and the Israeli services—they were mostly anonymous and invisible.

The name Hassan Nasrallah did not register on any "Be on the Lookout" printouts. His mugshot was not in the system. But the name Imad Fayez Mughniyeh was on file. Mughniyeh, a Shiite born in 1962, in the small farming village of Tayr Dibba four miles from Tyre, was a teenager when he volunteered in the ranks of Fatah to fight the Christians during the Lebanese Civil War. His specialty was sniping at women trying to find food for their families. He was good at killing and was recruited to serve in Force 17, Fatah's elite Praetorian Guard, as a bodyguard to Arafat's deputy. Mughniyeh's nom de guerre was *al-Fahad*, "The Leopard." Israeli intelligence captured the master log of all members of Force 17, though Mughniyeh had shed his fatigues and disappeared into the Shiite slums of south Beirut rather than board a ship taking Palestinian fighters to an overseas exile. His name was not associated with any new Shiite underground guerilla organizations.

The names of people of interest, the old-time usual suspects and new faces and previously unknown terror cells, were discussed at the staff meetings inside Dagan's Marjayoun HQ. HUMINT was the most valued commodity in the espionage bazaar of southern Lebanon, and A'man Unit 504 was king. Unit 504 was one of the most secretive entities in the IDF—it was called a mini-Mossad. Made up of Arabic-speaking officers who operated in confines of interest throughout the region, the unit consisted of analysts, handlers, case officers, and interrogators. There were existing networks of sources and assets that Dagan and A'man counterparts had built before Operation Peace for Galilee. New ones always had to be found and nurtured. The intelligence officers were the lifeblood of Dagan's entire organization. But the spies and their handlers could only report and log in what they knew or heard rumblings about. There were no absolutes in the espionage arena. Sometimes, vital information came too late to be used effectively.

Rumors of a massive explosion in Beirut reached Dagan's headquarters late on the afternoon of April 18, 1983—hours after the blast. At 13:04

in the afternoon, a Lebanese Shiite driving a GMC van packed with a ton of explosives accelerated his vehicle onto the curb on Avenue de Paris along the city's Corniche, crashing into the local guard booth at the U.S. Embassy's entrance, at the center of the U-shaped façade inside the circular driveway. The explosives, believed to have been made up of the powerful Pentaerythritol tetranitrate, or PETN, and propane tanks for added effect, created a shaped charge that caused the center wing of the building to collapse. The blast hit the chancery as the entire CIA Lebanon station was assembled in a secure conference room for a lunch meeting, killing eight of them. It was the single deadliest day in CIA history. Sixty-three people were killed that overcast Monday afternoon in Beirut in the suicide bombing.

An anonymous caller representing a never-heard-from-before shadow group named the Islamic Jihad Organization called the Associated Press desk in Beirut claiming responsibility for bombing the embassy. "This is part of the Iranian Revolution's campaign against imperialist targets throughout the world. We shall keep striking at any crusader presence in Lebanon, including the international forces."[11]

Just as they had in the bombing of the Israeli military compound in Tyre five months earlier, the new entity that the world would come to know as Hezbollah, the Lebanese Shiite Party of God, had eviscerated the U.S. intelligence presence inside Lebanon. The Reagan administration sent more peacekeepers to Beirut. The trap had been set.

Six months later, at 6:20 on the morning of October 23, 1983, a Shiite suicide truck bomber drove six tons of TNT into the barracks used by U.S. Marine Corps peacekeepers at Beirut International Airport. The explosive had been insidiously constructed, designed to propel the force of the blast and shrapnel upward, causing the building to collapse. Most of the Marines and sailors inside the building were asleep when the bomber struck. The attack killed 241 American servicemen—the deadliest day for the Marine Corps since Iwo Jima. The American peacekeepers, including those who'd manned the perimeter gate, had not had magazines in their M-16s, so as not to appear as if they were an occupying force.

Seconds after Beirut shook in the seismic force of the explosion, a suicide truck bomber hit the Drakkar building where French peacekeepers were stationed. The blast killed 58 paratroopers from the 1st Parachute Chasseur Regiment.

A month later, at 6:00 a.m. on November 4, 1983, a young man from a hilltop village recruited by Mohtashamipour and Mughniyeh drove a truck packed with TNT into the new Israeli military headquarters in Tyre. Protocols had been established to deal with suicide bombers, and the guards on duty fired over one hundred bullets at the speeding truck, but the driver was able to penetrate the main perimeter, reach the outer parking lot, and detonate his lethal payload. The Shin Bet command center was obliterated in the blast; tents where soldiers slept were vaporized. Fifty-nine people were killed in the second Tyre bombing—thirty-one of them were Lebanese detainees.

\*         \*         \*

Neither the Mossad, the Shin Bet, nor A'man appreciated the earthquake that had cut away the ground beneath them. The telltale signs were obvious, beyond the Khomeini posters that soon adorned the villages of the south, the cassettes of sermons in Farsi and Arabic that were distributed for free, and women who used to wear short dresses suddenly going out in public wearing the black abaya—money from unknown sources had flooded the Shiite communities. The poorest sector of the Lebanese mosaic was suddenly flush.

New schools, clinics, and mosques were built in impoverished hamlets. New tractors suddenly plowed fields. New cars, from dealerships in Damascus, suddenly appeared in family driveways. Mercedes was the vehicle of choice. Dagan did not put two-and-two together, failing to understand that money was the oxygen that fueled an underground terror movement, like the one in Iraq and Iran, where parents sent their children off to face certain death on the battlefield for the glory of sacrifice. For the remainder of his intelligence career, the nexus between cash and murder would be a central theme of Dagan's counterterrorism doctrine.

Money had always been a lubricant for information. A rucksack full of dollars or Lebanese pounds bought folders full of actionable intelligence for Dagan and his covert cells. Espionage was a business in Lebanon and loyalties were traditionally assigned to the highest bidder, but there were additional factors that turned Israel's clandestine campaign into an unwinnable struggle. Israel could not compete with the Khomeini revolution—and the zealous awakening of the Shiite faithful, particularly in the south, where the population had been disenfranchised for so long—and the clerics traveled from village to village with messages of resistance and martyrdom. The message emanating from Beirut and the Beqaa could not be silenced. Dagan decided to go after the messengers instead.

*　　　*　　　*

Major Saad Haddad died on January 15, 1984, at home surrounded by his wife Theresa and six daughters, following a long battle with cancer, which included medical treatments in Israel.[12] He was only forty-seven years old. Israel needed to honor its military comrades in arms and send a resounding message that the Jewish state would never abandon its Lebanese Christians and like-minded Shiite allies. Israel's top leadership—elected and military—paid their respects. A large contingent of IDF troopers arrived in Marjayoun at dawn to set up roadblocks and a defensive perimeter. The sounds of helicopters coming in for a landing muffled the rhythmic chimes of the bells in the church where the services were held.

Haddad's flag-draped coffin was surrounded by an honor guard of militiamen dressed in neatly ironed IDF surplus olive fatigues. Maronite nuns sat to the right of the casket in prayer, concerned over the fate of the besieged Christian minority. A who's who of Israeli political, military, and intelligence leaders filled the pews. Prime Minister Yitzhak Shamir and Defense Minister Moshe Arens sat in the front row, next to IDF chief of staff Lieutenant General Moshe Levy and the head of Northern Command Major General Orri Or. Meir Dagan sat in the first row, as well. Haddad had become a dear friend of his. He was a frequent guest at the Dagan home, and Meir brought his children to the militia commander's home in Marjayoun.[13]

The state funeral was held in a war zone. The Israelis who attended looked out of place as the mourners prayed and the priest spoke in Aramaic. The candles and incense were a new experience. Shin Bet agents assigned to Unit 730 appeared nervous throughout the ceremony. The men in safari jackets checked their watches, eager to return to the security of Israel. Snipers ringed nearby rooftops to deal with any threat.

Major Haddad's death signaled the end of an era and the launch of a new period of great uncertainty and challenge. He had swagger and charisma. His courage was unmatched. But the Shiites were on the march, and the stated objective of the 1982 invasion, peace for Galilee, would be defeated if terrorists—Palestinian or Iranian-backed—returned in force to south Lebanon to set up new bases of operations.

Dagan pondered his command and areas of responsibility and realized a proactive measure was called for. There was no shortage of worthy targets in the mountain villages where the yellow Hezbollah flags, decorated with the group's green fist and AK-47 logo, flew.

Sheikh Ragheb Harb was one of the most influential Shiite leaders, who had a traveling road show of fundamentalist incitement in southern Lebanon. He was the imam of Jibchit, a Shiite village twenty miles west of Marjayoun that had become a hub for the new Shiite underground movement. When Israeli soldiers were nowhere in sight, men openly brandished assault rifles. Gunfire and explosions could be heard at night, as young men who had never fired a weapon before were schooled in marksmanship and demolitions.

Harb was not a military commander in the newly formed Party of God. He did not lead active service units in the field, and he was not involved in the intelligence side of Hezbollah's growing networks or the Iranian emissaries in Baalbek, Damascus, and at the Iranian Embassy in Beirut. But he openly recruited new members to the organization, and he incited the young men to violence, preaching that it was their religious duty to kill Israelis even if it meant their death, which was sold as a guaranteed path to paradise.

Killing a cleric could backfire. There was a risk that the local population would construe Harb's assassination as a slight against the faithful, an unforgivable act that had to be avenged. But Dagan assessed that eliminating Harb, and men like him, would be preventative rather than punitive, and cause village imams to think twice about getting involved in a terrorist war. Israel could have no connection to his elimination. There was no shortage of men in south Lebanon who worked for the Israelis or who could be motivated to carry out a killing for a suitcase full of American dollars. Everything and everyone had a price in the country. Dagan did not want to overspend. He found two Lebanese agents who agreed to do the job.[14]

On the night of February 16, 1984, Harb returned to his Jibchit home. He drove himself. At a curve near a hill, as Harb slowed down, two men emerged from out of the darkness and sprayed his Mercedes with gunfire. A bullet to the head ensured that the thirty-year-old imam was dead.

The targeted killing of Sheikh Ragheb Harb was the opening salvo of Israel's war against Iran and Hezbollah—a bloody conflict that would consume Dagan for the next twenty-seven years. There would be many more assassinations and deaths on both sides. Dagan would fight this war in Lebanon, and he would take it to the far ends of the world.

# CHAPTER 14

# The Sharif of Lebanon

Wherever he served, no matter what his official job mission was, Meir Dagan made a point of assembling a small team of operators—men of like mind who could be sneaky, resourceful, and good with a suppressed weapon at close range—and who were on call for special assignments of targeted intelligence gathering and killing.[1] In Sinai along the Suez Canal and in Lebanon where he led the 188th Armored Brigade, there was always a small band of rogue warriors he traveled with who could be summoned for deniable direct action. Such men were busy in Lebanon. They were needed in the country's medieval landscape.

The noted bard Khalil Gibran once wrote, "You have your Lebanon and its dilemma. I have my Lebanon and its beauty. Your Lebanon is an arena for men from the West and men from the East. My Lebanon is a flock of birds fluttering in the early-morning as shepherds lead their sheep into the meadow and rising in the evening as farmers return from their fields and vineyards." But the real Lebanon was so much more than the beautifully crafted words of an acclaimed poet. It was a battlespace of boundless barbarity and betrayal—a flashpoint of such unimaginable savagery that had nothing to do with Israel, the Palestinians, the French, or even the Ottomans, or any of the landlords of a land defined by the phrase "Pity Thy Nation," but was all about faith and tribalism. Even combat-hardened men like Dagan were not prepared for the medieval religious hatred that flowed through the country's veins.

It was common for the Lebanon Liaison Unit commander to visit the front himself to talk to all sides along the religious, ethnic, and political divide, and get them to put aside their historic enmities and stop the internecine bloodshed that followed the political vacuum of the Gemayel assassination and the country's descent into chaos. Brigadier General Dagan's job description was both a spy coordinator's and a diplomat's.

During one of his tours of the fault lines where Palestinians, Sunnis, Shiites, Christians, and Druze intersected into absolute carnage, Dagan came across a Druze fighter wearing a uniform with a dazzling camouflage pattern and a bright red beret. The Druze militiaman was calm, almost nonchalant, but was standing over the rotting corpse of a Christian Phalangist militiaman and wore a devilish smile. It was hot, and the mugginess of a warm summer's day and the stench of decaying flesh summoned the flies and the feelings of utter sickness from the Israelis in Dagan's entourage. The Druze fighter took great joy in watching the Israelis begin to dry heave and perspire as nausea got the better of them. Sensing an opportunity to show off, he broke a branch from a nearby bush and stuck it into the swollen head of the dead Christian, using it as an impromptu skewer. He then offered a piece of the bloody mess to Dagan, asking if he had ever tasted a Christian's brain before taking a bite for himself. Dagan was aghast and did all he could not to hurl the breakfast he'd consumed hours earlier.[2]

He would never eat meat again.

*               *               *

The Lebanon Liaison Unit's mandate was to provide the decision-makers at IDF headquarters in Tel Aviv and the prime minister's office in Jerusalem with a clear picture of the situation in the besieged nation. But despite the all-encompassing capabilities of Israel's intelligence community—HUMINT, SIGINT, ELINT, and PHOTINT—Lebanon remained an unsolvable puzzle. The country's cruelty, fratricidal zeal, and forever shifting loyalties remained a mystery to the men ordered to keep northern Israel safe, for it had descended into full-blown chaos. Christian, Sunni, Shiite, and Druze militias were at war with one another. The Syrian military had returned to control the Beqaa Valley. Iran had become inextricably involved in a campaign against American and Israeli interests. In May 1983, the remaining Palestinian garrisons in Lebanon erupted into full-scale civil war when a mysterious Fatah officer named Colonel Saeed "Musa" Muragha launched an open rebellion against forces loyal to Arafat, who was fourteen hundred miles away in his Tunisian exile. Israel feared the rebels, known as the Fatah Uprising, would try to push toward Galilee. Few in A'man knew where they were.

Dagan felt that to be effective he needed to see what was going on beyond the safety of the IDF patrol. Israeli soldiers—let alone generals—were not permitted to travel north of the security zone, though. Any foray across the Awali River checkpoints required a series of upper-echelon approvals and demanded a rescue force, with Israel Air Force and special operations assets, standing by at the ready. Northern Command and the chief of staff Lieutenant General Moshe Levy would never have authorized Dagan to travel in harm's way. He knew too much. He would have made a priceless hostage. But Dagan was stubborn and, still to reach his fortieth birthday, confident that he was immortal. He did not run his idea up the chain of command, or seek anyone's permission. He went rogue.

Dagan summoned Colonel Sami Mutzafi Barak, his old friend from the days in Sinai and a Unit 504 veteran who was his section chief in Tyre, along with Lieutenant Colonel Reuven Ehrlich, his head of operations, that they were all going out on a recce of the terrain beyond the security zone to see if the Palestinian rebels were inching their way closer to Israeli lines and what other militias or state sponsors they were working with. Dagan knew all the warlords who controlled villages in the Shouf Mountains but Walid Jumblatt, the Druze chieftain who headed the secular Progressive Socialist Party and the dominant Druze militia. His father, Kamal, a force in Lebanese politics, had been assassinated by the Syrians in 1977, and Walid walked a fine line to keep the

Druze relevant and stay alive, which meant he worked with and against everyone. Dagan felt that he was *the* man to talk to. Mutzafi Barak and Ehrlich thought Dagan was kidding when he first proposed his plan. Traveling alone past dubious checkpoints and roads where men often disappeared was beyond dangerous—it was negligently foolish. But neither dared appeal the order.

A reliable and inconspicuous car was the camel of Lebanon's espionage landscape. The vehicle had to be sturdy, able to take a beating, and Le Mans fast when needed. Nothing exotic, nothing out of the ordinary. A former intelligence officer who served in Lebanon commented that a James Bond Austin Martin would not have been extremely useful for covert activity. The cars, like spies, had to have a cover story to help them make it through a militia checkpoint: a bill of sale, paperwork, and the proper registrations. When Dagan's men needed a vehicle, they stole one: break-ins and carjackings were risk-free in a nation where the police never ventured outside their barracks.

Mercedes, BMWs, and Audis were preferred—the Lebanese, especially those from groups known to carry AK-47s, loved German engineering. Volkswagens were less conspicuous. Dagan opted to use a Volvo 240 that his men had procured for the foray into the Shouf. It had about sixty thousand miles on it in case an inquisitive militiaman at a checkpoint wanted to check the odometer. It was battered enough to be inconspicuous. Volvos were considered the most mechanically reliable for covert ops even though their transmissions faltered in the steep inclines of the mountains.

The intelligence service drivers were not only experts behind the wheel but were all highly skilled Arabic speakers who'd mastered the slang and accents of the numerous Lebanese dialects. Dagan and Ehrlich were not fluent in the language, so the two masqueraded as European journalists. They did not have press accreditation, or any identification at all. A militiaman searching the vehicle would not have found a tape recorder, notebooks—not even a battered Nikon 35mm camera: the paraphernalia of a combat correspondent. All they had on them was a hardened black Samsonite briefcase that contained a Mini-Uzi 9mm submachine gun which, when its stock was folded, was only fourteen inches long; two thirty-round magazines; two Beretta M1951 pistols; two fragmentation grenades; and an emergency radio. The emergency kit was known as the James Bond bag, and was meant to give undercover espionage operatives a fighting chance should they find themselves in a desperate firefight.

Shortly after dawn on a cool spring morning in 1984, the four men crossed an IDF-controlled bridge over the Awali River and headed toward Moukhtara, a small mixed Christian and Druze town in the Shouf that was Jumblatt's birthplace and his seat of power. Dagan carried some money on him—tribute for checkpoints—and his trusted pipe. The tobacco was locally sourced. As Dagan drew on the pipe, the smoke inside the Volvo turned into a suffocating cloud. Men of respect always traveled around Lebanon with the windows up, opening them only when challenged at a roadblock.

The Israelis reached Jumblatt's headquarters only to learn that the warlord was not in. They met instead with Raja,* Jumblatt's chief of staff, who knew who Dagan was and was eager to accommodate his unscheduled request for a sit-down with his boss. Raja had his men prepare coffee and sweets for his guests while he figured out how to take the four to Aley, a mountaintop city that overlooked Beirut, where Jumblatt was expected. Dagan and his two officers were escorted into a camouflaged military Land Rover for the drive north. The Land Rover's driver and the operations chief, both armed with AK-47s, sat in the front seat. The three Israelis sat nervously in the back seat. Two other vehicles sporting heavy machine guns drove alongside. The three-car convoy traversed mountain roads near areas that were under the control of Syrian intelligence agents. Islamic Revolutionary Guardsmen traveled the same lanes in trucks that ferried weapons to Beirut and Shiite recruits to Baalbek for military irregular warfare training. Dagan clutched his Samsonite case and said to both Ehrlich and Mutzafi Barak that if the men in the front seat tried anything, they would kill them.[3] The Druze operations chief smiled dangerously and lit a cigarette as he stared into the rearview mirror. He spoke fluent Hebrew.

* A pseudonym.

The Israelis finally caught up with Jumblatt's motorcade along the Beirut-Damascus Highway. A roadside rendezvous was considered operationally safer; Syrian armor was stationed nearby, and Mercedes sedans carrying Syrian intelligence officers for a night out in the everything-goes Lebanese capital whizzed by. Jumblatt explained to Dagan that he had just been in Damascus in an audience with Syrian president Hafez al-Assad. The Syrian leader, known as the Butcher of Hama for his brutal crushing of an Islamic uprising in the city, was believed to have been behind the assassination of Jumblatt's father, Kamal, in 1977.[4] Assad let the Druze leader know that he was sitting in the exact chair that his father had years earlier before he was killed, a veiled reference that if he did not tow the Syrian line, he could meet a similar fate.

The message to Dagan was that although the Druze leader respected Israel's might, he feared Syria's resolve. The Israeli general and his officers were not in charge, and they were not safe.

Jumblatt ordered Raja to drive the Israelis back to Moukhtara and their awaiting Volvo but told him to take them near the Fatah rebel bases that had popped up across the Shouf, often under the protection of Syrian forces. The Israelis drove by several encampments, and Dagan counted the men and matériel he could see in the darkened distance of night. Lebanon was treacherous in the darkness. It was time to cross the Awali back to friendly lines.

*               *               *

That very night, after returning to Marjayoun, Dagan penned a detailed report to IDF HQ listing everything that had happened and everything he had seen with short- and long-term strategic risk assessments for Israel's presence in Lebanon included in the notes. Lieutenant General Levy was furious when the brief came across his desk. He could not believe that a brigadier general would risk himself and his junior officers, and expose himself to capture risk, on the whim of a personal adventure camouflaged as a fact-finding trip. Dagan, Levy assessed, was a cowboy gone rogue, who still did not realize that his position, representing Israel's tenuous presence in Lebanon, was political with regional implications. It was beyond the pale for a general to leave his post without preparing an on-call rescue force and without being monitored every step of the way with a secure line of communication.

Levy suspended Dagan pending further review and wanted Dagan kicked out of the army altogether, but Defense Minister Moshe Arens reinstated him after two weeks. Arens had a similar family story to Dagan's. A native of Kaunas, Lithuania, who emigrated to the United States with his family and served in the U.S. Army during the Second World War, Arens was an aeronautical engineer by trade who was as serious as they came when it involved Israeli security. He demanded efficiency and results, often regardless of how they were produced. The incident with Dagan was, on an otherwise illustrious military career, a notorious black mark that was ultimately swept under the rug.

But the incident humbled Dagan. Most importantly, it forced him to mature to the rank and the responsibilities he held. He would never risk himself or others again on a lark. The reprimand and the realization of how disastrous his decisions had been forced him to reassess his view of covert work and the responsibilities operations in the shadows entailed. A few weeks following Dagan's day trip into the Shouf, William F. Buckley, the CIA chief of station in Beirut, was kidnapped by Hezbollah gunmen as he prepared to head to the office at the U.S. Embassy in the Lebanese capital. His tortured corpse was dumped in a ditch seven years later.

# CHAPTER 15

# Major General

M eir Dagan took some time off after he finished his term commanding the Lebanon Liaison Unit. He continued his education and studied art in Safed, the highest city in Galilee, a spiritual hub for Orthodox Jews and a modern-day art colony. If he retired with the rank of brigadier general, he would have fulfilled an incredible military career of courage and sacrifice in the defense of the Jewish state. He could have tried his luck in the private sector, working for one of the country's defense firms; he would have been happy sitting in his studio in northern Israel, smoking his pipe, listening to classical music, and painting the memorably diverse faces that had left an indelible mark on him in his travels across the country. But the call of service still burned inside him. He was hopeful that he could reach the top of Israel's military pyramid and possibly make it to the post of chief of staff. That would have been an epic achievement for a man denied a slot in Sayeret Mat'kal. Meir Dagan returned to active duty.

Dagan's combat CV earned him a top-flight combat command, and he was awarded command of the 36th Division. The 36th Division was the Northern Command's frontline force of armor and infantry brigades. It was also the IDF's most active formation, situated opposite Syrian forces atop the Golan Heights and Hezbollah and other terrorist groups along the Lebanese frontier. His brigade and battalion commanders adored him, but Dagan often butted heads with the IDF's top brass. He was not afraid to challenge the orders—and thinking—of Major General Yossi Peled, his boss at Northern Command.[1] Peled, like Dagan, was a child of the Holocaust. He was born in Antwerp, and his parents had handed him off to a Christian family to save him. He survived and made it to Israel. His father perished in Auschwitz, and after the war his mother, burdened by the horrors of what she had witnessed, placed him for adoption with a Jewish family. Despite this similarity, the two officers did not see eye-to-eye on very much, and in battles of wills and personalities, Dagan always came out on top.

*               *               *

The rank of brigadier general was political—those left at that level were all in competition with one another for appointment to a higher slot on the path to possible promotion. Brigadiers needed friends, the proverbial "rabbi," among the decision-makers on the general staff as protection against the backstabbers determined to derail any rival. Peled could have destroyed Dagan's chances of higher rank, but in November 1987, unrest in the Gaza Strip turned violent, becoming a full-fledged uprising, or intifada. The unrest spread to the West Bank, where the various Palestinian factions in exile, primarily Fatah in Tunis, attempted to seize control of the chaos. At first, rocks and Molotov cocktails were thrown at Israeli police and military forces—followed by improvised daggers and spears. The images of Israeli forces using rubber bullets and live ammunition against protestors reversed the image of Israel as a David in a sea of Goliaths; Palestinian youths even used slingshots to hurl rocks at Israeli soldiers in a biblical irony. Israelis and Palestinians were killed.

Terror cells across the West Bank and Gaza sensed an opportunity and launched attacks with automatic weapons and explosives. The intifada became a full-blown Middle Eastern conflict. In the West Bank, an innovative paratroop officer introduced an under-cover counterterrorist unit, known as *Duvdevan*, or Cherry, in the fight against Palestinian terror cells and their commanders. The unit was a modern-day version of Dagan's Grenade Reconnaissance force from Gaza.*

During the intifada, a new phenomenon emerged inside the Palestinian movements—the emergence of powerful fundamentalist Islamic terror factions that were inspired by the Iranian revolution and the Egyptian Islamic Jihad's assassination of Anwar el-Sadat in 1981. In the 1970s, during the Grenade Recon's operations in the Gaza Strip, the Muslim Brotherhood's influence there was minimal and hostile toward the secular—communist—terror factions. The Islamists openly attacked the drug dens, bars, and brothels that Fatah and the PFLP frequented, administering a cruel punishment for their anti-Islamic way—pain usually inflicted courtesy of metal saws and hatchets. Israeli civilian administration officials even nurtured the fundamentalists, believing that they were a counterbalance to what they viewed as the greater danger—ideologically based Palestinian nationalist groups. Gazan clerics were even invited to appear on Israeli television and radio talk shows, to expound their views on men like Yasir Arafat and George Habash. One such pious figure was a quadriplegic named Sheikh Ahmed Yasin who would be instrumental in the founding of a group called Hamas—the Arabic acronym for Islamic Resistance Movement—in December 1987, a month into the intifada. The hatchets were now turned on Israeli forces and civilians, soon to be replaced by AK-47s and explosive vests.

The intifada was a military challenge for Israel and a public relations nightmare. The Palestinian riots provided cover to a growing terror offensive—much of it being directed from Yasir Arafat's new PLO nerve center in Tunis. The Israeli response was viewed in the media as oppressively heavy-handed. Yitzhak Rabin, the defense minister when the unrest began, was infamously quoted as ordering Israeli troops to break the bones of Palestinian protesters—Rabin denied that such a directive was ever given.[2]

The IDF chief of staff, Lieutenant General Dan Shomron, liked surrounding himself with special operations talent. Shomron, who

---

* The IDF also created an undercover force in Gaza, Unit 367, that was fittingly nicknamed "Samson."

had become internationally known for being the overall commanding officer for the rescue operation of 103 Israeli and Jewish hostages in Entebbe, Uganda, in 1976, knew that operators did not think like most conventional soldiers. They looked at the landscape with different eyes, perspectives, and an imaginative approach to solving strategic puzzles with daring tactical moves. Dagan's name always came up in discussions about men who had a statesmenlike appreciation of the strategic complexities facing Israel. Shomron, who had spent most of his career with the paratroopers, had commanded Dagan during the retaliatory strikes against the fedayeen in 1966. As the intifada raged with no end in sight, the chief of staff asked Dagan to serve as his counterterrorist advisor. Officers, even brigadier generals, did not refuse such requests.

The promotion out of the field and into the nerve center of the Israeli defense and military establishment was bittersweet for Dagan. He loved leading armadas of tanks on the plains of the Golan Heights during division-size exercises—he relished being the conductor of a massive orchestra of armored vehicles, artillery, and infantrymen on maneuvers and combat operations. When he was asked once if he missed his Nomex coveralls and tank commander's helmet, a huge smile came across his face, and his answer was "Of course,"[3] even though his body carried the damaging effects of two near-life-threatening injuries. Dagan endured unbearable pain when confined to the cramped spaces of a tank turret. He never winced in the company of others, even when hopping off the fender of a Merkava main battle tank in front of his brigade commanders.

But now he was in his forties and had learned how bad war was.[4] He brought this new and more mature thinking with him to his advisory posting with the chief of staff.

As part of that mission, he became a frequent guest at IDF headquarters in the Gaza Strip and inspected the units trying to contain the violence in the West Bank cities. He listened to division commanders of the same rank about the difficulties of applying a military solution to a problem that had a security and political dimension. Dagan asked the battalion and smaller unit commanders what they felt should be done; he talked to the conscripts and reservists who were on the front lines, absorbing the daily barrages of Molotov cocktails and gunfire, what they thought. "He made everyone, no matter what their rank, feel important," a former subordinate in the Mossad reflected. "The best ideas always came from the most unexpected of places and he was not one to dismiss anyone."[5]

The most impactful lesson that Dagan received came from the officers in COGAT—the IDF's Coordinator of Government Activities in the Territories. The office dealt with the local Palestinian political and religious leaders; they knew where the water wells were, which clan was involved in which businesses and illegal activities, and they understood the landscape better than anyone. Most of the COGAT officers were fluent in Arabic; many had degrees—some advanced—in Middle Eastern studies. They were the subject-matter experts who needed to be heard.

In Gaza, in 1971, the civil administration bureaucrats had been at war with Dagan when he led Grenade Recon. They viewed his counter-terrorist campaign as counterproductive to their efforts to bring about a semblance of normalcy to the Palestinians living there; he viewed the terrorists and the violence they perpetrated as the greatest single obstacle to most civilians ever having a chance at a peaceful and pros-perous future. Both sides were right, and, as he would learn later in life, both sides were also wrong. There were differences in the tactical and strategic policies, and now, he felt, was a time when he should listen, learn, and absorb whatever COGAT staffers could teach him. One officer in particular, Captain Udi Levi, gave the general a different perspective in his briefing. Levi discovered—much to the dismay and outright dismissal of senior IDF officers—that an entire shadow civilian infrastructure was quietly being built in the West Bank and Gaza. The new reality, known as the *da'wa*, Arabic for "the call to the believers to shelter beneath the faith," provided the necessities of life for members of the local population that accepted a fundamentalist view of Islam's place in Palestinian nationalism. The cash came from charitable orga-nizations. And to those who bothered to look, the money built new homes, opulent mosques, and bought new cars. It also paid for weapons, explosives, and safe houses used by terror cells.

The money flowed into the territories from the Middle East, as far away as Europe, and particularly from North America, where groups like the Holy Land Foundation, a not-for-profit group in Richardson, Texas, funneled charitable contributions to build a terror army in the West Bank and Gaza. Levi was able to connect the dots that the money—and not the fundamentalist fervor—was the oxygen fueling the violence. He sent reports up the chain of command to alert the higher-ups that financial warfare should be a weapon in Israel's counterterrorist arsenal. The only one who took him—and his thesis—seriously was Dagan. The two men would forge a close friendship and operational partnership lasting twenty years.

Fighting the money became a central theme of Meir Dagan's view of combating groups like Hamas and the PLO, though many in the general staff thought his ideas were eccentrically foolish. He stuck to his guns, though, disregarding the criticism and the inherent reliance on strategies that senior commanders enjoyed—tactical raids against targets that netted terrorists and their weapons; the more established door-kicking practices that were standard operating procedure but that did nothing to change the paradigm.

\*               \*               \*

In the autumn of 1991, Dagan was promoted to head of the Operations Command inside the General Staff—a position responsible for mapping out Israel's plans for war, emergencies, and covert actions, and assembling the IDF's recommendations needing the prime minister's authorization. It was an ultra-important post with enormous geopolitical implications— the job was, a former subordinate claimed, the IDF's deputy CEO."[6] Dagan's new office was inside the top command post in IDF headquarters, more affectionately known as the *Bor,* or the "pit," the underground nerve center where the most senior officers met. He dealt with the most sensitive military operations around the immediate frontiers of Israel and far beyond and was in direct contact with the country's three intelligence services. Much of what was discussed, reviewed, and submitted for government approval during this period remains classified.

One known mission, although details are still limited, involved the breakup of the Soviet Union and the fate of the two-and-a-half million Jews behind the crumbling Iron Curtain. The fear in the prime minister's office was that there would be pogroms—eruptions of nationalistic violence emanating from various segments of the population blaming the Jewish population for the chaos and disintegration of public order. It was feared that once the killing began, it would not end until a quarter of a million Jews were slaughtered. Prime Minister Yitzhak Shamir, a former underground leader himself, said that there would not be a second Holocaust on his watch.[7] He asked *Nativ*, Hebrew for path, a semi-secret office inside the prime minister's office that dealt with the Jews of the Eastern bloc as an underground railroad of sorts to help bring Russian Jews to Israel, to prepare a plan. Blueprinting a possible plan was handled at the Defense Ministry.

Defense Minister Moshe Arens was a man who demanded efficiency and results. But when the defense ministry approached the IDF asking about contingency plans to safeguard Russian Jewry, no one seemed interested. It was deemed too risky to involve the Israeli military in any action. The excuses heard at headquarters, Colonel (Res.) Ephraim Leor, a deputy of Dagan's in the operations section, would later recount was that "the IDF was too busy, the operation [to carry out any rescue bid—covert or otherwise—on European soil] was too risky, but Dagan would have none of it. He said we are doing it, and that was that."[8]

The tentative plan, code-named Operation Two-Wheeler, involved landing armed Israeli combat personnel inside the former Soviet Union and flying the Russian Jews out on IAF C-130 Hercules transports. It was not known if the authorities in the crumbling former Soviet republics would allow the Israelis to deploy to their countries. Dagan planned for all possibilities, including commando seizures of the airfields, and evacuation centers would have to process those wishing to flee, provide them with temporary food and shelter, and organize an orderly evacuation to prevent panic.

From his underground command post, Dagan summoned representatives from A'man and the Mossad and the air force. He also traveled overseas, incognito and on assignment, to assess the logistic difficulties of rescuing so many people in the chaos of a crumbling empire. There were large Jewish population centers in Moscow, St. Petersburg, and Kyiv. Jewish centers of life also existed in Moldova and Belarus, and far away in Baku, Tbilisi, Tashkent, and Bukhara in the former Soviet Asian republics. The coordination involved in rescuing everyone would certainly push the army, and especially the IAF, beyond their operational capacity. Dagan worked around the clock, ready to order assets into the air should the pogroms commence. They never did.

Between 1990 and 1992, nearly half a million Jews from the former Soviet Union reached Israel. Many more emigrated to the United States and Western Europe.

Moshe Arens never forgot that Dagan was the one officer who appreciated the importance of rescuing the Jews of Eastern Europe and acted accordingly. He promised to promote Dagan to the rank of major general, much to the chagrin of new IDF chief of staff Lieutenant General Ehud Barak.

Barak was the most decorated soldier in Israel's military history, a heroic commander of Sayeret Mat'kal, a man of boundless tactical courage and dare. He was also a cunning politician, earning the trust of Yitzhak Rabin, the new Israeli prime minister and defense minister. But he was not one of Dagan's many admirers. During the first Gulf War, when Israeli generals mulled a response should Iraq's Saddam Hussein carry out his threat to launch chemical and biological weapons at Israel, Dagan earned Barak's ire when he suggested bombing the dams over the Tigris and Euphrates Rivers,[9] flooding much of the country and destroying its agricultural output. Barak thought the idea was ridiculous; Dagan believed it to be a measured response that would enable Israel to respond demonstratively to unacceptable provocation without resorting to other means.*

Barak and members of his general staff preferred that Dagan end his military career as a brigadier general. But Defense Minister Rabin honored Moshe Arens's promise. He was named assistant director of

---

* Israel has never admitted—or denied—possessing weapons of mass destruction, including any response to accusations of it possessing a nuclear arsenal.

the Operations Directorate. On January 1, 1993, Meir Dagan, his wife, mother, and three children, ventured to Barak's office at IDF head-quarters for the official ceremony. Dagan smiled voraciously as Bina pinned his new rank to his epaulets, but the perennial outsider was still viewed as something of a stranger in the IDF even though he was near the pinnacle of command.

# CHAPTER 16

# Code Name Mango

A structure spanning the Jordan River near the village of Damiyah has existed since ancient times. Goods, people, and soldiers—especially soldiers—have crossed the waterway for centuries. Roman centurions from the east moved across an arch bridge when uprisings needed to be crushed in Judea. British colonial forces marched across the remnants of the ancient bridge in 1917 when the Ottoman Empire was defeated in the First World War. The Haganah blew it up in 1946; the Israeli military again, in 1967, during the Six-Day War. In 1968, the Israelis allowed the Jordanians to construct a narrow, prefabricated trestle over the Roman bridge to connect the East and West Banks and alleviate the bustle of traffic over the busier official Allenby Bridge. The water crossing is nothing more than an overpass over the drying streams of a once mighty river with pillboxes and rows of barbed wire concertina protecting both sides from one another. It was remote and sparsely used, making it ideal for covert meetings and clandestine travel across a border.

It usually took a little over an hour to drive from Jordanian military headquarters in the heart of Amman to the Damiyah Bridge. The route was barren in the summer and plush with vegetation in the winter and spring. There were no shortcuts—even for a staff car ferrying a general in a motorcade—because the twisting mountain roads are narrow and dangerous, with the lane dividers being something of a suggestion and not much more. It was a ninety-minute drive from IDF headquarters in the Kirya campus in downtown Tel Aviv to the Damiyah Bridge. A vehicle had to negotiate the horn-honking gridlock of traffic to leave Israel's largest city, cross the invisible green line separating the country's pre- and post-1967 war frontiers, and then take a circuitous path toward the Jordan Valley.

In the autumn of 1993, Major General Mansour Abu Rashid made the frequent trek from his headquarters at the Jordanian Armored Forces General Staff to the Damiyah Bridge to talk peace. His Israeli counterpart was Major General Meir Dagan, the assistant to the head of the IDF Operations Directorate.

*       *       *

It was a time of great hope and trepidation in the Middle East. Saddam Hussein's Iraq, a nation that aspired to acquire nuclear weapons to destroy the Jewish state and that had used chemical weapons against Iran and its Kurdish minority, had been defeated, albeit, not destroyed, by an American-led coalition that included an astounding forty-two nations that repelled the August 1990 invasion of Kuwait. Saddam Hussein unsuccessfully tried to drag the Jewish state into the war by launching SCUD missiles at Tel Aviv. Israel exercised self-restraint and did not allow the Iraqi invasion of Kuwait to become a pretext for another Arab-Israeli war.*

Perhaps the Gulf War's biggest loser was Yasir Arafat. The PLO chairman displayed his duplicitous opportunism when he supported Saddam

* In 1992, chief of staff Lieutenant General Ehud Barak convinced former prime minister Yitzhak Shamir and then prime minister Yitzhak Rabin that Israel had to send a message to the rest of the Middle East that SCUD missiles fired against the Jewish state would not go unanswered. Barak, the man who had led Sayeret Mat'kal and created its audacious way of looking at operational challenges, proposed a plan to assassinate Saddam Hussein. Code-named Operation Bramble Bush, the hit would consist of a Sayeret Mat'kal strike force masquerading as Iraqi soldiers who would attack the Iraqi dictator in his native town of Tikrit. The raid was green-lit at the prime ministerial level, but was scrubbed in November 1992 after five operators were killed in a dry run rehearsal that went horribly wrong.

Hussein, even likening the Iraqi attempts to reclaim what they insisted was theirs in Kuwait to Palestinian claims against Israel. The Kuwaitis—and the Gulf Arabs—never forgave Arafat. After Operation Desert Storm and the defeat of the Iraqi military, Palestinian workers in Kuwait, a sizeable force whose salaries supported families across the Diaspora, were given twenty-four hours to pack their bags and leave. The PLO tax on their salaries was a significant portion of the organization's operational budget and the millions kicked back to Arafat. More importantly, the Kuwaitis, Bahrainis, Emiratis, and Saudis, in the oil-rich states that bankrolled the PLO and its terrorist armies, cut off their generous subsidies to Arafat's army and political offices around the world. Overnight, the revolutionary coffers evaporated, causing hope in Jerusalem that the man who had professionalized Palestinianism into a pretext for acts of terror would soon be marginalized and forgotten. Arafat's dream of destroying the State of Israel had been obliterated, along with tens of thousands of smoldering Iraqi dead, in the smoldering scorched sands of the Kuwaiti desert.

The intifada fizzled without cash. But violence often looms inside a Middle Eastern vacuum. Hamas emerged as a force to be reckoned with.

Hamas did not have the military infrastructure that Fatah or the PFLP had enjoyed for many years. It lacked diplomatic acceptance and membership in the international fraternity of revolutionary and terror movements. But the fundamentalists had zeal and a unique brand of cruelty that they used both as a tactical and psychological weapon against Israel. The Majd, the Hamas internal security force that hunted down, tortured, and murdered collaborators with Israel was led by a sadistic enforcer named Yahya Sinwar. A young up-and-coming Hamas commander named Mahmoud al-Mabhouh headed a kidnapping unit, code-named 101 after Ariel Sharon's famed force, to abduct and murder Israeli soldiers.

On February 16, 1989, Hamas terrorists masquerading as ultra-orthodox Jews picked up Sergeant Avi Sasportas as he hitchhiked, a common practice for soldiers, in southern Israel. The men in the car subdued and beat Sasportas—his body was dumped in a remote ditch. Three months later, a Hamas squad abducted and murdered Corporal Ilan Saadon. The Shin Bet arrested the kidnappers, but the perpetrators never disclosed where the body was buried; Saadon's corpse was found seven years later.

Early one morning in December 1992, a Hamas kidnapping squad abducted and murdered Sergeant Nissim Toledano, a Border Guard policeman, as he walked to work in the city of Lod. His body was thrown into a gully; he had been tortured, and his body mutilated, before he was killed. Prime Minister Rabin had had enough. The IDF and the Shin Bet assembled a list of the Hamas leadership, rounded up 415 of them, and transported them to the no-man's-land north of Israel's security zone in southern Lebanon. The move would have horrific repercussions. Israel had inadvertently handed off the top military commanders of Hamas to the embrace of Hezbollah. Although Hamas was a Sunni group based on the principles of the Muslim Brotherhood and a mortal enemy of the Shiite Party of God, Iran's Islamic Revolutionary Guard Corps lived in a world where the enemy of my enemy is my friend and forged a military alliance with the Palestinians. President Bill Clinton urged Rabin to return the Hamas leaders to their homes in the West Bank and Gaza. The Israeli prime minister acquiesced, but not before the Hamas deportees received a crash course in suicide bombing tactics, counterespionage, and terror tradecraft from Hezbollah instructors.

The emergence of Hamas as a serious threat to Israeli national security was one of the factors that led to secret talks between Israel and PLO representatives. The process began in Oslo, the Norwegian capital, and soon evolved into trilateral negotiations with the United States. Before the Gulf War, such contact would have been unthinkable.

The negotiations were harsh and the people who sat at opposite ends of the table often felt as if their efforts were doomed to be unresolvable. But patience—along with King Solomon–like wisdom and the sheer might that only the United States of America could deliver—brought about a historic and unimaginable event on September 13, 1993, when Bill Clinton nudged a reluctant Yitzhak Rabin and a jovial Yasir Arafat to shake hands on the White House lawn.

The Oslo Accords, as the process became known, facilitated the prospect that Israel could reach peace and coexistence with other Arab nations. The hope was that the Hashemite Kingdom of Jordan would be the second Arab state—after Egypt—to sign a treaty with Israel. Although a formal state of war existed between Israel and Jordan, the 192-mile border between the two nations was peaceful; Palestinians and Jordanians crossed the Allenby Bridge to visit loved ones separated by the Jordan River and to trade goods.

For years, King Hussein maintained clandestine contacts with a long list of Israeli leaders and intelligence chiefs—from Golda Meir to Yitzhak Rabin. However, the Israeli defense establishment was wary about a rapprochement with Jordan. King Hussein had not joined the anti-Saddam coalition that included the Kingdom of Saudi Arabia and even the Syrians. Prime Minister Rabin needed to reassure the generals that peace could work. He summoned the IDF's assistant operations chief to his office to spearhead the effort. It was a task that Major General Meir Dagan enthusiastically accepted.

\*       \*       \*

British-trained and American-supplied, the Jordanian Armed Forces, the JAF, was the most professional fighting force in the Arab world. Its special forces were elite caliber; its intelligence service, the General Intelligence Department, worked side-by-side with the CIA and Britain's MI6; the GID also worked closely, albeit clandestinely, with the Mossad,[1] and were considered masters of HUMINT. Jordan was a tribal nation, and the armed forces were where the Bedouin clans flexed their muscle. The Bedouins were the backbone of the JAF and the GID, as were the country's minorities—the Circassians, Chechens, and Druze. They wielded enormous power inside the military. King Hussein, like Rabin, had to win their support to make peace with Israel work. It was not an easy undertaking. Many of the king's generals were young officers in 1967 when the IDF captured the West Bank and Jerusalem, the jewel in the kingdom's crown. The enmity ran deep. King Hussein entrusted Brigadier Mansour Abu Rashid to work with his Israeli counterpart to establish a rapport and turn mistrust and bitter feelings into cooperation.

Brigadier Abu Rashid came from the same generation as Dagan—they were warriors on opposite ends of the battlefield whose nations became defined by the Six-Day War. Abu Rashid had fought on the Jerusalem front in 1967 and against the Palestinian terror groups in the Black September of 1970. Like Dagan, a career soldier blessed with an extra helping of patriotism and confidence, Brigadier Abu Rashid was defined by his uniform and loyalty to his flag. He served in military intelligence for most of his career and believed himself to be an expert on all things Israeli. In 1993, he was the JAF representative to the United Nations Truce Supervision Organization, an observer force set up at the end of the 1948 Arab-Israeli War to ensure that armistice lines were not violated. The most important aspect of the job was to prevent small incidents from escalating into gunfire. In 1991, for example, when Iraqis fleeing Saddam Hussein's wrath in the wake of the Gulf War crossed Jordan attempting to reach a better life in Israel, UNTSO observers made sure that the IDF did not think the asylum seekers were terrorists trying to cross the frontier.

Baruch Spiegel, now a brigadier general, was Abu Rashid's IDF counterpart. A veteran Golani Brigade commander, Spiegel had been a battalion commander under Dagan's 188th Armored Brigade during the Israeli invasion of Lebanon. The two men struck up a friendship under fire and remained close.

Abu Rashid and Spiegel met near the Damiyah Bridge, often under United Nations auspices, to work on various issues of mutual interest. But when Rabin wanted to advance peace with Jordan, Dagan became personally involved. An informal but official meeting with Abu Rashid was scheduled.

The two men met at one of the oldest fish restaurants in Tiberias. The eatery, a favorite of IDF officers serving in the north, was on the promenade overlooking the Sea of Galilee. A UNTSO officer wearing a sky-blue beret was Abu Rashid's escort. The Jordanian general looked straight out of Hollywood casting in his neatly pressed khaki uniform. A chest full of decorations denoted a lengthy and distinguished career. His dark skin was accented by a thin military mustache. He wore a black beret. It was common to see United Nations peacekeepers in the restaurant. Few noticed the Jordanian officer. Dagan and Spiegel were already waiting at a remote table along the waterfront. "Dagan greeted me with an 'ahalan wasahalan' in his limited Arabic," Abu Rashid remembered. "I knew right away we could do business."[2]

Both men believed that if a peace deal could be struck between the two nations—and then nurtured into a friendship—it could change the strategic balance of power in the Middle East forever. "This was an assignment that Dagan had waited for his entire life," Spiegel remembered. "Dagan believed that war and the bloodshed it created should only happen when one was attacked. The chance to make peace meant everything to him."[3]

Usually, when generals gave gifts to one another, the custom was to exchange knives or some sort of article of clothing. Arab generals—especially those in the Gulf—coveted getting an Israeli-made Uzi submachine gun when clandestine meetings began with the presentation of gifts. The weapon was a symbol of Israeli military power and, in the Arab world at least, considered as highly prized as a rare and invaluable coin. But Dagan had something else in mind. When he left the Kirya to travel to the Damiyah Bridge to meet Brigadier General Abu Rashid, Dagan and Spiegel did not place a gift-wrapped box with a gold-plated dagger inside it or some other forgettable bauble in the trunk of their unmarked car. Instead, the two men drove to the Damiyah Bridge with small mango and avocado trees in the back seat. The Jordanians might have taken great pride in their martial background, but people who lived in the desert cherished anything that grew in the ground. "The Jordanians didn't know what a mango or an avocado was," Spiegel remembered. "From that exchange of the tree, Brigadier Abu Rashid's code name in the IDF files was Mango."[4]

The meetings between Dagan, Spiegel, and Abu Rashid became biweekly occurrences. The two developed a bond that could exist only between men who had seen the carnage of war, especially when each had once been the other's adversary, on the opposite side of the firing line. When they wiped a plate, as eating hummus is known in the region, and sat at their favorite table in Tiberias overlooking the Sea of Galilee, the men spoke philosophically about waking up one morning in a region that was nothing like the night before—a Middle East of peace, cooperation, and coexistence. From their perch, as the waiters brought course after course, it was possible to see the Golan Heights jutting up from the northern shores of the water. "Will Syria one day be part of a peace deal?" the two men asked, to challenge their imaginations.[5] Generals were allowed to dream.

It was important to the Israeli side that all the arrangements with the JAF—and the kingdom—be bilateral and without third-party involvement.

Against the wishes of the General Staff—and even some high-ranking members of Israel's intelligence community—Dagan charmed Israeli peace negotiator Elyakim Rubinstein, a former legal advisor to the Ministry of Foreign Affairs, to authorize a mobile phone to Brigadier Abu Rashid so that the two sides could communicate at will and without the elaborate mechanism of protocol.[6] Getting such a gift from Israel had political and security implications—there were no mobile telephones in Jordan at the time, and the signal would come from a nearby Israeli tower. Brigadier Abu Rashid had to get the JAF chairman of the joint chiefs of staff, Major General Abdul Hafez Kaabneh, to approve the phone, a cumbersome Motorola Dynatec 8000x, and get the king and military intelligence to sign off on it as well. Kaabneh had been head of Jordanian military intelligence and feared the device would be used for eavesdropping, but he approved Abu Rashid's request.

To help create a sense of transparency between the two sides, Dagan insisted that the Israelis bring Abu Rashid to Tel Aviv. Brigadier General Spiegel went to pick him up from the Damiyah Bridge on a warm sunny morning. Abu Rashid thought that the Israelis wanted to show off their miracle metropolis on the sea, for him to take in the sights of the beauties on the beach; the sea was something the virtually landlocked Jordanians cherished. But unbeknownst to the Jordanian general, he was driven straight to the "holy of the holies": the Defense Ministry and IDF headquarters campus in Tel Aviv.

The skyline of Tel Aviv was a universe away from the quaint hilly terrain of Amman; the drivers, though, were equally voracious, with a complete disregard for the rules of the road. Spiegel's staff car turned off Menachem Begin Boulevard toward Kaplan Street. The vehicle turned right, into a heavily fortified gate protected by young female soldiers in tan uniforms that included short skirts. The conscripts carried Uzi sub-machine guns and M-16 assault rifles. "Spiegel, *shu hada*?" Abu Rashid inquired in nervous Arabic, wanting to know what was going on. "This is the Ministry of Defense and IDF HQ," Spiegel replied, barely able to contain his smile. Major General Meir Dagan waited behind the gate, looking like a master pianist awaiting applause at a performance. The visit was historic, and Brigadier General Abu Rashid could not believe where he was. He trembled slightly and wiped the sweat from his brow as a nineteen-year-old female soldier, just as shocked to see a Jordanian army general as he was to see her, waved the car through the checkpoint.

The Jordanian general was ushered into the main headquarters without ceremony or fanfare. Dagan brought him upstairs, to a reception room where Major General Uri Sagi, the A'man director, and deputy chief of staff Major General Amnon Lipkin-Shahak, were waiting. Coffee and tea were served. A table full of the finest Israeli-grown fruit and an endless array of cakes allowed the men to snack while they introduced themselves. Like soldiers from any army, from any point in history, the men spoke about the battles they had fought, the friends they had lost, and the wounds they had suffered. Ultimately, the conversation always turned to what mattered most to these men—their children.

As the generals shared their personal stories and spoke of the challenges their nations faced in a part of the world where bloodshed was often unstoppable, Dagan lit his pipe and drank some tea, as former enemies talked like old friends. The men in different uniforms and religions placed forty-five years of war behind them. Everyone in the room felt there would be no turning back.

The day moved remarkably fast, as there was so much ground to cover. Dagan wanted to get Brigadier Abu Rashid to the Damiyah Bridge before sunset. It was a gesture of absolute reverence that a man of such importance should not be driven home in the darkness. Abu Rashid crossed the border quietly. Jordanian military intelligence officers were waiting to make sure his return was without incident or delay. The drive from the border back to JAF HQ took less than an hour. Major General Abdul Hafez Kaabneh waited in his office for the phone call from Abu Rashid. King Hussein was also waiting for the report.

The Jordanian monarch knew that Prime Minister Rabin wanted peace. The two men spoke regularly. But reaching an agreement was fraught with danger. King Hussein's grandfather, Abdullah I, had been murdered by a Palestinian assassin in 1951 after it was rumored that he was working on coexistence with the nascent Jewish state. The king was a teenager when he was coronated, and seven years after he assumed the throne, the FBI intercepted an Egyptian-led plot by a cabal of Jordanian army officers to overthrow him.[7] King Hussein knew that politicians might be the ones to sign accords, but armies enforced them. If Israeli generals were on board, it would be easier for the JAF's senior commanders to embrace the peacemaking efforts.

King Hussein received a detailed briefing from Abu Rashid that was laced with emotion. He spoke glowingly of his conversation with the generals, especially the effort made by Dagan, who spearheaded the initiative. Dagan's military CV was well known inside the palace, but his peacemaking desires trumped his ruthless reputation. King Hussein would remember Dagan's personal touch to peacemaking. So, too, did the king's brother, Crown Prince Hassan, and Hussein's eldest son, Abdullah, a colonel in the special forces. The Israelis learned of the Jordanian assessments. "We knew of the Jordanian excitement," Spiegel reflected.[8]

A week following the visit to the Kirya, Dagan was summoned to the office of Prime Minister Yitzhak Rabin for a briefing on his developing relationship with the Jordanians. Rabin was one of the founders of the Jewish state, a former chief of staff, and a man who had taken an enormous gamble in making peace with Arafat. Right-wing politicians viewed him as a traitor, an old man who had lost the fight in him. Dagan saw a man tired of the madness who wanted a formal peace—not a clandestine friendship like the one the prime minister enjoyed with King Hussein. IDF chief of staff Barak was present at the briefing, along with Ephraim Halevy, the London-born Mossad officer who had been Rabin's conduit to the Jordanian monarch. Some inside the intelligence bubble had dubbed Halevy "Lawrence of Arabia" because of his unique ability to forge ties and connections throughout the Middle East; Halevy was fascinated with the exploits of T. E. Lawrence during the First World War.[9]

The military side of the diplomacy was left to Dagan. His job was to sell the notion that the JAF was on board with other secret talks to formalize ties between the two nations. Dagan was always the center of attention, even in a room full of political and military superiors, and he articulated that Brigadier General Abu Rashid, representative of the other Jordanian generals and much of the military, was an advocate of a peace treaty and would not oppose it.

Formal negotiations for the peace treaty proceeded with great vigor. Ceremonies were planned in autumn of 1994 for the official signing of a treaty. Bill Clinton would be the master of ceremonies.

*          *          *

Baruch Goldstein was a Brooklyn-born physician who lived in the right-wing religious settlement of Kiryat Arba near Hebron. He served as a doctor in the IDF and was issued an Israeli-made Galil 5.56mm assault rifle. At dawn on February 25, 1994, Goldstein donned his fatigues, grabbed his weapon and extra magazines of ammunition, and drove to the Cave of the Patriarchs, a sight holy to both Jews and Muslims that had separate entrances to the synagogue and to the Ibrahimi Mosque. Because he was in uniform, the sentry outside the location did not challenge Goldstein. It was a Friday, and the mosque was crowded with over eight hundred worshippers gathered for the morning prayers.

Goldstein stood by the mosque's only exit and opened fire, aiming with every pull of the trigger, reloading several times during the carnage. When he paused to reload one more time, the survivors rushed him and bludgeoned him to death. Rioting erupted in Hebron and across the West Bank. More Palestinians—and Israelis—died because of Goldstein's act of senseless terror.

The Cave of the Patriarchs Massacre, one of the too-many-to-count acts of barbaric extremism that have plagued Israelis and Palestinians, claimed 29 dead and over 130 wounded. It was the excuse that Hamas had been looking for to launch a wave of suicidal terror that its commanders had learned from Hezbollah in the no-man's-land of south Lebanon. On April 6, 1994, forty days after Goldstein's rampage, the Muslim period of mourning, Hamas master bomb builder Yahya Ayyash, known by the Shin Bet as "The Engineer," rigged a 1987 Opel Ascona with an improvised explosive device that a suicide bomber drove into a school bus in the Jezreel Valley town of Afula, killing eight civilians and wounding fifty-five more. Ayyash's genius was turning inexpensive store-bought materials into TATP, or triacetone triperoxide, a witch's brew of high-yield explosives, made of acetone and hydrogen peroxide, that when mixed with nails, screws, bolts, rat poison, and batteries, created lethal payloads to be molded into potent suicide vests or crammed into backpacks.

A week later, a suicide bomber blew himself up in the Hadera central bus station, killing five and wounding thirty. Lebanon had come to Israel. Dagan and other members of the general staff and Israel's intelligence community who had worked tirelessly to ready the region for peace with Jordan feared the new wave of violence would threaten the prospects for coexistence.

Their fears were highlighted at 9 a.m. on October 19, when a suicide bomber from the West Bank wearing a powerful device built by Ayyash blew himself up on the No. 5 bus in the heart of Tel Aviv, killing twenty-two civilians and wounding one hundred more. The bombing came a week before Prime Minister Rabin, King Hussein, and President Clinton were to sign the peace accords between Israel and Jordan at the frontier between the two nations in the Arava Desert. The political mood in Israel was not one of beating swords into plowshares. Pedestrians who came to view the destruction of the city bus shouted, "Death to Arabs." The Israeli prime minister and the Jordanian monarch worked hard to sell peace to their skeptical nations.

The Jordanians brought bagpipers to the ceremony in the sands—homage to the British influence in their armed forces. Their generals—including Brigadier Mansour Abu Rashid—wore tan blazers and army ties. The IDF brought a marching band; the generals, like Chief of Staff Barak, wore their Class A's, though they looked casually dressed compared to their counterparts from across the river. King Hussein's Royal Guard wore sharp forest-green berets and neatly pressed sage fatigues; they stood out as they mingled with Israeli Shin Bet agents protecting

Prime Minister Rabin and U.S. president Clinton wearing suits and ties. Pentagon officials with a fruit salad of medals on their uniforms chatted with their Jordanian and Israeli counterparts. The audience was full of intelligence officers from the Mossad, the GID, and the CIA who had worked in the shadows for years and whose cooperation could now be more of an overt collaboration—and who tried to look nondescript. Folding chairs had been assembled in neat rows for the international who's who that converged on the ceremony. The two men who had helped make the day possible sat in the audience on their respective sides of the aisle far from the media's cameras.

The peace between Jordan and Israel has held firm through assassinations, terror attacks, another intifada, and even October 7. Playing a small role in bringing the two nations and their armies together was one of the proudest moments in Dagan's life as a soldier.

# CHAPTER 17

# The Call of Duty

There are only two dozen active-duty generals in the Israel Defense Forces at any given time. The rank is an exclusive club reserved for officers who have risen to prominence and power after decades of service and combat leadership. Membership in this exclusive circle is temporary, though. Typically, a major general serves in a command position for four years or less. There are always younger men, sometimes of greater skill and more impressive courage, eager to break into this league of extraordinary military minds, and there are those inside the group who believe they have their eyes on the prize: becoming a lieutenant general and chief of staff. A defense minister, part of the ruling coalition, recommends who is appointed the chief of the general staff.

Ten major generals have gone on to become defense ministers. Three chiefs of the general staff have been elected prime minister. The rank is a final hurdle toward the pinnacle of political power, or, in the case of many, lucrative job titles in government and industry.

Meir Dagan wanted to remain in the army and shoot for the top job. Staying in uniform and surviving the cut of attrition once the music stopped meant being appointed the head of one of the IDF's three geographic commands: Northern, Central, and Southern. Each covered regional threats and challenges; the head of any of the commands was responsible for the military forces under his control and the civilians living inside the area.

Northern Command was considered *the* best launching pad for onward promotion—and Dagan coveted the post. Moshe Dayan had been OC Northern Command before becoming chief of staff and defense minister. Yitzhak Rabin had also led the Northern Command, as had Mordechai Gur and Rafael Eitan. Yitzhak Hofi had taken his time at Northern Command, Israel's most strategic front, as a dress rehearsal for the job of Mossad director.

Dagan lived in the north, and he loved the area. Men who hovered near midlife did not want to uproot their families and relocate to new surroundings. He loved the challenge of Lebanon, outmaneuvering Syrian strongman Hafez al-Assad, and he knew that the Iranian dimension in the growing threat of Hezbollah to Israel would remain for years to come. And although he did not mention it too much, he wanted a second chance at what had nearly turned out to be a career-ending stunt in the Shouf Mountains.

The choice of who earned that coveted post was purely political. Lieutenant General Ehud Barak did not select Dagan for OC Northern Command. Barak gave the position to Dagan's former subordinate and close friend Amiram Levin, who just so happened to have also been the commander of Mat'kal, Barak's old unit. Barak, instead, offered Dagan Southern Command as a consolation prize. Although it was a challenging post that required the regional commander to interface with Arafat's Palestinian Authority and address security issues such as containing the growing presence of Hamas and Islamic Jihad in Gaza, the Southern Command's area was considered slow and sleepy, and Dagan wanted to be where the action was—in the north fighting Hezbollah and poised for a possible war with Syria.

Dagan learned of the offer while convalescing from back surgery. The news was a great disappointment. His thirty years of service had seemingly come to an end. He was fifty years old and at the precipice of a new existence—one that did not include playing a pivotal role in Israel's defense. And Israel was in trouble. There was a full-blown Palestinian bombing campaign targeting buses and cafés that killed scores of civilians. On January 22, 1995, three weeks after Dagan became a civilian, two Palestinian Islamic Jihad suicide bombers had killed twenty-one at a bus stop food stall in central Israel.

Old soldiers were mustered out of uniform quietly, without ceremonies or fanfare. Meir Dagan put in his papers at the Ministry of Defense and retired. He retreated to the studio in his home in Rosh Pina, a civilian. He listened to classical music, smoked his pipe, and painted. The oddest thing was to not wear a uniform and be saluted as he entered a military command.

*        *        *

It is a rite of passage for Israeli soldiers who have completed their three years of mandatory military service to take the cash bonus they receive once they are released from active duty and travel as far as they can away from the suffocating confines of Israel and the Middle East. After three years of duty in a state of permanent threat, the recess from the pressure and exhaustion of the army is a mental health requirement. Some travel to Goa in India for some transcendental meditation, free love, inexpensive beachfront lodging, and, of course, alcohol, sex, and drugs. Others backpack it to the Amazon rainforest and the snow-capped hills of the Andes. A Land Rover trek across Europe, into the former Asian republics of the Soviet Union, and then driving down all the way to the Far East was on Meir Dagan's bucket list. After years in Sinai, Gaza, and Lebanon, seeing the world one adventure at a time was exactly what the doctor prescribed. He ventured to the Urals with Yossi Ben Hanan, his closest friend in the world, who had retired from the army a year earlier. The trip was scheduled to take months—the two men were in no hurry to return to Israel. Thoughts of what to do the day they made it back were a million miles from their thoughts. They were living a dream.

The two were in Samarkand late at night on Saturday, November 4, 1995, when word reached them that the unthinkable had happened in Israel. Prime Minister Yitzhak Rabin had been assassinated in Tel Aviv after appearing at a large rally promoting the peace process with the

Palestinians. The Shin Bet's Unit 730 dignitary protection squad was the best in the world, or was that as much a fallacy as the idea that a Jew would not kill another Jew, even in the harsh political internecine chaos that erupted after the Oslo Peace Accords and the emergence of Hamas as a murderous entity intent on perpetrating mass slaughter. But when it became known that the assailant was a Jew, a right-wing zealot, the nightmare that unfolded inside the heads of men like Dagan, soldiers who sacrificed it all because the Jewish state was exceptional, hit them with almost unrecoverable force.

The two retired generals packed their gear and pushed their way onto the earliest flights to get back to Israel.

# BOOK FOUR

# SPY CHIEF

# CHAPTER 18

# On-the-Job Training

L egend has it that Golda Meir once engaged President Richard M. Nixon with her take on the differences between the United States and Israel. "You are the head of state for one hundred and fifty million Americans," the Israeli prime minister commented. "I lead a nation of six million prime ministers." Political discourse in Israel between the left and the right, the religious and the secular, those born in the country and who were of European descent, and those whose roots were in the Arab Diaspora, was often a bare-knuckle assault of pure animosity. Israelis watching the television news at night were embarrassed—sometimes aghast—by the behavior members of the Knesset displayed toward one another in their unfiltered attacks. The yelling, screaming, cursing, and even the scuffles were part of the country's way of governance, but assassinating elected officials was unthinkable. Jews did not murder their prime minister.

The Oslo Accords, the handshake between Yitzhak Rabin and Yasir Arafat, and the subsequent wave of Hamas suicide bombings, had ripped Israel apart. The fear and loathing it created was palpable and under-estimated.

Rabin was one of the founders of the Jewish state, a plank owner of Israel whose stock had been paid for in blood. No matter what one thought of him as a man or politically, he had dedicated his life to the State of Israel, and his murder was a point of no return for the country.

It can be argued that Israel has never recovered from that jarring pull of the trigger, making it more like other nations than an exceptional example of Jewish democracy and unity that had been at the center of the two-thousand-year dream of a return to Zion.

Someone had to pay.

Yahya Ayyash was the most wanted man in Israel for two long and bloody years—a mass-murdering boogeyman ghost whose suicide bombing campaign killed and wounded hundreds. He was a West Bank native and a master of disguise. To evade Israeli dragnets, he masqueraded as an old man and even a young woman. He found shelter in Gaza, in the territory under the control—and protection—of Yasir Arafat's Palestinian Authority.

The Shin Bet invested enormous resources to capture or kill Ayyash. On January 5, 1996, they finally got their man. In a brilliantly planned and executed operation, Shin Bet officers slipped a small and unnoticeable amount of military-grade high explosives into a Motorola flip phone that an asset would hand Ayyash. When the case officers were certain that the thirty-year-old Hamas engineer was talking on the phone, an electronic signal was sent to detonate the device. The force of the contained blast in the intricately designed device sent shrapnel fragments into Ayyash's brain and peeled off half of his face, killing him instantly. A quarter of a million Gazans attended The Engineer's funeral. Hamas vowed revenge.

The targeted killing of Yahya Ayyash was an act of necessary preemption to prevent future suicide bombers. It was also desperately needed vindication for the Shin Bet—the gatekeepers who prevented full-scale terror carnage on the streets of Israel. Shimon Peres, a forever veteran of Israel's Labor Party, Rabin's deputy, and the interim prime minister, appointed Rear Admiral Amichai "Ami" Ayalon, a former commander of the navy and someone who had spent most of his military career in the Flotilla 13 special operations unit, as the Shin Bet's new director before new elections were scheduled. Peres named Meir Dagan as his counterterrorism advisor—a position of top-level counsel.

Prime Minister Peres wanted a sober voice to guide him when making decisions based on the analysis received from the chiefs of military intelligence, Mossad, and the Shin Bet about counterterrorism strategies. Peres coveted the input of academics and career diplomats, but he held men with operational backgrounds closest to his heart.

The magnitude of rebuilding the Shin Bet and enacting measures to safeguard the Israeli public was enormous. Ayalon and Dagan were overwhelmed. Following the forty-day Muslim period of mourning, Hamas avenged Ayyash's killing. In one week at the end of February 1996, forty-five Israelis were killed and over two hundred wounded in four separate suicide bombings; two attacks targeted the same city bus route in Jerusalem.[1] The carnage was horrific—concentrated, indiscriminate, and unlike anything that had been seen before in the region outside of Beirut. It created a crisis of confidence in a nation whose pillars of security had already been shattered by the Rabin assassination.

Shin Bet director Ayalon had more on his plate than he could handle—counterterrorism, counterespionage, and especially the rehabilitation of Israel's internal intelligence agency after failing one of its core missions: protecting the prime minister from an assassin's bullet. Peres agreed. Ayalon created a Counterterrorism Bureau and promoted Dagan to lead it. It was a major opportunity for the general to prove his worth at the political appointee level.

Dagan gave the job three months—until, at least, the parliamentary elections in May, when Israelis would go to the polls to vote for Rabin's successor. It was the first time the electorate voted for party and prime minister on separate slates. Benjamin Netanyahu, the head of the right-wing Likud Party, won over 50 percent of the ballots and was elected prime minister. Netanyahu kept Dagan at the bureau. He liked the work the former general was doing.

*          *          *

The Counterterrorism Bureau was a blank canvas for Dagan. The office was supposed to be purely advisory—a watchdog group to review the activities of the various government agencies battling the terror armies and their state sponsors and prepare findings and recommendations for the prime minister's office. But Dagan was not a secretary. He had no intention of taking notes and writing memos. He was determined to make the bureau operational and coordinate over a dozen government agencies into talking to one another, working with one another, and working for him. It was a Herculean task facing depths of obstinate bureaucratic resistance. The larger agencies—the Mossad, the Shin Bet, and the IDF—resented it when outsiders stuck their noses in their day-to-day affairs. Smaller agencies—the police, the foreign ministry, and the tax authority—were bastions of bureaucratic autonomy where civil servants, not retired generals, ruled the landscape. Dagan would change the paradigm.

Dagan's bureau was housed inside the fenced-in walls of IDF head-quarters and the Defense Ministry in Tel Aviv, in the expansive campus known as the Kirya. Dagan's office was situated in a small Second World War–era cottage a safe distance from the main building. The structure, once used by the British Army during the dark days of the World War II, was later the headquarters for Israel's first defense minister, David Ben-Gurion, shortly after the creation of the Jewish state.*

The Counterterrorism Bureau had to be more than a one-man show to be impactful. Dagan recruited an inner circle of advisors, and each one had a special area of expertise, to make the office's mission effective. Ehud Yatom was brought on to spearhead issues of preventative physical security of individuals, facilities, and key infrastructure. Yatom was a controversial pick. In 1984, as Shin Bet operations chief, he had smashed the skull of a Palestinian terrorist following a failed bus hijacking;[2] he was also the brother of Danny Yatom, former commander of Sayeret Mat'kal and the newly appointed head of the Mossad.†

Dagan brought Elkana Harnof, a retired brigadier general and former head of A'man's Research Brigade who was Prime Minister Rabin's military secretary,[3] on board, to assemble reports and critical analysis of the changing terrorism landscape internationally. Avinoam Dagan,

---

* Ben-Gurion served as both prime minister and defense minister.

† In 2001 Prime Minister Ariel Sharon would task Ehud Yatom with heading the Counter-terrorism Bureau. The Israeli High Court of Justice ruled that he was unfit to serve as the government's point man on combatting terror, and the appointment was canceled.

a former high-ranking Mossad officer, was brought in to bring the office online with other international intelligence agencies, to forge operational cooperation. Sami Mutzafi Barak, Dagan's former officer in the Lebanon Liaison Unit, was recruited to serve as point man with the Palestinian Authority—with Jibril Rajoub's Preventative Security Force in the West Bank and with Mohammed Dahlan, Arafat's security chief in Gaza. Mutzafi Barak had been the IDF's military governor in Gaza at the height of the first intifada.

Collecting people was one of Meir Dagan's true talents. He was loyal to those he felt comfortable with and maintained close ties to friends even from childhood. He had a knack for identifying individuals with special skills and interests and embracing their unique personalities and skills—the more unconventional, the better. He mainly worked with people he liked to be around, though it did not mean the relationship was sycophantic. Captain Udi Levi, the COGAT officer he'd met a few years earlier, was one such individual. Levi believed that Israel could make a dent in the fight against terror if it targeted the money that financed weapons, explosives, and the salaries of cell commanders. Dagan was a believer. He commandeered Levi into the bureau and made him his operations chief. He created a new task force that would summon every one of Israel's government agencies to follow the terror money. A computer in the prime minister's office assigned a code name for this new entity—government red tape and bureaucratic protocol existed even in the secret world of counterterrorism. The code name was *tziltzal*, the Hebrew word for harpoon.

Tziltzal was a task force on paper only. It was a roundtable of representatives from the intelligence services, the military, the police, and a half dozen other government institutions. Dagan had to arm-twist to force the Mossad and the Shin Bet to send representatives to Tziltzal's regularly scheduled meetings. Most of the minutes of the Tziltzal meetings were dedicated to Hamas and the other Palestinian nationalist, ideological, and fundamentalist terror groups; significant time was dedicated to the multibillion dollars of American and European aid money propping up Yasir Arafat's malignantly corrupt Palestinian Authority. The Israeli entities were skeptical and resistant that bankrupting these groups was effective; direct action raids against safe houses and the targeted killing of high-value targets were far more satisfying.

\*     \*     \*

The Palestinian security forces, an integral component of the Oslo Peace Accords and President Clinton's foreign policy, became a pet project of the Central Intelligence Agency. Stanley M. Moskowitz, the CIA chief of station in Tel Aviv, and other officials flown in from Langley served as brokers during the meetings between Dagan's team and their Palestinian counterparts. The official sit-downs in Gaza and Ramallah, and the unofficial ones in some of Tel Aviv's most fashionable restaurants, were Dagan's introductory session to working with America's primary espionage service. The Americans were used to the trendy eateries in Israel's metropolis; the Palestinians loved the food, the cocktails, and the pretty waitresses. The trilateral meetings went well into the night—the armed security agents standing guard outside fooled the patrons into thinking that there was a high-level meeting of gangsters inside, making the establishment appear trendier among the status-hungry Tel Aviv crowd.

The CIA was far more than a mediator. The Agency was secretly training the Palestinian security services to interrogate prisoners,[4] augmenting what Arafat's legions already knew—and practiced brutally— with what they'd learned from the Soviets, the Romanians, the East Germans, the Syrians, the Libyans, and the North Koreans. The CIA program was highly controversial. It was designed to give Palestinian security and intelligence services—all twelve of them—an edge in battling Hamas and other fundamentalist forces, protecting America's investment in the Oslo Accords. Still, it was politically volatile, open to congressional oversight and hardcore criticism—America's spies training individuals who, less than three years earlier, had been considered terrorists.

Dagan and his office feared that the partnership—and the cash— would make Arafat's enforcers into a future military opponent of some measure should Oslo disintegrate into a full-scale conflict. Langley was adamant that news of the secret flights that ferried Palestinian security

officers to the United States for training, along with the hundreds of
millions of dollars of high-tech surveillance equipment to keep Arafat in
power, was kept far from the media—and that sensitivity made it suscepti-
ble to being compromised when it served Israel's purposes.* The program
was run from the Sensitive Compartmented Information Facility, known
as the SCIF, and other isolated rooms that housed the CIA presence in
the U.S. Embassy in Tel Aviv. Israeli government officials believed that
Moskowitz, a Bronx, New York–born Jew, went out of his way to favor
the Palestinians in the tense discussions. He was highly regarded in the
eyes of director of Central Intelligence George Tenet, though his reported
nickname inside Israeli intelligence was "the antisemite."[5]

Dagan did not believe it was in Israel's best interest to pick *this* fight
with the CIA. He was far more impressed by what stood behind the
chief of station—an espionage service with a budget and reach so vast
that it could waste billions on a side project with the Palestinians.

As Counterterrorism Bureau chief, Meir Dagan became a frequent
flyer, traveling across time zones to meet counterparts from like-minded
nations where Israel's fight against terrorism created a dialogue of common national interest. Mostly, though, he found himself in the United
States, almost always in Washington, D.C. He worked hard to improve
his English. He also needed to buy some suits.

The men and women who led American law enforcement received
Meir Dagan with the honor and respect he was worthy of. They checked
on him before his official visa was granted; retired generals and decorated
war heroes were always welcome in Washington. And Meir was different
than the typical Israeli military and intelligence officers who shuttled
back and forth across the ocean. He was amiable and self-effacing; humility was not a trait often found in many Israeli officials, especially one of
Dagan's accomplishments. He listened rather than lectured; he explained
rather than pontificated. He broke the ice with a sense of humor; he was
known for telling politically incorrect jokes. He was taken out to dinners

---

* The *Jerusalem Post* did the unthinkable on Christmas Day 1997, and outed Moskowitz
as the CIA chief of station in Tel Aviv—a move that, because of censorship laws in Israel,
is widely assumed to have been government-motivated and initiated. The Agency kept
him in Israel for another year.

at the Beltway's finest eating establishments, though he refused to say why he would never order prime rib or a burger. Dagan's trips to the Beltway brought him to the office of FBI director Louis Freeh, the heads of the DEA, Customs, the Marshals Service, and the Secret Service. He learned the art of diplomacy and establishing actionable partnerships, inviting key officials to Israel to see for themselves the threats that the Jewish state encountered and how they dealt with them while keeping a vibrant society safe, sane, and strong. When he could, Meir visited his older brother Eli, now a world-renowned microbiologist in Chicago. Eli had built a life in the United States, and raised a family. The two brothers did not see one another as much as they would have liked. Demanding careers got in the way of frequent reunions.

Dagan visited the U.S. Department of the Treasury to advance a unique agenda in the global fight against terrorism. He met with Ray Kelly, the former New York City Police Department commissioner appointed under secretary of the treasury for terrorism and financial intelligence by President Clinton. Kelly was a former Marine, and their shared military background made it easy for him to talk to Dagan. The Departments of Justice and the Treasury liked Dagan's new approach to fighting terror.

There were ongoing criminal cases against Palestinian charities throughout the United States that were bankrolling terrorism in the territories. Ramadan Abdallah Shallah, a professor at the University of South Florida in Tampa, went on to become the head of the Iranian-backed and Syrian-based Palestinian Islamic Jihad.[6] On the night of July 31, 1997, less than twenty-four hours after two Hamas suicide bombers killed sixteen and wounded over one hundred and fifty in Jerusalem's Mahane Yehuda market, two undocumented Palestinians from the West Bank were shot and wounded by the New York Police Department's Emergency Service Unit hours before they planned to carry out a similar bombing strike on a subway train in Brooklyn.

Dagan understood that the United States and Israel were fighting the same war but on different fronts. Israel, though, fought its wars differently. The Mossad was ordered to make sure the masterminds of the Jerusalem bombing never struck again.

*            *            *

On the afternoon of September 25, 1997, Jordanian police arrested two European-looking men in possession of Canadian passports following an altercation on the streets of downtown Amman. They had sprayed a mysterious substance, hidden inside an innocuous can of soda, toward the ear of a man walking out of his office in the Jordanian capital and the incident caused a commotion. The man who was hit with the fine liquid mist was Hamas leader Khaled Meshal, and he collapsed shortly after being exposed to the agent. The two men were Mossad agents, direct action personnel sent to the capital of a nation that had signed a peace treaty with Israel only three years earlier, and they were rushed into custody.

Meshal had been targeted following the lethal double-tap suicide bombing two months earlier in Jerusalem. Netanyahu summoned Mossad director Yatom immediately after the attack and wanted to hit Hamas decisively. Meshal was a legitimate high-value target—the same sort of terror leader responsible for the deaths of scores of civilians. Two years earlier, a Mossad team had eliminated Dr. Fathi Shiqaqi, the head of the Palestinian Islamic Jihad, while he was traveling through Malta. Shiqaqi was shot five times by two assailants with suppressed weapons, and the killing was attributed to Israel.[7]

Yatom convened meetings with his division and branch chiefs to draw up a list of possible targets. Jordan was close to Israel, convenient when mounting an extrajudicial killing, and King Hussein had little use for the fundamentalists, who he feared could become a religious force inside the country that would target his rule the same way that Palestinian guerrillas tried to in 1970, sparking the Black September civil war. It was decided that the Meshal hit would be what is known in the business as a "quiet operation," that made no noise, was 100 percent deniable, and would not be discovered until the assault team was safely back in Israel.[8]

Intelligence officers and operatives who embark on cross-border covert action to eliminate a hostile threat are issued with one universal instruction: do not get caught. The Mossad agents had broken the golden rule. Four other agents who supported the operation, fearing the dragnet was closing in on them, sought shelter at the newly opened Israeli Embassy in the fashionable al-Rabiah section of Amman. News of the botched operation reached Mossad headquarters within hours. Netanyahu phoned King Hussein, requesting he see the Jordanian monarch at once. No one in Jordan had bothered to inform the king of what had just transpired.[9]

King Hussein was livid that Netanyahu—and the Mossad—had such low regard for Jordanian sovereignty that they would stage a hit in Amman and endanger the fragile peace forged between the two former enemies turned strategic partners. The Jordanians and Israelis worked closely on security matters; the intelligence services of both countries, according to reports, fought Hamas, often together. The audacity of the Israeli plan was an insult to the Jordanian king and his people, and the fact that the Mossad director flew to Amman to request the release of agents—including two holed up at the Intercontinental Hotel, those who ran to the embassy—was a breaking point. Netanyahu was forced to fly to Amman and ask the king for forgiveness. The monarch refused to see him.[10]

The Israeli agents had sprayed a dose of synthetic fentanyl at Meshal, but the transdermal delivery did not kill instantly, and the Hamas leader lingered in a Jordanian hospital. Netanyahu sent Halevy, whose long history of back-channel workings with King Hussein was essential to clean up the mess. Halevy was Israel's ambassador to the European Union when Yatom summoned him into action to try to resolve the crisis. The Mossad veteran was even-keeled, urbane, and from a religious family. He viewed the Middle East methodically, and not passionately. He understood the precious strategic value of Israel's relationship with Jordan, and the king appreciated his work, and his temperament and sincerity.[11]

There was no time for nuance, though, and there was no urbane gentlemanly way to negotiate through the crisis. Meshal was dying on King Hussein's watch, and Israel had inadvertently and arrogantly humiliated its partner in peace. The Israeli government wanted to offer King Hussein weapons, or special types of munitions, as compensation for the transgression, Halevy recalled in an interview for Israeli television. He knew that the insult warranted a much steeper concession to help the Jordanian monarch retain his honor in the eyes of the Arab world. Halevy, on his own, offered the release of Sheikh Ahmed Yasin, the founder and spiritual leader of Hamas who was serving time on terror charges, in exchange for the release of the two Mossad agents held by the police and the remaining six operatives barricaded inside the embassy and the Intercontinental Hotel, after Yatom personally delivered the antidote for the fentanyl cocktail sprayed on Meshal.[12] Prime Minister Netanyahu reluctantly agreed to the terms, averting a possibly unrecoverable crisis.[13]

Halevy's espionage diplomacy worked. The two Israeli intelligence officers were spared from the hangman's gallows; the six other Mossad operatives were allowed to return home. The peace between Israel and Jordan was preserved. But Yatom, the Mossad's eighth director, could not recover from the scandal. A government commission was raised to investigate the Meshal assassination attempt. It concluded that Yatom had made errors in his handling of the operation; a panel member even recommended his dismissal.[14] Although the prime minister approved such missions, the assassination attempt in Amman had been bungled at the operational level, and Yatom preempted any official rebuke. He resigned from his post on February 25, 1998, after less than two years on the job.[15] A week before he stepped down, Swiss police arrested a Mossad agent caught attempting to tap the phone of a suspected Hamas operative in Bern. The operational arms of the Mossad were racing from one debacle to another. New and different leadership in the secret organization was warranted.

Danny Yatom was the first Mossad chief whose identity was public knowledge. His predecessors were known simply by the initial of their first name and they remained in the shadows until they retired. The new openness, a symptom some have said of the growing Western influence on Israeli society, opened the vacuum of Yatom's resignation to the public jockeying for insiders, and those inside the old boys' network of the security establishment, to quietly filibuster to fill the vacancy in support of their choice for the job. The names of several former generals were raised in the media. Dagan's name was not mentioned in the news-papers. He wanted the job more than anything. He felt he deserved the chance to lead Isreal's espionage service. He had dreamed of being in the Mossad, and leading the organization, ever since he was a teenager and he read the account of Adolf Eichmann's capture in Buenos Aires. Meir Dagan's hopes were bolstered when, days after Yatom resigned, he received a call from Jerusalem summoning him to the prime minister's office. Dagan was certain that the meeting was to interview for the vacant Mossad chief's position. He wore his best gray suit and headed toward the Israeli capital. The drive to Jerusalem from the Kirya took less than an hour. Dagan puffed nervously on his pipe the entire way.

Members of the prime minister's Unit 730 protective detail ushered Dagan inside the Aquarium, so named because the prime minister's office was enclosed in a fishbowl-like protective glass that anyone walk-ing past could peek into. There was a small waiting area for visitors where a staffer brought tea to Dagan. Punctuality was a religious virtue to him, and Netanyahu always kept people waiting—sometimes endlessly. Hours after the prescribed time, an aide ushered Dagan into the office.

The details of what was discussed behind closed doors remain unknown. Two hours after Dagan sat down with the Israeli prime min-ister, he was seen at his favorite falafel stand in Abu Ghosh, an Arab village on the main Tel Aviv–Jerusalem Highway, getting a quick snack. When he returned to his office in the Kirya, those who worked for him noticed he was emotionally deflated. He usually smiled in the office and was always upbeat, telling jokes and laughing, but he lit his pipe and was uncharacteristically silent. Dagan had learned that the prime minister selected Ephraim Halevy as Mossad's ninth director. It was a reward for Halevy's many years of exemplary service and his yeoman's work in diffusing the potentially map-changing crisis with Jordan; he was the first—and, to date, only—Mossad chief never to have served in the IDF. But that was not a major obstacle for Netanyahu, who was raised and educated in the United States, and was more comfortable speaking English than Hebrew. According to one of the prime minister's former chiefs of staff, he favored working with Anglos and Americans—espe-cially those with a religious upbringing.[16]

Netanyahu was not concerned that Halevy lacked an operational mindset and that he would focus more on research, intelligence gathering, and Mossad's relationship with friendly services around the world than on the unsavory but necessary violence sometimes needed in the spy business. But, to balance the agency's leadership, the prime minister saw to it that Amiram Levin was named Halevy's deputy.[17]

Dagan was dejected but resigned to the snub. He remained at the Counterterrorism Bureau for another year-and-a-half, forging policy and enhancing Israel's ties with friendly counterterrorist agencies overseas. Dagan worked closely with Prime Minister Netanyahu and learned the art of political power and statesmanship. He left the bureau in the summer of 1999 when Ehud Barak was elected prime minister.

Dagan was still a general—as a reservist, he commanded an corps consisting of several armored divisions and infantry formations for Northern Command—and at an age that was a safe distance from packing it in altogether. He was not ready to be a full-time pensioner. The millennium was approaching. In the Middle East, who knew what the next day would bring?

# CHAPTER 19

# The Architect

sraelis went to the polls on May 17, 1999, to vote for their next prime minister and government. The election pitted incumbent Prime Minister Benjamin Netanyahu of the Likud against opposition leader Ehud Barak, the head of the left-centrist Labor Party.

The left despised what they saw as Netanyahu's smugness and sound-bite ideology after his fiery rhetoric in opposition to the Oslo Peace Accords, and Yitzhak Rabin's leadership was viewed as the incitement that pulled the trigger of the assassin's pistol. But he also lost the support of his right-wing base for continuing Oslo and agreeing to the redeployment of Israeli forces in the contested and holy West Bank city of Hebron. Ehud Barak, the most decorated soldier in Israeli military history, IDF chief of staff, Yitzhak Rabin protégé, foreign minister, and, as of 1997, the new head of the centrist Labor Party, promised to usher Israel into the next century. In an odd reality that could only exist in Israel, Barak was Netanyahu's former commanding officer in Sayeret Mat'kal. And at the ballot box that warm day in May, the commander owned his former junior officer.

Barak won the prime ministership with an overwhelming 56 percent of the vote—a landslide by Israeli standards—but his party only managed to squeeze through twenty-six seats in the Knesset. To govern, he had to hodgepodge a fractious coalition of smaller left, centrist, and religious parties with special interests that did not coincide with the national agenda.

Israel's multiparty political system was designed for dysfunction, and Barak's mandate was tenuous and temporary. He wanted to change the country—and the region—forever. Desire is a dangerous dream to pursue in the Middle East—it is often a trip wire for disaster.

One of Prime Minister Barak's first initiatives was to order the unilateral withdrawal of Israeli forces from Lebanon. Israel had been stuck inside Lebanon for nearly eighteen years and was unable to extract itself from a lethal quagmire. The IDF controlled a narrow security zone north of the Israeli frontier that it held alongside the South Lebanon Army in a series of hilltop fortifications. IDF units clearing resupply routes and patrolling vital sectors found themselves under intense Hezbollah attacks. The Lebanese guerrillas became experts in irregular warfare, and they were master improvised explosive device makers. Casualties mounted. And there was no sign of a way out without returning the residents of northern Israel to the permanent threat of terrorist infiltration and rocket fire.

Following an accident involving two Israel Air Force helicopters in which seventy-three soldiers were killed in the worst aerial disaster in the country's history, a grassroots protest movement called Four Mothers was formed to urge the nation to withdraw from Lebanon before more of its sons and husbands were killed. It proved to be a potent political force, selling a powerful message of extrication.

The new prime minister wanted to extricate the armed forces from an untenable military predicament and focus on the Palestinian issue and domestic political matters. It was bold and, some have said, dangerously negligent, to abandon Lebanon to Hezbollah and Iran—a terror organization and its state sponsor that have sworn to wipe Israel off the face of the earth. Meir Dagan joined a long list of retired senior IDF generals and officers opposed to exposing Israel's north to incessant terrorist attacks, arguing that Hezbollah would force the IDF to return to Lebanon to fight another war—virtually the entire Israeli defense establishment opposed the move. They argued that while Barak was right that Israel had to get out of Lebanon, it would be foolish to think that it could extricate itself permanently from the dangers of the Lebanese landscape, because it would have to return, possibly repeatedly.[1]

The last Israeli combat units completed their withdrawal from Lebanon on May 24, 2000. IDF combat engineers used tons of explosives to obliterate the last of its fortified outposts. Israeli soldiers were relieved to no longer worry about being helpless targets inside the sights of a Hezbollah RPG. But less than five months later, on October 7, Hezbollah killed three Israeli soldiers patrolling the border and abducted their bodies back to Lebanon, holding their corpses hostage, bargaining chips in a ghoulish Levantine bazaar.[2] Meir Dagan and his contemporaries who opposed Barak's unilateral move were right: Israel would have to return one day to Lebanon—perhaps larger and more demonstrative than before.

*       *       *

Prime Minister Barak's other initiative—to once-and-for-all end the impasse impeding a final peace accord with Yasir Arafat and the Palestinians—would have an equally disastrous and more immediate outcome. In July 2000, President Clinton convened a summit at Camp David to memorialize the Oslo Accords into a lasting arrangement that would forever change the Middle East. Clinton shepherded Prime Minister Barak and Palestinian Authority President Arafat through tense negotiations, as small armies of advisors shuttled between the rustic cabins carrying maps and charts. Barak offered the Palestinians 96 percent of the West Bank and all of Gaza. Arafat was even offered what had always been a non-negotiable for Israeli governments—East Jerusalem as the capital of a newly established Palestinian state. The deal was everything that Arafat had always professed he wanted. But the Palestinian Authority balked, unable or uninterested in getting enough when, it became evident, he wanted more. He wanted it all. In 2024, Clinton would reflect, "You walk away from these once-in-a-lifetime peace opportunities, and you cannot complain twenty-five years later when the doors were not all still open, and all the possibilities were not still there. You cannot do it."[3]

Violence is language in the Middle East—senseless and irreparable bloodshed is the prose that narrates a political process. Arafat needed a military victory to erase what he saw as the Palestinian humiliation when the State of Israel won its war of independence in 1948—what was referred to as the *Nakba*, or disaster. Arafat wanted a war.

On September 28, Likud leader Ariel Sharon made a provocative visit to the Temple Mount in Jerusalem. It was a spark intended to light a fire under the Israeli electorate to demonstrate the rights of Jews to visit anywhere in the holy city. It had the opposite effect, though. Sharon's publicity stunt set ablaze a petrol-soaked brush fire that Arafat and Hamas had tactically prepositioned. Fiery protests soon turned into gunfire. The Palestinian rage became the second intifada. It would end with suicide bombings and thousands of dead. The hope of Oslo—the dream that Israelis and Palestinians could coexist in two states—had been murdered.

The intifada's eruption eroded the fractious political pillars of Barak's government. His poll numbers dropped. Barak resigned from office on December 9. Elections were called for February 2001.

Ariel Sharon, sensing that his goal of becoming the Israeli prime minister was near, asked Meir Dagan, his old friend and trusted junior officer, to handle polling for him on election day. Dagan did not like politics. His beliefs were right of center, but he disdained the backdoor deal-making of how Israelis governed; he found it all distasteful. Unlike many former generals, Dagan had never thought to run for office. But, out of work and looking to help his mentor, he agreed. The polling work was organizational, demanding the talents of someone with the experience to handle multiple problems simultaneously. It was Dagan's first entry into the political trenches, and he excelled at it. Sharon won the direct election for prime minister by a landslide. On March 7, 2001, he was sworn in as the eleventh prime minister of the Jewish state.

\*       \*       \*

When Sharon took office, forty-eight Israelis had been killed in the second intifada. That number would soon skyrocket. On June 21, 2001, twenty-one Israeli civilians—namely high school students out for an evening of dancing—were killed when a Hamas suicide bomber detonated his lethal payload at the entrance of the Dolphinarium disco on the Tel Aviv shore. Two months later, on August 9, fifteen men, women, and children—including seven members of a single family—were killed when a Hamas suicide bomber dressed as a hippie inside the Sbarro pizzeria in downtown Jerusalem detonated the explosive device he was carrying concealed in a guitar. Israel was overwhelmed by the terror onslaught. It was impossible for people living outside the country to comprehend how a democratic state could function living in indiscriminate carnage. And then came a cloudless Tuesday morning in September in New York City with bright blue skies.

The al-Qaeda attack against the United States on September 11, 2001, transformed Israel's war against Hamas and Arafat's insurgent armies from a local conflict into one of West's battlefields in the new Global War on Terror. By the time U.S. forces were fighting the Taliban and Osama bin Laden's armies in Afghanistan, Israel had retaken West Bank cities following the suicide bombing of a hotel during Passover in which thirty civilians were slaughtered. Israel was no longer alone in the fight.

*       *       *

At the halfway mark of every Mossad director's four-year tenure, he begins to search for a new deputy, someone the prime minister of Israel will strongly consider as a replacement when his term ends.[4] A deputy director is not a lock for the job, just a front-running candidate. The following year, the Israeli prime minister begins his search, reviewing the long list of names for consideration as the next spy chief. The lengthy printout soon becomes a short list.

Prime Minister Sharon was given three names to consider in early 2001. The first was Ilan Mizrahi, Halevy's deputy and a thirty-year veteran of the intelligence agency who was an expert in the Arab world and had spent most of his career in Tzomet, the Mossad branch that ran agents. The second name seriously considered by the prime minister was Major General Shlomo Yanai, a decorated armored officer who had been seriously wounded in the Sinai Desert and who headed the

IDF's Planning Directorate. The final name under consideration was Hagai Hadas, the head of Caesarea, Mossad's operational branch, who had reportedly resigned in 2002 following a disagreement with Halevy.

Sharon realized that intelligence organizations must reinvent themselves periodically, especially when dramatic global events mandated change. He understood that the Mossad needed new direction, and a new type of leader, to position itself at the tip of the spear of the post-9/11 universe. Ephraim Halevy had been an effective and respected head of the Mossad, especially in enhancing the organization's relationships across borders with other members of the international intelligence fraternity—in particular covert ties to similar services in the Arab world—but the Mossad had to be proactive and creative, a dynamic force to meet the threats of the challenging times. Sharon wanted a general in the director's chair with enough trigger time to develop a bold strategic mindset based on tactical experience—a warrior with unquestionable courage and who was unafraid to shake up the organization from within. Ariel Sharon wanted Meir Dagan, who was serving as the new prime minister's national security advisor.

When Sharon shared with confidants in the defense establishment that Dagan was his first and only choice, it ignited a firestorm of discontent. Mossad insiders who wanted the job or wanted their preference to assume the director's chair began rumbling, anonymously, to the press. The Mossad was a government bureaucracy where those entrenched inside it were against being overseen by outsiders, especially perennial outsiders with a reputation for rogue ruthlessness. Negative articles about Dagan soon appeared in Israel's voraciously aggressive press. Commentators mocked Dagan's military career. "One prominent journalist," one of Dagan's closest comrades in the intelligence community later reflected, "even went on television and said that all Dagan was good for was killing. Another prominent defense report summed up the campaign by penning an article titled 'Meir Who?'"[5]

Several cabals, consisting of the ambitious, those with scores to settle, and those on the brink of retirement who maintained influence among their protégés, created a disruptive mood inside the organization, and it expressed itself openly when news filtered down that Dagan would be their next boss. Part of their issue was the concern that the appointment was a quid pro quo, payback for Dagan's work for the Sharon election campaign in 2001. The heads of the intelligence services were selected based solely on competence and strategic capabilities, and never for any other sort of consideration, and the fear was that Sharon had selected Dagan purely out of the desire to politicize the espionage service and place a loyalist at the helm. But others, including former director Yatom, dismissed those suspicions as irrelevant. "It would be wrong to deny Dagan the position based on his work on the campaign," Yatom would later reflect. "Dagan helped Sharon out of friendship [two former comrades in arms], and not out of any political consideration."[6]

The simmering of malcontents and naysayers made noise, but nothing else. Ariel Sharon was not the kind of man to let anyone get in the way of a tactical decision. Generals rarely took no for an answer, and Meir Dagan would not allow backstabbers to keep him from his dream assignment. On September 10, 2002, Prime Minister Sharon announced that Meir Dagan would be the tenth director of the espionage service.

A special government committee to approve high-level posts reviewed the appointment. Dagan appeared before the panel, as did others who spoke on his behalf, including Defense Minister Benjamin "Fuad" Eliezer, a veteran special operations reconnaissance officer and a retired general. The head of the left-wing Meretz Party testified against the appointment, claiming that it was a mistake to place one of Sharon's lackeys in charge of an organization so vital to Israel's security. Outgoing Mossad director Halevy* commented that while Dagan was worthy of the posting, *he* would have preferred to promote someone from within the organization.[7] The committee approved the appointment. Dagan's lifelong dream had been fulfilled.

*                    *                    *

Dagan took an apartment in Tel Aviv close to headquarters. Rosh Pina was almost one hundred miles from the Mossad's campus, and the

* Prime Minister Sharon subsequently appointed Halevy as his national security advisor.

daily commute—nearly two hours on a good day—was unrealistic. At home in northern Israel, with the energy of a man half that age the fifty-five-year-old Dagan packed boxes with his personal effects and photos he would bring to his new office. He placed his favorite books into the boxes. He would not part with the titles on history, science, the Arab world, and art, especially books about Vermeer, his favorite artist, which followed him everywhere. He loved fountain pens and pipes. The two items would assume a prominent portion of the real estate on his large desk. Lastly, Dagan carefully packed the framed portrait of his maternal grandfather being mocked and abused by the SS moments before he was executed. As he looked out his office window and saw the shoreline in the distance, Dagan understood the gravity of his new responsibility. He would be responsible for the safety of Jews worldwide.[8] The symbolism of his appointment was not lost on the man born inside the ashes of the Holocaust.

A former Dagan deputy described the transition from private citizen to Mossad director as a crash course of intensive immersion. There were endless briefings on the internal structure of the organization, and the bureaucracy that each piece entailed, ranging from the cost of the maintenance staff to equipment that was on order, from high-tech gadgets of a classified nature to what was spent annually on stationery, entertainment, travel, and even ammunition.

The new director met the commanders and foot soldiers of his clandestine army. In the get-to-know-you sit-downs, Dagan was always personable. He was inherently interested in people and their life stories and had the uncanny ability to remember the names of people's spouses and children as if they were his own. But he was also blunt, and his sledgehammer approach was new to Mossad veterans who were not used to such directness. Dagan hated to be finessed. If he asked a direct question, he expected a straightforward reply even if it was not what others thought he wanted to hear. He expressed his impatience with a raised voice and swore with a skilled cadence. He would punctuate his frustration by slamming a forceful hand on his desk.

A long list of veterans did not want to be part of the service with Dagan as director—the number of resignation letters overwhelmed the human resource department. Dagan was unfazed by the organizational brain drain. He had come across people in the army and in the counterterrorism bureau whose talents were overlooked and dedication unexploited, who he knew would be perfect for the work of espionage. Once in the director's chair, he deputized like-minded military officers, CPAs, Arabists, and other unconventional thinkers into the Mossad.

Dagan was briefed by the branch heads about ongoing operations, missions in the planning stage, and the agency's international relationships. There were introductory calls to make to the heads of friendly services that the Mossad dealt with in North America and Europe—the CIA, Canada's CSIS, Britain's MI6, France's DGSE, and Germany's BND—and even the *Sluzhba vneshney razvedki Rossiyskoy Federatsii*, the Russian SVR.

There were also calls to the heads of the Middle East services from countries that Israel maintained official diplomatic ties with, such as Jordan's GID and Egypt's GIS, and with the heads of the espionage services from Arab and Islamic nations that did not recognize the Jewish state but whose intelligence and security services, according to reports, maintained long-standing covert ties to their counterparts in the Israel. Those were the calls—and the relationships—that Dagan enjoyed the most. His dream was to use his office to advance Israel's acceptance as an open partner in the Arab and Muslim world.

The incoming Mossad director received instructions on the office's security protocols that would follow him everywhere he went. He had a personal protection detail and would be driven around in a fortified vehicle. As one of the most important men in the country, Dagan would be protected by armed agents wherever he went. He was known throughout the building as having a creative mind and meticulous approach to detail, like an architect. It became his calling card.

\*　　　\*　　　\*

On October 30, 2002, a small reception was held inside Prime Minister Sharon's office to honor outgoing chief Ephraim Halevy, and to welcome

Meir as the tenth director of Israel's foreign espionage service. He had joined a very exclusive and distinguished club.

A small buffet table was prepared with finger food and soft drinks. Bina and the three children were there along with Meir's parents, Shmuel and Mina. The prime minister was elated. His and Meir's friendship, forged under fire, spanned thirty years, and defined the bond between commander and young officer that civilians could find hard to understand but those who served considered unbreakable. Dagan was beaming at the ceremony, but he appeared out of uniform. The gray suit did not fit properly; his white shirt could have been ironed better, and his navy-blue polka-dot necktie seemed wrinkled. The job would demand a new wardrobe. But fashion was irrelevant to Dagan. That day, as Sharon and Halevy raised a glass of red wine to usher in a new era in Israeli intelligence, Dagan's ear-to-ear smile was infectious. Noa had never seen her father so happy.[9]

A few weeks after Dagan assumed the title of head of the Mossad, he presided over a small event at headquarters to honor an outgoing branch chief and to welcome his replacement. Food was served, and the agency's catering branch had worked overtime to impress the new director. Speeches were given. Testimonials underscored the most memorable moments of a career in service to one's country followed by some more lighthearted reflections on the man's replacement. The new branch chief was tall and handsome, and his outward appearance had become his calling card inside the Mossad. Veterans of the service, especially those who did not want Dagan occupying the director's office, began whispering among themselves as they glanced at the new boss sitting in the front row. "*Kama zman hu yahzik ma'amad?*" some voices whispered in the darkened hall, "How long will he last?"

When it was Dagan's turn to address the assembled branch chiefs, unit leaders, and intelligence officers, he glanced around the room, cleared his throat, and spoke about the irrefutable fact that the organization's greatest weapon was its personnel. He twisted his serious face slowly into a devilish smile, and closed, "Attention! I am short and fat with a large belly, and I am bald. But I am the head of the Mossad and will be here for a long time."[10]

Silence followed Dagan's self-effacing moment of candor and confidence. The guests that night left headquarters under the darkened winter's night sky, somewhat unsure of the man who had been thrust upon them and their organization. The men of Meir Dagan's security detail were puzzled, as well. Their protectee was not leaving the building. As they doubled back inside to check on him, they saw the new Mossad director going to every one of the workers who had made the evening possible and thanking them for their work. Dagan spoke to each waiter, cook, busboy, and cleaner, treating each one with respect usually reserved for heads of state. It was a small gesture, a sign of egalitarian identification that a man from the streets had made it to the director's office. Dagan wore that distinction as a badge of honor.

No matter how late he left the office, Dagan always showed up to work when the day's new sun rose. Being the *Ra'msad*, the acronym for the head of the Mossad, became the pillar of his existence.

Meir Dagan always defined his background as coming from a generation that, in his words, history had screwed up—a generation that gave everything and asked for nothing in return. He had fought in three conventional and countless irregular wars. He had lost many friends in battle; any warrior who had seen such horrors and survived engagements with the enemy is a changed human being. His parents had survived Hitler's genocide. When he entered his office, often nursing a cup of tea with lemon, he would glance at the framed portrait of his grandfather moments before he was murdered and appreciate the meaning of the espionage service he led and the sacrosanct mission he had to carry out.

As a child, Dagan used to wonder how the six million Jews who were slaughtered in the Holocaust did not fight back. He would later realize that they had no alternative. Now, on his watch, the Jewish people had an alternative. On his watch, Jews would no longer be the victims. There was a price that Israelis paid for being Israelis; for being Jews. He was now able to make sure that anyone who targeted his countrymen—his people—would pay a steep price.

CHAPTER 20

# At the Head of the Table

The Kenyan port city of Mombasa was a particularly popular destination for Israeli tourists. Situated on the shores of the Indian Ocean, Mombasa was a historic trading post that bridged a bygone remnant of British colonial Africa with the Asian subcontinent. The climate was tropical, and the beaches were pristine. It was close enough to Israel for flights from Ben Gurion International Airport to be affordable; far enough from the confining reality of a nation under permanent siege to appear exotic. The shekel fared well on the African black-market exchange rate. Hebrew was widely heard on the safari trail. Arkia, Israel's second-largest airline, flew a chartered special once-a-week shuttle to Mombasa's Moi International Airport. A stay at the Israeli-owned Paradise Hotel, with its cheap rooms and generous breakfast buffet, was part of the flight package. The Israeli government did not have any outstanding security alerts concerning Kenya, even though it was in proximity to both Somalia and Sudan—two known hubs of transnational terrorism.

On the morning of Thursday, November 28, 2002, guards manning a security barrier at the entrance to the Paradise Hotel stopped three men of Arab appearance driving toward them in a Mitsubishi Pajero. One man emerged from the vehicle and blew himself up at the gate. The two remaining men burst through the gate and crashed into the lobby of the hotel, detonating several hundred pounds of explosives hidden

209

in the back of their car. Dozens of Israeli tourists were checking into the Paradise. They had arrived an hour earlier on an Arkia chartered flight. Seventeen people—including three Israelis—were killed in the blast. Another eighty were critically wounded.

As Kenyan policemen and soldiers rushed to the scene of devastation, Arkia Flight 582 to Tel Aviv was taking off from Moi International Airport. The Boeing 757 had reached an altitude of one thousand feet when the crew in the cockpit noticed the flash and smoke trails of two missiles launched from the ground and gaining height and proximity to the climbing airliner. Terrorists on the ground had fired two SA-7 Strella Soviet-produced shoulder-launched antiaircraft missiles designed to shoot down combat jets and helicopters. The SA-7s were one of the most widely proliferated MANPADS (man-portable air-defense systems) in the Third World but were poorly maintained by the terror armies. The SA-7 was reliable, but miraculously the two missiles launched at the Arkia jet missed their target, and the airliner landed in Israel without incident.*

A shadowy group called the Palestine Army took responsibility for the Mombasa attack, but the perpetrators were from the Somalia-based al-Qaeda in East Africa. A year following September 11, Osama bin Laden thought that targeting Israelis would enhance his appeal in the Arab world.[1] Meir Dagan was in the director's chair for less than a month when al-Qaeda attacked the two Israeli targets in Mombasa.

Meir Dagan issued two imperatives when he entered office: target Iran's nuclear aspirations and take a proactive role in the American-led Global War on Terror. Iran was the priority; stopping the spread of al-Qaeda and its allies was a strategic priority for what had become a Western world war against fundamentalist terror. Dagan wanted to hit the ground running and get to work immediately but found the espionage service was not operationally ready for an aggressive campaign far from the country's borders.

---

* The two terrorists who fired the SA-7 were never caught by Kenyan authorities. They reportedly fled to neighboring Somalia, where they played a significant role in setting up the notorious al-Shabab fundamentalist al-Qaeda terror offshoot that would perpetrate scores of attacks against Kenya and other targets across eastern Africa.

The Mossad was still recovering from the fallout of the Meshal Affair, and was not running on all cylinders, a longtime veteran reflected. Institutionally, it had become apprehensive and risk-averse. Director Halevy prioritized intelligence gathering over decisive action and deprioritized the special operations that had propelled the organization for fifty-three years. "It had lost its self-confidence," a former division chief recalled. "It no longer took chances."[2] The Mossad was not a think tank; the spy service was never meant to be an army of analysts working on policy assessments. Its mandate and reputation demanded that it carry out James Bond–like exploits. The failed assassination of Khaled Meshal stunted the service. The challenge Dagan faced was reinventing it into a bold fighting force—one built in his image that could meet the threats Israel faced in the post-9/11 world.

*          *          *

The Mossad had multiple official mandates. It was responsible for the secret collection of intelligence beyond Israel's frontiers; preventing Israel's enemies from developing and equipping themselves with unconventional weapons; thwarting terror activity against Israeli and Jewish targets overseas; developing and maintaining secret diplomatic and intelligence relationships outside of Israel; assisting Jewish communities needing to escape repressive discriminatory antisemitic regimes and immigrate to Israel; producing strategic, political, and operational intelligence for Israel's elected leadership; and carrying out clandestine special operations worldwide.[3] Unofficially, it handled all the covert gray areas required to safeguard the Jewish state.

The size of Mossad's manpower and budget are classified, but the service is structured into divisions and sections. The Mossad fields five operational divisions: Tzomet, Tevel, Caesaria, Keshet, and Research and Analysis.

*Tzomet*, the Hebrew word for intersection, is the service's HUMINT force. It runs agents, assets, and sources globally. According to published accounts, it is the service's largest arm.[4]

*Tevel*, Hebrew for world or universe, is responsible for international espionage relationships, with friendly—and some not-so-friendly—foreign intelligence services.

Caesaria, named after a Roman city in Israel on the Mediterranean coast, is Mossad's special operational arm, comprised of combatants—men and women—with advanced tactical skills. These are the best trigger pullers in Israel—usually recruited from veterans of the three tier-one units in the IDF's Order of Battle (the army's Sayeret Mat'kal, the navy's Flotilla 13, and the air force's Shaldag unit), or individuals from top-flight commando units that have a propensity for adventure and dare.

*Kidon*, Hebrew for bayonet, is the direct-action sub-unit within Caesaria; described in various platforms as Mossad's assassination unit, Israeli journalists have to preface any reference to it with the words "according to foreign reports" to never acknowledge its existence from a source inside the Jewish state.[5] Kidon handles the most sensitive missions of extreme prejudice, specializing in eliminating high-value targets. The unit, also referred to as Wrath of God, became legendary after it hunted down the Black September terrorists in Europe and the Middle East who were responsible for murdering the Israeli athletes during the 1972 Munich Olympic Massacre.

*Keshet*, the Hebrew word for arch, is the Mossad's SIGINT arm. The Research and Analysis division provides a strategic assessment of the intelligence the other operational forces gather and process for the head of Mossad to use in highest-level discussions with the prime minister and political leadership. Dagan wanted this division to come out from behind the safety of their desks and bring ideas, based on their delving deep into all types of intelligence, for the Caesaria and Tzomet teams to act upon.

The spy service also had regional and topic-specific desks to gather and disseminate information. These included Strategic, Hostile Terrorist Activity, Military (Syria and Hezbollah), Political, and most importantly, Iran. Dagan also brought Tziltzal into the Mossad organization chart. He wanted to cut off the steady flow of cash, the camouflage of straw companies, and the illicit bank accounts and transfers that terrorists used to support their murderous attacks.

The Mossad also fielded support personnel, protective security personnel, human resource administrators, maintenance crews, and cooks. It was an army—Dagan's army.

The new director wanted to know everyone personally. He spent long hours in his office, drinking endless cups of tea, puffing away on his pipe, and reading everyone's personnel file. Dagan became consumed with the job—staying late, arriving early, and spending less time with his family than he had while he was a brigade and division commander; he spent one night a week, Friday, at the family home in Rosh Pina, opting to leave late Saturday night so that he could be the first one in the office on Sunday morning, the start of the Israeli workweek. "He was a commander and not a manager," E.,* his former chief of staff, commented. "This was new for the organization."[6] And, as a combat leader, Dagan wanted to know what his officers were learning in preparation for them being sent into harm's way. "He made a point of participating in every training course given to his officers," E.A.,[†] the former Mossad head of instruction, remembered. "He wanted to know everything."[7]

It was difficult for many veterans to adjust to Dagan's abrupt and regimented leadership style. He demanded punctuality from everyone. Being even one minute late was unacceptable to him. In his weekly meetings with division and section chiefs, once the door to the secure meeting room was closed, it was closed. Dagan would not let late staffers—even high-ranking ones—walk into a meeting already in progress, no matter what the excuse. There were no exceptions.

Dagan demanded that whoever was sitting in front of him, whether in a secure conference room or his office, speak candidly. He always looked straight into the eyes of the person opposite him. Dagan did not tolerate it when someone would tell him what they thought he wanted to hear rather than the truth, no matter how unpleasant the candor could be. "He judged people by their courage and creativity," a former head of Tevel reflected.[8] The conversations were personal and professional. Smoking was prohibited inside headquarters, but that did not apply to

* Identity withheld for security reasons.

† Identity withheld for security reasons.

the director. Once Dagan began inserting his favorite tobacco inside one of the many pipes on his desk, followed by the striking of a match, the person sitting in his office knew that the room would soon fill with a cloud of smoke. No one dared complain.

The conversations were as much a chance for service personnel to learn about the director as they were an education for Dagan. He believed he should know what everyone did in the organization and how they did it. He felt most comfortable with the operational side of the building, especially with the men and women of Kidon, because he knew the impact of covert activity. As he liked to joke, one of technology's great innovations was the 9mm pistol. But he was equally interested in the linguists and analysts, as well as the work of the computer staff.

The one-on-one meetings yielded details of small problems of importance that the new director wanted to remedy. He discovered that many intelligence officers in the organization were religiously observant. These men and women found themselves stretching the boundaries of their faith and service when deployed beyond Israel's frontiers. These issues were as simple as not having the chance to pray three times a day, or they could be as complex and soul-searching as eating food that was not Kosher or even having to have sexual relationships outside their marriage to maintain a cover. Dagan was never religious, but he understood the power of faith and the beauty of the scriptures. He did not want his intelligence officers and operatives conflicted and he did not want them to lose their operational effectiveness, so he hired a rabbi, Y.,* the agency's first-ever full-time religious official, to provide spiritual solutions to day-to-day clandestine issues.[9]

Much to Dagan's chagrin, he learned that the Mossad was highly compartmentalized. Intelligence officers, field agents, technical staffers, and analysts operated in multiple self-contained mini-universes. The organization was so secret that the different divisions did not share their projects, operations, and findings with their counterparts. The rigid structure, and the culture it fostered, hampered the cross-pollination of ideas and capabilities. Intelligence locked in a vault or encrypted in

---

* Identity withheld for security reasons.

a computer that only one person knew the password for was wasted. Combining the various divisional capabilities—HUMINT, SIGINT, special operations, and cyber—was a vital force multiplier—a necessity for a small espionage service that faced threats on a global front. It was a mindset forged in Dagan in Gaza thirty years earlier and one that he tried to instill in the organization he now led.

Dagan also discovered that the organization had lost what he felt was its sense of initiative. It was content to sit back and wait for things to happen. He wanted Mossad personnel to adopt a special operations mindset and show how it could be more innovative, daring, and audacious than the reputation it had nurtured through past exploits. He demanded that the spy service be built around outside-the-box thinkers with a penchant for the spectacular who craved action and achieved results. There were no Queensberry rules for spying in Meir Dagan's espionage universe. He would not allow the words "fair fight" to enter the vernacular at headquarters. Intelligence work was dirty and manipulative; operations required guile and strength; people were killed.

Dagan pressed section chiefs and other intelligence specialists to seek out missions and initiate actions. It was uncommon for the head of the Mossad to walk around headquarters, knocking on doors, sitting opposite someone's workstation, and finding out what they were doing. He pushed people; lit fires under them. Working for the Mossad was not a right, it was a privilege, and one that mandated results.

In the first few months as Mossad director, 155 Mossad employees—from every field and division—resigned. Ostensibly, it was due to a change in the Israeli pension laws for civil servants, but that was a smoke screen. Dagan was shifting budgets to focus on clandestine work, and many wanted nothing to do with it.[10]

Those who remained and did not want any part of the paradigm shift were reassigned, demoted, or let go. Many veterans retired rather than be part of what they saw as a disaster in the making. It did not matter to Dagan. He poached the IDF, the Shin Bet, and other commands and services for the best and brightest, bringing in many of the soldiers and spies he had collected throughout his career—from his time in Gaza, the Lebanon Liaison Unit, and the Counterterrorism Bureau.

*          *          *

The head of the Mossad chaired a forum known simply as *Va'ra'sh*, the acronym for *Va'ad Rashei Ha'Sherutim*, or Committee of the Chiefs of Services, that also included the A'man commander, the head of the Shin Bet, and, sometimes, the prime minister's military secretary and the head of the National Security Council. It dated back to the early days of the Jewish state when survival depended on a steady flow of accurate intelligence that helped the new nation fend off numerically superior enemy armies—information, and knowing what to do with it, was a potent force multiplier. This triad worked together mostly, a common front against those that threatened the Jewish state, although their authorities and zones of interest sometimes overlapped, and the men and the forces they led could compete. The head of the National Security Council also had a permanent seat on this committee, as did, situationally dependent intelligence representatives from the Foreign Ministry and the Israel National Police.

The Israeli intelligence community did not have a singular government minister overseeing all the services. The Mossad and Shin Bet chiefs work directly for the prime minister; the A'man commander worked under the defense minister. There was no mechanism to control operations or settle disputes between the services. "The prime minister does not intervene in problems involving the territorial arguments of the intelligence services," former Mossad deputy director Hagai Hadas explained.[11]

The traditional paradigm was that A'man was the Mother Ship, and the two other services supplied it—and its Research Division—with information. The head of A'man and the commander of 8200, even the Shin Bet director, did not want the Mossad to depart from its traditional role of supporting their strategic efforts, and they tried to fight Dagan's determination to take a wrecking ball to the accepted way of doing things.[12]

Dagan was concerned that a revolt inside the Mossad, and among the other two arms of Israel's intelligence triumvirate, could become a public embarrassment for Sharon, and he requested a one-on-one meeting with the prime minister to discuss his plans. Public pressure, especially from the press, never bothered Sharon. On the contrary, he enjoyed the free-for-all atmosphere; he loved the fight. Sharon never doubted Dagan; never second-guessed him. His marching orders to his Mossad chief were simple: "Get it done!"[13] The bond between the two men was unbreakable.

Everyone in headquarters had heard the story of the legendary security cabinet meeting when Dagan was national security advisor, shortly after Sharon was elected prime minister. Dagan walked slower than most because of the constant state of pain from his war wounds, and he did not like to be seen using a cane. At this meeting, as the ministers and IDF brass walked into the cabinet meeting room for a closed-door session, shuffling for a good seat, Dagan walked in and sat at the far end, opposite the prime minister. "Come sit next to me at the head of the table," Sharon told him. "Mr. Prime Minister," Dagan replied, "wherever I sit *is* the head of the table." Cabinet officials, military representatives, and even the stenographers were aghast by Dagan's unabashed arrogance. But it thrilled Sharon. He broke out in a loud baritone laugh and smiled for the remainder of the meeting.

\*        \*        \*

The Mossad received a budgetary bonus to stake its membership in the Global War on Terror fraternity.[14] Dagan put the resources to good use. News reports began to appear with accounts of people with blood on their hands and those who were planning new acts of carnage mysteriously ending up dead. The first to go was Mohammed al-Masri, a senior al-Qaeda operative who set up shop inside the Palestinian Ein el-Hilweh refugee camp in southern Lebanon. A veteran of the war in Afghanistan and a known member of Bin Laden's terror group, he was a charismatic figure who was given the job of recruiting Palestinians in Lebanon to join the global jihad. A bomb placed near his bean shop killed him as he was about to walk to prayers in the local mosque.[15]

The next to die was Izz el-Deen al-Sheik Khalil, a senior Hamas commander in Damascus. Khalil was an operational liaison between the terror cells in the West Bank and Gaza, and the organization's political and financial command echelons overseas. He had just left his villa in the affluent al-Zahraa section of the Syrian capital to head to his office on September 26, 2004. He sat in his brand-new white Mitsubishi Pajero for the drive downtown, put the key into the ignition, and fiddled with the radio to find a song of his liking. After he answered a call on his mobile phone, a powerful explosion ripped through the car, turning the SUV into a twisted pile of burning steel. A powerful explosive device had been placed under the driver's seat.

The bombing came a month after a lethal Hamas double suicide bombing in the southern Israeli city of Beersheba that killed sixteen people and wounded over one hundred. Israel did not ever deny or admit* its role in the assassination of its enemies, but, after Khalil's killing, Ra'anan Gissin, Prime Minister Ariel Sharon's spokesman, claimed, "We have no knowledge of this incident." He would add, "Our long-standing policy has been that no terrorist will have any sanctuary and any immunity. They're in a very risky business, they live in a rough neighborhood, and [they] should not be surprised when what they plan for others befalls them."[16]

Targeted killings in the Mossad vernacular are referred to as "Negative Treatment." The Middle East was a target-rich environment for such attention.

---

* This policy would change after October 7 and "hits" across Lebanon, Syria, and Iran that the government of Israel took credit for.

# Friends, Enemies, New Alliances

E lhanan Tannenbaum was a shifty Israeli businessman and opportun-
ist who was lured to Abu Dhabi on October 3, 2000, to partake in a
narcotics deal that would help alleviate the inescapable debts that he had
accrued. The transaction—and travel—were arranged by a close friend,
an Israeli Arab, who unbeknownst to Tannenbaum, was a Hezbollah
agent. Tannenbaum also happened to be a colonel in the reserves.

Tannenbaum was flown to Brussels, where he was handed a forged
Venezuelan passport, before continuing to Abu Dhabi on a Gulf Air
flight. In the United Arab Emirates, he was subdued, drugged, and
smuggled to Lebanon: a hostage in Hezbollah's marketplace of captives
and anguish. Four days later, a Hezbollah special operations squad
crossed Israel's northern border and ambushed an IDF patrol. The
terrorists killed three Israeli soldiers—Staff Sergeant Adi Avitan, Staff
Sergeant Benyamin Avraham, and Staff Sergeant Omar Sawaid—and
abducted their bodies so that they could be bartered off at a hefty profit.
The leaders of Hezbollah knew how to penetrate the armor of the Israeli
mindset. They understood the value that Israel's leaders—and civilians—
placed on human life and in recovering their dead. Live hostages were
better than dead ones, but bodies also had worth. Hezbollah wanted

to test the value of its newly acquired hostage currency in the open Middle Eastern marketplace.

The pillars of Israel's counterterrorism strategy have always been that the Jewish state does not—and never would—negotiate with terrorists. Close to one hundred Israeli civilians and soldiers were killed during the 1970s—in places like Maalot, Entebbe, Glilot Junction, and Nahariya—in rescue raids attempted by the IDF and the national police because the government did not barter with barricaded killers. The message was clear: Israel would act defiantly and with unrivaled daring instead of negotiating with hijackers and murderers. Israelis, even those flying on a foreign airliner, were considered soldiers: the government would do everything in its power to secure their release, but it would not negotiate with those who held them hostage.

The paradigm changed in 1979. Israel released seventy-six imprisoned Popular Front for the Liberation of Palestine General Command terrorists in exchange for one Israeli soldier captured during the 1978 Operation Litani.* In 1985, the PFLP-GC once again extorted a lopsided prisoner exchange with Israel when Israel swapped three soldiers captured by the terror group during Operation Peace for Galilee for fifteen hundred terrorists serving lengthy sentences in Israeli prisons for heinous acts of bloodshed. Among those released were Kozo Okamoto, one of the three Japanese Red Army gunmen responsible for the 1972 Lod Airport Massacre, and Sheikh Ahmed Yasin, the quadriplegic founder of Hamas. The exchange opened the floodgates for lopsided prisoner exchanges between terror groups and Israel.

---

* One of the men released in that exchange was Hafez Kassam Dalkamoni, a Syrian-born (some say Palestinian-born), high-ranking operative in the PFLP-GC who was implicated in the bombing of an American troop train in Hedemunde, West Germany, in 1987. He was arrested on October 26, 1988, as part of the German BKA's "Operation Autumn Leaves," in the city of Neuss, along with other members of a PFLP-GC bomb-building cell. The devices they were building were identical to the device that would bring down Pan Am 103 over Lockerbie, Scotland, two months later killing a combined 270 people in the air and on the ground. Dalkamoni was sentenced in a West German court to fifteen years in prison for terrorism offenses. Although Libya has been identified as the key perpetrator of the Pan Am bombing, many in the intelligence and legal community are convinced that the pro-Syrian and pro-Iranian PFLP-GC played a major role in the act of terror.

Rabbi Ber Slushni, Meir Dagan's maternal grandfather, was ridiculed by the SS moments before he was executed in occupied Poland during the Holocaust. The image—of a family member, a Jew, who was humiliated and helpless—would be a driving force behind Dagan's military and intelligence career, prompting him to adhere to a faith of Never Again, and was displayed in his office at Mossad HQ, visible to service personnel heading into harm's way.

Meir (child closest to the left), his brother Eli, and their parents, photographed near Dzierżoniów, Poland, during a summer vacation, before the Huberman family made aliyah in 1950.

August 1963: Meir Huberman is conscripted into the ranks of the IDF.

4

Smoke billows as Israeli paratroopers from Meir Huberman's brigade depart the West Bank village of Samu following a retaliatory strike against Palestinian guerrilla bases on November 13, 1966. The counter-guerrilla battles he fought as a young soldier and officer would greatly impact his tactical senses later in his military and espionage career.

5

Posing as a PFLP operative infiltrating Gaza via Lebanon courtesy of a fishing boat, Meir Huberman (left) and his Grenade Recon team prepare to set sail for an operation.

6

The *Sayeret Rimon*, Grenade Recon, unit pin.

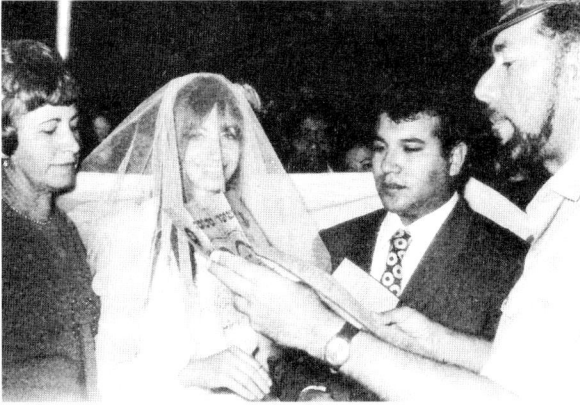

7

A professional soldier's salary made marriage and the dream of owning an apartment a reality: the wedding of Meir and Bina Huberman.

8

Major Meir Dagan, seen at a desert command post in the early hours of the Yom Kippur War, during the IDF's effort to stave off the Egyptian Army's advance into Sinai on October 6, 1973.

9

Centurion (Sho't) tanks from Meir Dagan's 188th Armored Brigade push up the Lebanese coast toward Beirut, June 1982. The Shiites and Hezbollah, the Iranian-supported Party of God, would soon turn on the IDF and embark on an ongoing guerrilla and terror campaign against Israel.

Colonel Meir Dagan (center), the commander of the 188th Armored Brigade, poses with Brigadier General Yossi Ben-Hanan (right) and Major General Haim Nadel (left) on the road to Beirut.

IDF chief of staff Lieutenant General Rafael "Raful" Eitan and Bina Dagan pin the rank of brigadier general onto the epaulets of Meir's Class A tunic during a ceremony at IDF headquarters in Tel Aviv on November 22, 1982.

Brigadier General Meir Dagan (far left), commander of the Lebanon Liaison Unit, attends the funeral for Major Saad Haddad, South Lebanon Army commander and Israel's stalwart ally in the counterterrorist wars along the northern frontier on January 16, 1984. Prime Minister Yitzhak Shamir, Defense Minister Moshe Arens, and former Defense Minister Ariel Sharon attended the services.

Prime Minister Ariel Sharon (left) and National Security Advisor Meir Dagan meet with U.S. special envoy Anthony Zinni and U.S. ambassador to Israel Dan Kurtzer on December 5, 2001, in Jerusalem.

Soldier and his commander: Prime Minister Ariel Sharon congratulates Meir Dagan upon his appointment as Mossad director on October 30, 2002.

Espionage Diplomacy: Masoud Barzani, president of the Kurdish Regional Government, hosts Meir Dagan in Erbil. The Kurds were long-standing allies of Israel and an instrumental component of the Mossad's containment of Iran and its nuclear ambitions.

In July 2006, Israeli Air Force commander Major General Eliezer Shkedi briefs Prime Minister Ehud Olmert on the capabilities of the F-16I fighter bombers at an air base in the northern part of the country. A year later, Olmert's confidence in the intelligence brought to him by the Mossad and his faith in the IAF airmen allowed the prime minister to authorize Operation Orchid, the destruction of the Syrian nuclear reactor in al-Kibar near Deir ez-Zor on September 6, 2007.

An FBI wanted poster for Hezbollah commander Imad Mughniyeh—the world's foremost terror mastermind, who was responsible for some of the most catastrophic attacks against American, Israeli, and other targets through a twenty-five-year reign of suicide bombings, kidnappings, and wars.

Meir Dagan shares a moment of laughter with President George W. Bush in the prime minister's residence in Jerusalem, during a state visit to Israel in May 2008. The two men admired one another and enjoyed their one-on-one discussions—their friendship allowed unprecedented American-Israeli intelligence cooperation.

On February 17, 2010, a Hamas terrorist stands guard in the Jabaliya refugee camp at a memorial for Mahmoud Al-Mabhouh, the group's procurement and clandestine warfare chief who, according to published accounts, was assassinated by a large Mossad hit team in Dubai on January 19, 2010.

Prime Minister Benjamin Netanyahu applauds outgoing Mossad director Meir Dagan at a ceremony passing the reins of command to Tamir Pardo in January 2011.

21

Prime Minister Benjamin Netanyahu, President Reuven Rivlin, and other dignitaries bid farewell to Meir Dagan, who was buried with full military honors at the Israeli Military Cemetery in his hometown of Rosh Pina in northern Israel.

22

Iran's Islamic Revolutionary Guard Corps parades a Zolfaghar ballistic missile past a reviewing stand in Tehran on the forty-fourth anniversary of Saddam Hussein's 1980 invasion of the country. Meir Dagan dedicated his tenure at the Mossad to preventing Iran's vast ballistic arsenal from ever having nuclear-tipped warheads.

Hezbollah paid close attention to the skyrocketing retail price of hostages—dead or alive—on the Lebanese exchange. Israel held high-profile Hezbollah and Palestinian prisoners. Sheikh Hassan Nasrallah, the Hezbollah leader, wanted to make a deal that would humiliate Israel in the eyes of the Arab world. Meir Dagan inherited the Tannenbaum file and the plight of the three soldiers killed and whose remains were held by Hezbollah when he became Mossad's director.

Because of the international complexities of negotiating with terror groups, the Mossad had to conduct communications using trusted channels among its international espionage allies. In the case of Hezbollah, the *Bundesnachrichtendienst*, or BND, the German Federal Intelligence Service, was pressed into service to act as the go-between.

The BND and the *Bundeskriminalamt*, or BKA, the German Federal Criminal Police Office that was akin to the FBI and the Shin Bet, had strong networks in Lebanon and the Arab world. Germany's espionage and counterintelligence services had worked closely with their Israeli counterparts since the creation of the Jewish state. Gerhard Conrad was the German intelligence officer entrusted with maneuvering through the mistrust and posturing. He was a veteran Arab and Islamic affairs specialist inside the BND who had served clandestinely in Damascus before assuming the lead in the hostage affairs office.[1]

Conrad and his BND team shuttled back and forth between Berlin, Beirut, and Tel Aviv to hammer out a prisoner exchange that would be acceptable to both sides. The Mossad—and Meir Dagan—did not believe that Tannenbaum was worthy of the effort. He was a drug dealer, a petty hustler, and someone who had placed himself and his country in terrible jeopardy. Israel wanted its resources used in some sort of exchange with Hezbollah to release—or at least return the remains of—Captain Ron Arad, an IAF navigator captured in Lebanon in 1986 after being forced to eject from his aircraft that Amal, a Shiite militia, seized in 1986 before handing him over to the Shiite Party of God and the Iranians. The Mossad invested a great deal of effort in locating Arad. A'man and the IDF mounted deep-penetration high-risk Sayeret Mat'kal operations to abduct two Hezbollah commanders—Sheikh Omar Adel Karim Obeid and Mustafa Dirani—who had held Captain Arad hostage or knew of his whereabouts, including corroborating the fears that the navigator had been flown to Tehran.

In the Mossad scope of understanding, returning Arad—preferably alive—was the fulfillment of a pact between Israel's leaders and its soldiers that no man or woman would ever be left behind. But if Israel released Obeid and Dirani for Tannenbaum and the three slain soldiers, it would lose its trump card in trying to bring Arad home. There were heated debates at headquarters—and in the prime minister's office—examining the virtue of exchanging Israel's most valuable trading chips for the return of a trafficker. Dagan opposed striking a deal for Tannenbaum, and let the prime minister know his feelings. "How many Israelis and Jews would be slaughtered by the killers Israel would have to release?" Dagan asked, former subordinates in the Mossad remembered.* Future events would prove him right.[2]

But Prime Minister Sharon decided that Israel had to do whatever it took to bring Tannenbaum and the remains of the three slain servicemen home.[3] "What are we going to do?" a former Mossad officer remembered the prime minister saying. "He's a Jew. We can't just leave him there."[4]

On January 29, 2004, under extraordinary security, with German counterterrorist forces and armed Israeli agents ringing the tarmac, the exchange was executed. Israel released four hundred Palestinian prisoners and the remains of fifty-nine Hezbollah terrorists killed in southern Lebanon, including the body of Sheikh Hassan Nasrallah's eldest son. Simultaneously, in a scene reminiscent of Cold War spy exchanges at Checkpoint Charlie in Berlin, Israel flew twenty-nine prisoners—including Obeid and Dirani—to Cologne on an Israel Air Force plane and parked at a remote corner of the airfield next to a German Air Force

---

* Dagan would later justify his opinion at the time, claiming that 231 Israelis were killed by the men freed for Tanenbaum and the bodies of the soldiers. The number of innocent lives lost in the pantomime of this deal with terrorists would pale in comparison with the carnage that would follow the aftermath of future prisoner exchanges, especially the 2011 deal for Gilad Shalit exchange, in which 1,027 Palestinian terrorists, including Hamas chieftain Yahya Sinwar, were released for one seized soldier. The ramifications of the 2023 and 2025 post–October 7 prisoner releases will take years to realize.

aircraft that had arrived carrying the bodies of the three slain Israeli soldiers and Tannenbaum. German foreign minister Joschka Fischer thanked the security services for their work, and noted how Germany was a trusted intelligence partner for such sensitive endeavors.[5]

Trust is essential in the intertwining relationships among members of the international espionage fraternity. Maintaining the interservice working relationships—even alliances—falls on the shoulders of the men and women who lead these organizations. Meir Dagan accepted this mission with unbridled enthusiasm.

*          *          *

The Mossad splits the world into two camps: base nations and target countries. Base nations are the nations with which Israel maintains full diplomatic relations. Target countries are enemy states in the region, as well as those in the Arab, Muslim, and Third World that—publicly, at least—do not recognize the Jewish state's right to exist.

Improving and expanding the working relationship with the Arab intelligence services was a strategic imperative to Dagan's foreign policy. It was driven partly by personal predilection. He was fascinated by Arab culture, art, and music, and was jealous of the Arabic-speaking officers who worked for him and had such mastery of the language. In turn, he fascinated the Arabs. Dagan personified what they thought Israelis were like—determined and stubborn, blessed with an extra helping of confidence, uncomfortable in a suit and tie, but more than making up for their lack of style in chutzpah, that uniquely and not necessarily Israeli brand of arrogance.

There was more to Dagan's thinking, however, than a mere interest in Arabic culture. Before he had entered office, his predecessors engaged the Sunni Arab world in transactional espionage diplomacy. The emirs, kings, and generals did not trust the Palestinians, especially Arafat, who made a career, and billions stashed in offshore accounts, in extorting cash and favors from the wealthy states; these leaders feared the more radical elements inside the national liberation movements, who hated their pro-Western regimes as much if not more than they despised

Israel. They provided Israel with tidbits of intelligence when it suited them, to help keep the Palestinian groups in their place. The Mossad in turn provided the Arab rulers with information useful to their survival and introduced Israeli technical knowledge in the spheres of irrigation and agriculture, medicine, and most of all security. This was how the Mossad won hearts and minds in the Arab world for years.

The vision of Israeli and Arab states working side by side on joint ventures, like the Mossad routinely did with the BND in Germany, was considered revolutionary inside headquarters; some veterans considered it blasphemy. The Arabs were useful, but they were still hostile entities that did not recognize Israel's right to exist. Dagan refused to accept that argument. The secrets in the Mossad vault were useless unless they yielded results, and if that meant gambling on working with present enemies who could be future allies, then so be it.

*          *          *

The Hashemite Kingdom of Jordan was the center of Meir Dagan's vision of the Middle East and Israel's place in it. The country, the most moderate nation in the Arab world, was a buffer for Israel against threats in Syria, Iraq, and Iran. The General Intelligence Department in Jordan was the best espionage agency in the Arab world, carrying out operations beyond Jordan's frontiers and internal security inside the kingdom. The GID specialized in HUMINT and had excellent sources inside the tribal-run areas along the country's borders with Iraq and Saudi Arabia. The Jordanians viewed Israel—and its military prowess—as an extension of its security.

Neither side could ever admit that its security and intelligence services worked together, but since both countries shared enemies and faced similar threats, the need for the relationship was obvious. These ties, formed after the 1967 Six-Day War, preceded the peace treaty, and survived countless diplomatic hiccups: Israel was poised to come to Jordan's aid during the Black September civil war when Syrian armor poured across the kingdom's northern border. King Hussein traveled to Tel Aviv to warn Prime Minister Golda Meir that the Egyptian and

Syrian armies were about to launch a surprise attack in 1973.[6] King Hussein and Prime Minister Yitzhak Rabin were friends; the affection that both men displayed toward one another was genuine. The Jordanian monarch came to Jerusalem to eulogize the assassinated Israeli leader at his funeral on November 6, 1995. On February 8, 1999, Prime Minister Benjamin Netanyahu led a sizeable Israeli delegation to Amman to pay respects at the funeral of King Hussein. The delegation included Ephraim Halevy, the monarch's close friend of many years.

When he became the head of the Mossad, Meir Dagan's counterpart in the GID was Saad Kheir, a man whom CIA director George Tenet described as a "superstar."[7] Kheir was a dapper man of Savile Row blazers and ascots, debonair with an overcompensating polish. Dagan was the antithesis of pretentious, who felt far more comfortable wiping a plate of hummus and ful with a basket full of pita than he did at a Michelin-starred restaurant.

Kheir was called Basha, the Arabic pronunciation of Pasha, a throwback to the Ottomans. While in Amman, Dagan was honored with the same title. Both men made names for themselves battling Palestinian terrorists. The two men had daunting items of interest to cover that impacted both nations.

Al-Qaeda in Iraq, led by the Jordanian-born Abu Musab al-Zarqawi, had placed the Hashemite Kingdom in its crosshairs. A sociopath who relished the carnage of catastrophic bloodshed, al-Zarqawi was a criminal who masterminded several notable terror plots in Jordan, including the "millennium plot" to blow up the Radisson SAS Hotel in Amman on New Year's Day in 2000.* Zarqawi's network was behind the 2002 assassination of Laurence Foley, a senior administrator of U.S. International Development in Amman, and an ambitious plot—foiled by Jordanian intelligence and its elite CTB-71 counterterrorist unit—to use three large trucks filled with close to twenty tons of mixed industrial chemicals, explosives, and even nerve gas, and crash them into the U.S.

---

* In 2005, al-Qaeda in Iraq succeeded in their desire to attack the five-star hotels in Amman when, on November 9, 2005, suicide bombers struck the Radisson SAS, the Grand Hyatt, and the Days Inn hotels, killing six and wounding close to two hundred.

Embassy in Amman, a soccer stadium filled with spectators, and GID headquarters.*

Iran was also a shared strategic concern to both Israel and Jordan. Following the United States–led international coalition that invaded Iraq in 2003, after Iran began to make its moves and flex its influence from the Persian Gulf nations, across the Middle East, to its Hezbollah proxies in Lebanon on the Mediterranean Sea, King Abdullah famously coined the phrase the "Shiite Crescent."[8]

Protocol dictated that the heads of services deal directly, but the Mossad director's true relationship with Jordan was with its king. The two men could not have come from more different backgrounds—one a king and a graduate of Sandhurst, and the other the son of Holocaust survivors who learned command undercover in Gaza—but they spoke the language of warriors and struck a deep friendship. Both men were soldiers and connected in a way that only men who wore a uniform and carried the burdens of command could. Dagan and King Abdullah shared similar military career trajectories: each had worn the black beret of a tank officer, and both had made names for themselves in the dark arts of special operations.

Dagan became a frequent guest in the king's palaces. The director of the Mossad was impressed by the military precision of the *Hamza Ibn Abd Al-Muttalib*, the Royal Guard Brigade, dressed in their sharply pressed sage-green fatigues and green-colored berets, moving in a choreographed maneuver of protective muscle. He was also enchanted by the pageantry of the king's sword- and dagger-carrying Circassian guards, adorned in their cold-weather black uniforms, heavy wool hats, red capes, and leather boots. The visits to the Jordanian capital were clandestine—steps were always taken to keep the meetings secret and far from the prying eyes of the press. The Jordanian monarch and the director of the Mossad understood one critical fact vital to both nations.[9]

---

* Abu Musab al-Zarqawi was killed on June 7, 2006, in a safe house in Baqubah, Iraq, after he was hunted by Task Force 145, a combined unit of U.S. and British Tier 1 special operations units with assistance from the GID. Before his death, al-Zarqawi shuttled between Syria and Iran—anywhere that served to attack the West, Jordan, and Israel.

King Abdullah and Meir Dagan were both born on January 30, albeit seventeen years apart, and they always tried to share their birthday dinners. "It said a lot about the relationship between the two men that Meir wanted to spend his birthday with the king and not his family or friends," one of Dagan's division chiefs commented, "and it said a lot about the king's appreciation for Meir the man and the leader that he would choose to share the birthday meal with the head of the Mossad."[10] When circumstances did not permit an in-person celebration in Amman, the two men met on neutral ground or called one another to exchange best wishes.

*          *          *

Jordan might have been Meir Dagan's favorite stop in the Middle East, but his travels took him everywhere in the region. The Mossad did not have an air force, and because of the nature of the visits—and their locations—military aircraft, adorned with the blue Star of David and the white background of the IAF roundel, would not have been suitable. When Dagan, or another high-level delegation from the Mossad, needed to visit the "cousins," an Israeli term for Arabs (as well as the Arab term for their Israeli counterparts), they flew on private jets that were on loan from wealthy tycoons and billionaires. This was the Mossad's version of NetJets. Affluent Israelis were always more than happy to help a national cause. It never hurt to be in the good graces of the intelligence services.

Egypt was also vitally important to Israel's intelligence triumvirate. The Egyptian General Intelligence Service dealt with A'man and the Shin Bet on matters concerning the Gaza Strip, Hamas, and their connections to the outlawed Muslim Brotherhood and al-Qaeda-linked groups in the Sinai Desert and the African mainland. The Mossad, it has been reported, worked with the GIS about matters beyond Gaza—the Red Sea, the Horn of Africa, and the Maghreb, wherever the interests of both countries converged.

Omar Suleiman was Egypt's legendary spymaster. He had a reputation for Machiavellian brilliance and pure ruthlessness. Like Dagan, he was personable and distant from the stilted demeanors of Western diplomats and intelligence chiefs. Both came from humble beginnings and proved their worth in military uniforms, reaching positions of great command and importance. Suleiman was President Hosni Mubarak's right-hand man and the second most powerful figure in the country. Dagan was Prime Minister Sharon's most trusted counsel. *Foreign Policy* magazine called him the Middle East's top "spook."[11]

*        *        *

In 2002, when Meir Dagan was announced as the new Mossad director, one of the first congratulatory cables that the new spy chief received came from King Hassan II of Morocco and his head of intelligence Ahmed El Harchi. The Kingdom of Morocco did not have a formal peace treaty with the State of Israel, but that was just a formality.* The clandestine relationship between the two countries—and their respective espionage services—was the worst-kept secret in the Middle East.

The cooperation and dialogue dated back to the early 1960s. Israel wanted to safeguard Morocco's thriving Jewish community and ensure they could immigrate to the newly formed state; code-named Prepare, the clandestine operation, carried out by the Mossad and the American-based Hebrew Immigrant Aid Society, paid for close to one hundred thousand Jews to leave the country and emigrate to Israel via ports of call in Italy and France.[12] As payback for the king's benevolence, the monarch asked the Mossad to assassinate Mehdi Ben Barka, a vocal and charismatic opposition leader. Although Mossad chief Meir Amit did not get approval for the "give-and-take" killing, Prime Minister Levi Eshkol did permit the Israeli spy agency to locate Ben Barka.[13] He disappeared from the streets of Paris in 1965.

---

* As part of the Abraham Accords, Israel and Morocco signed the declaration formalizing full diplomatic relations between the two countries on December 22, 2020. Trade, tourism, and mutual projects flourished—El Al and Royal Air Maroc flew routes between the two countries. October 7 and the war in Gaza lowered the public temperature of the relationship—flight routes were suspended—but military and security cooperation intensified. In July 2024, Morocco agreed to acquire a spy satellite from Israeli Aerospace Industries in a one-billion-dollar deal.

A tacit agreement to allow the migration of Moroccan Jews to Israel forged close-knit contacts and strategic cooperation. Israel sold the Moroccans espionage service expertise and French-made surplus equipment, and the Moroccans provided Israeli intelligence with a foothold in North Africa.

Although King Hassan II sent five thousand Moroccan soldiers to fight alongside Egyptian and Syrian forces in the 1973 Yom Kippur War, he openly met with Israeli leaders when other Arab leaders who did not have peace treaties with Israel were shunned from doing so, hosting numerous Israeli prime ministers in very public summits. Prime Minister Ehud Barak ventured to Morocco with a sizeable Israeli delegation to attend King Hassan's funeral in 1999; the Moroccan monarch had admired the Jewish people and the capabilities of Israel's spies.[14] According to published accounts, the Mossad, along with Morocco's foreign espionage service, the DGED (*Direction Générale des Études et de la Documentation*) was close to assassinating Osama bin Laden in 1995, shortly after an al-Qaeda-linked attempt on the life of Egyptian President Hosni Mubarak in Ethiopia.[15] Cooperation between the two services continued into the new millennium.

The Mossad was always entrusted with representing the Israeli government in countries with which Israel did not possess diplomatic relations. The warm relationship between Rabat and Jerusalem continued with King Hassan's son, Mohammed VI. Meir Dagan was adamant that the covert ties be strengthened under his watch. Events precipitated his diplomatic efforts.

On May 16, 2003, twelve al-Qaeda-linked terrorists carried out five synchronized suicide bombings in the Moroccan city of Casablanca, killing thirty-three and wounding over two hundred. Two of the five bomb sites were Jewish landmarks. Meir Dagan flew to Rabat shortly after the terror attack—the deadliest in Moroccan history—to show solidarity with the Moroccan king and his intelligence service.[16] Dagan did not speak French or Arabic, a hindrance when dealing with the Moroccans, for whom English was not common, but that was for the interpreters to sort out. Dagan represented a brand of Israeli might and resolve that King Mohammed VI respected, a message that needed no translation.

Israel and Morocco were under attack by fundamentalist terror forces tied to Muslim Brotherhood ideology. Hamas and al-Qaeda were identical in the threat they posed and the bloody means they used to achieve their objectives. Adding to Dagan's concerns, Iranian intelligence and elements of its Quds Force special operations espionage arm placed sub-Saharan Africa in its crosshairs. Lebanese expatriates across the northern half of the continent, from the Western Sahara and Mauritania to the eastern stretches of Sudan and Somalia, were particularly helpful in expanding Tehran's troublemaking. The Iranians were less interested in the schism between Shias and Sunnis,[17] and more focused on menacing pro-Western governments, especially those with secret ties to Israel.

Wherever Dagan traveled in the region to meet with his counterpart in the intelligence services of the Gulf states, North African nations, and elsewhere in the Islamic world, his mission was to speak for the State of Israel's short-term needs and long-range aspirations. Every new friendship mattered; no potential alliance was dismissed. Dagan met with the leaders of the Peshmerga in Erbil, in Kurdistan, and ventured to Baku in Azerbaijan to forge a covert partnership with the country's foreign intelligence service. The former Soviet republic, a Muslim nation with seemingly endless oil wealth, was called the Casablanca of the Cold War against Iran because it was inundated with Western spies keeping tabs on Russia and Iran. The Azeris liked the distinction and the attention it warranted, especially from Meir Dagan's Mossad. According to published reports, Israeli agents operated on the ground there.[18]

The covert traffic in the air was two-way: the Arab spy chiefs wanted to visit Israel just as much as Dagan enjoyed visiting the desert sands of the nearby kingdoms. When they landed in Israel, these anonymous travelers were driven straight from the tarmac to Mossad headquarters in awaiting sedans with blacked-out windows to obscure the exact location of their destination. Escorts ushered the VIPs into a special elevator to the director's office. On special occasions, Dagan went downstairs to welcome his guests. The hospitality was diplomatic theater—a four-act play of respect, honor, friendly talk, and brass-tacks business. Some of the visitors, depending on the circumstances, fulfilled lifelong dreams of visiting Jerusalem. Others were happy to see Tel Aviv's famed beaches.

Dagan was an ebullient host, but every visitor was greeted with a history lesson about the black-and-white photograph on his wall. Dagan wanted his guests—the princes, the royal emissaries, and the generals—to see Never Again with their own eyes and hear the personal account of the Holocaust from the Mossad director's lips inside one of the most important locations in the Jewish state. It was hard to dismiss the reality of Israel's permanence in the Middle East after spending thirty minutes in the director's office—exactly as he intended. Dagan did not need to sell the merits of working with Israeli intelligence to Sir Richard Dearlove, the head of Britain's MI6, or George Tenet, the head of the CIA. August Hanning, the president of the BND, did not require history lessons and strategic guidance. The Arab and Muslim national spy chiefs needed reinforcement to expand on existing relationships and face the dangers of the new Middle East together with Israel. Just as he intended to change how the Mossad did business, Meir Dagan hoped to lay the foundations for a new Middle East.

*     *     *

The director of the Mossad was an emissary, an ambassador, and, in the covert market of intelligence wheeling and dealing, a traveling salesman. "He was always on the go, heading from one bilateral meeting five time zones away to another urgent conference with his counterpart from a friendly nation closer to home," a former aide recalled.[19] The Mossad director traveled with a small protective detail and, sometimes but not always, with a few aides, which made booking flights less of a headache for the agency's travel office. He always flew first or business class; his favorite seat was 1A, the window. El Al was the preferred airline: security on board and at the gate were airtight. The Israeli national carrier only flew to fewer than fifty destinations worldwide, and often overbooked flights, forcing the director to fly on the flag carriers of other nations, always those who maintained a working intelligence relationship with Israel.

The trips were an adventure for Dagan, who loved to explore new countries. The five-star hotels were regal, a perk of his position, but he was a man who spent years sleeping on an army cot, and a motel room with a reading lamp was luxurious enough for his tastes. Those who worked for him remember he loved to visit Asia the most. In Thailand, he found Gullati, an Indian tailor in a backroom shop in downtown Bangkok, who made his suits to his custom order. El Al flew to that Thai capital, so there was always an excuse to stop in the city on a layover and find the time to be measured for a dark gray single-breasted. Dagan recommended Gullati to everyone who worked in the Mossad. It was quite the referral.

Not all of Dagan's travels were to meet his counterparts in the international intelligence fraternity. He also visited his troops in the field, reviewing their prep work for ongoing missions, running through every step of an operation with the team, to see that the plan had merit. Division chiefs had to get the director's approval for a plan—Dagan had to get the prime minister to sign off. "It was a big thing to have the boss come on-site and visit a safe house or what we would use as a springboard. Everyone was excited to have him there," Ram Ben Barak, his former head of operations and a future member of Knesset, would comment. "He truly seemed to enjoy being back in the field in the middle of all the action."[20] He knew the mood in a command post before a mission was always tense, especially those in treacherous locations. He engaged with the people around him, wanting answers to reinforce everyone's confidence. But he also cut through the tension with jokes and a smile trying to make everyone feel at ease.[21]

Sometimes, during these trips, Dagan was forced to travel in disguise, but he was a hard man to hide. A former head of the counterterrorism desk remembered that "wigs, even fake mustaches, were sometimes employed, but Israel being Israel, where everyone knew everyone else, he would be ushered to the gate in a masquerade only to have someone walk by who had served under him in the army, and yell, 'Hey Dagan, how are you? Remember me?'"[22]

The Israeli Ministry of Defense classified Meir Dagan as a wounded warrior, a man with a hundred percent disability from wounds suffered during his years in active service. But he never complained about his condition. Sitting in a car for long stretches was excruciating for him. So was getting in and out of taxis; even negotiating the escalator at a metro station could be difficult. He never slowed the pace, even though his schedule was grueling. The travel, jet lag, and the pain of walking from various points in an airport terminal took a terrible toll on his body, but he never allowed it to hamper his stature as a warrior; he refused to be driven in a cart or wheeled anywhere, even though each step caused debilitating pain. Younger officers were amazed by his stubborn resilience.

Dagan was harsh on himself and viewed anything but true immersion in the job, no matter how painful, as an excuse; a dereliction of duty at what he saw was his life's calling. No matter how tired he was or what ungodly hour of the day his flight from wherever landed, his car took him straight to headquarters. "If his flight landed at Ben Gurion International Airport at 5:30 a.m., he was chairing a meeting in his office at 8:30," a former Mossad division chief added.[23] "In the eight-and-a-half years that he was the director of the Mossad," former head of Tevel David Meidan, whose code name in the service was Primo, commented, "he never took a vacation."[24]

The Mossad director's daily, weekly, and monthly calendars were always full—meetings with the prime minister, day-to-day obligations at headquarters, and covert day trips around the region packed Dagan's day, with little chance to sneak away. But Dagan always found the time to attend the memorial services of his friends, comrades, and soldiers killed in 1967, 1973, and Lebanon. Showing his respects to the families of the fallen was holy to him—far more important than celebrating the Jewish holidays. He seldom traveled on Fridays—the day reserved for personal conversations with employees, from his division heads to the cleaning staff. "He knew who was getting divorced, who was celebrating a son's bar mitzvah and a daughter's wedding, and he remembered the minute details he heard and genuinely cared. He was not feigning sincerity. He viewed everyone in the organization as family," remembered E.,* a former chief of staff at headquarters. "He followed up days, weeks,

---

* Identity withheld for security reasons.

and months later, asking for updates. Everyone was important to him. It was remarkable."[25]

No matter where he ventured, regardless of which spy chiefs and royal family members he had met during the week, Dagan was back in Rosh Pina for Friday night dinners with the family. He sometimes returned home with a new wardrobe and the odd souvenir, but as far as Bina and the kids were concerned, he never left Tel Aviv. There was a complete firewall between his work and the family. None of them knew what he did, whom he shook hands with, or what was happening in his office. They knew better than to ask where he had been or where he was going.

# The Race to Stop the Bomb

It took two minutes for fourteen Israel Air Force fighters and bombers—eight F-16As and six F-15As—and the twelve two-thousand-pound Mk. 84 unguided bombs they carried to destroy Saddam Hussein's nuclear reactor in Osirak, near the Iraqi capital of Baghdad on June 7, 1981. The operation was code-named Opera. It took two days for the editorial page of *The New York Times* to respond with absolute alarm over the Israeli move, the first time in history that one nation had destroyed the nuclear capabilities of another. The article was titled "Israel's Illusion" and stated that "Israel's sneak attack on a French-built nuclear reactor near Baghdad was an act of inexcusable and short-sighted aggression."[1] The apoplectic assault on the Israeli raid was shared by the editors of newspapers across the world. British prime minister Margaret Thatcher called the raid "a grave breach of international law."[2] President Ronald Reagan was beside himself, unable to comprehend how the upstart Jewish state, the recipient of such generous American aid, could launch such a preemptive attack without informing the White House. Jeane Kirkpatrick, Reagan's ambassador to the United Nations, was one of Israel's most vocal advocates in the administration. But the Iron Lady of

U.S. diplomacy was instructed to condemn Israel's raid on the Osirak reactor at an emergency Security Council meeting.*

Menachem Begin's decision to order the destruction of Iraq's nuclear reactor and its ability to produce weapons-grade material that could annihilate Israel, defined the resolve and scar tissue that the prime minister was built from. He was barely five feet tall, but when it came to what he saw as his responsibility of safeguarding the Jewish state and its people, he was a giant of defiance. He did not care that President Reagan temporarily embargoed further shipments of F-16 fighter bombers to the IAF. The sentiment among officers of a certain generation, men like Meir Dagan, who was then the head of the South Lebanon Area, was that Prime Minister Begin had an extra helping of overdue chutzpah, and he shoved his middle finger in the face of the entire world, and they were thrilled by it. Begin proclaimed once and for all that the Jews of yesterday, the Jews of the shtetl, and the Jews of being pitied rather than being feared, were part of history, not the present. Israel would have to define what the country needed to do to defend itself. The rest of the world be damned.

Twenty years later, though, when he sat in his office overlooking the sea and pondered what the Mossad needed to do—and could do—to stem the despots in the region from acquiring weapons of mass destruction, Meir Dagan took a more parochial approach to Begin's effrontery. Israel, the Mossad, could not wave its middle finger in the face of the rest of the world—especially the Americans—and rid the Middle East of a nuclear threat. It needed partners, especially from the world's only true superpower.

*          *          *

In 1981, it had taken the Mossad several years to try to sabotage Saddam Hussein's nuclear program clandestinely. The supply chain of expertise

---

* A decade later, following Saddam Hussein's invasion of Kuwait, then Defense Secretary Dick Cheney would say that the Israeli raid on Osirak made the work of the international coalition to stop Iraq's aggression much easier.

and materials was European, making it easier for Israeli agents to penetrate. But when intelligence indicated that Saddam Hussein's reactor was about to go hot, preemptive military action was called for. Operation Opera had been a perfect storm of spot-on intelligence, calculated dare, and the luck of retaining the element of surprise against an arrogant enemy. There were no guarantees that lightning would strike twice. Israel and the Mossad had to remain vigilant. It would not be caught off guard and awake to a new dawn in the Middle East with the country facing the possibility of a mushroom cloud annihilation triggered by a nearby Arab or Islamic nation seeking the Jewish state's destruction.

Pakistan joined the nuclear weapons club* on May 28, 1998, after conducting five underground tests in the Chagai region, a remote desert area in the southwest of the country near the Iranian and Afghan frontiers, fulfilling a thirty-year quest to build the "Islamic Bomb."[3] The father of Pakistan's bomb, Dr. A. Q. Khan, was more than merely a nuclear scientist. He was a dangerous peddler of the most sensitive weapons of mass destruction secrets to the highest bidder: Dr. Strangelove with a slew of offshore bank accounts. Khan took his centrifuge designs to the open market and found generous customers in Pyongyang, Baghdad, and Tripoli selling Armageddon for dollars and dinars, without, it is alleged, the knowledge of the Pakistani government.[4]

Dr. Khan found an enthusiastic client in Tehran. The Iranians were determined to build the Shiite Bomb and turn the Islamic Republic into a nuclear regional superpower.

The Shah of Iran—with the assistance of the U.S. government—had introduced the notion of the country having atomic energy in the late 1950s. The Shah feared that the country's oil supply would eventually run out and they would need a fallback solution for the nation's energy needs. The nuclear goals changed following the arrival of the Ayatollah Khomeini. The Islamic Revolution, especially after the brutal Iran-Iraq

* The list of nations with nuclear weapons currently includes the United States, Russia, China, the United Kingdom, France, India, North Korea, and Pakistan. Although widely believed to possess a nuclear arsenal, Israel has never admitted this and has repeatedly declared that it will not be the country to introduce such weapons of mass destruction into the region.

War in which, according to some estimates, half a million soldiers and civilians were killed, needed an insurance policy to safeguard the regime. To justify diverting vital national funds into a nuclear weapons program, the mullahs promised to destroy Israel and liberate Jerusalem. With the help of Khan's illicit technology sales, Tehran jump-started the program.

Four Mossad directors watched Tehran's nuclear aspirations turn from a notion to an actionable plan. They tracked the movement of Iranian scientists, and attempted to provide the prime minister with accurate assessments of how viable a Shiite bomb was. The Iranians had learned the lessons of Operation Opera and spread their sites across the country. Installations were dug deep inside mountains or burrowed hundreds of feet underground. It would be difficult, if not impossible, for the Israel Air Force to deliver a knockout blow. When Meir Dagan entered office, the question was when, not if, Iran would cross the nuclear threshold. Stopping the effort was an imperative.

Dagan had been in office for less than a year when in 2003, Libyan leader Muammar Gaddafi revealed to the world that Tripoli was far along in the pursuit of a nuclear weapon. The Western intelligence agencies—the CIA, MI6, the French DGSE, and Italy's SISMI (the Military Intelligence and Security Service, *Servizio per le Informazioni e la Sicurezza Militare*)—did not have much of an inkling as to how close the North African leader was to the bomb.

Libya, like all of Dr. Khan's client states, was a global pariah that used its vast natural resources to finance many of the world's most notorious terror groups; its intelligence service had carried out numerous acts of mass murder, such as the bombing of Pan AM Flight 103 over Lockerbie. International sanctions strangled its economy. The Libyan leader was viewed as a madman, gallivanting with a phalanx of female bodyguards, proclaiming himself the King of Kings of Africa,[5] but he was not crazy.

The Americans had let it be known that nations inside the proclaimed Axis of Evil would face overwhelming military might if they produced, stockpiled, or threatened to use unconventional weapons. The cruise missiles and bombs began landing in Baghdad on the night of March 20, 2003. The George W. Bush White House used the September 11 attacks in the United States as an opportunity to warn terrorists and rogue regimes that a new world order had been declared. The U.S.-led invasion of Iraq terrified the Libyan dictator. He thought coming clean and rehabilitating himself in the eyes of the West was a path to regime survival.[6]

As far as Meir Dagan was concerned, Israel could not tolerate more surprises like Libya.

Unlike the Libyan dictator, Iran's leaders were not motivated by madness and mayhem. The ruling regime in Tehran led a fundamentalist religious nation, fueled by the fanaticism of a violently medieval Islamic revolution. The country's oil wealth funded a foreign policy of regional expansion and chaos. The men who pulled the strings were a cabal of clerics fighting an ancient war of Shia religious legitimacy and a more recent vendetta against the West—primarily the United States and Israel—for supporting the shah. The rulers of the new Islamic Republic were nothing more than a tyranny-enforcing Mafia-like army of clerics, regime enforcers like the Islamic Revolutionary Guard Corps, paramilitary militias, and an army of regional proxies that were easy to manipulate and purely disposable.

The Iranians not only believed in martyrdom—a force far more dangerous than Gaddafi's megalomania and Saddam Hussein's desire to intimidate the other Arab leaders—but they also promoted it as a pillar of their national doctrine. As far as Jerusalem was concerned, Tehran could never be allowed to turn its chants of "Death to Israel" into a viable military objective. The challenge facing Israel was how to deny their aspirations. The IDF believed that a more spectacularly ambitious rendition of Operation Opera to destroy all of Iran's nuclear enrichment facilities was not yet feasible and would require American assistance. It was assessed that the United States, already embroiled in wars in the Muslim world in Afghanistan, Iraq, and elsewhere in the global battlefield of the War Against Terror, would be against the overreach and overextension of a full-scale confrontation with Iran. The campaign to stem Tehran's march to the bomb would be carried out in the shadows by brave men and women.

*     *     *

The easiest solution for the Mossad would have been to identify, locate, and eliminate the Iranian military commanders who ran the nuclear endeavor and the scientists who would make it work. The actions would need to be deniable, but there was a precedent for such a preemptive policy.

In the early 1960s, Egyptian president Gamel Abdel Nasser imported an all-star team of West German rocket scientists and former Nazi officials, the men behind the V1 and V2 projects for Hitler, to develop and manufacture long-range ballistic missiles to be used against Israel. The Mossad was fresh off its storybook capture of Adolf Eichmann in Buenos Aires, and Isser Harel, one of the founding pillars of Israeli intelligence, became consumed by the Holocaust and efforts by the largest Arab state to annihilate the Jewish state.

The Mossad, along with A'man's mysterious Unit 188 special tasks force, blueprinted Operation Damocles, the targeting of the Germans for assassination. In Cairo, throughout Egypt, and in Western Europe, the prominent Germans involved in the project received letter bombs, a bullet to the face, or ended up dazed and confused, kidnapped for interrogation back in Israel. According to published accounts, the Mossad even recruited Otto Skorzeny,[7] the Waffen SS *Obersturmbannfüher* who had been Hitler's go-to special operations wizard, leading, among others, Operation Oak, the daring September 1943 rescue of Benito Mussolini.

Damocles became one of the most controversial operations in Mossad history. Assassinations failed; innocent people were killed. Israeli intelligence officers were arrested in Switzerland, and the campaign became public and a scandal in the country that cost Harel his job and, ultimately, the prime ministership of Israel's first leader, David Ben-Gurion.[8] The belief was that Harel's Mossad had exaggerated the threat posed by the ambitious—though ultimately unsuccessful—Egyptian missile program. Meir Amit, Harel's successor, utilized diplomacy and break-ins to undermine Nasser's grand scheme, stealing cargo containers of documents and learning more about the project than even the Germans involved in building the missiles for Cairo knew.

Spy chiefs must fulfill two primary missions for the political leadership that appointed them to office: keep the victories secret and minimize the public damage of their failures. Dagan felt that one of his jobs, in addition to protecting the State of Israel, was to insulate Prime Minister Sharon from political embarrassment. He would act dynamically against Iran, but cautiously.

For all the bluster surrounding Meir Dagan, and his misclassification as a man who slept with a dagger between his teeth, he viewed the planned taking of another life as a measure of absolute last resort. He was not religious and did not consider the position of Mossad chief as an extension of a divine authority dispensing justice; the calculated elimination of another human being could never be solely punitive. That was the official line, at least. Neither Dagan nor any member of the Mossad ever shed a tear when a terrorist with blood on their hands was killed in a shootout with the IDF or one of the Border Guard police special operations units while resisting arrest or in an airstrike, but dispatching a team to terminate a target was always preventative: someone who had masterminded mass murder in the past and continued to plot catastrophic attacks in the future was permissible, albeit almost always deniable.

Dagan had no intention of giving his officers the James Bond license to kill. Negative Treatment came with an enormous burden of responsibility and moral clarity. To emphasize this, Dagan gave all his division chiefs, senior officials, and any guest who came to his office—or whose office he was a guest in—a copy of Christopher R. Browning's book *Ordinary Men: Reserve Police Battalion 101 and the Final Solution in Poland*, published in 1992.[9] The book chronicles a German reserve rear-echelon battalion dispatched to the town of Jozefow in Poland in 1942. The soldiers were too old and too out of shape for combat duty, but they were professionals, and yet they proceeded to massacre tens of thousands of Jews. Dagan found great meaning in the work, not only because it was about an area of Poland where his parents were from, but also because it spoke of overreach and the infectious peer pressure of violence. Dagan believed it served as a sober warning.

As hesitant as the Mossad director was in taking lives, he was averse to risking them. It is likely that Dagan, like most of his generation, suffered from a form of PTSD. The men who fought in the 1973 war, absorbing the surprise two-front attack in what was known as the October

Earthquake, were haunted by the psychological scars of battle. The talk of psychological scars was frowned upon; it was a sign of weakness, especially in men of a certain rank, where military advancement was determined by capability, courage, and machismo. But Dagan had killed men with his bare hands, up close and personal, and he had watched men, *his* men, die. No one emerged from that trauma unscathed.

Dagan brought those internal scars with him to the Mossad. Dispatching his officers to Iran was a great conflict for him. If one of them were captured, there was no doubt that the agent would be tortured and killed. The Islamic Revolutionary Guard Corps loved show trials and public executions. The favored method of state murder was hanging—suspects, the guilt or innocence did not matter, were hoisted by their necks on industrial cranes until the lifeless body of the accused stopped struggling one hundred feet above a Tehran square. Israel and Iran had never exchanged spies. There was no Checkpoint Charlie where enemy agents were swapped. Intelligence operatives were killed. Even their remains were never returned.*

Dagan, contrary to his swashbuckling reputation, was risk averse. And, as he revealed in a documentary about his career and final struggles that appeared on Israeli television in December 2024, he had a psychological yardstick he used to gauge whether to send an Israeli into harm's way. "I called it the Dan Dagan exam," he explained, the test named after his son. "Would I send my son on this mission?"[10]

There were plenty of allies that Israel had in its campaign against Iran. From its inception in 1949, the Mossad had invested great resources to curry contacts with non-Arab groups in the region. Known as the Periphery Strategy, it at first centered around Turkey and Iran. After

---

* Every Israeli intelligence director has worked to return the body of Eli Cohen, the Mossad's man in Damascus. On May 18, 2025, on the sixtieth anniversary of his execution in Damascus, the State of Israel revealed that a daring Mossad operation in Syria had recovered 2,500 pages of documents and personal effects, virtually the entire archive on Eli Cohen. The material brought back to Israel included handwritten letters from Cohen to his family, photographs, and other materials that Syrian intelligence had assembled. Prime Minister Benjamin Netanyahu and Mossad director David "Dadi" Barnea presented the findings to Cohen's widow, Nadia. At the time of this book's writing, Cohen's remains have yet to be returned to Israel.

THE RACE TO STOP THE BOMB

the Islamic Revolution, when Israel became the Little Satan and Iranian counterintelligence agents suspected everyone of working for the CIA or the Mossad, the focus turned to the multitude of discriminated against minority ethnic groups who had religious and territorial scores to settle with the mullahs in Tehran and would be willing to work directly—or indirectly—for Israel or Israeli agents masquerading as a Western third party. The Turkmen, Baluchis, Azerbaijanis, Zoroastrians, and Kurds held ancient enmity with the Persians and later Iranians.

The forty million highly fractious Kurds were the world's largest stateless ethnic group. They were native to the mountains across southeastern Turkey, northwestern Iran, northern Iraq, and northern Syria—real estate that the Mossad was extremely interested in—and they were fiercely independent and exceptional warriors. Historically mistreated inside the boundaries of every nation they lived in, the Kurds identified with how Israel managed to build a thriving nation surrounded by enemies who wanted its destruction. Many men who would go on to serve as Mossad directors, like Shabtai Shavit, spent time in, according to foreign reports, the agency's spy station in Kurdistan. Dagan visited the Kurdish leaders, including political and military commanders, including Masoud Barzani, to solidify the clandestine working relationship. The Barzani clan, the most powerful and important Kurdish dynasty, had been dealing with Israeli intelligence for over half a century.[11]

In Erbil, the capital of Iraqi Kurdistan, Dagan, like the Mossad directors who had ventured to meet their counterparts in the Kurdish militias, was treated as a head of state. Spy chiefs, especially former generals, were always more respected than the elected heads of state. The Kurds had a reputation for being fierce, loyal, and unbelievably stubborn—the very type of people Dagan loved most.

\*       \*       \*

The Kurds and the Sunni Arabs were essential allies against Iran. Still, if Israel was going to stop Tehran from reaching a nuclear threshold, the Mossad's most important friends were in the West and particularly in the United States.

THE ARCHITECT OF ESPIONAGE

The CIA was a fortress of the blue-blooded elite. It was historically male and Protestant, populated by families of means, who did not display overtly sympathetic feelings toward the Jewish people, let alone the State of Israel and its oil-interrupting fixture in the Middle East. There were a few exceptions: high-ranking CIA officials who valued expanding the cooperation with the Israelis. James Jesus Angleton, the legendary KGB-mole hunter, saw enormous benefit in establishing close intelligence ties with the Jewish state's nascent yet highly effective spy agency; Angleton ran what the Agency called the "Israel account."[12]

CIA director William Casey, appointed by President Ronald Reagan and a veteran of the OSS, America's intelligence arm in the Second World War, admired Mossad's capabilities and believed the Israeli spy agency was a force multiplier for America's global security needs. In 1984, the Mossad and Israeli intelligence assets in Lebanon, including the South Lebanon Liaison unit headed by Dagan, dedicated enormous resources to locating William F. Buckley, the CIA station chief in Beirut, kidnapped and ultimately murdered by Hezbollah.[13]

George J. Tenet, the Queens, New York, son of Greek immigrants, was the sixteenth director of Central Intelligence to deal with Israel and the man who greeted Meir Dagan when he visited Langley for the first time as the head of the Mossad. A graduate of the Georgetown School of Foreign Studies, the CIA director had worked with the administrations of three prime ministers—Netanyahu, Barak, and Sharon—and Mossad directors Yatom and Halevy, and was believed to display a measure of mistrust toward the Mossad, fearing that Israeli intelligence had planted a mole inside the ranks of the Agency.[14]

Meir Dagan and George Tenet should have hit it off, but the two never clicked. Tenet, it was reported, felt that Dagan was playing him, manipulating him for some self-serving goal.[15] "Meir never had the same kind of bond that he would have with other CIA chiefs or other heads of services," a former subordinate commented, "but it never became an impediment to business, it just meant things flowed at a more protracted pace."[16]

The meetings between the two service heads were always cordial and designed to be productive. Dagan admired the American ability to be carefree, a wonderful symptom of the people who lived in a super-power, and that is why the conversation almost always focused on Iran. To contain the Iranian ambitions Dagan spearheaded a multi-pronged approach that involved political pressure, economic warfare, espionage, sabotage, and if necessary, direct action.

Tenet, confirmed unanimously by the U.S. Senate on July 11, 1997, was Clinton's man in Langley, not Bush's.[17] His term had been extended as the Agency recovered from the shock of 9/11. Tenet was capable and a dedicated leader, but the hope at Mossad headquarters was that the man—or woman—that President George W. Bush would appoint would be more understanding of Israel's concerns and show greater operational appreciation of its capabilities.

A nuclear Iran was not solely an Israeli issue: it impacted every pillar of American foreign policy, including the defense of NATO. Dagan, Israel's point man in dealing with Tehran's quest for the bomb, knew that Israel could not stop the Iranians alone. It would need the partnership of the United States, its president, and its intelligence services.

# BOOK FIVE

# SPYMASTER

# The Disruptors

The first light of the new winter's day appeared over the Tel Aviv skyline at 6:36 a.m. It was January 30, 2005, a Sunday and the start of the Israeli workweek, and Meir Dagan had been at his desk before the first rays of sun spanned its light over the Mediterranean shoreline. His driver and security detail routinely collected him from his Tel Aviv high-rise while the city that never slept was deep in slumber. He always appeared energetic when entering his protected vehicle, even though his guard and driver did all they could to keep from yawning. Dagan was mission-driven, and it propelled him.

Meir Dagan turned sixty that day. The birthday was a milestone for anyone, but for a man who had spent so much of his life under fire, the special day was indeed a landmark achievement. A retired general should have been relishing his birthday with family, surrounded by grandchildren, enjoying a quieter time in the golden twilight of life, working as an incredibly well-paid CEO for a defense firm, raking in an impressive high-six-figure salary in the private sector, and thinking as much about his art studio and grandchildren as he did about the next board meeting. But he was at his desk, nursing black tea in a glass cup as the Russians drank it, and smoking his pipe while reviewing breaking intelligence from around the region. Early that morning, a British Royal Air Force C-130K Hercules transport had been shot down by Sunni insurgents over Baghdad, killing all ten soldiers on board, and there were rumblings across the entire Middle East in the two months since Yasir Arafat died of a mysterious illness in Paris. Dagan somehow managed to find the time to share some cake in his office with well-wishers. He celebrated the latter part of the day with the King of Jordan.

There were days, though, when Dagan never went home. Late-night meetings turned into secure calls with time zones seven hours behind and five hours ahead. Aides sometimes found him at work at his desk at three in the morning reading pages, making notes, and humming Russian folk tunes that had been coopted into Hebrew; he was transfixed by classical music, and the rousing hymns of the Soviet Army from the Second World War, his daughter Noa reflected years later at a memorial for her father.[1] He would grab a few hours of shut-eye on his office sofa. Soldiers were masters at turning any flat surface into a suitable bed. He was still a tank officer at heart, or at least that was how he viewed himself.

Dagan did not expect his staffers to work the same hours he did, but many chose to follow the boss's lead. He was harder on himself than he was on those who worked for him. He felt the job was too important to surrender to such human frailties as exhaustion, and nothing, not the pains his battered body felt, or calls from family and friends to slow down, would convince him otherwise. The way he saw the world, there were not enough hours in the day, and it was his job to catch up against the clock. He was too old and far too stubborn to change his ways.

Many of those who worked closely with Dagan during his first years on the job, the division chiefs and senior staff members, thought that he was a terrible director. "He was all over the place," one former division chief commented, "he came in like an elephant and did not realize he was in a store selling the finest Czech crystal."[2] "He tried to change the world overnight when such high aspirations usually take forever," another added.[3] But he learned on the job, admitted where his style faltered, and did whatever it took to be the successful head of an espionage agency.

It took a few years, but Dagan became a force to be reckoned with inside the Security Cabinet—a forum created by law in 1999 to outline and implement diplomatic and national security policies. The Security Cabinet consisted of the prime minister, defense minister, foreign minister, justice minister, finance minister, and internal security minister. The three intelligence chiefs, the IDF chief of staff, and other generals and officials were often invited to address the group. Dagan, because of his personality and closeness to Prime Minister Sharon, at first appeared cocky to some, even to those who knew him. But he matured. Dagan streamlined his act. He honed his passions and strategic outlook and became a sought-after consigliere for Israel's leaders and others. High-level visitors to the Jewish state wanted to meet with Dagan more than the prime minister. Guests from the Arab world and beyond wanted to hear his opinion on matters besides espionage and tradecraft. His guests did not want to leave the office;[4] fifteen-minute meetings stretched into an hour. The delays shipwrecked his calendar.

*          *          *

The back-and-forth inside the Security Cabinet and the work of the heads of the three intelligence services during those first few years were driven by the Global War on Terror and, particularly, Israel's specific battlefield in it: the second intifada. The Palestinian campaign even took on a transnational component, when, at shortly before 1:00 a.m. on the morning of April 30, 2003, two British nationals of Pakistani descent with open sympathies to al-Qaeda[5] carried out the suicide bombing of Mike's Place, a pub on the Tel Aviv beach promenade, adjacent to the U.S. Embassy and popular with Americans and Anglos. Hamas and Arafat's al-Aqsa Martyrs Brigade had masterminded the suicide strike.

The second intifada consumed Prime Minister Sharon's years in office. The number of counterterrorist operations brought before his desk for approval—the targeted killings, the arrest raids inside sensitive locations such as mosques, and other executions of tradecraft carried out far from Israel's borders—was numbing. There were high-profile targeted killings of Hamas officials, including its leader, Sheikh Ahmed Yasin, who was freed from prison in 1997 in the prisoner swap that followed the Mossad's failed assassination of Khaled Meshal in Amman. Yassin, confined to a wheelchair, was hit by Hellfire antitank missiles fired by IAF AH-64 Apache helicopter gunships as he departed a mosque in Gaza City after morning prayers on March 22, 2004.[6]

Counterterrorist and undercover special forces units carried out nightly operations against Palestinian terror targets throughout the West Bank and the Gaza Strip; Hamas began to dig tunnels for the smuggling of weapons and for offensive use along the frontier with Egypt near the city of Rafah. The attacks, though, continued. Israelis were killed in catastrophic attacks inside the country. Dagan was convinced that it was time to put his pet project, covert financial warfare, to the test.

Dagan understood that money was a lethal weapon for terrorists and that defeating it could be achieved bloodlessly, behind the scenes, and in a way that would be digestible to the media, because Israel needed endless validation of its self-defense actions in the courts of international public opinion. When, thirty-plus years earlier, Dagan had engineered a new brand of warfare in Gaza, undercover operations were designed to unmoor the terrorists, make them feel unsafe in locations where they were the masters. Following and drying up the bloodstained millions that enabled Israel's terrorist foes to kill not only unnerved the men behind the attacks but also humiliated them. Without cash or access to Islamic means of moving money underneath the established financial radars, terror chieftains could not rent safe houses, hire bomb building engineers, or pay salaries.

Following the money that terrorists used to endanger Israeli national security and trying to destroy it was the specific reason Dagan brought Tziltzal, his pet project, into the Mossad Order of Battle. The task force had worked with police entities, counterintelligence services, and tax authorities across the globe. They could talk to everyone, because they were an asterisk—not confined to any specific jurisdiction—and a footnote to larger enterprises, ensuring national security. Tziltzal was small, but its numbers were also deviously inclined and possessed a mindset like Dagan's that killing an enemy did not necessarily have to involve putting an explosive device under a car seat. Members of Dagan's team often wondered if 9/11 would have happened if the radical zealots recruited by Khaled Sheikh Mohammed for Bin Laden had not been able to pay for travel and flight training. "If you took away the dollars and dinars made available to the terrorists," a former member of Israeli intelligence commented, "they'd only be disgruntled men with hate in their hearts, only wishing they had the cash or credit to kill you, and we aren't in the business of winning hearts and minds."[7]

There were basic ways that the terrorists financed their operations that involved Islamic charities, Islamic money transfers called *Hawala*, and even something as simple as IOUs. There were ingenious ways that mercantile activity was camouflaged into money laundering, including the use of goods bought and sold through China, and even skimming profits from the sales of weapons and drugs. The destination for most of the money was the Middle East's complex banking networks and their branches inside Gaza and the West Bank, handled by men who possessed the encrypted account numbers.

The West Bank and Gaza were outside Mossad's jurisdictional responsibility, but that was irrelevant to Dagan. He spearheaded efforts for the army and police to join in on his follow-the-money crusade.

On February 25, 2004, Tziltzal spearheaded a large-scale operation in Ramallah targeting banks that held terror accounts. The operation, code-named Green Lantern, involved hundreds of Israeli counterterrorist policemen, IDF special operations commandos, and Shin Bet agents.[8] The Arab Bank branch in Ramallah was targeted, as were several branches of the Cairo-Amman Bank. The Jordan-based Arab Bank was of particular interest to Dagan and Tziltzal. Abdul Majid Shoman, the son of the Arab Bank's founder, was Arafat's private wealth manager and handled all the Palestinian Authority's investments and vast holdings, much of it skimmed from benevolent aid emanating from the United States and the European Union. He was a Palestinian nationalist and religious, and even took a tax from the salaries of bank employees, 5 percent of their monthly wages, that he called the "Support the al-Aqsa Intifada Fee."[9] The bank held accounts belonging to Hamas-affiliated terror cells responsible for the suicide attacks across Israel; 177 Israelis had been murdered in 2003 alone.

Green Lantern netted forty million shekels* of cash that Tziltzal and the security services claimed emanated from Iran, Lebanon, and Syria— millions of dollars in cash and an intimate glimpse of the secretive world of money transfers, offshore accounts, and how Hamas moved money around. The money in the accounts went to the acquisition of weapons, explosive materials, safe houses, getaway cars, and forged IDs, which cost money, but also to pay bomb builders and cell commanders, who earned salaries, and the families of terrorists killed or incarcerated, who received monthly stipends. Before Dagan became Mossad director, Tziltzal had worked closely with the U.S. Department of the Treasury to combat terror financing; Dagan was a regular at the U.S. Department of Justice, allying with like-minded agencies fighting a common struggle, even before 9/11. But Operation Green Lantern outraged the Americans, especially President George W. Bush. Reportedly, he was livid that the Israelis had lowered themselves to become bank robbers. U.S. ambassador to Israel Daniel C. Kurtzer likened the operation to something John Dillinger would have done.[10]

Prime Minister Sharon and Foreign Minister Silvan Shalom dealt with the American blowback. Sharon could not claim ignorance as a defense against Bush's ire, because he had, after all, approved of the operation. Dagan thought that the furor was laughable. He had engineered the raid of the West Bank financial institutions because, as Willie Sutton once reflected, "that's where the money was."[11]

Green Lantern reaped enormous intelligence dividends. The material obtained was used operationally by the Shin Bet and the IDF, overseas by the Mossad, and even in U.S. federal courts, by attorneys and NGOs that Tziltzal had conveniently enlisted in the fight against terror financing. U.S. law allowed American citizens[12] to sue terror groups and the nations that financed them for damages in court.† The legal cases involved evidence that Tziltzal provided to the plaintiff's attorneys and

---

* Approximately $10 million.

† Numerous lawsuits would be filed against the Arab Bank by American citizens harmed during the second intifada. In August 2015, the Arab Bank reached a confidential settlement with 597 victims or relatives of victims in twenty-two of the attacks.

received widespread media attention in the United States and the Middle East, precisely what Dagan wanted.

Mossad security officials urged the director not to disseminate the material in the public domain, but Dagan wanted everyone, media and decision-makers worldwide, to learn of the bank accounts, corresponding American banks, and the sheer volume of transfers that racesd across deserts and oceans to purchase AK-47s, buy explosive materials, or pay the families of suicide bombers who killed civilians. Tziltzal became that megaphone. Following the money and separating it from the terror chieftains was not as sexy as other aspects of espionage work, but it was effective.

*          *          *

Four plus years into the second intifada, Prime Minister Sharon understood that Israel did not have a Palestinian partner for peace. Terror groups that worked under the command of Yasir Arafat's Palestinian Authority and his Fatah political and military umbrella were full-fledged perpetrators in the carnage witnessed on the streets of Israel. Sharon also realized that Israel faced two choices when dealing with the uprising and the territories ceded to the Palestinian Authority in the Oslo Accords: annexation or separation. Much to the horror of the right flank of his party, the prime minister opted for separation.

Gaza was the center of the Israeli plan, and the fighting there focused on the protection of the Israeli citizens who lived in twenty-one settlements established after the June 1967 war and stopping the smuggling of arms and money under the border with Egypt in tunnels. Sharon saw little strategic value in holding the area any longer. In the summer of 2005, Israeli police and military forces removed nine thousand settlers from their homes. The forced evacuation, dubbed Operation *Yad Le'Achim*, or "Give the Brothers a Hand," was viewed by his Likud Party as the ultimate betrayal. On September 11, 2005, the last Israeli soldiers departed the Gaza Strip. The conscripts locked the gates to the frontier crossing under a brutal autumn sun. The combatants hoped and prayed they would never have to return. The young men, weary veterans by the time they reached their twentieth birthday, would be forced to return nine years later as reservists.

Two weeks after the withdrawal, rebels within the Likud, led by former prime minister Benjamin Netanyahu, attempted to oust Sharon as its leader. He barely survived the motion. Reading the writing on the wall, Sharon resigned as the head of the Likud, dissolved the Knesset, and created a new centrist-right political party known as *Kadima*, Hebrew for forward. Elections were called. Sharon was determined to retain the prime ministership with a Kadima-led coalition.

But the seventy-seven-year-old Sharon was not a healthy man. Morbidly obese and faced with the stress of internal Israeli politics and leading a nation at war with the Palestinians, the prime minister suffered a debilitating hemorrhagic stroke on January 4, 2006. Surgeons saved his life, but he was placed in a medically induced coma and remained in a vegetative state until his death eight years later.[13] Meir Dagan was at his desk at dawn on January 5, 2006. Upheaval and uncertainty could invite Israel's enemies to start trouble, and the Mossad needed to be on a war footing. His pipe was already lit when staffers entered the office. He did not let the others see him saddened or preoccupied by what had happened to Sharon or the possible crisis that Israel would face. Connected to machines was no way for a warrior to live, Dagan thought; it was not how a man like Sharon, for all his pluses and minuses, would have wanted to part this world.

# Meirke

P olitics was in Ehud Olmert's DNA. His father had served in the Knesset as a member of the right-wing Herut Party founded by Menachem Begin. He was conscripted as an infantryman, but a nagging injury prevented him from completing basic training. He became a military journalist for the army newspaper and, as a reservist during the Yom Kippur War, was attached to Major General Ariel Sharon's headquarters, launching a thirty-year friendship with the future prime minister. Olmert was already a member of the Knesset himself, having been elected to the parliament before the outbreak of the fighting in 1973. He advanced quickly up the rungs of the Likud hierarchy and was even appointed a minister without portfolio in the government of Yitzhak Shamir.

When the Likud was voted out of power in 1992, Olmert ditched national politics for a while and ran to be the mayor of Jerusalem. The city was a trip wire of faith and religious ownership—a volatile intersection of the world's three monotheistic religions, which made it, at least on paper, impossible to govern. Olmert was the first Likud candidate to win the city's mayoral election. He served two terms before returning to the Knesset as a senior member of the Likud.

Olmert remained loyal to Ariel Sharon when Kadima was formed and became the party's number two. Following Sharon's incapacitation,

Olmert became acting prime minister. Kadima won twenty-nine seats in the 2006 elections, making it the country's largest party. Two months later, after successfully forming a coalition government, Ehud Olmert was sworn in as Israel's twelfth prime minister in an election where less than 65 percent of the country's eligible voters bothered to go to the polls.

*          *          *

Meir Dagan was midway into the final year of his four-year term when Olmert began his term as prime minister. The two men could not have been more different: Olmert, the party apparatchik and political insider with a hint of blue blood in him, and Dagan, the perennial outsider and career soldier. Olmert was polished, a true politician, who measured the benefits and blowback of every word he shared. Dagan was still rough around the edges when it came to the trappings of higher office. But the two men meshed beyond most expectations. Olmert had seen Dagan in action inside the closed-door sessions of the Security Cabinet when the most important matters of the day were covered. The Mossad chief was always direct and laced every topic with strategic insight. He was thought-provoking with the ministers rather than confrontational. Most importantly, as far as Olmert saw it, "there was nothing bullshit about him."[1]

Shortly after taking office, Olmert met with his Mossad director to discuss the pressing matters of the day, and the template of their working relationship was established. "I told Meir that I want him to tell me the truth, not what he thinks I wanted to hear, otherwise I couldn't trust him," Olmert recalled. "I also told him that any failures will be mine, and all the successes would belong solely to the Mossad."[2]

Olmert did not have a military background or the institutional experience of dealing with the high-pressure stakes of combat, but he had an uncanny grasp of what it took to lead an organization like the Mossad. As Tamir Pardo, Dagan's deputy and a future head of the Mossad, once described the essence of the director's job, "The head of the Mossad conducts a huge philharmonic orchestra, with most of the musicians being soloists, talented soloists, each of whom can perform alone on stage. But to achieve a result, you must take the group and organize it as an orchestra that knows how to play at the right pace, when to enter and exit, and when to stop."³

Olmert oversaw an intelligence service dream team. Shin Bet director Yuval Diskin, who replaced Avi Dichter before the pullout from Gaza in May 2005, was considered a gifted espionage chief. The head of A'man, Major General Amos Yadlin, was a decorated F-16 pilot and one of the eight airmen in the entire IAF handpicked to take out the Iraqi nuclear reactor in 1981. But Dagan was his favorite. Inside the prime minister's office, the intelligence chiefs were never referred to by their given names but rather by their titles. It was a sign of respect. Olmert, though, showed genuine affection toward Dagan. He called him "Meirke," a nickname of reverence and pure admiration.

On May 23, 2006, shortly after forming his government, Olmert traveled to the American capital to meet with President George W. Bush. A visit to the White House was mandatory for Israeli prime ministers—a pilgrimage to secure and safeguard the strategic alliance between the two nations. Negotiations with the Palestinian Authority always topped the public agenda; American presidents from Carter to Bush always felt compelled to be *the* leader of the free world to cement a once-and-for-all deal ending the Arab-Israeli divide, though none had ever been successful. There were signs of promise that accompanied Olmert's visit to 1600 Pennsylvania Avenue: the unilateral Israeli withdrawal from Gaza and a sense that the second intifada was slowly coming to an end.

Olmert, like Sharon before him, was convinced that Iran sought the bomb and that the Islamic Republic would stop at nothing to become a nuclear power. Ostensibly, both leaders were on the same page. "The prime minister and I shared our concerns about the Iranian regime's nuclear weapons ambitions," Bush told reporters with Olmert at his side. "The United States and the international community have made our common position clear: We're determined that the Iranian regime must not gain nuclear weapons."⁴

Olmert brought Dagan with him to emphasize to the White House the sense of urgency and that Israel's strategy moving forward would be no-nonsense, built around an aggressive intelligence service campaign to thwart Tehran's ambitions.

Meir Dagan was not a stranger to meeting world leaders, though sitting down with the president of the United States was different. Dagan had been kept out of view during the photo op session and the press conference following Olmert's one-on-one with Bush, working in the West Wing with his counterparts and being far from the telephoto lenses of the White House Press Corps.

Bush had a folksy way about him, a disarming familiarity that camouflaged his privileged upbringing in what can be best described as American royalty. He called everyone "Buddy." But Dagan also had the natural ability to engage whomever he met with an inherent extra helping of charm. He was naturally likeable, reachable, and downright unpretentious. President Bush, a Dagan deputy remembered, was particularly enamored of the Mossad director's uninhibited everyman ability, endearing himself with an off-color joke, something he was famous for, and always asking questions before suggesting solutions. Mostly, though, Bush found it remarkable how Dagan would always use the word *Dvash*, Hebrew for honey, when describing how sweet life was. That was enlightening to a man of faith like the president.[5]

Decision-makers who sat across from Dagan him were impressed by his knowledge and appreciated him doing his homework. His military background was an added plus to men outside Israel. "President Bush liked to be surrounded by military men and war heroes," Olmert reflected, "and Dagan impressed him."[6] Another general who impressed President Bush was Michael Hayden. Two weeks before Olmert arrived in Washington, Bush nominated Hayden as the next director of Central Intelligence.* Hayden had almost forty years of intelligence experience in the U.S. Air Force and, later, at the National Security Agency. His specialty was covert information acquisition; most of his career was in the Air Force Intelligence, Surveillance, and Reconnaissance Agency.[7]

Dagan and Hayden would become close. Their friendship would change the paradigm of how the CIA and Mossad worked together. An intelligence relationship that had endured its ups and downs became a full-fledged operational partnership. The alliance came at a critical time.

* Porter Gross, who replaced George Tenet, resigned on May 5, 2006.

\*            \*            \*

The tank crew from the 188th Armored Brigade's 71st Battalion stationed along the Gaza frontier, near the Kerem Shalom Border Crossing, did not hear the entrenching tools digging underground 330 feet from the barbed wire barriers of the frontier fence, at 5:00 a.m. on the morning of June 25, 2006. They did not hear the seven men whispering in Arabic; neither did the Bedouin soldiers from the IDF's Desert Reconnaissance Battalion manning their positions at a nearby observation post. The sun was thirty minutes from emerging over the eastern horizon, and it was hard to stay alert after a night of guard duty. The whizzing of incoming mortar shells shattered the silence, as did seven men in camouflage fatigues and green Hamas bandanas emerging from a small opening in the ground and charging the tank and the OP. The Merkava tank's commander and loader were killed in the assault; the driver was seriously wounded. The gunner, a lanky nineteen-year-old corporal named Gilad Shalit, was injured in the attack, dragged into the attack tunnel, and taken into captivity in Gaza.

Hostages seized by terrorists involved the Mossad. News reached Meir Dagan later that morning. It was Sunday, the first day of the workweek, and he was at his desk. The news infuriated him. The 188th was his old outfit. The following day, Hamas acknowledged that it was holding the young corporal hostage. A team was assembled at headquarters to assess options and engage Mossad's international partners, primarily the Egyptians and the Germans, to start the stuttered dialogue that would bring the soldier home.

The Shalit kidnapping was a dry run—a harbinger of much worse to come.

On June 29, the foreign ministers from the G8\* nations met in Moscow—a preparatory session of diplomacy, cocktails, and review of topics that would be discussed at the thirty-second such summit, slated to begin in St. Petersburg on July 15. This was Russia's first chance to host

---

\* The G8 nations included Canada, France, Germany, Italy, Japan, Russia, the United Kingdom, and the United States. Russia permanently left the G8 in 2017.

the grand meeting of the world's foremost industrialized democracies, even though its admission to the group was something of an anomaly, considering it was not a democracy and lacked the national wealth and industrial weight of the other members. President Putin planned a lavish event filled with pomp and ceremony as a show of Russia's new global prominence. But Iran's nuclear issue was high on the G8 agenda—President Bush and the Europeans were concerned that the economic sanctions were not quite harsh enough to sway the Grand Ayatollah Sayyid Ali Khamenei and his generals at the Islamic Revolutionary Guard Corps from building an atomic arsenal. A diversion was called for; it helped to have proxies on standby.

At 9:00 a.m. on the morning of July 12, 2006, Hezbollah artillery batteries in southern Lebanon launched a fusillade of Katyusha 122mm rockets at Israeli positions in northern Israel. The unprovoked barrage was a ruse. Members of Hezbollah's commando entity, the Radwan Force, were lying in ambush on the Israeli side of the border. Their mission was to attack an Israeli patrol, kill as many as they could hit, and then seize soldiers, dead or alive, to be held for ransom. The mission, conceived by Imad Mughniyeh, the arch terrorist responsible for blowing up two American embassies and the Marine Corps barracks in Beirut twenty years earlier, had been enthusiastically approved by the group's leader, Sheikh Hassan Nasrallah.

Two IDF HUMVEEs (high mobility multipurpose wheeled vehicles) were hit by antitank fire as they approached Signpost 105 along the frontier. The vehicles, manned by reservists, were sitting ducks. Three Israeli soldiers were killed in the attack, and two—Sergeant Ehud Goldwasser and Sergeant Eldad Regev—were mortally wounded. Their badly battered bodies were dragged back across the border into Lebanon. Five Israeli soldiers were killed in battles to prevent the Radwan attackers from disappearing into the south Lebanon countryside with their ghoulish trophies. Full-scale combat erupted hours later. The Second Lebanon War was underway.

Of the men who rushed to the Defense Ministry in Tel Aviv to attend an urgent convening of the Security Cabinet in the prime minister's satellite office, Meir Dagan was one of the few who had ground experience in Lebanon. Olmert was not a career military man and had no experience leading a nation that suddenly found itself at war. The defense minister, Amir Peretz, was a labor unionist, who had been named to the post solely as a reward for bringing his Labor Party into Olmert's coalition; he had been an ordnance officer in the paratroop brigade, but was not a frontline combat leader and had no experience in managing a behemoth like the Israeli military. IDF chief of staff Lieutenant General Dan Halutz was an air force officer, a veteran F-4E Phantom pilot, with no ground combat experience. The IDF, coming off six incessant years of campaigns against Palestinian terrorists in the second intifada, was worn thin and exhausted; supply stores were depleted and neglected. The army was not prepared for another conflict. Neither were the intelligence branches. Neither the Mossad nor A'man had had any inkling that Hezbollah was preparing for a major incursion. The Mossad's counterparts in the United States, Europe, and the Arab world had also been blindsided. Imad Mughniyah's file was pulled. It was always active.

The Security Cabinet's initial fear was that Hezbollah would transport the kidnapped Israeli soldiers out of the country, like Ron Arad, never to be heard from again. Prime Minister Olmert authorized immediate Israeli airstrikes: IAF F-16s cratering the runway at Beirut International Airport. The Beirut-Damascus Highway, the lifeblood of vehicular traffic between Lebanon and Syria, was also targeted with sustained IAF aerial bombardment. The IDF mobilized its reservists, and the citizens of northern Israel scampered to their fallout shelters as thousands of Hezbollah rockets were fired into Galilee. Israel was once again at war, and the Mossad now had three hostages that it had to locate and negotiate for. No one in Dagan's headquarters knew if the captives were dead or alive.

*        *        *

The conflict, known as the Second Lebanon War, became a quagmire for both Hezbollah and Israel. In 1982, it took the IDF a week to reach the outskirts of Beirut. In 2006, Israeli forces faced great adversity and significant casualties in advancing a few dozen miles. Hezbollah—and Iran—had spent years preparing for a ground war with Israel. The Shiite Party of God fielded the most disciplined, combat-ready, and well-equipped military force in the Arab world. Its fighters were fanatics, believers in martyrdom, but they were also expertly trained, tactically superb, and fierce combatants; they were also armed with the latest communications gear and man-carried antitank missiles, capable of inflicting enormous damage on advancing Israeli forces.

The ground campaign became a slugfest and a meat grinder where every inch of territory was paid for in blood. Hezbollah did not have an air force, but it boasted a sizeable missile force that was used with great effectiveness against Israeli civilian population centers across the northern third of the country. Ballistic missiles were even fired into Haifa, Israel's third-largest city. Tens of thousands of Israeli civilians living in Galilee and the northern reaches fled their homes. Those who stayed were sequestered inside bomb shelters. Some agricultural communities, especially among the Israeli Arab community, had no structural protection where it was safe to sit out the missile onslaughts. Shin Bet director Yuval Diskin was quoted as telling a closed cabinet security forum that "government systems in northern Israel had completely collapsed during the rocket attacks." The cost of rebuilding the damage inflicted by four thousand rocket and missile strikes was estimated at over two billion dollars.[8]

Throughout the war, inside the Defense Ministry, or the Aquarium in Jerusalem, the men who led Israel's military and intelligence services argued with cabinet ministers and other politicians and military officers about how to prosecute the war against Hezbollah. Meir Dagan sat in the Security Cabinet and tried to reason with Defense Minister Peretz and Chief of Staff Halutz that an effective way to expedite an end to the fighting and deal Hezbollah a decisive blow was to target the network of banking institutions that enabled the terror group to pay salaries, receive wire transfers, and buy weapons and explosives. In fifty-eight years of constant wars with its neighbors, Israel had never bombed an Arab bank from the air. The IAF did not have those targets in its files, but the Mossad did.

Meir Dagan did not differentiate between a terror chieftain planning an attack and his banker, who facilitated the means to perpetrate mass murder. Both men posed a threat to the country. Tziltzal's intelligence officers identified a series of financial institutions that Dagan argued before the Security Cabinet needed to be hit immediately. They included the Beit al-Mal, Hezbollah's unofficial treasury office with branches across the country; branches of Albaraka and Fransabank throughout Beirut and Lebanon's largest cities; and the MEAB, or Middle East Africa Bank, a key laundering entity in Hezbollah's global empire of Iranian money and profits earned from more creative sources, such as counterfeiting and narco-trafficking.* Other financial centers populated Dagan's bank of suggested targets. Some worked with corresponding American banks. Any large-scale Israeli military operation targeting Lebanese banks, especially those that did business in the United States, risked the anger of President George W. Bush, who did not like it when Israel engaged in, as one former CIA officer claimed, "Middle Eastern Jesse James bullshit!"⁹ As it was, President Bush, overextended with campaigns in Iraq and Afghanistan, had to divert the Sixth Fleet to Lebanon so that U.S. Marines could evacuate American citizens from the war-torn country, and he did not want additional headaches from the allies in Israel.

The IDF wanted to focus solely on military targets: command and control facilities, rocket launchers, missile silos, and fortified positions. Olmert wanted to hit Hezbollah's ability to rain an indiscriminate missile blitz on Israel's cities; the damage and death from such attacks were significant. Dagan was often so exacerbated by the generals and ministers not listening to his argument that if Hezbollah lost its ability to pay the salaries of its fighters or rebuild Shiite homes damaged in

---

* Hezbollah was classified by the U.S. Drug Enforcement Administration as one of the world's largest and most dangerous drug cartels, moving South American cocaine money from Venezuela to Damascus and then on to Beirut for dissemination around Europe and Asia. The Shiite Party of God also made millions in cigarette smuggling in the United States, placing its operatives in the crosshairs of criminal investigations by the Bureau of Alcohol, Tobacco, and Firearms, along with other federal law enforcement agencies.

the combat, Sheikh Nasrallah would be forced to end the fighting, that he would yell inside the behind-closed-door session.

It took two weeks for Dagan to convince the prime minister, who had to authorize the air strikes, to hit the banks. But Dagan's relentless campaign ultimately paid off. "Dagan had no intention of stopping until he got his way," a former deputy head of Tziltzal explained. "He was very persuasive when he knew everyone else was wrong."[10]

On July 25, two weeks into the fighting, IAF F-16 and F-15 squadrons received their targets from headquarters. The young pilots and the older reservists assembled at the preflight briefings received instructions to obliterate their objectives but pinpoint and minimize collateral damage. To prevent innocent civilians from being hurt, the IAF dropped leaflets warning bank employees that a strike was imminent; IAF commanders surmised that a fifteen-minute heads-up would give anyone inside the chance to flee, but that the time frame was too short for Hezbollah operatives to remove the cash or back up their computers. By the time, the F-15s and F-16s returned to their bases across Israel, over a hundred million dollars in various currencies had been incinerated.[11] The images of smoldering bills flying around city centers across Lebanon were sur-real. The strikes permanently damaged Hezbollah's reputation that they were the only force in the country that could protect the interests—and life savings—of the Lebanese people.

With the runways at Beirut International Airport rendered inoper-able by Israeli bombs, and Israeli special operations units ambushing vehicles all along the road routes connecting Lebanon and Syria, Iran could not replenish the cash Hezbollah lost in the bombing of the banks. Sheikh Nasrallah's legions did not operate on American Express. "We know that they are looking for money," Brigadier General Dani Arditi, Olmert's counterterrorism advisor and an old friend of Dagan, told NBC News. "They are very desperate to have some cash and [now] they don't have it."[12]

Hezbollah's commanders maintained their zeal and desire to kill Israelis; they just did not have the loose cash needed to pay the salaries of the men on the front lines. Two weeks after the banks were hit, Hez-bollah sued for a ceasefire. Dagan had been vindicated. His directives helped shorten a war and save the lives of young men at the front and civilians in their homes. He did not dare to light his pipe inside the prime minister's office or any of the Security Cabinet get-togethers as a gleeful gesture of "I told you so"; that was beneath the office. And it was unnecessary. The prime minister realized Dagan had been correct all along.

And Hezbollah's hierarchy realized that it had made a fatal mistake in launching the war. "We did not think, even one percent, that the capture would lead to a war at this time and of this magnitude," Nasrallah told Lebanon's New TV channel. "If I had known on July 11 that the operation would lead to such a war, would I do it? I say no, absolutely not."[13]

Nasrallah would never see daylight again. He lived in bunkers, some as deep as 330 feet below ground, throughout south Beirut, the notorious Dahya section of the city, where Shiite clerics and Hezbollah officers lived. He knew that Israel—and especially its intelligence services— would never forgive him for the unnecessary carnage of 2006 and would one day find an opportune moment to prevent him from continuing a war against the Jewish state and the West at the behest of his paymasters in Tehran, and to convince his successor that continuing and escalating the hostilities would come at an enormous cost.

# The Other Sons of Abraham

During the months that followed the end of the fighting in Lebanon, Dagan and the head of Tevel traveled east to the United Arab Emirates. The oil-rich nation assembled from seven smaller semi-independent emirates had built a peaceful hodgepodge of unimaginable wealth and tranquility in the violent seas of the Arabian desert. Dubai, a city of Metropolis-size dreams and steel towers, was its flagship—a billboard to the world that Arab money did not have to translate into fundamentalist terror. Dubai was a global vacation magnet, a landing spot for European expatriates, their money, and their Western lifestyles. Dubai International Airport, known by its code of DXB, sported a mall where travelers connecting to their flights could purchase a Lamborghini. Emirates, the local airline, became one of the largest in the world and even sponsored soccer teams for millions of dollars in the United Kingdom and Europe. Sheikh Mohammed bin Rashid al-Maktoum, the country's prime minister, was a man guided by a billionaire's pragmatism that it would be a sin to allow the Iranian desire to expand its Shiite Crescent into the playground of the rich and famous.

Initial formal contact between the Mossad and the UAE's two security services, the Signals Intelligence Agency and the State Security Department, was made in 2005 while Sharon was still prime minister. It was crucial to Israel's strategy to muster into a cooperative bloc the Sunni states who viewed Tehran as a dangerous nuisance. A more serious effort was made in 2006 after the Second Lebanon War, when Dagan visited Dubai and Abu Dhabi to forge an operational espionage connection between the two countries.[1] Dagan arranged to open a small satellite office in the UAE to promote Israeli medical and defense products and a convenient way to foster Israeli and Emirati regional strategic thinking to form a common front against Iran.[2]

David Meidan, the Egyptian-born head of Tevel, was Dagan's frequent travel partner on trips across the Middle East. "We used to sit in a car for hours on end, driving through the desert, moving about under the radar, just us two, relying on maps and sometimes landmarks and the occasional road sign. Meir loved to talk about history, art, and subjects that were not part of what an intelligence chief should focus on, but he enjoyed knowing 'something' about 'everything.'"[3]

One time, Meidan would recall in a memorial to Dagan a year following his death, "we were driving in the desert, one of these endless drives *somewhere* in the region where I cannot mention, and I had to go and relieve myself. I knew enough about my travel partner not to leave the vehicle without my passport and money. As I ventured behind a rock, I heard the engine being gunned, and the car disappearing into a cloud of smoke and dust. That was Meir. A few minutes later he returned, smiling, and asking, 'You didn't think I'd leave you here, did you?'"[4]

According to reports, Dagan visited Oman, Kuwait, and other nations where there was mutual interest. Dagan, though, was always suspicious of the Qataris. The tiny but über-wealthy Persian Gulf emirate masqueraded itself as a forward-thinking pro-Western nation seeking peace in the Middle East. Dagan saw through them, identifying the country and its pro–Muslim Brotherhood leaders as the "real problem" in their attempts to placate everyone. Dagan even suggested to his counterparts in the United States that they would be better served if the Pentagon removed its bases from Qatar.[5]

The key to Mossad's outreach in the Arab world, especially against Iran, was the Kingdom of Saudi Arabia.[6] The Saudis were a critical, albeit behind the scenes, component in the creation of a Jewish-Sunni alliance to stem the nuclear aspirations of the Supreme Leader in Tehran and his roundtable of national security insiders, spy chiefs, and IRGC commanders who ran the Islamic Republic and profited from the chaos it caused.

According to published accounts, official face-to-face contact was made between Meir Dagan and the Saudis after the Second Lebanon War.[7] The Saudis always felt a sense of ownership in Lebanon: protectors of the Sunnis, business partners with the Christians, and employers of the Shiites. In the heyday of the Middle East when only conventional armies fought wars, Lebanon was a Saudi playground, a mooring dock for their yachts before pushing west toward Monte Carlo. The destruction that Iran and Hezbollah had brought upon the country for a senseless act of abduction terrified them, and the royal family feared it was a harbinger of what the rest of the region faced. The kingdom let it be known, through espionage circles, that it supported Israel's war against Hezbollah, a carefully worded message that it supported the defeat of one of Iran's proxy armies.[8]

The meeting was held in Amman, secured by Jordanian intelligence, and under the auspices of the king. On September 13, 2006, Prime Minister Olmert and Mossad director Dagan flew to the Jordanian capital to meet Prince Bandar bin Sultan al-Saud, a member of the royal family, the secretary general of the National Security Council, and, for over twenty years, the Saudi ambassador in Washington during the administration of four American presidents. He was so close to the Bush family, George H. W. and George W., that his nickname in Beltway circles was "Baby Bush." It is suspected that this was not the first meeting between Dagan and his Saudi counterparts. Secret talks at the intelligence service level were reported to have transpired in Europe and the United States.

Prince Bandar bin Sultan al-Saud became the Saudi point man for covert discussions with Israeli intelligence.[9] He was rare among the Saudis, especially only five years after fifteen of his countrymen had been among the nineteen 9/11 hijackers, in that he embodied pragmatic moderation. He was as comfortable playing hardball with a senator as he appeared while talking to Larry King on CNN. Bandar understood the American mindset and its political layers so well that it was joked that he spent more time in the halls of Congress than most elected representatives. He was also a darling of the defense establishment—arms sales to the kingdom were good business. Bandar was a player and a skilled politician—two factors needed when handling a secret relationship. He also had the full support of King Fahd bin Abdulaziz Al Saud.

The details of the talks in Amman are secret, though Iran was most likely the primary topic discussed. Reports indicate that the Israelis wanted overflight freedom should the decision be made to remove Iran's nuclear sites militarily; this is not confirmed.[10]

The Saudis were technically at war with Israel, but this was a trivial detail for two nations living in a region besieged by fundamentalist forces and threatened by emboldened Shiite armies on the march in Iraq. The Middle East was built on a foundation of marriages of tribal convenience used for temporary fixes. The trips were so secret that the flight paths flown were circuitous, often involving changing planes in third countries to throw off any surveillance and security breaches.*

A former U.S. State Department special agent who served in the Middle East once commented that in Arab eyes, it was less important *who* you were but rather the *size* of your protective detail. Gunslingers depicted power and prestige. Dagan was the exception to that rule. When he flew to target nations at the invitation of the ruler of a country like the Kingdom of Saudi Arabia, he traveled light, his detail confident in the armor of secrecy and discretion. There was honor among the spy chiefs. The safety of a guest, especially a secret one of such unrivaled importance, was a sacred pledge. "Dagan did not travel with an army of personal protection specialists when he visited countries that officially, at least, were hostile to us. He did not have to," a former high-ranking member of Tevel claimed.[11]

Rapport was everything in the face-to-face conversations and sensitive discussions behind the inner sanctums of the palaces. Each side

* Officially, these trips were all top secret—deniable by both the Israelis and the Saudis. An exception to this was a trip conducted in November 2020 by Prime Minister Benjamin Netanyahu and Mossad director Yossi Cohen to the Saudi coastal city of Neom to meet with Crown Prince Mohammed bin Salman and U.S. Secretary of State Mike Pompeo.

took stock of the person opposite him, examining facial responses and body language, listening to the timbre of the other's voice, and gauging his sincerity. Dagan was real, something the Saudis were not used to. All he wanted from them was their strategic friendship in combating a common enemy to make the region safe for his grandchildren.

*     *     *

Meir Dagan's four-year term was due to end as 2006 was placed in the rearview mirror. The end of a director's term was when the boards of major defense companies usually sent out feelers wanting to know what size signing bonus it would take to lure a man like Dagan into the CEO's chair. Dagan never thought much about money, other than realizing he had never made a fortune. The only paycheck he ever earned belonged to the state. Offers flew about. They did not interest him much. He thought about painting, sculpting, and spending time up north in Rosh Pina, a pensioner with a military disability.

Prime Minister Olmert should have also thought about who would replace Dagan. All prime ministers review names and recommendations when a director's term is near its end. But Olmert had no intention of letting Dagan leave his side. The prime minister extended Dagan's term by two years.

# Alpha!

The Mossad did not operate in a world of hysterical eyes or hyperbolic content. The stakes were too high for an espionage service to base its operations and assessments on political grandstanding or popular sentiment. An intelligence service could not exaggerate a threat for convenience or dilute danger to meet a particular narrative.

The Mossad did not believe that Iran pursued nuclear weapons to expedite paradise-seeking Armageddon. "First and foremost," Dagan once explained, "the nuclear card is an insurance policy to guarantee the regime's survival and deter foreign powers from trying to overthrow the regime." Secondly, nuclear weapons guaranteed Iran's status as a regional and global power and the dominant military superpower in the Islamic world. This, according to Dagan, aligned with Khomeini's scheme to make the Shiite revolution attractive to the Sunni world. But perhaps just as important, in Dagan's eyes, was that Iran's quest for the bomb stemmed from a pragmatic resolve that emanated from the eight-year-long Iran-Iraq War, where hundreds of thousands of Iranians were killed, Saddam Hussein's forces used chemical weapons against Iran, and Iraqi long-range ballistic missiles were launched at the country's population centers inflicting unimaginable horror. Nuclear weapons were to be Iran's deterrence, its insurance policy against the powers that sought the destruction of the Islamic state.[1]

Iran was an economically sanctioned but potentially oil-rich nation with a population of ninety million people. Syria, on the other hand, was a poor and malignly corrupt nation of twenty-three million people, without grand religious aspirations. The Syrians were not as ambitious as the Iranians: they wanted a nuclear strike capability for the sole reason of ensuring the survival of the Assad family dynasty.

*          *          *

Syria was a frontline enemy state that occupied a significant amount of attention from each of Israel's intelligence services. Although relatively poor, Damascus financed Palestinian and Lebanese terror groups operating inside the confines of Israel, making Syria a concern for the Shin Bet. The Syrian military, positioned opposite Israeli lines atop the Golan Heights, was a powerful force to be reckoned with that was made up of Russian hardware and advisors and was a target nation for intelligence gathering and operations by A'man and the IDF's special operations community. Syria's role in the geopolitical axis of evil that was anchored in Iran was the purview of the Mossad. "The Mossad's most important mission," Dagan would reiterate, "was to thwart the proliferation of unconventional weapons in the arsenals of Israel's enemies, and it carried out operations to achieve that strategic mandate."[2]

*          *          *

The Mossad began following telltale hints that Damascus was embarking on a weapons of mass destruction program shortly after Dagan entered office.[3] Hafez al-Assad, the former Syrian Air Force officer who had run the country since 1970, had died on June 10, 2000, ending a bloody thirty-year reign. He was succeeded by his son Bashar, a British-trained ophthalmologist who had been living in London until 1994, when his father's first choice for an heir, the elder brother Bassel, drove his Lamborghini at over one hundred miles an hour into a wall. The younger Assad, who had not lived in Syria for years, underwent a crash course in the family business; he received command of the military's elite 41st

Brigade, part of the Republican Guard's 4th Division, whose sole mission was brutal suppression of any threat to the regime and to protect the capital and the Assad family palaces from angry mobs.[4]

The branches of Israeli intelligence did not know what to make of the young Assad when he assumed power on July 17, 2000. He was a thirty-five-year-old novice, soft-spoken and gawky, removed from the day-to-day sinister measures needed for a member of a small religious minority to rule a nation of fractured ethnicities and political persuasions. There was even hope in Israel that the new Syrian leader would introduce reforms and Western-style changes and possibly be amenable to ending the fifty-year state of war between the two nations. Shortly after moving his family into the presidential palace, Assad even allowed limited internet access to the Syrian population. Boutique hotels opened in the capital; internet travel bloggers flocked to Aleppo and Homs to view the ancient markets and enjoy Syrian hospitality for the new Western adventurers. Some referred to the minuscule freedoms granted as the Damascus Spring.

Large-scale Western investment never materialized. Neither did most of the advertised freedoms. Hezbollah and Iranian representatives moved about the capital as if they owned it. Damascus was an armed camp of soldiers loyal to the Assad family and the ruling Baath Party, all enforced by thugs from Syrian Air Force Intelligence, the primary force of state security which imprisoned citizens without charges, tortured inmates, and made thousands disappear. And then the North Koreans arrived.

The emissaries from Pyongyang found it hard to hide their presence in Syria. The visiting contingents were usually in uniform, though when trying to blend in, they were adorned in ill-fitting warm-weather clothing produced in China that made them look like low-budget tourists. The North Koreans had been state sponsors of numerous Palestinian terror factions that operated in Syria, and high-level visits did not immediately spark concern. A'man, Unit 8200, and the Mossad monitored events closely, but there was nothing concrete that Israeli intelligence could act upon. The American NSA passed along information that they had intercepted telephone traffic between the Syrian desert and Pyongyang, the North Korean capital.[5] Britain's MI6, reportedly, had an agent inside the Syrian military, and he told his handlers that there was something suspicious underway in the northeast desert. The information was shared with the Mossad, but there was little to go on.[6]

The American and Israeli services could not figure out why the North Koreans were leaving an electronic footprint in northeastern Syria, in the center of nothing but a desert, and not in Damascus or Latakia, where Russian freighters and warships docked.

The intelligence-gathering effort trying to connect the dots between the North Korean "tourists" and the Syrian military continued, but nothing actionably conclusive indicated that the Assad regime was working on a nuclear reactor. Activities against Syria continued, but the information was scattered and nonspecific. IAF reconnaissance flights continued to fly over the region; other images, indigenously obtained or acquired through partners in the United States, were examined.

Dagan summoned a meeting with all the division heads. The men and women gathered in the SCIF were adamant that something of that nature could not be happening inside Syria without Israel knowing anything about it, and that the organization did not have to take the information seriously. Dagan lit his pipe, filled the no-smoking room with a cloud from the fragrant tobacco, and said, "Nonsense." They would treat the tip as genuine, take the threat seriously, and build an operational plan to determine once and for all, yes or no, what was happening in Syria. The British information, the Mossad would learn, was wrong. But the exercise set off alarm bells inside headquarters. Increased SIGINT and PHOTINT capabilities were utilized, and new human sources had to be identified and recruited. The intelligence-gathering campaign targeting Syria was intensified by both A'man and the Mossad.[7]

The possibility of weapons of mass destruction in the hands of the new and hostile regime in Damascus required an all-hands-on-deck effort by A'man and the Mossad, and that became part of the challenge. The two intelligence services were competitors, and the rivalry could be petty and sometimes ugly. Both Dagan and Yadlin were opinionated and strong-willed and demanded that their views be validated. There was historical bad blood between the two services, sentiments that were exacerbated after Dagan became Mossad director. Military intelligence, according to accounts, had to convince Dagan and his division chiefs of the pressing urgency involving the Syrian issue;[8] the reality was that there were speculations, uncertainties, and the need for a unified front.

To enhance the effort, special operations teams—Mossad and IDF—were dispatched to Syria to try to bring back eyes-on-target intelligence about where possible nuclear operations could be located. The three IDF tier-one units—Sayeret Mat'kal, Flotilla 13, and the IAF's Shaldag—worked closely with all facets of Israeli intelligence. The top-secret missions were conducted all over the target nation. The process was slow. Operations, especially those deep inside Syria, always required the prime minister's approval. HUMINT sources sometimes yielded nothing but money and time that was wasted.

The hunt for the elusive Syrian smoking gun dragged on, and Dagan grew impatient. He tasked his division chiefs to blueprint an operation that would either confirm the intelligence of nuclear activity in Syria so that it could be decisively dealt with tactically or, if no such threat existed, allow Israel's security arms to move on and drop the concern.[9] Two subjects of interest emerged on Dagan's radar. The first was Brigadier General Muhammad Suleiman. A member of a wealthy Alawite clan whose official title was special presidential advisor for arms procurement and strategic weapons, Suleiman was also the facilitator for the Syrian military's connection to Iranian intelligence and Hezbollah.[10] There were those in the Arab intelligence services circles who suspected that this was accentuated by his blond hair and fair skin, prompting his nickname of the "Imported General."[11] He spoke for President Assad in all matters concerning national defense and did not have to seek government approval for any action needed by his many top-secret programs. He was considered paranoid about his security. Suleiman traveled in armored limousines with a sizeable protective detail and disdained the use of telephones and computers. He was considered a hard target.

Ibrahim Sudki Othman, the head of the Syrian Atomic Energy Commission, was an easier mark. He was an engineer and not trained in precautionary tradecraft like security and safeguarding his information. He traveled alone on a regular passport and flew commercially; his itineraries, even hotel bookings, were easily obtained by those who knew how, and he journeyed freely and frequently to London and Vienna. The Mossad monitored General Suleiman but focused on Othman.

*                    *                    *

In February 2006, Ram Ben Barak, the head of Keshet, learned that the Syrian atomic chief would travel to Vienna. Operations had been mounted before trying to get to Othman, but none had yielded results; the effort continued. A large team of Mossad agents was waiting; former deputy Mossad chief Tamir Pardo, on loan to the IDF and the National Security Council, was summoned to lead the team.[12]

Othman was placed under near-hermetic surveillance in the Austrian capital. Teams of Mossad agents—men and women—monitored his every move, trying to assemble a pattern for him, to determine what times he left his hotel room, so that it could be searched. Mealtime was considered the safest time to enter his room and go through his possessions; housekeeping did not roam hotel floors in the evening, and he was known to leave his briefcase containing his files and laptop in the room when he ventured out to one of the expensive eateries in Vienna.

Multiple teams of agents watched Othman as he ordered drinks, ate a lavish meal, and then treated himself to a Viennese coffee and dessert. The Israelis sat inside the restaurant with him, on the street, in his hotel, and throughout the lobby, watching his every move. In Othman's room, the Mossad officers found a treasure trove of documents, photographs, and folders. Everything was laid out on the bed, photographed, and then returned to its place. His laptop, though encrypted, was easy to enter. The contents of his hard drive were copied, and eavesdropping malware was placed inside it that would allow the Mossad to follow his work, contacts, and emails moving forward. The Israeli agents even found Othman's mobile phone recharging under the bed.

There was so much information stored in the hotel room that Othman managed to complete his dinner and head back to his room while the Israeli agents were still working inside it. There is usually a window, the target thirty seconds from returning, when an operation commander must order *Hadal*, to "cease," and remove his agents from being uncovered. The intelligence team managed to extricate itself from the room before Othman entered the lobby elevator. Had Othman resisted the last cup of coffee and the piece of strudel and returned to his hotel room five minutes earlier, the operation would have been aborted, and the intelligence bonanza lost.

The sheer volume of information acquired from Othman's laptop and phone was vast. It took a small army of nuclear technicians and topographical experts several days to process and analyze the raw data uncovered in Vienna. There were photographs and charts, even blueprints. The haul provided irrefutable proof that the Syrians had paid the North Korean government two billion dollars[13] for the construction of a carbon copy of the Yongbyon nuclear reactor seventy-five miles north of Pyongyang. Photos of Othman and Chon Chibu, a top engineer in North Korea's nuclear program, were on the Syrian's mobile phone in Vienna. The reactor, at al-Kibar, was still under construction and was situated a little more than half a mile from the Euphrates River near the desert outpost town of Deir ez-Zor in northeastern Syria. The facility was camouflaged by its ordinariness: a false roof and walls had been constructed around the sarcophagus of the under-construction reactor[14] to make it look like a large warehouse where agricultural equipment was stored. There were no fences around the encampment—no military footprint at all, not even antiaircraft emplacements. Canals siphoning off a flow from the Euphrates had been dug to provide the reactor with coolant waters for the core. It is believed that only a few men in all of Syria knew of the project.

On March 13, 2007, Meir Dagan telephoned Prime Minister Olmert requesting an urgent meeting. The Mossad director's tone was short and urgent. His words were straightforward, out of place for the banter the two men usually exchanged under less critical circumstances. Dagan arrived in the early evening after most staffers had already left for the day. Olmert looked concerned and inquisitive; Dagan was all business. He produced a bulky manila envelope from his satchel and placed photographs and charts on his desk. "What am I looking at?" Olmert asked. Dagan's response was sharp: "A secret Syrian nuclear reactor." Olmert was shocked by the revelation. Although the Israeli prime minister was currently under investigation for financial improprieties, Olmert had weeks earlier asked Recep Tayyip Erdogan, the then–prime minister of Turkey, to reach out to the Syrian president to see if he was interested in conducting secret peace talks.[15] Before the prime minister could ask about Israel's options, Dagan responded, "It needs to be destroyed."[16]

According to the Mossad assessment, an opinion that A'man concurred with, Israel had a six-to-eight-month window before the reactor was completed and went hot—the significance being that attacking the site after it was operational risked radioactive fallout and a Chernobyl-like polluting of the Euphrates River. "For a thousand years," Dagan would reflect in one of his last interviews on camera, "every time a child in Syria or Iraq died of cancer, the world would blame Israel."[17] The political and diplomatic repercussions that Israel would encounter would be enormous and irrevocable, the manifestation once again of the centuries-old blood libel of Jews for unspeakable atrocities.

Olmert felt compelled to update the Americans. Twenty-six years earlier, Menachem Begin did not tell President Reagan that IAF F-16s were heading to the Iraqi reactor at Osirak. The failure to notify Washington caused a rift in the burgeoning bilateral relations and an increasingly inseparable strategic partnership. Dagan and a small team of analysts were dispatched to Washington, D.C. Dagan's job was to sell the deal to the Americans. Prime Minister Olmert would handle the political matters between heads of state.

*          *          *

CIA director General Michael Hayden had not been told why Meir Dagan needed to see him urgently. The reason behind the meeting request was cryptic.

Dagan and Hayden admired one another professionally—they first met in 2003, shortly after Dagan became the head of the Mossad and Hayden headed the National Security Agency. The two men spoke the same language—intelligence professionals always did—and they respected one another. They became friends and allies, quite an accomplishment given the constraints of their positions and the sensitive nature of the material they handled. Hayden called Meir General Dagan. The Mossad director referred to Hayden by his military rank, as well. The two men, Hayden remembered, spoke once a week, and Dagan visited him frequently, usually offering ideas for joint operations. The CIA director remembered Dagan's absolute professionalism and soldier-like straightforwardness. As much as they liked one another and as close as the Mossad and the CIA had become following 9/11, there was always some distance that had to be maintained. "We had to be careful," Hayden reflected, "because sometimes the Mossad did things we didn't do."[18]

Hayden did not know what kind of presentation Dagan would bring. He ordered a projector prepared in an offline room on the seventh floor just in case. But, in a very to-the-point Israeli way, the Mossad director brought copies of the photos and diagrams seized in Vienna, in a simple white looseleaf binder that looked like it had been used all year by a high school student.

Hayden was left speechless by what he saw. He was shocked by the intelligence presented to him and embarrassed that the CIA had missed it. The sting of Iraq and the WMD debacle was still felt at Langley. American troops were fighting sixty miles away across the border from the reactor. The meeting lasted over an hour. Dagan never told Hayden how he had obtained the material in his binder. The CIA director felt that Dagan knew more than he was letting on: that was part of the game. Israel had insight into Syria that the United States could not have assembled, but the Mossad did not have the stockpile of information that the CIA and the other arms of the American intelligence community had warehoused over decades of active espionage work.

Hayden knew that Dagan's next stop was the White House. The CIA director called Vice President Cheney to warn him that the intelligence the Mossad director was bringing was earthshaking. Dagan could have gone directly to the White House with the material, but he never wanted intelligence from Israel going through the filters of political echelons before it reached Langley.

Meir Dagan and his team stayed in the better hotels when visiting Washington, D.C. Still, being served to highlight his importance made him uncomfortable. When Dagan looked at himself in the mirror, even before a meeting at the White House to discuss an issue crucial to the security of Israel, he saw a soldier—and military rations were good enough for him. He always chose to walk a few blocks to a deli, an enhanced bodega, for a cheese sandwich and a tea, before beginning his day of high-level impactful meetings. The deli was his one abandonment of protective tradecraft.[19] The Mossad director felt safe in the American capital.

Steven Slick, a twenty-eight-year veteran of the CIA's clandestine service and special assistant to the president, as well as senior director for intelligence programs and reform on the staff of the National Security Council, remembers that Dagan was playful during the meeting in the West Wing, as he shared the intelligence with national security advisor Stephen Hadley, deputy national security advisor Elliott Abrams, and Vice President Dick Cheney. The meeting was held in Hadley's office, with the Israelis and Americans sitting on a sofa and the vice president perched on the edge of a large blue wing chair next to a polished coffee table.[20] He skimmed through the material and was alarmed by the Israeli intelligence. "What do you think this is?" Dagan asked as he flipped through the binder. "What about this?"[21] The Mossad director did his best to be dramatic. In the West Wing, a stone-faced Cheney looked on as Dagan was asked about what needed to happen next. His response was simple: "It needs to be destroyed."

Meir Dagan made his pitch. The case he presented, the tenor of his voice, and the knowledge that the Mossad director did not exaggerate the material, did not turn the exchange between the Israeli intelligence chief and the American vice president into theater, and yet was adamant that the only resolution acceptable to his country was the reactor's complete obliteration, led Cheney to concur. A year earlier, in the fall of 2006, after the North Koreans conducted their first nuclear test, President Bush had warned of Pyongyang's dangerous proliferation of nuclear and missile technologies to places like Iran and Syria. U.S. intelligence would later determine that the construction of the al-Kibar reactor began in 2002.[22]

The discussions ended inconclusively—there were no firm commitments to attack, though Prime Minister Olmert thought it would be best for the Americans to destroy the Syrian reactor. It would be a

ALPHA!                                    283

political form of recovery from the WMD misstep, and it would send a
resounding message to Tehran that they were well advised to abandon
any hope of reaching the nuclear threshold. The American view was
that the United States did not want to get involved in another Middle
Eastern campaign, especially one that risked escalating into a regional
war. But the White House also did not want Israel to start a major military conflict. Meir Dagan was resolute that if Israel and the United States
did not acknowledge the strike on Syria, or what was hit, Assad would
not be able to mount the public and domestic support he would need to
launch a retaliatory strike in response to the destruction of the al-Kibar
reactor. The Mossad director understood the invaluable importance of
Israel's strategic relationship with the United States and that it was the
Jewish state's greatest asset, but there were lines in the sand. Allowing
al-Kibar to stand was one such line.

Working groups were established to explore the issue and collaborate
at the bilateral level. The American team became known as the Library
Group, since they met, in secret, in the White House Library. Secretary
of State Condoleezza Rice, brought into the mix, reportedly had lost
her respect for the IDF following its performance against Hezbollah
in the summer of 2006, and was against any military action targeting
Syria, especially one conducted by Israel with American knowledge.
During the Second Lebanon War, when President Bush convened a
national security meeting to discuss the conflict and Vice President
Cheney wanted to let Israel finish off Hezbollah, Rice had replied, "If
you do that, we'll be dead in the Middle East."[23]

The secretary of state held great sway with President Bush. She
demanded that the Syrian reactor be handled diplomatically. Secretary of Defense Robert Gates, someone who was viewed in Jerusalem
circles as being less than sympathetic to the State of Israel, was against
any American—or Israeli—action against al-Kibar. President Bush had
to assess what was best for the United States and he had to round up his
cabinet members into some form of consensus. Cheney was the only
member of the inner circle who knew what had to be done.

The team in Israel was called the Box. The group consisted of Olmert;
Defense Minister Amir Peretz, and then later Ehud Barak when he

assumed leadership of the Labor Party and became the new defense minister; IDF chief of staff Gabi Ashkenazi; A'man head Amos Yadlin; IAF commander Major General Eliezer Shkedi; and Meir Dagan.

The group met every Friday afternoon, the start of the Israeli weekend, to try to keep the assembly secret from prying eyes. Every one of the Box participants had to sign a letter at the end of each meeting swearing not to divulge anything discussed, and that included the prime minister. The group was far from being unified, however. Barak was seen as problematic, and possibly self-serving. He was vehemently against any attack. He wanted to delay any strike until the spring of 2008, some say for personal political reasons after seeing Olmert's legal standings closing in around him. Olmert was shocked, even horrified, that Barak considered it all right to hit the Syrian reactor even after it went hot.[24]

At the end of July 2007, President Bush telephoned Olmert on a secure line. Bush, as was his trademark with world leaders and those he was fond of, referred to Olmert as "Buddy." The American president stated that his people had reviewed all the scenarios and that there were three options before both nations: an American attack, an Israeli attack, and diplomacy, and Bush and his inner circle opted for a diplomatic solution. Bush said that he would send Condoleezza Rice to Israel to launch the process. Olmert was aghast; it was as if he had been punched in the gut and then kicked for good measure. Composing himself, the Israeli prime minister applauded Rice's diplomatic skills, but told Bush not to send her, adding "We'll deal with this on our own."[25]

Although Dagan and members of his team traveled back and forth to the United States, where the countries updated each other with advanced intelligence, Israel was, indeed, alone. Plans were intensified to take out the al-Kibar reactor.

*         *         *

The IDF prepares contingencies—plans that the chief of staff, the defense minister, and ultimately the prime minister must approve. The prevailing notion in the Kirya was that the Syrian reactor would be taken out in an Osirak-like air strike. But there were other contingencies thought of, including a massive special operations raid to take over the location, "acquire" whatever intelligence could be loaded into choppers, and then the entire complex would be wired with explosives. IDF tier-one units were reportedly sent into the Syrian desert[26] to reconnoiter the terrain and prepare landing sites for pilots who would need to be rescued. The IAF losing one of its aircraft over Syria was a nightmare scenario, as it would eliminate any chance that the Israeli government had to deny its involvement in the reactor's destruction. The IAF also did not want its aircraft shooting down any Syrian warplanes scrambled to intercept the blips on their Russian air defense radars; dead Syrian airmen or soldiers would also incriminate Israel in the raid. The desire was for Damascus—and Syria's allies in Iran and North Korea—to guess which nation was responsible. The IAF had been preparing for the operation for six months.[27]

*　　　*　　　*

The IDF and the intelligence arms were still honing down the best possible attack scenarios when Dagan received an urgent call from Washington, D.C., on September 5. It was the afternoon in Israel—just after nine in the morning in D.C.

At an open house at the Israeli Embassy on International Drive, Fox News reporter James Rosen had asked an Israeli diplomat about the Syrian reactor in the desert. The embassy political officer said nothing, but he alerted the declared Mossad representative, who rushed to the SCIF and called Dagan.[28] The mere chance that there had been a leak somewhere in the Beltway risked everything—surprise was key. The Mossad chief called the prime minister, who summoned an emergency session of the cabinet and the Box. Major General Shkedi was confident that the IAF could destroy al-Kibar, and he expressed the attack plan in meticulous detail and with a reassuring sense that to the pilots involved this was all very routine. The vote to launch the attack was unanimous. The operation was code-named *Sahlab*, Hebrew for Orchid.

The prime minister went to bed for a few hours that night before heading to the Kirya and the "Pit," the underground command and control center where the raid would be watched in real time. Dagan had stopped to grab a falafel from his favorite spot near the main Tel Aviv–Jerusalem Highway and returned to the office before assembling with the prime minister and the IDF hierarchy deep under the Kirya at 23:00. Large-screen televisions and computer terminals illuminated the room. The prime minister sat in silence as eight aircraft—four F-15Is and four F-16Is—took off from Ramat David air base in the north for their circuitous route over the Mediterranean and then into northern Syria along the border with Turkey—a flight path IAF commanders believed would not be tracked by radar; for good measure, IAF electronic warfare aircraft blinded Syrian air defenses.

At approximately 00:40 on the morning of September 6, the lead pilot uttered the word "Arizona," the code that seventeen tons of precision munitions had been dropped on the al-Kibar reactor. The pilots then uttered the word "Alpha" repeatedly, the IAF term for when a bomb hits the dead center of its mark.

Major General Shkedi saluted Prime Minister Olmert when the planes returned safely to Israel. Olmert hugged him in return.

Olmert rushed to a secure telephone and had a staffer connect him to President Bush. Bush was on a tour of Australia, and his ability to talk freely was diminished. But Olmert could not hold back. "Remember that thing in the desert we spoke about?" the Israeli prime minister asked. "Well, it's not there anymore."[29]

*     *     *

Israel did not prepare for a large-scale war before launching Operation Orchid. The Syrian military possessed over five hundred SCUD missiles aimed at Israel—each carried a warhead of high explosives that weighed a ton. The Syrian missiles could hit every target in Israel—from the Red Sea resort of Eilat to the heart of Tel Aviv. Any mobilization of the IDF's Homefront Command would have set off alarm bells; a raid on a nuclear reactor 280 miles from central Israel could have set off a panic. But Dagan was certain that if Israel did not boast about the raid, the Syrians could deny that the reactor was ever there or that it had been destroyed and would not feel compelled to retaliate.

But the raid could not be kept secret. An externally mounted six-hundred-gallon fuel tank from one of the F-15s had been jettisoned for technical reasons and landed inside Turkish territory. Saudi newspapers reported on a strike in northeastern Syria, but the details would take weeks and months to emerge.

President Bashar al-Assad did nothing. Israel's soldiers—and its soldier spymaster—had been right in their assessments.

The question of Syrian retaliation and a larger Middle Eastern war was the principal reason behind CIA director Hayden's opposition to the Israeli intentions. Hayden and Dagan rarely disagreed and never in public. Syria was the exception. Dagan and the Israelis, Hayden would later admit, were right. The two men would not disagree on operational matters again. Quite to the contrary, the events that transpired on the night between the 5th and 6th of September 2007 solidified the relationship between Israel's Mossad and the CIA.

Considering the events that would transpire in Syria in the years to follow—the Arab Spring, the Syrian Civil War, and the emergence of ISIS, the few hours that the Mossad spent sifting through a hotel room in Vienna one cold February evening might just have saved the Middle East from a fate even worse than a regional war.

# Code Name Wild Child

The Second Lebanon War was a blow to the IDF and Israeli intelligence. The Hezbollah cross-border attack had instigated thirty-four days of incessant combat that saw Israeli cities targeted by enemy missiles for the first time since the 1991 Gulf War, resulted in 121 soldiers and 44 civilians killed, with thousands wounded in the fighting inside southern Lebanon and in Haifa and Galilee. The bodies of two Israeli reservists were warehoused like stock merchandise by Hezbollah, to be traded for an exorbitant fee that would pain the very foundations of the State of Israel's ethos to its citizens that terror would never be allowed to prevail. Hezbollah's capabilities—and its intentions—had been misread by the Mossad and A'man.

The war had rewritten the flow chart of espionage priorities. Iran, Syria, and the Shiite Party of God formed, a triumvirate that the Israeli intelligence community labeled the Radical Front[1] providing the Islamic Republic with a terror deterrence to protect its nascent nuclear program. Hezbollah became an urgent intersection of the Mossad's two primary responsibilities: preventing Israel's enemies from acquiring unconventional weapons and fighting terrorism. There was hell to pay, but the question was who would get the bill.

Not many members of Mossad's leadership made it home to see their families in the weeks and months that followed Lebanon. The long days at headquarters often blurred into all-night events. Senior intelligence officers brought their shaving gear and a change of clothes to the office to be fresh and ready for those days when one day became another.

On one cold and stormy night, when it was too late to go home and too early to start the new day, Dagan held court in his office for a few of the men on his counterterrorism team, including a new member of the staff who had been poached from A'man to spearhead the fight against Hezbollah. The men talked about what had happened to Israel's once daunting deterrence and the black eye that the IDF had endured because of the overall failure in the summer war. More importantly, they brainstormed ideas about what could be done to show Israel's enemies in Beirut, Damascus, and Tehran that they would soon face a wrath of preemptive action.

Dagan liked these informal sessions of free thinking where his most trusted officers would be unafraid to talk about ideas, no matter how crazy, to see what might stick. The men drank water and tea and chatted while waving away the clouds of suffocating smoke from Dagan's pipe. Significant espionage operations did not always originate in the weekly roundtable of division heads discussing world events and breaking intelligence revelations. Brilliant and often game-changing ideas for operations, especially those that took years to incubate from conception to execution, also emanated from casual discussions inside a car, or in the director's office at some ungodly hour.

Dagan and his section chiefs talked into the night over the soundtrack of classical music that always filled the background in his office. As the men talked and yawned, one of them blurted out, "Why don't we just kill them all?"[2] Dagan liked it. There was no doubt in his mind that Imad Fayez Mughniyeh, the Hezbollah head of special operations and Iran's man in the organization, would top the hit list.*

* Up until the intelligence operations mounted against Hamas and Hezbollah in the months—and years—following October 7, 2023, the State of Israel would neither deny nor confirm its role in any of the extrajudicial killings its intelligence services carried out beyond the country's frontiers and outside the West Bank and Gaza Strip. In the aftermath of October 7, though, in the wake of highly complex direct-action operations carried out in Lebanon and Iran, representatives from the Israeli government began

A'man referred to Mughniyeh as "Maurice."[3] In the Mossad, his code name was Wild Child.[4]

*          *          *

Imad Mughniyeh was an arch-terrorist—an evil practitioner of no-holds-barred violence who was both a sociopath and a diabolical tactician. He was born in the small farming village of Tayr Debba, just east of the outskirts of Tyre, on December 7, 1962. Although Mughniyeh came from a prominent Shiite clan, his parents were poor, simple but religious folk who worked the land. Imad was known as a devilish child who had a remarkable singing voice and was rumored to have memorized the entire Quran and to enchant local clerics by serenading them with religious passages.

The young Mughniyeh was obsessed with guns, and when Palestinian guerrillas took over parts of southern Lebanon after they were kicked out of Jordan in 1971, the young boy became enamored of the swagger and muscle of the Palestinian fedayeen, even though they abused the Shiite villagers. The reports of raped women, and husbands and fathers disappearing into the night, mattered little to him. He wanted to fight. In 1976, at the height of Lebanon's Civil War, Imad Mughniyeh volunteered into the ranks of Fatah.* He was only fourteen years old.

The battle lines in Lebanon's fratricide might have been drawn along religious lines, but there was nothing pious in the bloodletting—especially among the Palestinian groups. The use of drugs and alcohol by the fedayeen, and the sexual promiscuity with female fighters, were anathema to Mughniyeh's strict Shiite upbringing. Rather than being

---

to take credit for strikes in Lebanon, Syria, and Iran, those carried out by the Mossad during the current conflict as well as some—like Mughniyeh's—that had taken place years earlier. In September 2024, former prime minister Ehud Olmert admitted that the Mossad had assassinated the Hezbollah chief in 2008.

* According to author Kai Bird, in his book *The Good Spy: The Life and Death of Robert Ames*, Mughniyeh was recruited into Fatah by Ali Hassan Salameh, the head of the Black September Organization and the architect of the Munich Olympics Massacre, who was also a CIA asset.

repulsed by it, it energized him. The teenager excelled at killing. He had not reached his eighteenth birthday when Mughniyeh was offered a spot in Force 17, Arafat's Praetorian Guard and special operations unit. He was, it is believed, trained in the Soviet Union in the basics of dignitary protection. He would travel throughout the Middle East as a member of Abu Iyad's detail. Iyad, the nom de guerre of Salah Khalaf, was Arafat's deputy and the man who created Black September.*

In the summer of 1982, as Israeli armored columns—including Dagan's brigade—pushed into the Lebanese capital, Imad Mughniyeh broke into the Interior Ministry and destroyed his file, including his birth registry information and the photograph he had submitted for his identification card. He then shed his lizard-pattern camouflage fatigues, ditched his AK-47, and disappeared into the Shiite slums of south Beirut, where he would blend into the destruction and chaos. He would emerge in the months that followed indoctrinated by Khomeini's revolution and eager to be one of its armed emissaries bringing an Iranian-style war of sacrifice and martyrdom to Israel and the Western powers—the United States and France—that were now situated in Lebanon as part of a peacekeeping force. Islamic Revolutionary Guard officers used the Iranian Embassy in Beirut and a deserted army barracks in Baalbek as a base of operations.

It was Imad Mughniyeh—along with Ali Akbar Mohtashamipur, an Iranian cleric and ambassador to Syria—who turned Shiite rage into one of the most lethal terror armies in history.[5] It was Mughniyeh who recruited Ahmed Qasir to inaugurate suicide bombings as a weapon of choice in November 1982. The success of the destruction of the Israeli military headquarters in Tyre made Mughniyeh Iran's man in Lebanon's shadow Shiite army.

Mughniyeh's résumé constituted some of the most heinous acts of terror of the 1980s and 1990s. Among the acts of mass murder that Mughniyeh blueprinted: the suicide truck bombing of the U.S. Embassy in Beirut in 1983; the bombing of the U.S. Marine Corps barracks at

---

* Abu Iyad was assassinated by a gunman from the Abu Nidal Black June Organization, under the orders of Saddam Hussein.

Beirut International Airport and the French paratrooper headquarters in the Lebanese capital in October 1983; the bombings of the American and French Embassies in Kuwait City; the kidnapping and murder of CIA station chief William Buckley in 1984; the bombing of the U.S. Embassy in Beirut in 1984; the kidnapping of Westerners in Lebanon; the hijacking of TWA Flight 847 and the murder of U.S. Navy diver Robert Stethem in 1985; the kidnapping and murder of U.S. Marine Corps colonel William Higgins; the bombing of the Israeli Embassy in Buenos Aires; the bombing of the Argentine Israel Mutual Association Jewish community center in Buenos Aires in 1994; and the bombing of the U.S. barracks in Khobar Towers in Saudi Arabia in 1996.

There were dozens of other lethal attacks around the world. Mughniyeh was also behind the deadly suicide-bombing guerrilla war waged against Israeli forces in south Lebanon from 1985 to 2000; he masterminded the abduction of Israeli soldiers and Elhanan Tannenbaum in 2000, and was the engineer of the 2006 Second Lebanon War. Ehud Yaari, a famed journalist and one of Israeli media's foremost Arab experts, categorized Mughniyeh as one of the most lethal terrorists in the region's history.[6]

There were arrest warrants for Imad Mughniyeh issued in a dozen countries—he was a wanted man in Jordan, Kuwait, and Saudi Arabia. The U.S. State Department's Diplomatic Security Service's Rewards for Justice program offered a five-million-dollar reward for any information that led to his apprehension; he topped the FBI's Ten Most Wanted List.

Meir Dagan always felt a sense of responsibility for Mughniyeh's crimes. As a deputy brigade commander in 1978, during Israel's mini-invasion of south Lebanon, the future Mossad director had met the sixteen-year-old Mughniyeh one morning in the village of Bazouriye. Dagan's tank force was hunting Fatah operatives who had shed their uniforms and were hiding among the Shiite villagers when the local imam greeted him pledging peace and promising that there would be no trouble in his village. "He brought his sixteen-year-old relative with him, an unimpressive teenager with a distant gaze," Dagan remembered. The old man wanted to make sure nothing happened to his cousin."[7] "He's in Fatah, the imam said," Dagan would recall in one of his last on-camera interviews, "but it wasn't in his heart."[8] The imam was begging that the Israeli soldiers not take young Imad away. "I believed him," Dagan confessed, "anyway, we didn't know what to do with those we already had in custody."[9]

Early in Olmert's prime ministership, the new leader and his Mossad chief spoke about short-term objectives and long-term goals for the espionage agency. The top item on the agenda was requesting authorization to hunt down Mughniyeh and kill him—the authorization was known as a *Daf Adom*, Hebrew for Red Page. Dagan explained that eliminating Imad Mughniyeh would save Israeli lives, as well as innocent civilians in the West. The prime minister gave his intelligence chief the green light to move forward. Events in Lebanon in the summer of 2006 intensified Dagan's desire to rid the world of the terror mastermind.

*         *         *

Meir Dagan was not the first Mossad director to place Mughniyeh inside the crosshairs. In 1994, when Shabtai Shavit was the service head, a bomb killed Fouad Mughniyeh, Imad's younger brother, to draw the elusive Hezbollah operations chief out in the open at the funeral. Imad sensed an ambush and stayed cleared of the procession. Mossad officers respected his uncanny sixth sense. He adhered to strict tradecraft for self-preservation. He used couriers and maintained close company with a cabal of Iranian intelligence chiefs and Syrian military commanders.

Mughniyeh drove events in the Middle East, ultimately becoming the head of Hezbollah's international operations and a de facto senior commander in Department 900, better known as the Quds Force, the special operations and intelligence branch of Iran's Islamic Revolutionary Guard Corps. The Quds Force had been created in 1979 to export the Islamic Revolution beyond Iran. His closest working partner was Quds Force commander Qassem Soleimani, who led the clandestine warfare unit since 1997.[10] Soleimani, like Mughniyeh, was considered a genius at his craft.

For decades, the Mossad, the CIA, the GID, the Saudi GIP, and virtually all the European intelligence services attempted to get close to Mughniyeh and find an Achilles' heel, some perversion or fault, that could be used as the first sketch of a complex intelligence operation against him. Psychologists analyzed his crimes and the raw known facts about him; experts in Islam attempted to understand Mughniyeh's faith, though it was determined that his sole belief was anchored in Iran's conflict against the West and Israel.

He was forty-four years old when he masterminded the kidnapping raid that sparked the 2006 Second Lebanon War and supervised Hezbollah's support of Shiite rebels battling American and coalition forces in Iraq. The signs of middle age had begun to show. His guerrilla-style beard no longer concealed the onset of a double chin. He had gained weight; his paunch was uncharacteristic for a man who led a global terror army. He underwent a midlife crisis, seeking sexual reaffirmation of his once mighty manhood among the beautiful women in Beirut, Damascus, and Tehran. He began granting interviews, primarily to beautiful young female journalists who fawned over his achievements.[11] He took on mistresses, multiple ones, though it is believed that some of these women were provided to him by the Quds Force, as a reward for his dedicated service against the United States and Israel in Lebanon and Iraq.[12]

After the 2006 Lebanon war, when the arms of Israeli intelligence became laser-focused on Mughniyeh, vanity had gotten the better part of his cover. He abandoned the one rule of tradecraft that had kept him two steps ahead of the spies: he became addicted to his mobile phone. It was hard to maintain girlfriends and woo journalists with couriers. The women sent messages to Mughniyeh's pager, and he had numerous mobile phones, the must-have equipment when needing to send late-night text messages or the odd nude photograph.

In early 2007, Israeli intelligence acquired one of Mughniyeh's mobile phone numbers. Some accounts list the find emanating from A'man's Unit 8200 and a SIGINT intercept; others indicate that a Mossad asset in Lebanon handed the information off to his case agent.[13] Mughniyeh always carried his mobile phones with him; Nokia was the brand of choice because they were small, unobtrusive, and robustly reliable. He

was worried more than anything else that his wife, Saadi Badreddine,*
who was also a cousin, might read the messages and discover his infi-
delity. Damascus became Mughniyeh's love nest—the Syrian capital was
close enough to Beirut to be convenient and far enough from his wife
to be discreet. He frequently met with Brigadier General Muhammad
Suleiman and Qassem Soleimani during visits to the Syrian capital.

*       *       *

Locating one of Imad Mughniyeh's telephones and using it as a hom-
ing beacon to monitor his every move was the needle in the haystack
that the Mossad—and others—had been seeking for over twenty years.
Dagan, who viewed Mughniyeh as his arch-nemesis, wanted the Hezbollah commander dead. But Israel was not alone. Up until September
11, 2001, Imad Mughniyeh's Hezbollah had killed more Americans than
any other terrorist group in the world, and the United States wanted vengeance: the bombing of the barracks in Beirut was the single deadliest
day for the Marine Corps since the storming of Iwo Jima in 1945. The
CIA wanted payback, as well. Mughniyeh had eviscerated the agency's
presence in Lebanon in the U.S. Embassy in Beirut in 1983; the kidnapping and cold-blooded murder of Chief of Station William F. Buckley
could never be forgiven. Meir Dagan understood America's thirst for
revenge, even though, officially, the Mossad never killed anyone for
retribution.

* Hezbollah was always a clan-driven operation. Mughniyeh's brother-in-law, Mustafa Badreddine, was recruited into the organization in 1983. An explosives expert
who helped construct the massive truck bomb that killed 241 American marines and
sailors on October 23, 1983, he was arrested in Kuwait following the December 1983
bombings of the American and French Embassies. Kidnapping Westerners in Beirut
was an attempt by Mughniyeh to secure his brother-in-law's release; Badreddine walked
to freedom in 1990, after Saddam Hussein invaded Kuwait and the jails were emptied.
Badreddine, rumored to have had hundreds of mistresses across Lebanon and Syria,
was believed to have been behind the massive bomb that killed former Lebanese prime
minister Rafik Hariri on February 14, 2005. When Badreddine was killed at Damascus
Airport on May 12, 2016, he was one of the top commanders in the organization. No
nation has ever taken responsibility for the deadly blast.

But Dagan also understood that since Damascus was where Mughni-yeh abdicated his security protocols for the pleasures of the flesh, Syria would be where any attempt on the Hezbollah chief would need to be made. In Beirut, Mughniyeh was a ghost. He wore camouflage fatigues and sometimes dressed in all black, blending into the slums of south Beirut. In Damascus, he was a playboy and a player—dining at the city's famed eateries and wearing designer fashions.

Whenever senior Israeli intelligence and special operations person-nel met with their American counterparts, Hezbollah and Iran were uttered in the same breath. Mughniyeh's name was always said in terms of elimination. But hypothetical ideas turned into realistic scenarios as a response to Hezbollah's use of Iraq as a killing ground for American servicemen. It became clear to the Pentagon as well as Langley that Hezbollah once again posed a significant danger to America's policy in the Middle East.

It is not known precisely when Meir Dagan pitched the idea of a joint Mossad-CIA operation to Michael Hayden. Many inside the Mos-sad were furious at the director for involving the Americans; it was a severe breach of Israeli independence and operational integrity. Dagan hushed the uproar as nonsense. He preached the virtue that intelligence that went unused was a waste of resources and possibly lives that were risked obtaining it. According to reports, the Mossad director shared the Israeli intelligence about Mughniyeh's phone with Hayden. It did not take long for the CIA to be on board.

For operational and diplomatic reasons, involving the Americans made tactical sense.* The United States maintained embassies in both Beirut and Damascus, providing American intelligence personnel with diplomatic cover that was denied to the Mossad. The CIA's HUMINT and SIGINT capabilities in the region were vast. The CIA also maintained its own special operations army, the Special Activities Division, and Langley often used assets belonging to the Joint Special

---

* The U.S. government has never admitted or denied any role in the assassination of Imad Mughniyeh. The Israeli government has not claimed American assistance either.

Operations Command, JSOC—which included the U.S. Army's 1st Special Forces Operational Detachment-Delta, or Delta Force, and the U.S. Naval Special Warfare Development Group, more commonly known as SEAL Team 6—to assist in delicate and dangerous missions in enemy locations.

Forging a joint operation with Israel's closest intelligence ally was a coup for Dagan. It had never been attempted before because the expansion of intelligence sharing to joint participation was considered far-fetched in many circles. The CIA insisted that America's role in Israeli operations be deniable and legal. Hayden needed presidential authorization to move forward, President Bush needed Attorney General Michael B. Mukasey and National Security Advisor Hadley, along with the Office of Legal Counsel at the Justice Department,[14] to sign off on CIA involvement in targeting Mughniyeh, so that the administration would not violate Part 2.11 of the 1981 Executive Order 12333 signed by Ronald Reagan prohibiting assassinations.[15] The Americans also insisted that there be no collateral damage. Mughniyeh—and only Mughniyeh—was to be harmed, even if the Israelis could take out other high-value targets in the process.

It was decided that a car bomb would be used to kill Mughniyeh. Details of American participation remain vague. The CIA built the device and tested it over twenty times at a secluded site in North Carolina to ensure that the blast radius would not kill bystanders.[16] The CIA would transport the device through a diplomatic pouch from Jordan, and then into Syria by road, and then provide Israeli agents on the ground with the explosives and added surveillance support. Israeli agents bought a new silver Mitsubishi Pajero SUV in Lebanon that would be used to deliver the bomb. The Pajero was driven to Damascus, where the device, described as highly sophisticated, was inserted into the vehicle in a place where it would be difficult to detect, and then parked on the street around one of the target buildings so that police and neighbors would become accustomed to it. According to Ehud Olmert, the explosives were planted in the bumper.[17]

Both Hayden and Dagan monitored the progress of the joint effort. Israeli assets on the ground focused on the house of one of Mughniyeh's mistresses in the Kfar Sousa neighborhood of Damascus, an upscale area of luxury high-rises and five-star eateries. "The only reason why you maintain a girlfriend and spend the money lavishing her with gifts and promises of a future is to visit her," an Israeli intelligence officer explained, "and Mughniyeh had damn good taste."[18] Mughniyeh also frequented a second apartment, also in a luxury high-rise, where he would meet Muhammad Suleiman and Qassem Soleimani. Teams of agents surveilled the locations around the clock. Cameras were installed around the addresses to send real-time images back to headquarters. Apartments were rented, providing advantageous views of the two locations Mughniyeh was likely to walk past. The routine allowed Mossad officers to create a forecast of arrivals and departures. Mughniyeh had become a man of routine, carnal desire, and a schedule. When he was near Damascus, the Pajero was always positioned to be in the center of the kill zone.

Neither the Mossad nor the CIA knew precisely when Mughniyeh would visit Damascus, but the intended operational date was sometime in January or February. The agents waited, as did the intelligence service directors. Too many things could go wrong. In Langley and Tel Aviv, the spies were nervous. Imad Mughniyeh crossed the border between Lebanon and Syria midday on February 12, 2008.

That evening, at approximately 9:00 p.m., Mughniyeh, Suleiman, and Soleimani met at the safe house apartment. The men traveled light with armored motorcades and a phalanx of bodyguards; plainclothes security agents from Syrian Air Force Intelligence did not cordon off the street. Suleiman and Soleimani* left first. Mughniyeh came down later. At 10:45 p.m., as the Hezbollah commander made his way toward his car and walked past the Pajero, a signal was sent from Tel Aviv, detonating the lethal payload. A fireball illuminated the Damascus sky, followed by screams and sirens.

Prime Minister Ehud Olmert was flying from Berlin back to Israel following a state visit to Germany on a chartered El Al airliner when

---

* Qassem Soleimani was killed twelve years later, at just after midnight on January 3, 2020, outside Baghdad International Airport. He was killed by missiles fired by a CIA MQ-9 Reaper drone.

he received word that Imad Mughniyeh had been killed.[19] Olmert had given Dagan the green light to get it done.

Meir Dagan forbade any celebrations following the Negative Treatment of an enemy target. Champagne bottles were never opened, and no one dared clap. "We are not Gods," he used to tell his officers. "The taking of another life is a last resort and nothing to rejoice over," his former head of training remembers. Dagan never authorized a citation or a medal for any operation that resulted in the death of a legitimate target.[20]

There was, though, a sense of relief and closure. There was no arguing about the significance of eliminating Mughniyeh. He was irreplaceable to Hezbollah. The director of Mossad wondered how many innocent lives would now be spared with Mughniyeh no longer in the game.

After U.S. ambassador to Iraq Ryan C. Crocker received details of Mughniyeh's assassination on SIPRNet* hours after the blast in Damascus, he commented, "All I can say is that as long as he drew breath, he was a threat, whether in Lebanon, Iraq, or anywhere else."[21] Crocker had served in Lebanon in the 1980s at the height of Hezbollah activities against the United States and had lost friends and comrades killed at the hands of Mughniyeh.

Nearly a quarter of a million Shiites swarmed the streets of Beirut to attend Imad Mughniyeh's funeral. Sheikh Hassan Nasrallah, speaking from a bunker somewhere in the city, warned Israel that it would face a lethal wrath for the murder. But Hezbollah did not retaliate for the death of Imad Mughniyeh: not because of a lack of desire, but because their capabilities had been significantly degraded, and perhaps forever weakened. Following the 2006 war, the assessment in numerous relevant offices in the Israeli intelligence community was that Imad Mughniyeh had emerged as the conflict's true winner. But after Hezbollah failed to perpetrate a response to Mughniyeh's death, it became apparent that Israel had inflicted more damage on the Party of God than was

---

* The system of interconnected computer networks used by the U.S. Department of Defense and the U.S. Department of State to transmit classified information.

realized, and that only a dedicated intelligence effort to eradicate the leadership of the Iranian proxy could result in the group's eradication. But intelligence work is the labor of patience and perseverance. The conversation on Dagan's couch that would inspire the imagination and turn it into an actionable plan took years to percolate.

Once again, the Syrian government was horrified by how easily its secrets and the country's integrity had been penetrated by Israeli intelligence. Five months after the al-Kibar reactor had been destroyed, Israel showed the Assad regime that it had the power to operate with impunity and carry out a high-profile killing in the heart of Damascus.[22]

*          *          *

Air Force One landed in Israel on May 14, 2008. Five months earlier, in Jerusalem, the forty-third president had reiterated American and Israeli fears about Iran. At a question-and-answer session during a red-carpet event, Bush said, "Iran was a threat, Iran is a threat, and Iran will be a threat if the international community does not come together and prevent that country from having the know-how for a secret weapon."

President George W. Bush, in the final months of his second term, wanted to pay his respects to a nation that had been a staunch ally in the international war on terror, the effort to stop Iran—and others—from acquiring nuclear weapons, and a great many other matters of mutual concern, but the one man he truly wanted to see was Meir Dagan. There was a lot to talk about.

The American president wanted to show his appreciation to the Mossad director on a family matter. George H. W. Bush had been the director of the CIA before being elected president. The murder of William F. Buckley was a crime that had needed to be answered, and the killing of Mughniyeh, long overdue, brought closure to the American intelligence community. Bush, Olmert, and Dagan met at the prime minister's residence on Balfour Street in Jerusalem. The three men joked and spoke about family, and how the spies and the spymasters had ushered in a new era in Israel's relationship with the United States, a full-fledged alliance of interoperable necessity.

*          *          *

There are no handshake deals that end terror wars, only intermittent pauses between moments of anguish and loss. On July 16, 2008, after nearly two years of intelligence service negotiations led by the Mossad and European services, the bodies of Ehud Goldwasser and Eldad Regev were returned to Israel. The two reservists, mortally wounded in the Hezbollah attack that sparked the 2006 war, had been held by Hezbollah. Negotiators for the Shiite Party of God never let their Israeli counterparts know if the two men were dead or alive. The Mossad assessment was that they had died shortly after being taken captive.

The remains were returned to Israel's northern border. Prime Minister Olmert joined the widows of the two men in a somber ceremony. The moment of closure was a painful chapter for Dagan. The price that Israel paid for the two slain servicemen was the release of Samir Kuntar, the then teenager who murdered the Haran family in 1979, launching the planning for Operation Olympia and the eradication of the PLO leadership in Beirut. Kuntar, forty-six years old when released, was Druze, but Hezbollah greeted him back in Lebanon as a conquering hero. After the assassination of Imad Mughniyeh, Sheikh Nasrallah needed to create new heroes.* In Gaza, news reports of the two Israeli servicemen returned home in coffins sparked celebrations in the streets as Hamas gunmen handed out candies and sweet pastries.[23]

*          *          *

Six months after Mughniyeh's assassination and three months after Bush's last visit to Israel as the president of the United States, Brigadier

---

* Kuntar was killed on December 19, 2015, in an air strike in Jaramana, Syria, during the country's civil war. He had been fighting with Hezbollah in support of the Assad regime. Israel never claimed responsibility for his death.

General Muhammad Suleiman was shot and killed as he hosted a dinner party at his lavish seaside villa along the Mediterranean coast near the city of Tartus. Reportedly, he had been shot in the head and neck by an Israeli raiding party, ostensibly operators from Flotilla 13. When asked years later about Suleiman's death, Dagan did not share any details, only commenting, "I heard that something had happened to him."[24]

# New Bosses, Different World

The prevailing consensus among many in the Mossad is that Ehud Olmert was the best prime minister ever for the spy service. His decision-making was decisive and courageous. He protected his director and those who served under him with boundless energy. Olmert might have been a politician, but he was a patriot. And the men and women in the Mossad knew that he would do everything in his power to use the resources at his disposal to protect the State of Israel. "The organization doubled in size and capabilities under his leadership," former deputy Mossad director Ehud Lavi remembered."[1]

But in July 2008, Olmert, facing a slew of corruption investigations that would ultimately send him to prison, said he would not contest the leadership of his Kadima political party in the primaries scheduled for later that year. Tzipi Livni, the foreign minister who had served in the Mossad for four years in the 1980s, a member of Kidon,[2] assumed the party leadership. She would attempt to retain the prime ministership in the upcoming elections slated for February 2009. Her principal rival was Likud Party chairman Benjamin Netanyahu. The former prime minister, whose political fortunes had been crippled following the 1998 elections, but who had made a startling comeback after shining as a cost-cutting finance minister in Ariel Sharon's cabinet, had made stopping Iran from becoming a nuclear power a centerpiece of his national security outlook.

Elections were held on February 10, 2009. Tzipi Livni's Kadima Party won more seats than the Likud, but Netanyahu was able to form a governing coalition. He became prime minister on March 31, 2009.

Mossad veterans with many years of service behind them, especially those who served during Olmert's prime ministership, were of the consensus that George W. Bush was the best president that the Israeli defense and intelligence establishment ever had. Bush did not give Israel carte blanche to do whatever it wanted; he reined in Israel when actions could undercut American policies and objectives in the Arab world. But he allowed the strategic alliance between the two nations, especially their intelligence services, to thrive. Bush's second term, though, was coming to an end. American voters went to the polls on November 4, 2008, with a historic choice between the Republican candidate John McCain, the Arizona senator and former prisoner of war, and the Democratic Party's choice, Barak Obama, a senator from Illinois, and the first African American to ever seek the country's highest office. Obama won a historic victory. He was sworn in on January 20, 2009.

One of the new president's first moves was to nominate a new head of the Central Intelligence Agency. Obama chose Leon Panetta, a former congressman from California who had served as President Bill Clinton's director of the Office of Management and Budget and White House chief of staff, to head America's foreign espionage service. Serving as a first lieutenant in the Army Intelligence Corps was the limit of Panetta's clandestine experience, but he was highly versed in the Beltway universe. Panetta was confirmed as CIA director by the Senate on February 12; it was, coincidentally, the first anniversary of the Mughniyeh hit. Vice President Joseph R. Biden, Jr., came to Langley to swear him in a week later. Biden stood before the marble wall at headquarters, where eighty-nine stars honored CIA officers killed in the line of duty. The symbolism of the wall was disrupted by Biden's comments about the Agency's behavior during the eight years of the terror wars. "The Bush administration's intelligence policies gave al-Qaeda a powerful recruiting tool," the vice president stated.[3] CIA officers in the room, the frontline warriors in the clandestine campaigns against transnational terror, were not quite sure what to make of Biden's comments. Meir

Dagan and his staff at headquarters did not know what to make of the new American administration and the new CIA director. Dagan arranged to travel to Washington, D.C., and meet his new counterpart at Langley. The Mossad travel secretary coordinated the trip with the Israeli Embassy in Washington. Dagan would fly to the United States at the end of March.

The rapport between Meir Dagan and Michael Hayden had been unique, almost uncharacteristic. Dagan was boisterous and outgoing, while Hayden was far more reserved and soft-spoken. Yet the two men were professional soldiers who pushed the American-Israeli intelligence relationship into a partnership that bordered on the intimate interoperability of the Five Eyes Anglosphere intelligence alliance. Dagan studied up on Panetta. The CIA director did the same. "I knew that the intelligence relationship was close and that we were working as partners on several issues on terrorism and Iran," Panetta remembered. "I identified him as an old soldier who'd been around a long time, and [someone] who also understood politics."[4]

Meir Dagan arrived at CIA headquarters on an unseasonably cool afternoon at the end of March 2009. He was ushered by a private elevator to the seventh floor and a waiting room where the new director would greet him. It had been decided to have a working lunch, a casual get-to-know-you session between Dagan, the director, and their closest staff members. The Agency's protocol office had done its homework. The vegetarian menu consisted of an appetizer of baby greens with crispy chickpeas and red onion straws, with Madras curry-ginger vinaigrette, and an entrée of soy-grilled tofu with fried vegetables and sriracha ponzu dipping sauce; dessert consisted of a blood-orange sorbet with fresh berries and cashew tuille.[5] Dagan was impressed by the catering effort and the consideration of his dietary restrictions.

Panetta, like Dagan, was the son of immigrants. The son of Calabrese parents, the CIA director was built on the foundation of hard work and the American dream, and he saw something of his family in the head of the Mossad. "Dagan reminded me of my father. He did not have a great deal of education, but knew what life was all about," Panetta stated. "He [Dagan] was a hard worker, and always talked the truth, with a very pragmatic sense about him, knowing what needed to get done. Dagan had all these qualities, plus the benefit of a long experience of understanding and dealing with others: those up to no good and those who were good people."[6]

Lunch was served on a long conference table. The CIA hosts sat on one side, the Israelis on the other. The seating arrangement was based on rank. Panetta and Dagan used the working lunch to gauge each other. Both men were good at reading people. Panetta was more interested in the policy end of running an espionage service, establishing Obama's vision of the world in how the CIA operated. According to published reports, Dagan wanted no disruptions in the covert operations the two services were involved in, such as the cyber effort against Iran's nuclear reactors known as Operation Olympic Games and including the release of the Stuxnet worm[7] that targeted Siemens machines involved in controlling the speeds of centrifuges,* as well as other joint campaigns to battle al-Qaeda, Hezbollah, and other mutual enemies. The Mossad director also spoke of the need to enhance the economic sanctions that were crippling Iran and forcing them to crawl rather than sprint toward the finish line of producing enough weapons-grade plutonium for a device.

The two men agreed that the Mossad and the CIA needed to work together on this common goal and that they would meet frequently and talk several times a week. "Dagan hated walls, but loved bridges," Tevel chief David Meidan remembered.[8] Dagan believed in working with like-minded people and nations for the common good and wanted to invest whatever capital he could to support the continuation of the close bonds between the CIA and the Mossad.

One of Panetta's first overseas trips as director was to Israel. Dagan wanted to sit down with him before Netanyahu assumed office so that he could brief the new prime minister on details about how the new CIA director would work with Israel. Dagan arranged for a working meal, like Panetta had prepared for the Mossad director at Langley. Amos Yadlin joined Dagan in hosting the CIA chief. It was a large dining

---

* Neither the CIA nor the Mossad has ever taken responsibility for Stuxnet or any other cyber worms that the Iranians found in the computers that serviced their reactor project.

party; the food was catered to appeal to Panetta's Italian immigrant roots. The mood was businesslike, and there were numerous items to review on the agenda. But the roundtable reminded the CIA director of his family dinners in California, sitting around in the kitchen, when his parents talked about the day's events.[9]

Coffee was served and the mood relaxed with the arrival of sweets and fruit. The chitchat at the table quickly turned from talking about pressing issues into friendlier discussions about the pressures of the job. The CIA was still dealing with al-Qaeda, and Panetta asked Dagan what he would do about the terror group. Dagan, Panetta remembered, did not hesitate with his answer. "I'd kill them," the Mossad director responded, "and I'd kill their families."[10] Panetta never knew if the Mossad chief was joking or serious. Spymasters, even the closest of allies, held their cards close to the vest, and preferred their friends did not know what the other was planning.

Two years later, the CIA located Osama bin Laden in Abbottabad, Pakistan, and with the help of SEAL Team 6, killed him and members of the terror leader's family in a daring late-night raid.

The camaraderie between the spy chiefs would be essential in the joint efforts against Iran and the fight against terrorism: the relationship between the new American president and the incoming Israeli prime minister was fraught with hostility.

Prime Minister Benjamin Netanyahu arrived at the White House on the morning of May 18, 2009. It was a warm spring day, but the frost inside the Oval Office would set the tone of Israel's relationship with the United States for the next eight years. Netanyahu wanted to talk about Iran and the need for a united front against Tehran. The American president wanted to talk about a lasting peace with the Palestinians, and Obama lectured the Israeli prime minister, threatening him, that there were to be no more Jewish settlements in the West Bank.

\*          \*          \*

There were three scenarios where the head of the Mossad sat down with the prime minister in the Aquarium office. The head of the Mossad had a regular seat at the Security Cabinet meetings when ministers responsible for Israel's defensive policy and strategies convened. Some gatherings were scheduled long in advance—sessions to review policies toward regional issues—while others were ad hoc, scheduled at an hour's notice, to deal with developing threats.

The Mossad chief also had to get the prime minister's approval for *every* operation carried out by the spy service. Most of the authorizations were done remotely—and securely. But for larger plans, especially those involving grave risk and national danger, the Mossad director came with an entourage of division chiefs and staffers, often coming to the office with the needed charts and maps to sell an operation.

The prime minister's calendar also included weekly personal and work meetings with his espionage chief. The Mossad director always came to these sit-downs with his chief of staff; the prime minister, his military secretary, and a stenographer would join them behind closed doors and discuss a range of issues. It was common for the prime minister and the Mossad chief to grab a few minutes alone, just the two men behind closed doors. The three others would wait in the hallway until summoned back into the room.

Netanyahu, his former chief of staff explained, "held the Mossad in enormously high regard, and respected and appreciated their capabilities and vision."[11] But the prime minister had inherited Dagan, and he was compelled to work with him until his term ended. It was not an ideal situation and one that created great tension. Dagan was in the sixth year of his second term when Netanyahu formed his government. He had developed a sense of confidence and gusto when he walked the halls of power. Dagan carried with him a powerful gravitas that threatened the prime minister, who, although a master politician, found it hard to trust and befriend others. Exacerbating the chasm between the two men was Ehud Barak, who, as part of the coalition that Netanyahu assembled, was the defense minister. Barak and Dagan had a history, one that was not conducive to collaboration.

There were elements of Netanyahu's way of doing business that frustrated Dagan, and they reached breaking points during the meetings in the Aquarium. Dagan viewed punctuality as a religion, and if a meeting was scheduled for 10:00 a.m., he was there at 9:45 a.m.: it was a matter of respect more than anything else. But Netanyahu's tardiness was notorious and well known. Dagan and his chief of staff would be led into the Aquarium, where a secretary would direct the two to a waiting room with a Persian rug, a sofa, and a small table. Tea and coffee would be served. Time dragged on. Sometimes the prime minister ran a half hour behind schedule; sometimes longer. Dagan would kill time by chatting with the national security advisor or the military secretary. But the wait continued.

There were times when Netanyahu was running so late, E.,* Dagan's chief of staff, remembered, that the Mossad director would just grab his bag, call his driver, and return to headquarters, always stopping for a falafel or some other takeout to bring back to the office.[12] There were too many urgent national security matters to contend with to be sequestered in a waiting room, sipping tea and wasting time.

Dagan had admired Sharon and Olmert because they were decisive decision-makers. Both men deliberated the risks and benefits of high-risk operations, often asking very tough questions when it came down to authorizing a mission far from the country's borders, but they never hesitated to render a decision either way. Netanyahu, a former division chief stated, hemmed and hawed, often refusing to give Dagan a resolute yay or a nay for a particular operation, gesturing with his head rather than giving an answer. "Does your head say yes or no?" Dagan would ask, Olmert remembered him sharing with him once.[13]

Netanyahu appreciated the need for Dagan's clandestine service leadership at the helm of the Mossad for the fight against Iran, and in October 2009, he extended Dagan's tenure by another twenty-four months.[14]

*     *     *

Months before Operation Orchid, Meir Dagan had presented U.S. undersecretary of state R. Nicholas Burns, a veteran Foggy Bottom insider and former ambassador to NATO, with a five-step plan for

---

* Identity withheld for security reasons.

expediting a regime change in Iran, the most effective way the Mossad director believed that Iran's race to the bomb could be stopped without massive military action.

The first step was public and political, make Iran an issue before the United Nations Security Council and warrant an international consensus and crippling economic sanctions.

The second involved the expansion of covert action: cyberwarfare, financial warfare, espionage, sabotage, and direct action, preemptive Negative Treatment of key Iranian individuals involved in nuclear development.

The third measure was strict international controls and law enforcement pressure to restrict countries from selling technologies and equipment to Iran that could be used in nuclear weapons development. The fourth involved suffocating economic sanctions—crippling, bankrupting, and inescapable measures that would hobble the regime and force the citizens of the country, the vast majority of whom did not support the mullahs, to rise. These measures included seizing the fortunes of the mullahs and the IRGC senior echelons held in foreign banks, preventing them from traveling, and even liberating their fortunes through a wide array of clandestine schemes. This also meant applying the same financial pressures to the international partners of the program—European salesmen, Asian shell companies, and African money laundering schemes.

Dagan believed that the combination of all these steps happening together could expedite regime change in Tehran—something that the United States, the Europeans, and especially the Gulf States, had wanted since the downfall of the shah.[15]

Time was not on the West's side, though. The Iranians were racing toward building the bomb. And that posed a separate set of challenges and limitations. Israel did not have the military capabilities in the Middle East at the time to take out the facilities and any kinetic action needed to be done with the United States, and that was unlikely during the Obama administration. Although a nuclear Iran was not solely an Israeli issue, the brunt of the dirty work fell on the Jewish state and its intelligence services.

The Iranians were wise students, though. They had learned the lessons of al-Kibar and Osirak. The Iranian reactors and research facilities were spread across the country in multiple hardened facilities. Two enrichment facilities would have to be destroyed to take out the nuclear weapons program. The Nantanz nuclear facility, outside the holy city of Qom, was Iran's principal uranium enrichment site. Most of the Nantanz facility was underground, buried 160 feet below a mountain, defended by antiaircraft missile launchers and artillery batteries. Fordow, a former Islamic Revolutionary Guard missile base turned uranium enrichment facility, was the second-largest development site. Parchin, an Iranian missile testing facility some twenty miles southeast of Tehran, was key in coordinating weapons-grade material with the delivery systems to fire them at Israel.

Dagan hoped that the Mossad's clandestine efforts would be able to stall Iran until the rest of the world or the Iranian people changed the paradigm. According to published accounts, the Mossad reached Iran's most secret sites and carried out operations to undermine the nuclear program's very sense of security. But the missions were fraught with danger. Dagan used to sit with those he was about to send into harm's way in his office, underneath the photo of his grandfather, and tell them the risks and the operation's overall chances for success. He never sugarcoated peril; he never said to any agent that if they were captured, the State of Israel would deny any knowledge of their existence. If a mission went south and the intelligence officer was arrested, the Mossad would do everything possible to obtain their release. But the Israeli capabilities to return a captured spy were limited.

It was Dagan's theory that Israel was at war with Iran, but the battles had to be covert. Ingeniously planned operations of a clandestine nature lowered the possibility of a conventional conflict. Virtually all the proactive intelligence efforts undertaken by Israel against Iran were classified—even those that in the Israeli media were mentioned "as according to foreign reports."

As far back as Ariel Sharon's prime ministership, Dagan had wanted the Mossad to assume leadership in stifling Iran's nuclear ambitions, and the agency led the effort in direct action, joint operations with friendly services like the CIA, and choking off vital financing to the Islamic Republic. Dagan traveled wherever his presence could make a difference and met anyone in power who could help the world rid Tehran of its nefarious plans. The director of Mossad visited his counterparts across the region and traveled on state visits with the prime minister to talk to world leaders. Prime Minister Olmert took Dagan to Russia to help in his efforts to persuade President Putin to halt Russian military assistance to the Iranians. The Russians were Iran's principal arms suppliers, and the plea was to stop selling advanced air defense weaponry to Tehran. "Putin liked Dagan and respected him as a former intelligence officer and as a man of courage and integrity," Udi Levi reflected. "The Russian president preferred to talk business with the head of the Mossad more than with an elected official."[16] The Mossad chief also traveled with Netanyahu to talk to Putin about ways of slowing the Iranian march toward a nuclear threshold.

Meir Dagan reportedly visited Riyadh in the spring of 2010 to establish a regional consensus that would join the American and European efforts to stymie the Iranian effort and assist the Mossad in any clandestine action it and the IDF would need to take against Tehran.[17]

*          *          *

Prime Minister Netanyahu pushed the Iran issue in every forum he could—domestically, to the Israeli electorate, and internationally, at the United Nations General Assembly, the White House, and on Capitol Hill. Netanyahu spoke of a military option, a preemptive strike, a notion that the prime minister and Defense Minister Barak promoted with a sense of urgency.

Meir Dagan had learned a valuable lesson from his combat experiences in Lebanon. There were limits to military power, and overreach was a threat to Israel's democracy. War was a last resort. "It [the strike] will be followed by a war with Iran," Dagan would later say. "It is the kind of thing where we know how it starts, but not how it will end."[18]

A preemptive raid against Nantanz, Fordow, and Parchin would require special munitions that the United States did not provide. The

GBU-57, or the Massive Ordnance Penetrator bomb, would only enter U.S. military service in 2011. The IAF, at the time, lacked the aerial refueling capabilities and stealth aircraft to reach the targets undetected and the ability to rescue pilots downed by antiaircraft fire. Hezbollah was hit hard in 2006, but it was not vanquished; it still had tens of thousands of missiles aimed at Israel's population centers, and Israel did not yet have a high-tech antimissile system in place. Iran would launch missiles, as well. "Iran isn't Iraq, Iran isn't Lebanon, and Iran isn't Syria," Tamir Pardo explained, "it's a whole other reality."[19]

There were political considerations, as well. There were tens of thousands of American soldiers in the Middle East, many stationed in countries the Israeli aircraft would have to fly over on their way to Iran. The diplomatic fallout, the Mossad assessed, could be overwhelming.

In 2010, Netanyahu and Barak's talk of war came eerily close to reality. Dagan and Shin Bet director Yuval Diskin were outspokenly against Israel mounting a unilateral preemptive strike, taking the discussions in the Security Cabinet with the utmost severity. There was a theory, some Netanyahu insiders have mentioned, that the bluster was a Sayeret Mat'kal–inspired posture to show the world that Israel meant business and to prod the international community into action.[20] IDF chief of staff Lieutenant General Gabi Ashkenazi, a former infantryman regarded as a tough-as-nails soldier, also placed roadblocks in front of the political leadership, strongly arguing against the merits of an attack. Dagan claimed that going to war would violate Israeli law and could not be done solely by the prime minister and his minister of defense.[21] The prime minister's powers were not open to debate, though the Israeli democracy, Dagan firmly believed, had human safeguards for just such scenarios.

In the end, the security chiefs prevailed. Israel did not attack Iran.

\*          \*          \*

The United States continued to take the lead in the diplomatic and economic campaign against Iran. Dagan was determined that the Mossad would do whatever it could to delay and dissuade the Iranian quest.

Israel, according to published accounts, took the more direct approach. On January 12, 2010, Masoud Alimohammadi, a senior scientist in Iran's nuclear project, was killed in a Tehran suburb by an explosive-laden motorcycle parked near his car. No one ever assumed responsibility for the blast. During Dagan's tenure as director of the Mossad, five key scientists involved in Iran's pursuit of the bomb were killed.[22]

Many more would die in the years that followed.

# End of Term

f ever there was a candidate for Negative Treatment, Mahmoud al-Mabhouh was it.*

Al-Mabhouh, one of fourteen children, was born in the Gaza Strip in 1960. He was seven years old when Israeli tanks rolled into Gaza; he was in his teens when he joined the Muslim Brotherhood. The Brotherhood had been outlawed by Egypt, though allowed to thrive by the IDF and the Shin Bet, who saw the pious men as convenient rivals of the nationalistic and ideologically focused Palestinian terror groups. Al-Mabhouh was a bruiser, physically imposing and good with his hands. He lifted weights and boxed; he had a reputation as an enforcer, someone who used violence against those who opposed the Brotherhood in the political turf wars that the various Palestinians fought among themselves. In 1986, the Shin Bet arrested al-Mabhouh on suspicion of belonging to a terrorist organization. An assault rifle, grenades, and hundreds of bullets were found in his home. Hamas was the Muslim Brotherhood's underground army.

Members of the fundamentalist terror group did not do well behind the walls of Israel's security prisons. Most of the inmates belonged to

---

* The State of Israel has never taken *official* responsibility for the killing of Hamas commander Mahmoud al-Mabhouh.

Fatah or one of the popular fronts. Al-Mabhouh displayed a penchant for cruelty behind bars, taking out rivals when needed. He claimed to have been tortured there, but he made a name for himself as a prisoner, and when he was released and returned to Gaza, he was welcomed back into the ranks of Hamas with great fanfare. The Islamic resistance movement had become a force to be reckoned with during the first intifada. It took on more members than it could absorb. Al-Mabhouh assembled a small band of like-minded muscle into a force he named Unit 101, whose sole mission was kidnapping and murdering Israeli soldiers. His partner was Yahya Sinwar, the feared Hamas enforcer, whose penchant for cruelty had earned him the nickname "the Butcher of Khan Younis."

Their first victim was Sergeant Avi Sasportas, a paratrooper. He was kidnapped in southern Israel on February 16, 1989, by Hamas terrorists masquerading as Orthodox Jews; the soldier was thumbing a ride, trying to get home on leave. Three months later, al-Mabhouh and his team abducted and murdered nineteen-year-old Corporal Ilan Saadon. They reportedly photographed themselves stomping on the dead soldier's corpse.[1]

The long arm of Israeli intelligence had never managed to catch up to al-Mabhouh. He evaded massive dragnets in Gaza. He fled to Egypt, and then Libya, Algeria, and Jordan, before being deported to the embrace of Hamas headquarters in Damascus. He displayed great skill with numbers, taking charge of the organization's budget for weapons procurement. The Iranians liked him. He was the man behind attempts to smuggle freighter vessels full of missiles and explosives to Gaza during the second intifada. He was the mastermind of the Hamas rocket and missile program and was one of the key liaison officers connecting the Gaza-based terrorists with Hezbollah in Lebanon. In 2007, after Hamas took over the Gaza Strip in a bloody coup against Fatah and the Palestinian Authority, al-Mabhouh was instrumental in building the Hamas rocket arsenal; the materials were smuggled from Egypt through a series of large tunnels. By the end of 2007, Hamas and the Palestinian Islamic Jihad had fired close to three thousand rockets against the Israeli population centers of southern Israel.

Hamas had transitioned from suicide bombers to terror tunnels and short-range rockets, and al-Mabhouh worked hard to expand the range of the terror group's missile development. He established a sophisticated smuggling route from Iran to Sudan, and then to Egypt, Sinai, and Gaza, through the expanding network of smuggling tunnels. In January and February 2009, the IAF launched pinpoint air strikes against Iranian Islamic Revolutionary Guard trucks and facilities in Port Sudan on the Red Sea, where the Iranian ships carrying the Hamas ordnance docked. The IAF flew over eight hundred miles to hit their targets.[2] The Israeli operation, code-named Birds of Prey, also involved intelligence and commando assets and reportedly killed thirty-nine IRGC and Hamas operatives.[3] Iran and Hamas had turned Sudan into a terror hub.

The Mossad viewed Mahmoud al-Mabhouh almost in the same light as it regarded Imad Mughniyeh—a target whose importance to a terror group and Iran was unmatched and irreplaceable. Meir Dagan presented al-Mabhouh's name to the Heads of Services Committee as a target for consideration. The assignment, according to reports, was handed to Caesaria, and operational plans were drawn, redrawn, reviewed, dry-run, and prepared for the director's approval.

As published, a Mossad asset somewhere in the Middle East had inserted a Trojan horse into al-Mabhouh's laptop, allowing Israeli intelligence to monitor his every move. He developed a travel pattern, flying across the Middle East and using Dubai as his primary connecting hub; the Hamas commander liked Emirates airline, especially its business class product and use of the airport lounges for comfort. He preferred to stay at luxury hotels and did not travel with a security package of bodyguards.

The Mossad was no stranger to Dubai. The city and emirate were undergoing a massive construction boom. Five-star hotels, shopping malls, and office buildings that reached the skies were being built there. Tourists and businessmen flooded the country. Forty million people flew in and out of Dubai in 2009; 140 airlines flew in and out of the massive airport, one of the world's largest and busiest. It was an easy location to insert teams of agents without great fanfare or peril. A hit on al-Mabhouh was considered low-risk.

Sometime in November 2009, Dagan brought the mission to the prime minister for final review and authorization. Netanyahu gave his Mossad director the green light to proceed.[4] Al-Mabhouh's code name in the Mossad files was Plasma Screen.[5]

\*          \*          \*

Mahmoud al-Mabhouh traveled to Dubai on January 19, 2010, on Emirates Flight 912 from Damascus. To conceal his identity, he used Palestinian travel documents in the name of Mahmoud Abdul Raouf Mohammed.* EK912 landed at 3:15 p.m.; the airport shuttle car took al-Mabhouh to the Al Bustan Rotana, only five minutes away. He was checked into his room by 16:00. Israeli agents were waiting at the hotel. They watched the reception agent hand al-Mabhouh his plastic magnetic room key. Surveillance followed him as he opened the door to Room 230.

The progression of the operation was monitored closely at headquarters.

Before and after al-Mabhouh landed, a large force of Israeli agents, men and women, carrying a library of passports from numerous European countries, had arrived in Dubai from embarkation airports across Western Europe, on numerous foreign airlines. The spies were young. No one was over forty years old; most were in their twenties. They stayed at separate hotels around the city. UAE immigration officials at the airport, dressed in their snow-white dishdasha robes and ghutra headdresses, did not notice any issue with the travel documents. Twenty-nine of the agents were on the ground in Dubai. Twenty-six of them were believed to have used counterfeit or fraudulently obtained passports.[6]

Rotating teams followed al-Mabhouh's every step in Dubai, tailing him to the City Centre Deira Shopping Mall and then to a meeting at the Iranian consulate. Mahmoud al-Mabhouh was last seen alive at 8:24 p.m. on closed-circuit television in the hotel. Elements of the Mossad direct

* Although Palestine is not recognized in most Western circles as a sovereign state, Palestinian passports are recognized in the Arab world.

action team began leaving the Al Bustan Rotana two minutes later. The
Caesarea agents departed Dubai that evening. They took separate flights
to Hong Kong, Johannesburg, Frankfurt, and numerous other European
destinations, before finding a route back to Israel.

It is believed that al-Mabhouh was overpowered in his room, given
a muscle relaxant, and then asphyxiated. The Mossad agents managed
to leave the room and yet lock it from the inside. There were no signs
of a struggle when the housekeeping staff found his body the following
afternoon; the Do Not Disturb sign had kept them from entering Room
230 earlier that morning.

*          *          *

The taking of Mahmoud al-Mabhouh's life took only a couple of minutes.
Preparing for the operation—acquiring the documentation and identities,
monitoring the target's computer, and blueprinting the mission's every
move—took almost a year and involved countless man-hours. Tactically,
Operation Plasma Screen was a success. Intelligence operations are not
always judged by results, though. Sometimes, they are remembered for
the political fallout they create. The killing of Mahmoud al-Mabhouh
turned into a mess.

The Dubai Police at first thought that the body in Room 230 had died
of natural causes. A heart attack was suspected. But when investigators
discovered who the man in the morgue was, detectives began pulling
CCTV coverage at the hotel, the airport, and throughout the city.* It
did not take them long to connect twenty-nine faces that intersected
with the victim's movements throughout the city, even though there
were almost seven hundred hours of video to review and analyze.[7]
Within days, Lieutenant General Dahi Kahlfan Tamim, commander of
General Security for the Emirate of Dubai, chaired press conferences

* The al-Mabhouh assassination was not the first "hit" in Dubai carried out by a foreign
intelligence service that was caught on the city's near-hermetic network of cameras.
On March 30, 2009, Sulim Yamadayev, a former Chechen general, had been shot and
killed by anonymous assailants as he left a car park in Dubai. Two assassins working
for the Russian FSB were arrested for the murder.

with audiovisual support. The faces of the Israeli agents and the corresponding passports they used were plastered on the front pages of newspapers worldwide; the passports were from countries that did not need visas to enter the UAE.[8] Many of the passports belonged to actual people who had no idea their identities were being used.

Governments friendly to Israel were outraged that their passports had been used illegally, fraudulently, and for an extrajudicial killing. Israeli ambassadors were summoned to the foreign ministries in Berlin, Paris, London, and elsewhere to answer for the transgression. Intelligence insiders claimed Operation Plasma Screen had been an abject failure because of the publicity it attracted and the firestorm it created, stating that it was poorly planned, terribly conceived, and sloppily executed.[9] "With the advances in facial recognition software and other technologies, the operation in Dubai was the last of its kind and marked the end of an era," Ehud Lavi, a veteran Mossad officer and commander in the Tzomet and Caesaria branches, said. "It will be hard for intelligence agents to remain anonymous any longer when carrying out such assignments."[10]

Meir Dagan, though, was satisfied. None of his agents were arrested, and al-Mabhouh was dead. And that was more important than anything that could be cleaned up by politicians and diplomats later.

Prime Minister Netanyahu stood by his espionage chief, though the debacle was just the out he was looking for to rid himself of the pesky Dagan. But, it is believed, Netanyahu could not forgive the Mossad director for his insolence in opposing the plans to attack Iran. And with Dubai, Netanyahu had the political justification to deny Dagan another two-year term extension. Meir Dagan became a lame duck intelligence chief. His service to the State of Israel had come to an end.

*          *          *

At 10:00 a.m. on January 2, 2011, the cabinet was assembled for meeting number eighty-five of Prime Minister Benjamin Netanyahu's government. There were seven items on the agenda. A farewell to Meir Dagan topped the list.

Dagan wore a dark gray suit. He looked like a banker, though he wore a Casio Pathfinder watch, favored by special forces soldiers, to retain his military image. Dagan sat to the prime minister's right, the seat of honor. The spy chief looked relaxed, almost jovial. "Today," the prime minister proclaimed to the ministers assembled around the packed conference table, "we are saying goodbye to Meir, the head of the Mossad, after eight years serving as the head of the Mossad, dozens of years of service to the IDF, and as the prime minister's counterterrorism advisor. I wondered how I could thank you for your great contributions to the security of Israel." The prime minister spoke of how he remembered sitting in the director's office at Mossad headquarters, seeing the photo of Ber Slushni hanging in his office, and *finally* understanding what made Dagan tick. Netanyahu hugged Dagan, thanking him. Applause broke out in the room.

Dagan sat as he thanked the prime minister in a prepared address. He was uncomfortable speaking publicly. He did not talk about himself, but rather his successor, Tamir Pardo, who had served as his deputy for almost six years. Dagan talked about the men and women of the Mossad and their work on behalf of Israel's survival. The work was lonely, he explained, and they operated without the backup of tanks and combat aircraft and often carried out the job with the knowledge that they could be captured without any chance of rescue. Their only cover was their quick wit, cover story, and courage. He ended by reiterating the need to defend the people of Israel and the State of Israel.[11]

Meir Dagan always looked at the world through the eyes of Israel, and he looked at Israel through the eyes of the Jewish nation.

Meir Dagan left the prime minister's office, and later Mossad headquarters, with a sense of regret and relief. He had not been able to bring back the bodies of Eli Cohen, the Mossad's man in Damascus, nor could he provide the Arad family with closure by returning the navigator home for a proper burial. He left the Mossad after eight challenging and sometimes spectacular years with Israel's enemies, namely Hezbollah and Syria, weakened, and he had delayed Iran's quest for nuclear weapons. He fulfilled his mission of keeping weapons of mass destruction out of the hands, even if temporarily, of Israel's enemies, and his agents terminated those who had killed innocent civilians and who were still planning future crimes.

Meir Dagan returned the swagger to the Mossad and made the Jewish state's enemies fear the imagination and sheer audacity of Israel's spies. He used personality and reputation to advance Israel's ties with its Arab neighbors, never forgetting that Israel lived in the Middle East and would have to work with those neighbors. His efforts helped to lay the tracks for what would eventually become the Abraham Accords. Most importantly, Meir Dagan played a critical role in strengthening the strategic bonds between the Mossad and the CIA, and, in essence, between Israel and the United States.

Dagan knew that one day, in the whirlwind of a terrible crisis that posed an existential threat to the country and the Jewish people, the alliance he had significantly strengthened would be needed.

The forty-eight years he spent serving his country took a toll on Meir Dagan. He lost precious and unrecoverable time with his wife, children, and grandkids. He returned home an old and tired soldier, but he had no plans to fade away.

# CHAPTER 30

# A Warrior's Epitaph

On a cool March night in 2015, seven months after a small war in Gaza against Hamas ended in stalemate, Meir Dagan did something that made him very uncomfortable and caused him to tremble in fear: he addressed eighty thousand Israelis in the heart of Tel Aviv at a political rally meant to jar the country out of what he felt was a dangerous and possibly unrecoverable vortex. Israel was adrift, mired in political conflict and what the former Mossad director saw as self-serving leaders who threatened the country's very existence. "Israel is a nation surrounded by enemies, but I am not afraid of enemies," Dagan said. "I am frightened by our leadership. I am afraid because of the lack of vision and loss of direction. I am frightened by the hesitation and the stagnation. And I am frightened, above all else, of the crisis in leadership. It is the worst crisis that Israel has seen to this day."[1]

Dagan served three prime ministers during his tenure as Mossad chief. He saw the virtue behind those who thought ten years into the future and those who worked solely for their political base. Toward the end of his years as Mossad chief, and in the later years before his death, Dagan feared that the divisive appeal of populism and the collateral damage of political overreach threatened to destroy the foundation of Israel's democracy. He expressed his concerns over Netanyahu's leadership, behind closed doors when he was the head of the Mossad, and then, as a citizen, with a megaphone at rallies and through the media to vocalize his fears that Israel was in peril from elected officials who lacked accountability and that the country deserved better.

Meir Dagan was purposely apolitical. He had never belonged to a party—not on the right or the left. He practiced pragmatism and integrity. His only core belief was that the Jewish state and the Jewish people needed to be protected. In private, and even in the company of elected leaders, he often repeated *Ha'Mamlacha Ze Lo Ha'Melech*, the "Kingdom is Not the King," when speaking of Netanyahu, fearing the prime minister was leading Israel down a disastrous path. Dagan often reminded Netanyahu that although the Mossad director answered directly to the prime minister, he, like all Mossad directors, served the State of Israel. But now he felt compelled to lend his voice, demanding a better future for the country. His bout with cancer made his voice quiver as he addressed the thousands who had traveled across the country to hear him speak. Dagan was no longer the larger-than-life bulldozer. He had lost a lot of weight and looked like a shell of his former self. He was dying, and he knew he was quickly running out of time.

\*          \*          \*

Life after the Mossad had been busy for Dagan. He did something he did not like to do—he frequently spoke to the press. He gave interviews, appeared on Israeli television, and was even featured in a segment of the CBS News program *60 Minutes*, interviewed by Lesley Stahl. He tried his hand at business, serving on the advisory board of Black Cube, a private intelligence company with offices in Tel Aviv and London that became controversial because of some of its clients in Hollywood, Eastern Europe, and Africa: Harvey Weinstein; Joseph Kabila, the president of the Democratic Republic of the Congo; and Hungarian strongman Viktor Orbán. Dagan was listed as the company's president but did little in its day-to-day operations. "When you say, 'The president of my company is Meir Dagan,' there is no better entrance card to any club you choose," a former high-ranking Israeli veteran of the country's defense and security industry told *Forbes*.[2]

Dagan also consulted and served on the boards of companies and organizations determined to keep nuclear weapons out of the hands of the Iranians. But he was not a very good businessman, having never managed an entity that chased money as an objective. "He felt that he owed something to his wife, kids, and grandchildren," Udi Levi, his subordinate and close confidant, admitted. "Public servants always get the feeling into retirement that they missed out on providing for their families."[3]

In early 2012, doctors found that Dagan was suffering from an aggressive form of liver cancer. He underwent intensive sessions of chemotherapy. In Israel, the United States, and elsewhere in Europe, the former Mossad director was too old to receive a liver transplant. Former world leaders and those in power tried to pull strings for Dagan. President Obama and Prime Minister Netanyahu were unsuccessful in their attempts.

Alexander Lukashenko, the dictator of Belarus, was able to help. Dagan had met him during his time at the Mossad, and connections, even with despots, sometimes came through. The retired intelligence chief received his new liver in October 2012. The kings and emirs of the Middle East wanted to help. King Mohammed VI of Morocco offered Dagan and his family one of the royal palaces in the Atlas Mountains for his convalescence.[4] He received similar offers from Jordan and the Emirates. The operation bought him a little over three extra years and helped rekindle Meir's relationship with his brother Eli, who had become a world-renowned scientist specializing in cancer research, cellular differentiation, and adult stem cell research. Eli visited his ailing brother in Israel, and Meir visited the Huberman home in Chicago in between therapy sessions in the United States.

Meir Dagan was sober about his condition and chances of beating the disease. He accepted his fate, began to bid farewell to his friends and loved ones, and continued to work. He became a relentless critic of Netanyahu, but the conflict was one of leadership; it was never personal or laced with any personal ambition. Had he not fallen ill, he might have entered politics. His closest friends always warned him that he had led too honest a life to dirty his legacy by throwing his hat into the ring of a system crueler and nastier than anything he'd encountered in the shadow wars he led in the army and at the Mossad.

The talk of a life of elected service was not meant to be. The cancer returned, harsher than ever. The disease battered his diminishing frame, but not his spirit. He fought to the end, though cancer proved to be the one foe that Dagan could not vanquish. Meir Dagan passed away on March 17, 2016. He was seventy-one years old.

*         *         *

Rosh Pina is a small hillside hamlet of three thousand people in Upper Galilee established in 1878. Residents live in modest stone homes, some of which date back to the days of the Ottoman Empire, with lovingly manicured gardens and rock fences. Its mountain air is crisp and refreshing. Rosh Pina boasts art galleries and spas, attracting bohemians and tourists alike with a special brand of Zen-like enchantment. Life there can be tranquil, even though the melodies of chirping birds are sometimes interrupted by the roar of combat aircraft. Rosh Pina sits less than ten miles from the Lebanese frontier and only a forty-minute drive from the Syrian border.

Over the years, Rosh Pina became a popular home for military officers assigned to the commands protecting Israel's north. The professional soldiers needed a place to live, where they could raise a family, close to their bases near the Lebanese and Syrian front lines. Many fell in love with the location and decided to call Rosh Pina their permanent home. Meir Dagan was one of them. It was there that he wished to be buried.

Dagan's flag-draped coffin was laid in state at Mossad headquarters. It was the first time in the service's history that such a salute was afforded to a former chief.[5] An honor guard of senior Mossad intelligence officers, his most trusted deputies, stood stoically at attention while past and present members of Israel's intelligence fraternity walked past the coffin and paid their final respects, as the spy agency's rabbi recited from the Psalms.

Meir Dagan was saluted as a spymaster. On March 20, he was buried as a soldier.

A convoy of army vehicles and a police escort had transported his flag-draped coffin up north. Like all communities in Israel, regardless of their size, Rosh Pina has a military cemetery. It was founded in June 1948 to bury ninety-five soldiers who were killed repelling the Syrian army that invaded the state following Israel's declaration of independence. But the cemetery grew. There would be more wars and more fallen to bury. The tombstones are made of polished sand-colored stones and etched with the soldier's name, place of birth, and where and when they were killed. The graves face north and south. It is a solemn place, situated along the slope of a hill, marked by a towering blue-and-white Israeli flag overlooking the Hula Valley and the Golan Heights.

Men who fought with Dagan across the atlas of Israel's wars—Gaza, Sinai, and Lebanon—and who survived to talk about it, filed into the cemetery to honor their fallen commander and comrade. They were in their sixties and seventies; their feats of daring and valor were now just memories. Their swagger was slowed by age.

Bina Dagan and her children requested that the funeral not be broadcast live on television.[6] Part of the reason was family privacy, but part was that members of the intelligence community would not have to worry about their faces being broadcast and their identities revealed. An A-list of past and present political leaders and generals came to Rosh Pina. A commentator for Israel's Channel 1 said, "Never before had so many of Israel's heroes been gathered in one place."[7]

Prime Minister Benjamin Netanyahu, President Reuven Rivlin, Defense Minister Moshe Ya'alon, and Mossad chief Yossi Cohen were all present. They sat next to Dagan's immediate family in the front row, under a white tarp turned gray by the rainfall, awaiting their call to deliver a eulogy. "You taught us that the State of Israel has to prevent a second Holocaust," President Rivlin commented. "He once told me that he hoped that he did everything in his power to prevent such a thing from ever happening again."[8] He concluded by stating that Dagan was the greatest among the giants."[9] Former president Shimon Peres said, "Meir, you never surrendered. Not to a drawn sword, the bitter truth, and you never stopped in the struggle to achieve peace."

Mossad director Yossi Cohen, known by his code name Model, whom Dagan had appointed to head the Tzomet intelligence-gathering division, also spoke of his former boss. "He dedicated his life to the Mossad totally and completely," Cohen remembered. "He will be remembered as one of the best and most influential Mossad directors. He knew how to pass on to us, the members of the Mossad, precisely what he planned. He would sometimes remove himself from an area where we were operating and the command post to allow us, the commanders, to act with freedom." Then, switching to a personal reflection, Cohen concluded, "He was a person who took things to heart, and he had a wide heart. He tried to hide it from me, but his heart was broken, tears filled his eyes, and his voice quivered when he spoke about his comrades who fell in battle and about the genocide of the Jewish people in the Holocaust."[10]

Even Prime Minister Netanyahu, whose contentious relationship with Dagan became very public, spoke glowingly of his former spy chief. Netanyahu spoke of the outside-the-box intelligence operations that Dagan would present to him for authorization, reminiscing that some of them were beyond the boundaries of imagination, they were so spectacular. The operations, the prime minister emphasized, personified the Israeli chutzpah, Dagan's chutzpah. In a rare moment of magnanimity, Netanyahu thanked Dagan for his dedicated service to the people of Israel, reciting a passage from a poem by Shlomo Skulsky about Rosh Pina, Dagan's beloved home, that captured the essence of the man: "You do not conquer the top of the mountain if there is no grave on its slope."[11]

Six major generals representing the different branches of the Israel Defense Forces served as pallbearers. It was the same rank that Dagan had achieved in uniform. The men lowered Dagan's coffin, a simple pine box, into the ground of the land he so loved, as a military rabbi recited from a prayer book. An honor guard of young conscripts from the Armored Corps lined up and raised their M-16 rifles toward the darkening skies of the approaching winter's dusk, to offer a gun salute. Dagan's son and his brother, Eli Huberman, recited the kaddish, the mourner's prayer. A simple placard with the IDF emblem, Dagan's serial number, and rank, surrounded by daisies and other flowers, marked his grave.

Over one thousand people attended the funeral. They were aging comrades in arms and contemporaries of the spy world wanting to pay their respects to a fearless gunslinger and a man of boundless strategic vision who represented a generation of Israeli warriors that was more a part of the nation's past than its future. Former CIA director Leon Panetta remembered his old friend's legacy as "one of total loyalty to the mission of protecting the security of Israel. He would do whatever was necessary to make sure that Israel's enemies would never succeed, and in the process built an intelligence operation that was second to none."[12] The men and women who served under him would agree. To them, he was their battlefield commander and one of the most important and impactful directors to lead Israel's spies.

# Never Again

Eli Huberman was seven months old when the Germans marched into Łuków on September 9, 1939. His parents, Shmuel and Mina, trapped at the onset of yet another of history's attempts to annihilate the Jewish people, found themselves helpless and scared for the safety of their newborn and their extended families. But they were offered a lifeline. They fled Poland and headed east, surviving the Holocaust. They would not feel truly safe until 1950, when the family, along with their second-born, Meir, made aliyah to the new State of Israel, a nation built to ensure the survival of the Jewish people.

Kfir Bibas was nine months old on the morning of October 7, 2023, when Hamas terrorists stormed the gates of Kibbutz Nir Oz. His parents, Yarden and Shiri, were also helpless the moment the murders began. Yarden was savagely beaten and dragged off to the tunnels of Gaza, where he would remain a hostage for 484 days. Shiri, holding Kfir and his four-year-old brother, Ariel, was last seen clutching her two babies as terrorists manhandled them before taking them into captivity, where the three would be brutally murdered. The Bibas family's lifeline was supposed to have been the impenetrable might of Israel's military, intelligence, and security service shield.*

* Yarden Bibas was freed from Hamas captivity on February 1, 2025, during the fourth

October 7, 2023, was the bloodiest day for the Jewish people since the end of the Holocaust, and it happened on Israeli soil—inside the nation whose primary mission was to prevent such history from being repeated. One thousand, one hundred and ninety-five men, women, and children were killed that terrible day: civilians, soldiers, police officers, and first responders. Approximately two hundred and fifty Israelis, the dead and those still alive, were abducted and taken to a miserable fate of torture, neglect, and starvation in the tunnels underneath the Gaza Strip. Nine-month-old Kfir Bibas was the youngest hostage; the oldest was eighty-six years old and had survived Hitler's Europe. Men and women of all ages were raped and sexually molested that day and for the weeks and months that many would spend in captivity. The accounts of barbarity—the beheadings, mutilations, and desecrations of the dead—are still impossible to fathom, even though many of these unspeakable crimes were filmed on GoPro cameras and mobile phones carried by the terrorists and broadcast, live, on social media for the world to see.

October 7 was far more than a terrorist attack. It was an invasion. Hamas and Islamic Jihad terrorists blasted through border fences and utilized underground tunnels to cross into Israel. Others came by air using motorized paragliders; frogmen landed on beaches from the sea. A barrage of thousands of rockets aimed at Israeli towns and communities supported the blitz. Gunmen from the Nukhba Force, the Hamas special operations spearhead, were equipped with advanced weaponry and the best personal kits that money could buy. The terrorists came with food and cargo pockets full of Captagon, the Iranian-bankrolled, Hezbollah-distributed, and Syrian-produced amphetamine that gave users superpower rage; the attackers came with medics, hoping to tend to their wounded, hurt fighting off the Israeli counterattack. It took the Israeli military and police almost three weeks to recapture the towns, agricultural communities, and forward military bases that had been seized.

round of hostage release talks. During his 484 days as a prisoner, starving and being tortured in the tunnels under the Gaza Strip, he repeatedly asked about his wife and kids. His captors said they were okay. They had, though, been brutally murdered shortly after being abducted; the babies, a forensic analysis revealed, were killed with "bare hands." Their bodies were returned to Israel on February 20.

In 2021, two years before the vapor trails of Hamas rockets punctuated the morning's sky over southern Israel and close to four thousand heavily armed terrorists invaded twenty-two communities in the Gaza Envelope, Hamas leader Yahya Sinwar asked the Iranian Islamic Revolutionary Guard Corps for five hundred million dollars to destroy Israel and two years in which to do it.[1]

Fifty years and a day before October 7, on the Jewish holy day of Yom Kippur, the Egyptian and Syrian armies launched a devastating surprise attack to strike Israeli lines along the Suez Canal and atop the Golan Heights. The conventional armies that overran Israeli positions on October 6, 1973, were sent into battle to undo the last war's humiliation and set the stage for a political settlement. On October 7, 2023, the invaders were terrorists, men who were dispatched to undo the very creation of the Jewish state by displaying such unprecedented butchery that the carnage would draw all of Israel's enemies into a united front and set the entire Middle East ablaze.

In 1973, the signs of impending doom had become apparent to Israel's intelligence services and the country's political leadership, but what became known in Hebrew as *Ha'Kontzeptzia*, the conception that the Arab armies would never dare attack the army that had vanquished them six years earlier in the Six-Day War, led to fatal overconfidence and debilitating miscalculations; Israel's strategic thinking had become stagnant, one resting on previous laurels and optimism. Two thousand, five hundred soldiers were killed in eighteen days of intense combat. Meir Dagan was a by-product of that war and what became known as the October Earthquake. The men who rushed toward the Golan Heights or deep into the Sinai Desert could never forget the trauma of being caught so dangerously by surprise. He could never shake the memories of all he had witnessed in war, but he would take the lessons learned with him as he rose through the ranks and in the eight years he served as director of the Mossad.

In 2016, an Israeli Ministry of Defense memo elaborated that Hamas intended to move the next confrontation to Israeli territory and that an attack from Gaza would likely involve hostage-taking and occupying several communities.[2] Just two years before October 7, Israel managed to get hold of the Hamas playbook that detailed the precise makeup of the attack, down to specific details about the houses in the targeted communities. The document, code-named Jericho Wall, was a forty-page playbook dismissed by analysts and mid-level commanders who viewed the terror blueprints as grandiose wishful thinking.

Meir Dagan preached, to anyone who would listen and from a mountaintop if given the microphone, that intelligence gathered but ignored, locked in a file cabinet somewhere and not shared, was wasted. But in the weeks leading up to October 7, surveillance soldiers serving at observation posts along the border with Gaza, mainly female conscripts, reported Hamas preparations for an invasion. Their commanders scoffed at the notion that something sinister was imminent; they were women, what did they know? Many of them were butchered, raped, and abducted on October 7.[3]

History has proven that overconfidence and arrogance are Kryptonite for intelligence agencies and the nations they serve. The seismic ruptures of October 7 were far worse than those experienced in the smoldering collateral damage of October 1973. The perfect storm self-inflicted disaster was compounded by political hubris and strategic malpractice. In 2015, when an ailing Meir Dagan took the stage at the same square where, twenty years earlier, Prime Minister Yitzhak Rabin had been assassinated and warned that he was fearful of the country's leadership and its lack of vision, the former Mossad director's prescient warning spoke of such a disaster. The details of Israel's October 7 intelligence failure will take years to analyze and perhaps decades to be declassified. The collapse was system-wide and catastrophic. The Shin Bet and A'man shared the intelligence and operational responsibility for the Gaza Strip and the West Bank, and history will allocate to them—and to the political leadership that allowed the intelligence to be ignored and its strategic miscalculations to guide the nation's defenses—the responsibility they are due.

Israel, like any nation attacked by an enemy wishing to seek its destruction, went to war after October 7, just as Yahya Sinwar had calculated. The Israeli counterattack into Gaza, one designed to destroy Hamas and see to the release of the two hundred and fifty hostages, was dubbed the Swords of Iron War. It pitted the might of a conventional army against an unconventional enemy that had spent billions of dollars of American and European benevolence, and billions in Qatari pocket change, to build a subterranean network of tunnels, some dug deeper than stations in the London Underground, to be used as launching pads for a fight against the IDF. Hamas used the civilians of Gaza as human shields, intentionally sacrificing its men, women, and children, for social media snippets illustrating Israeli aggression and disregard for human life. As evidenced by the mass protests on college campuses across the United States and protests and demonstrations around the world, Sinwar's strategy weakened Israel, but it did not bring it to its knees.

As of July 30, 2025, twenty-two months since October 7, the war in Gaza continues. Hamas still holds Israeli hostages, alive and dead, human bargaining chips to guarantee the terror group remains in control of Gaza.

\*          \*          \*

Gaza was but a piece of a much larger, and far more complex, regional undoing. The Israeli intelligence services viewed Hamas as a lethal foe but never an existential threat to the survival of the Jewish state. That distinction was designated to Iran, its nuclear program, and the development of its terror proxy Hezbollah as the most powerful army in the Arab world.

In the fall of 2006, during that rainy late-night shoot-the-breeze session inside Meir Dagan's office at Mossad headquarters in the predawn hours before a new day, when his trusted division chiefs were discussing what to do about Hezbollah and the words "kill them all" were uttered, the idea was not hyperbole. The words were a marching order. It began with the assassination of Imad Mughniyeh. The rest would have to follow. Meir Dagan's Mossad took upon itself a massive project to enter every facet of Hezbollah's world—its financial practices,\*

---

\* In 2008–2009, in an elaborate campaign by Tziltzal involving a dupe hedge fund manager, the Mossad initiated a Ponzi scheme operation that saw Hezbollah leaders, including Sheikh Hassan Nasrallah, lose close to a billion dollars from their personal fortunes.

its leadership, their personal and sexual practices, and their other personality shortcomings—that could be used against key members of the
Shiite Party of God and, at a moment of opportunity, deliver a crippling
blow that the group would never be able to recover from.

It was common practice for intelligence services, including Israel's,
to recruit assets of convenience rather than necessity. Dagan would have
none of it. The resources needed to be targeted and invested in locating
sources, nurturing them, and then finding their weaknesses, had to be
directed toward individuals who could yield specific intelligence from
the inside, and not merely what could be gleaned from signal intercep-
tions and other more sensitive cyber techniques. The spy game was a
human enterprise based on frailty and manipulation. It was always said
in the Mossad that agents were primarily recruited because of sex or
money. But these individuals of interest often allowed themselves to be
targets of compromise because of carelessness.

Hezbollah paid Shiite civilians to store weapons and explosives in
their homes, paying them a stipend as rent, compensating them for
tunnels and bunkers built under their houses and farming fields. Procurement for the Shiite army was handled by companies managed by
Hezbollah leaders and their relatives, who were eager to skim hefty profits from the importation of weapons, gear, and even communications
devices. When money changes hands, people of interest are exposed.
And that sparked an idea inside headquarters to target the Hezbollah
supply chain, including walkie-talkies and beepers.[4]

In 2006, as part of the after-action battlefield autopsy conducted
by the IDF and the arms of Israeli intelligence, to review the shortcomings of Israel's counterattack and generate a list of lessons learned
that could be used in any future conflicts, a few items of operational
interest emerged. One of them was that Hezbollah's frontline forces
were equipped with uniform gear, especially tactical vests that were procured through an import-export firm run by one of the Party of God's
cronies, and that the communications gear carried an iCOM IC-V82
VHF encrypted walkie-talkie, which had been selected as the group's
radio of choice because it fit inside a pouch on the upper left-hand side
of the load-bearing equipment, near the heart. This provided the idea

of intercepting the transmissions and broadcasts, knowing intentions and operations in real time, along with an outside-the-box series of "what if we could . . . " notions about booby-trapping the supply chain of radios. Unit 8200 and the Mossad went to work.[5]

A massive network of human sources was developed inside Lebanon and beyond, targeting Hezbollah following an intensive recruiting drive. HUMINT developed SIGINT, and vice versa. Dagan would have liked immediate results against the Lebanese terrorist group, but he realized that the most effective espionage work was gradual. The seeds planted into the Mossad's operational to-do list would continue and accelerate after Dagan left office, under the supervision and guidance of Tamir Pardo, Yossi Cohen, and David "Dadi" Barnea, the head of the Mossad on October 7.

The Arab Spring and the Syrian Civil War opened an enormous window into Hezbollah for Israeli intelligence. Iran dispatched Hezbollah units into the bloody fratricide to help protect the regime of Bashar al-Assad from ISIS, Kurdish rebels, and other fractious ethnic and religious militias in Syria trying to survive the carnage. The Syrian battlefield developed into a superpower proxy war with both the United States and Russia supporting different sides, and it was also an open book for the intelligence agencies. The amount of SIGINT and HUMINT shared between the friendly services, those in the West and their counterparts in the Arab world, was vast. Adding to the espionage landscape, Hezbollah, engaged in brutal combat and enduring significant losses, overlooked the legendary tradecraft secrecy that the terror group was known for.[6] The funerals of Hezbollah operatives killed in Syria were broadcast on Lebanese television, and the faces of commanders were seen, and their drivers photographed; commanders spoke on their mobile phones with their liaison officers in Damascus and Tehran.

Israel's intelligence efforts against Hezbollah intensified in the years that followed, and especially after the discovery of the "Galilee Plan," a bold initiative ordered by Nasrallah to dig attack tunnels under northern Israel and send thousands of his best fighters, commandos from the Radwan Force, into the communities opposite the Lebanese frontier to seize ground and take hostages, an operation that Hamas would copy and execute on a smaller scale.

"Intelligence work," a former U.S. intelligence officer once explained, "is a cocktail of brilliance, dare, initiative, and opportunity, but the missing ingredient is always dumb luck."[7] When, in 2014, iCOM stopped producing the walkie-talkie that so conveniently fit into the pouch of the tactical vest Hezbollah had no intention of changing, it allowed the facets of Israeli intelligence to inject itself into the terror group's supply chain, manufacturing the devices rather than merely sabotaging them. Mossad shell companies were created, and the radio reverse-engineered with one minor modification: a lethal amount of PETN explosives placed within the batteries, connected to a signal in Israel.[8] All that would be needed was a situation that would warrant a green light from the prime minister to detonate thousands of the devices.

Pagers were next.

In 2018, it was reported that a technical officer at Mossad headquarters drafted a plan to insert explosives into the pagers used by Hezbollah operatives, but that the idea was nixed because the terror group relied more on cellular phones for day-to-day communications and that off-the-shelf beepers were too fragile for field use.[9] When, at the directive of Iranian counterintelligence officials, Hezbollah limited its telephone use and, instead, sought a way of having its people receive information rather than transmit it so that prying ears could listen, a new pager option was set in motion. As with the iCOM walkie-talkies, the Mossad established shell companies in Europe and Asia, primarily a manufacturer in Taiwan called Gold Apollo and an exporter based in a suburban part of the Hungarian capital called BAC Consulting. The pager, known in the Gold Apollo sales catalog as the AR-924 Rugged, was pitched to Hezbollah's purchasing agents as robust and rugged enough for military use.[10] It was shockproof and waterproof, with a remarkably long-lasting battery. When Hamas launched its October 7 invasion of Israel, thousands of the fully functional pagers were on the hips of Hezbollah's terror army.

Sheikh Hassan Nasrallah, who had reluctantly confessed that he would never have authorized the kidnapping of two Israeli soldiers in

2006 had he known that Israel would level most of the Shiite stronghold of south Beirut in response, did not want to join Hamas in its war on Israel launched on October 7, but he could not stand idly by either. Honor was important among what was referred to as the Axis of Resistance, even though both the Iranians and Hezbollah were perfectly content fighting Israel to the very last Palestinian. On October 8, Nasrallah authorized limited rocket fire against Israeli military and civilian positions. Israel responded in kind, though arguments against launching a full-scale retaliation against Hezbollah were muted by the attempts to prioritize the Gaza fighting and, at the urging of U.S. president Joe Biden, kept the conflict from expanding into a regional war with Iran or possibly others.

Israeli defense minister Yoav Gallant, a former major general with a lengthy military career in special operations, urged Prime Minister Netanyahu to authorize the Mossad to detonate the beepers in coordination with a large air strike planned for Lebanon on October 11. But the aircraft, already armed and in the air, were called back after Biden and Netanyahu spoke by phone.

The Mossad waited and continued its clandestine campaign against Hezbollah, keeping the pagers and the walkie-talkies at the ready.

The Mossad, A'man, and the IDF took out multiple high-ranking Hezbollah and Iranian officials, including the likes of Fuad Shakr, the organization's second in command, killed in an air strike on his Beirut home on July 30, 2024; Shakr, who sat on the Hezbollah military council, played a central role in the bombing of the Marine Corps barracks on October 23, 1983.* Reportedly, the Mossad had learned his whereabouts thanks to pillow talk and amorous phone conversations with four of his mistresses.[11]

---

* On April 1, 2024, an Israeli air strike destroyed an Iranian Embassy complex in Damascus, Syria, that served as the nerve center of the Islamic Revolutionary Guard Corps' effort in directing Hezbollah operations against Israel. Iran responded with a massive rocket, drone, and ballistic missile attack on the night of April 13. Israeli air defenses, and the antimissile efforts of the United States, the United Kingdom, Jordan, and other Gulf states, shot down most of the incoming Iranian ordnance. On October 1, Iran launched over two hundred missiles at Israel, most directed at IAF bases, in response to the July 2024 assassination of Hamas leader Ismail Haniyeh in Tehran, an operation carried out, it has been reported, by the Mossad.

But as the war in Gaza appeared to be winding down in the autumn of 2024, there was fear inside Israeli intelligence that Hezbollah counterintelligence officers suspected something was wrong with the pagers they carried. Fearing a use-it-or-lose-it moment, Prime Minister Netanyahu gave the Mossad permission to strike. At 3:30 p.m. on September 17, Hezbollah operatives across Lebanon and Syria received a page of great importance. Some were shopping for groceries when the alarm sounded, others grabbed their devices and held them close to their eyes to read every word being transmitted; because the pagers were designed for military use, they were larger than store-bought devices and needed two hands to be used. The subsequent explosions took out the eyes and hands of anyone holding the pagers but yielded limited collateral damage to innocent bystanders, including the children of several Hezbollah operatives. Those who wore the AR-924 on their belts had their testicles blown off. In many cases, the explosions were captured by surveillance cameras, and the footage of the detonating Trojan horse went viral. Emergency rooms were flooded with men who had lost fingers, eyes, and other parts of their anatomy. Sheikh Hassan Nasrallah was in his operations center, hundreds of feet underground, when the pagers of those standing near him detonated.

The next day, as some of those killed in the attack were buried and Hezbollah commanders issued strict directives to their forces to discard the pagers, the iCOM radios began exploding all over Lebanon. The combined pager and walkie-talkie operation killed close to 50 members of Hezbollah and crippled an astounding 3,500 others. In an interview with CBS News, former CIA director Leon Panetta, a man who had admired Meir Dagan and the Mossad, called the operation a form of terrorism.[12]

Hezbollah never recovered from the Mossad operation.

On September 20, Ibrahim Aqil, commander of Hezbollah's elite Radwan unit and a member of the Jihad Council, was killed in an Israeli air strike in Beirut. He had been wanted by the CIA and the U.S. State Department for his role in the bombing of the U.S. Embassy in April 1983 and the attack against the Marine barracks six months later; there was a seven-million-dollar reward on his head.

Sheikh Nasrallah would be next. He had spent eighteen years underground, sequestered in a series of bunkers so deep below the surface of Beirut's streets that he felt impervious to any attempt by the IAF to target him. But Israeli intelligence had so penetrated the terror group's command-and-control inner circle that Nasrallah's whereabouts, once a mystery, were tracked. On the night of September 27, a flight of IAF F-15s and F-16s dropped over eighty bombs onto his underground lair in south Beirut, destroying the subterranean fortress and everyone inside it. The operation was code-named New Order. Many of Nasrallah's top lieutenants were killed alongside him.

The IDF had entered southern Lebanon days earlier, determined to decapitate the military juggernaut that Iran and Hezbollah had built along Israel's northern border. There would be no repeat of October 7 in Galilee.

*       *       *

The evisceration of Hezbollah's leadership with exploding pagers and walkie-talkies, followed by the elimination of Sheikh Nasrallah and virtually the organization's entire hierarchy, pinpoint strikes initiated by dead-center intelligence gathering, sparked a rebel resurgence in Syria and the ouster of Bashar al-Assad and the Baathist regime there. By taking on Hezbollah and laying the framework to take it out, Israel, led by the Mossad, had the chance to deliver a blow to the principal pillar of Iran's regional strategy that would prove devastating to its ability to threaten Israel and its neighbors. Meir Dagan could never have realized, not in his wildest dreams, that the late-night talk in his office, the talk of kill them all so that Hezbollah could no longer kill Israelis, Americans, or others, would change the Middle East forever.

Meir Dagan spent a lifetime in uniform and in and out of the shadows, fueled by the belief that if Israel was strong and vibrant, it was guaranteed that Jews would never again be led to their wholesale slaughter. He would have been devastated by the abject failures of October 7, but he would have been reassured by how Israel recovered from the shock and horror to emerge a more daunting foe to the enemies that wish to wipe the Jewish state from the face of the earth.

It has been said that the efforts of Meir Dagan and the agency he led played a critical role in stalling Iran's march to the bomb by a decade or so—the extent of that work materialized in June 2025 during the Israeli and, later, American bombing campaign against Tehran's nuclear weapons program. The building blocks that Dagan instilled at the Mossad helped cripple a terror army that held the Middle East hostage. History has proven that there will always be a diabolical force intent on destroying the Jewish people and that the State of Israel is a last line of defense against such threats. If the work and courage of Dagan and many like him can keep a senior citizen from enduring the shackles of a dungeon prison and give toddlers in a kibbutz the chance to have a future free of fear and terror, then perhaps his life's work of Never Again will have been realized.

# Rising Lions and Midnight Hammers

In the early morning on June 13, 2025, waves of Israeli combat aircraft attacked a lengthy list of nuclear, Islamic Revolutionary Guard Corps, and missile defense targets across Iran. The armada of F-35I, F-16I, and F-15I warplanes flew over a thousand miles from their bases to hit their targets. IDF spokesperson Brigadier General Effie Defrin relayed that over two hundred Israeli warplanes were involved in the opening strikes, hitting over one hundred targets. By sunrise that morning, the IAF was already mounting its third wave of attacks. The Israeli operation, code-named Rising Lion, achieved complete surprise. The Israeli decision to launch was prompted by intelligence that Iran had made great strides in the uranium enrichment needed to weaponize its nuclear program.

The IAF eviscerated Iran's command and control capabilities, killing the country's top generals and defense officials, in a coordinated strike with the arms of Israel's intelligence services. Before IAF fighters and bombers penetrated Iranian airspace, teams of Mossad agents, who had covertly set up forward operating bases across Iran, launched a blitz of drones to take out the advanced Russian-made air defense batteries that ringed vital installations, including reactors, IRGC bases, and high-value targets. The Israeli mastery of the aerial battlespace over Iran was rivaled by the Mossad's incredible penetration of the shadows. Israeli intelligence assembled unprecedented and intimate information about Iran's top military decision-makers, including the military's chief of staff and several generals, the men who advised Supreme Leader Ayatollah Ali Khamenei. Israel also targeted the key Iranian nuclear scientists who were critical in advancing the country's program. Most were killed in their beds in precision attacks that left little collateral damage. The chaos and confusion sowed by the Israeli attacks and the complete obliteration of Iran's ability to defend its skies allowed Israeli pilots the freedom of action to strike numerous targets critical to Iran's centers of nuclear and offensive military gravity. Israeli intelligence knew who the players were, where they lived, and how to efficiently target them. It was revealed that IDF special operations units were on the ground in Iran.

Iran responded the way Israel had expected, with volleys of ballistic missiles targeting Israel's civilian population. But the Islamic Republic no longer fielded its proxy defensive shields. Hamas was damaged in Gaza, Hezbollah's stranglehold in Lebanon had been shattered, and the Assad family's dynasty in Syria had been overthrown. The Shiite militias in Iraq wanted no part in risking the wrath of Israel or the United States; even the Houthis in Yemen, who had used the war in Gaza to do Iran's bidding since October 7, 2023, restricted their response to lobbing only a few missiles and drones at Israel. Iran fired approximately six hundred missiles at Israel and over one thousand drones. Iran was still engaged in the indiscriminate missile warfare strategy it had used forty years earlier in the war against Iraq; Israel was fighting a twenty-first-century campaign. Most of the Iranian missiles were intercepted by Israeli, American, and even Jordanian air defenses. Some got through. Twenty-eight people in Israel were killed in the strikes, and thousands were wounded; the property damage is estimated in the billions of dollars.

On June 22, U.S. Air Force B-2 stealth bombers dropped fourteen GBU-57 Massive Ordnance Penetrator bombs on the Fordow nuclear enrichment facility buried deep below a mountain outside Tehran. U.S. Navy submarines fired multiple BGM-109 Tomahawk Land Attack Missiles at nuclear targets in Natanz and Isfahan. The American strike was code-named Operation Midnight Hammer.

President Donald J. Trump announced a ceasefire between Israel and Iran two days later.

Intelligence analysts will assess the damage inflicted on Iran's nuclear program by both Israel and the United States and make determinations about how effective the campaign was. This was the third time in history that the State of Israel had thwarted or significantly downgraded the nuclear capabilities of an enemy nation intent on its annihilation. The challenge now, as former A'man chief and a pilot who had personally flown the sortie to destroy Iraq's nuclear reactor, Major General Amos Yadlin, wrote in *The New York Times*, is the need to "leverage military action into a broader diplomatic initiative that aims for a strong, enforceable agreement rolling back Iran's nuclear program, including assets that will remain intact."[1]

*       *       *

In 2002, when Meir Dagan took over the Mossad, he vowed to use the agency's resources to not only gather intelligence on Iran's nuclear ambitions but also to proactively delay, thwart, deter, and destroy components of Tehran's program. Dagan enlisted the support of Israel's allies in the international espionage community, especially the CIA. Good intelligence work requires patience. Sometimes, the investment in manpower and technology can take years, even decades, to bear fruit.

Less than a week after the twelve-day war with Iran came to an end, Mossad director David "Dadi" Barnea made a rare public appearance, thanking the men and women of the organization, as well as the IDF, for their work in Operation Rising Lion, and offering his gratitude to the CIA. "Objectives that once seemed imaginary have now been achieved," Barnea stated. "We will continue to keep a watchful eye on all known Iranian projects—we are intimately familiar with them—and we will be there, just as we have been until now."[2]

# Acknowledgments

I met Meir Dagan one time. It was in September 2015, while I was working as a coauthor on a book about Tziltzal, also known as Harpoon, the financial warfare unit he had created before becoming the head of the Mossad. His battle with liver cancer was in its third year, and he was no longer the mountain of a man he had once been. There must have been a million things on his mind the night we met, but once in his company, his guests became the focus of his attention. He was a patient, kind, and gregarious host. He was known to take guests to the balcony of his high-rise apartment in Tel Aviv to enjoy the amazing vista that stretched for miles, but a once-in-a-twenty-year desert heat wave and sandstorm had swept across the Middle East, and Tel Aviv was covered in an eerily thick red cloud of unbreathable dust. It did not make a difference, because the view of the bright lights and big city, and all points around, would have been as interesting as Meir's wit, insight, and kindness. Cancer would claim his life six months later, but he was generous with his time. He did not like to speak about his past exploits, especially anything connected to secrets and his clandestine work, but was outspoken when it came to discussing Israel's future and making plans. He was a fighter to the end.

Meir Dagan was a man of courage and convictions who dedicated his life to the defense of Israel and the protection of the Jewish nation.

As remarkable as he was on the battlefield or in mapping out complex intelligence operations with strategic forethought and daring, he was also an everyday man who appreciated, respected, and honored people of all types—from world leaders to maintenance workers at Mossad headquarters. Although he was blessed with an extra helping of natural charisma that made him the center of attention in any room he walked into, he was humble and worried more about those he was responsible for than himself. The loyalty to his soldiers and intelligence officers was an unbreakable and lifelong bond, and those who knew him share a universal affection and appreciation for the man. While working on this book, the one phrase heard from everyone I interviewed was "We miss Dagan indeed and urgently need someone like him among our leaders." Those who knew Meir Dagan and worked for him are very protective of his legacy, and I feel great honor and responsibility for having received their trust and support to tell part of the story of an amazing soldier, spy chief, and patriot.

This book would not have been possible without the support and guidance of Dr. Udi Levi, one of Dagan's most trusted and beloved deputies. Udi gave this project his blessing, and he gave me his trust. Udi's assistance was vital in assembling the interviews and material needed to make this book a reality. I am forever grateful for his friendship and kindness. Udi connected me to Meir's son, Dan, who made this book possible. Words cannot express my gratitude to Dan for his patience and kindness in sharing about his father. I also want to thank Meir's brother, Eli Huberman, who generously shared the family's history with me.

I wish to offer special thanks to former prime minister Ehud Olmert for taking the time to talk to me about the partnership he forged with Meir Dagan. The former prime minister's affection for Dagan and the admiration he felt toward his former spy chief's contribution to Israeli security are inspiring. I also wish to thank former Mossad director Tamir Pardo for his time and for sharing his unrivaled insight into the threats Israel and the West face and what it is like to lead an espionage service. Many of the deputy directors, division chiefs, and senior officers who worked at the Mossad were kind with their time and in sharing their reflections on what it was like to serve under Dagan. Some of those who have allowed me to thank them include Ram Ben Barak, Zohar Palti, Eyal Hulata, David Meidan, Eshel Armoni, Haim Tomer, and Ehud Lavi, among many others. I am grateful for their generosity, support, trust, and friendship. Many men and women who spoke to me and operate in the shadows—in Israel, elsewhere in the Middle East, in Europe, and in the United States—have asked to remain anonymous for obvious reasons. They know who they are, and I want all of them to know that their help was indispensable, and I am profoundly grateful for everything they have done on my behalf.

I wish to thank Meir's comrades in arms from his days in Gaza, the 1973 War, Lebanon, and while he worked on the IDF General Staff, at the Counterterrorism Bureau, and as national security advisor to Prime Minister Ariel Sharon, for taking the time to share their memories with me for this book. A heartfelt thanks to Shmuel Paz, Hagai Hadas, Ephraim Sneh, Eyal Ben-Reuven, Baruch Spiegel, Dani Arditi, and especially Sami Mutzafi Barak for their time and expertise. I also wish to thank retired major general Mansour Abu Rashid, Meir's partner in peace, for his memories and assistance.

Meir Dagan believed in partnerships, in pursuing common goals and strengthening alliances, especially with the United States. I wish to thank two former directors of the Central Intelligence Agency—General Michael Hayden and Leon Panetta—for taking the time to talk to me about a member of the intelligence fraternity and a partner they admired and enjoyed working with. I would also like to thank Marc Polymeropoulos, a twenty-six-year veteran of the Agency and operations in the Middle East, for his reflections and guidance. A special thanks to former U.S. Department of State Diplomatic Security Service special agent Fred Burton, my coauthor on past and future projects, for his insight and expertise.

I want to thank Nitsana Darshan-Leitner and Avi Leitner for introducing me to the world of Tziltzal and forging many relationships with Meir Dagan's inner circle. I also want to thank Ari Harow, a veteran of Israel's political world and someone whose vast knowledge is surpassed only by his kind spirit and eagerness to help, for assisting me with his expertise and memories, and Ziv Koren, one of the world's top photojournalists, for his guidance with illustrative issues concerning this book.

This book would not have been possible without Colin Harrison, my editor at Scribner, who believed in this project and offered assistance and direction throughout the process, an undertaking that began before October 7 and that was written throughout the conflict. It is an absolute pleasure working with Colin.

My desire to write about Meir Dagan's life and service became a book because of the intrepid efforts, editorial expertise, and knowledge of my literary agent, Doug Grad. Besides being a fellow Queens native, diehard Mets fan, and friend, Doug knows this business inside and out, and, at a time when projects (positive and accurate ones) about Israel were not easy to sell, Doug found this book an amazing home. I am truly thankful.

Lastly, and most importantly, I want to thank my wife, Sigi, and my three wonderful children for their tolerance in sharing their lives with someone who writes for a living. The process of turning mountains of papers, months of research, gigabytes of interviews, and endless hours on airliners crossing oceans and continents can be stressful, and their love, support, and understanding are indispensable and most appreciated.

# Glossary

A'dal: Acronym for *Aizor Drom Lebanon*, the South Lebanon Region unit

A'man: Acronym for *Agaf Ha'Modi'in*, the Military Intelligence Directorate of the Israel Defense Forces

BKA: The *Bundeskriminalamt*, the German Federal Criminal Police Office

BND: The *Bundesnachrichtendienst*, the German foreign espionage service

Caesaria: The Mossad branch responsible for espionage operations in target (enemy) nations[1]

CIA: The U.S. Central Intelligence Agency

CSIS: The Canadian Security Intelligence Service

DGED: The *Direction Générale des Études et de la Documentation*, Morocco's General Directorate of Studies and Documentation, the kingdom's foreign espionage service

DGSE: The *Direction générale de la Sécurité extérieure*, France's foreign espionage service

DIA: The U.S. Defense Intelligence Agency

DNI: The U.S. Director of National Intelligence

DTX: The *Dövlet Tehlükesizlik Xidmeti*, the Azerbaijan State Security Service

EGIA: Egypt's General Intelligence Agency, the *Gihaz El Mukhabarat El 'Amma*

**FSB:** The *Federal'naya sluzhba bezopasnosti Rossiyskoy Federatsii*, the Federal Security Service of the Russian Federation

**GID:** The General Intelligence Department of the Hashemite Kingdom of Jordan

**GIP:** The General Intelligence Presidency of the Kingdom of Saudi Arabia

**GRU:** Russian military intelligence, the *Glavnoje upravlenije General'nogo shtaba Vooruzhonnykh sil Rossiyskoy Federatsii* (Main Directorate of the General Staff of the Armed Forces of the Russian Federation)

**IDF:** The Israeli Defense Forces

**Katsa:** Acronym for *Ktzin Isuf*, or gathering officer, the title used by the Mossad for a field intelligence officer

**Kidon:** The direct-action force that, according to published accounts, operates under the command of Caesaria[2]

**MI5:** The Military Intelligence Section 5, or Security Service, Great Britain's domestic counterintelligence and counterterrorist agency

**MI6:** The Military Intelligence Section 6, or Secret Intelligence Service, Great Britain's foreign espionage agency

**MIT:** The *Millî İstihbarat Teşkilatı*, Turkey's National Intelligence Service

**NSA:** The National Security Agency, United States

**NSC:** Israel's National Security Council

**NSH:** The National Security Headquarters in the Prime Minister's Office, Israel

**NSIS:** The National Security Intelligence Service, Kenya

**QSSA:** The Qatari State Security Agency

**Radwan Force:** Hezbollah's special operations force (also known as Unit 125)

**Rasha:** The Mossad's division head forum

**RAW:** The Research Analysis Wing, India's foreign espionage service

**Shin Bet:** The *Sherut Ha'Bitachon Ha'Klali*, or General Security Service, Israel's domestic counterespionage and counterterrorist intelligence service

**SVR:** The *Sluzhba vneshney razvedki Rossiysko Federatsii*, Russia's foreign intelligence service

**Tevel:** The Mossad's international liaison branch

**Tzomet:** The Mossad's HUMINT branch

**Tziltzal:** The Mossad's financial warfare unit, also known as Harpoon

**Unit 504:** The Israeli Military Intelligence HUMINT force that runs agents behind enemy lines

**Unit 730:** The Shin Bet's dignitary protection unit

**Unit 8200:** The Military Intelligence Directorate force responsible for clandestine data-gathering operations, signals intelligence, code decryption, cyber warfare, electronic surveillance, and technological innovation, similar in scope and importance to the American NSA

**Unit 9900:** The Military Intelligence Directorate's terrain analysis, mapping, and visual intelligence (VISINT) gathering and analysis division

**Va'ra'sh:** Acronym for *Va'adat Rashei Ha'Sherutim,* or Committee of the Chiefs of Services, the coordinating commission for the heads of Israel's three intelligence services

**Ya'ka'l:** Acronym for *Yechidat Kishur Levanon,* or Lebanon Liaison Unit

# Notes

INTRODUCTION The World View from the Head of Mossad's Office

1 Bruce Riedel, "Enigma: The Anatomy of Israel's Intelligence Failure Almost 45 Years Ago," Brookings, September 25, 2017.
2 "A conversation with the former director of Israel's Mossad, Shabtai Shavit," The Atlantic Council, March 11, 2021 (https://www.youtube.com/watch?v=L7fnn fG07O8).
3 Interview with Udi Levi and Dan Dagan, Israel, December 28, 2023.
4 Shira Rubin, "As It Planned for Oct. 7, Hamas Lulled Israel into a False Sense of Calm," Washington Post, December 6, 2023.
5 U.S. Department of Justice, "The 9/11 Commission Report: Executive Summary," 2004.
6 "Meir Dagan, Israeli spy chief—Obituary," Telegraph, March 18, 2016.

PROLOGUE Away from the Office One Sunny Fall Day

1 Ari Harow, My Brother's Keeper: Netanyahu, Obama, and the Year of Terror and Conflict That Changed the Middle East Forever (New York: Post Hill Press, 2024), p. 145.
2 Herb Keinon, "Netanyahu to Meet Putin, Return Before Shavuot," Jerusalem Post, May 13, 2013.
3 Interview, Herzliya, January 2, 2024.
4 https://obamawhitehouse.archives.gov/issues/foreign-policy/presidents-speech -cairo-a-new-beginning.
5 Interview with Ari Harow, former chief of staff to Prime Minister Netanyahu, New York, July 16, 2024.
6 Interview, Tel Aviv, November 18, 2024.
7 Harow, My Brother's Keeper, p. 146.

8 Interview, Tel Aviv, November 15, 2024.
9 https://www.youtube.com/watch?v=_v6Ol_CbASs&t=966s.

CHAPTER ONE **Proof of Life**

1 Interview with Eli Huberman, Chicago, April 11, 2024.
2 Interview with Eli Huberman, Chicago, April 11, 2024.
3 Interview with Eli Huberman, Chicago, May 3, 2025.
4 Interview with Eli Huberman, Chicago, April 11, 2024.
5 Interview with Eli Huberman, Chicago, April 11, 2024.
6 Ellen Brazer, *I Am Meir's Brother: Biography of a Family Separated by Destiny*, (TCJ Publishing, 2021).
7 Brazer, *I Am Meir's Brother.*
8 Brazer, *I Am Meir's Brother*, p. 21.
9 https://www.jta.org/archive/300-czech-jews-leave-italy-for-israel-vessel-to-pick-up-tripolitanian-jews-en-route.
10 David Remnick, "The Vegetarian: A Notorious Spymaster Becomes a Dissident," *New Yorker*, September 3, 2012.
11 Interview with Eli Huberman, April 11, 2024.

CHAPTER TWO **Newcomers**

1 *The American Jewish Yearbook*, Volume 53 (American Jewish Committee, 1952), pp. 421–429.
2 Interview with Eli Huberman, Chicago, April 11, 2024.
3 Interview with Eli Huberman, Chicago, April 11, 2024.
4 Interview with Eli Huberman, Chicago, May 3, 2025.
5 https://history.state.gov/historicaldocuments/frus1952-54v09p1/d728.
6 https://www.baba-mail.co.il/video.aspx?emailid=26105.
7 Interview with Eli Huberman, Chicago, April 11, 2024.

CHAPTER THREE **Soldier**

1 Electronic interview with Eli Huberman, May 9, 2025.
2 https://www.idf.il/en/mini-sites/our-soldiers/uri-ilan-a-heroic-idf-soldier-who-was-captured-by-the-syrians-left-behind-a-message-for-his-country/.
3 "*Shloshim Le'Moto Shel Meir Dagan*," Kan 11 (Israel Broadcast Authority), April 14, 2016.
4 Ronen Bergman, "*Hekarti Harbei Rashei Memshalot. Af Ehad Me'Hem Lo Haya Tahor Ve'Kadosh. Aval Hayta Lahem Tchuna Meshutefet: Ke'She'Hem Higiyu Le'Nekuda She'ba Ha'Interest Ha'Ishi Naga'a Be'Interest Ha'Leumi—Ha'Leumi Tamid Gavar. Rak Al Shnayim Ani Lo Yachol La'Hagid Et Ze: Bibi Ve'Barak*," "I met many prime ministers. None of them were pure. But they all shared a common attribute: when their personal interests touched on the national interests, the national interests always won" *Yediot Aharonot*, April 8, 2016.

5 https://www.paratroops.org.il.
6 Electronic interview with Eli Huberman, May 9, 2025.

CHAPTER FOUR **Combat Leader**

1 Major Charles B. Long (USAF), "Analysis of the Six Day War, June 1967," Air Command and Staff College Air University, Maxwell AFB, Alabama, October 1984.
2 Report of the Secretary-General on the withdrawal of the United Nations Emergency Force, UNEF I withdrawal (16 May–17 June 1967)—SecGen report, addenda, corrigendum DOCUMENTS A/6730 AND ADD.1–3 (Original Document—June 26, 1967).
3 Carl F. Salans, "Gulf of Aqaba and Strait of Tiran," *Proceedings* (U.S. Naval Institute), December 1968, Vol. 94/12/790.
4 John Quigley, *The Six-Day War and Israeli Self-Defense: Questioning the Legal Basis for Preventative War* (Cambridge, UK: Cambridge University Press, 2013), p. 60.
5 https://history.state.gov/historicaldocuments/frus1964-68v19/d130.
6 *Ariel Sharon Mefaked Ugda Mesaper al Mesimotav Be'Milhemet Sheshet Ha'Yamin*— Israel State Archives—June 30, 1967, File No. 3632-1.
7 James Reston, "Washington: Nasser's Reckless Maneuvers; Cairo and Moscow, the U.S. Commitment the Staggering Economy Moscow's Role," *New York Times*, May 24, 1967.
8 Uri Milshtein, *Ha'Historia Shel Ha'Tzanhanim—Kerech B*, (Tel Aviv: Shalgi Publishing, 1985), p. 869.

CHAPTER FIVE **The New World Order**

1 "A Brief History of Gaza's 75 Years of Woe," Reuters, October 11, 2023.
2 David Hurst, *The Gun and the Olive Branch* (London: Futura Publications, 1977), p. 282.
3 *"Shloshim Le'Moto Shel Meir Dagan."*
4 Ron Ben Yishai, *"Mivtza Ha'Hista'arvut Ha'Leyli Be'Retzu'ah ImMeir Dagan: Kach Husal Ha'Terror Be'Aza Be'Shnot Ha-70," Ynet*, March 19, 2021.
5 Ben Yishai, *"Mivtza Ha'Hista'arvut."*
6 Ronen Bergman, *"Ha'Zikiyot Shel Meir," Yediot Aharonot Sheva Yamin*, April 5, 2017.
7 Bergman, *"Ha'Zikiyot Shel Meir."*
8 Dr. Uri Milshtein, *"Rimon Helem: Kach Hisla Yisrael Et Ha'Terror Ba'Retzu'a Be'Shnot Ha'70," Maariv Sof Shavua*, January 23, 2016.
9 Yaakov Bar-On, *"Ha'Tahpusot, Ha'Egadchim, Ve'Hatiyulim Be'Drom Levanon: Bato Shel Meir Dagan Mitgaga'at," Maariv*, September 10, 2018.
10 Interview with Sami Mutzafi Barak, Israel, August 28, 2024.
11 *"Shloshim Le'Moto Shel Meir Dagan."*
12 *"Shloshim Le'Moto Shel Meir Dagan."*
13 Yoav Tilon and Eli Michelson, *"Yechidot Meyuchadot Le'Lemida Ma'archatit Be'Tza'ha'l," *IDF Dado Center Journal, January 2016.
14 *"Shloshim Le'Moto Shel Meir Dagan."*
15 Interview with Shmuel Paz, Israel, June 25, 2024.

CHAPTER SIX  Chameleons and Trigger Pullers

1 Yossi Melman, *"Yesh Eizeshe'u Ne'um Shel Khrushchev Me'Ha'Va'ada,"* *Haaretz*, March 7, 2006.
2 Bergman, *"Ha'Zikiyot Shel Meir."*
3 Interview with Shmuel Paz, Israel, June 25, 2004.
4 Interview with Sami Mutzafi Barak, Israel, August 28, 2024.
5 Aviad Glickman, *"Meir Dagan Nizkar Be'Sayeret Rimon: Haragnu Esrot Rabot,"* *Ynet/Yediot Aharonot*, November 8, 2011.
6 Interview with Shmuel Paz, Israel, June 25, 2004.
7 Interview with Shmuel Paz, Israel, June 25, 2004.
8 Interview with Shmuel Paz, Israel, June 25, 2004.
9 https://www.shaked424.co.il/%D7%A4%D7%A6%D7%99-%D7%92%D7%99%D7%91%D7%95%D7%A8-%D7%9B%D7%99%D7%A4%D7%95%D7%A8.html
10 Interview, Haifa, June 17, 2024.
11 Remnick, "The Vegetarian."
12 Interview with Shmuel Paz, Israel, June 25, 2004.

CHAPTER SEVEN  The Director and His Theater of Dirty Tricks

1 Major General (Res.) David Maimon, *Ha'Terror She'Nutzach* (Tel Aviv: Steimatzky, 1993), p. 42.
2 Ben Yishai, *"Mivtza Ha'Hista'arvut."*
3 Interview with Shmuel Paz, Israel, June 25, 2004.
4 Interview with Shmuel Paz, Israel, June 25, 2004.
5 https://www.youtube.com/watch?v=wBPzTQNLdTM.
6 Uri Milshtein, *Rimon Helem.*
7 Shlomo Gazit, *Trapped Fools: Thirty Years of Israeli Policy in the Territories* (Routledge, London, 2003), p. 62.
8 *"Shloshim Le'Moto Shel Meir Dagan."*
9 Bergman, *"Ha'Zikiyot Shel Meir."*
10 Ron Ben Yishai, *"Mivtza Ha'Hista'arvut."*
11 Interview with Shmuel Paz, Israel, June 25, 2004.
12 "The Spymaster Speaks," *60 Minutes*, CBS, March 11, 2012.

CHAPTER EIGHT  Curtain Call

1 Hurst, *The Gun and the Olive Branch*, p. 311.
2 Glickman, *"Meir Dagan Nizkar Be'Sayeret Rimon."*
3 Glickman, *"Meir Dagan Nizkar Be'Sayeret Rimon."*
4 Glickman, *"Meir Dagan Nizkar Be'Sayeret Rimon."*
5 Nitsana Darshan-Leitner and Samuel M. Katz, *Harpoon: Inside the Covert War Against Terrorism's Money Masters* (New York: Hachette, 2017).
6 Nitsana Darshan-Leitner interview with Bina Dagan for the book *Harpoon* (location unknown), May 9, 2017.

CHAPTER NINE  Behind Enemy Lines

1  Dr. George W. Gawrych, "The 1973 Arab-Israeli War: The Albatross of Decisive Victory," *Leavenworth Papers, Combat Studies Institute,* No. 21, 1996.
2  Mitch Ginsburg, "Account of King Hussein's 1973 War Warning Still Deemed Too Harmful to Release," *Times of Israel,* December 12, 2013.
3  Amir Oren, "A Model of Military and Civilian Courage Dies," *Haaretz,* April 20, 2004.
4  Eyal Lavi, *"Gibor Milhemet Yom Kippur: 'Kvar 31 Shana Tzahal Lo Mesapek Et Ha'Schora,"* NRG, September 13, 2013.
5  Avraham Arnan, *"Pe'ilut Kommando Mitzri Be'Milhemet Yom Ha'Kippuring—Du'h Tahkir,"* IDF Archives, File No. 144/1041/1984.
6  https://www.youtube.com/watch?v=anyicFI7Xl4.
7  https://www.youtube.com/watch?v=anyicFI7Xl4.
8  Amatzia Chen, *"Milhemet Yom Kippur – Az Ha'Yom,"* News1, October 19, 2015.
9  Arnan, *"Pe'ilut Kommando Mitzri Be'Milhemet Yom Ha'Kippuring."*
10  Iddo Shejhter, "Tour of Duty: When Leonard Cohen Serenaded Ariel Sharon on the Battlefield," *Haaretz,* March 22, 2022.
11  Interview with Shmuel Paz, Israel, June 25, 2024.
12  *"Shloshim Le'Moto Shel Meir Dagan."*
13  David T. Zabecki, "Slugfest on the Suez," Historynet, November 1, 2017.
14  Gordon F. Sander, "The Arab-Israeli War 50 Years Ago Brought Us Close to Nuclear Armageddon," *Washington Post,* October 10, 2023.
15  https://www.youtube.com/watch?v=FYDlo5_egvs&t=166s.
16  *"Shloshim Le'Moto Shel Meir Dagan."*


CHAPTER TEN  Northern Armor

1  "Arab Terrorists Slay 18 in Raid on Israel," *Virgin Islands Daily News,* April 13, 1974.
2  Hillel Kuttler, "The Legacy of the Maalot Massacre," *Tablet Magazine,* May 14, 2024.
3  *"Shloshim Le'Moto Shel Meir Dagan."*
4  Aluf Ben, *"Dagan Ve'Hamesima Ha'Bilti Efshari,"* Haaretz, December 7, 2010.
5  Ben, *"Dagan Ve'Hamesima Ha'Bilti Efshari."*
6  Ben, *"Dagan Ve'Hamesima Ha'Bilti Efshari."*
7  Interview, New York, August 22, 2024.
8  *"Dagan, Ha'Milhama Ha'Aharona,"* Episode 2, Yes TV, December 2024.
9  Amir Oren, *"Meir Dagan: Ha'Outsider She'Balam Et Harpatknotam Shel Yotzi Ha'Sayeret Netanyahu Ve'Barak,"* Haaretz, March 17, 2016.
10  Ronen Bergman, *Rise and Kill First: The Secret History of Israel's Targeted Assassinations* (New York: Random House, 2018), p. 235.
11  *"Ptzatza Be'Etztadion Ve'Koach Dag Maluach: Ha'Nisionot Le'Hisool Arafat,"* Ynet, January 24, 2018.
12  Bergman, *Rise and Kill First,* p. 241.
13  Ronen Bergman, *"Be'Rega Ha'Aharon: Lama Butal Ha'Mivtza Le'Hisool Arafat?,"* Yediot Aharonot, 7 Yamim, November 13, 2020.

14 Interview with Ephraim Sneh, Tel Aviv, June 20, 2024.
15 Bergman, "*Be'Rega Ha'Aharon.*"
16 https://www.wilsoncenter.org/blog-post/lesson-the-1981-raid-osirak.

CHAPTER ELEVEN  **Lightning**

1 Interview with Udi Levi and Dan Dagan, Israel, December 28, 2023.
2 Michal Margalit, "*Met Be'Tisha Be'Av: Ha'Einayim Me'Achorei Ha'Shir 'Tulik',*" *Yediot Aharonot*, May 4, 2014.
3 Interview with Baruch Spiegel, Haifa, June 16, 2024.
4 Ofer Aderet, "What Historical Mossad Files Reveal About 'Israel's Most Planned War,'" *Haaretz*, September 8, 2022.
5 Richard Zoglin, "Did a Dead Man Tell No Tales?," *Time*, October 12, 1987.
6 Bob Woodward, "Alliance with a Lebanese Leader," *Washington Post*, September 29, 1987.
7 Uri Misgav, "Behind the Scenes of the Mossad's Mad Attempt to Change the Face of Lebanon," *Haaretz*, September 15, 2022.
8 Shabtai Shavit, *Head of the Mossad: In Pursuit of a Safe and Secure Israel* (Notre Dame, Indiana: University of Notre Dame Press, 2020), p. 86.

CHAPTER TWELVE  **Bloody Beirut**

1 Interview with Eyal Ben-Reuven, Tel Aviv, June 26, 2024.
2 https://www.youtube.com/watch?v=OUcmxbhJ7Ik.
3 Interview with Eyal Ben-Reuven, Tel Aviv, June 26, 2024.
4 "*Ani Nishba Helek B.*"
5 "*Shloshim Le'Moto Shel Meir Dagan.*"
6 https://www.youtube.com/watch?v=OUcmxbhJ7Ik.
7 "*Shloshim Le'Moto Shel Meir Dagan.*"
8 Ze'ev Schiff and Ehud Ya'ari, *Israel's Lebanon War* (New York: Simon and Schuster, 1984), p. 190.
9 "*Ani Nishba Helek B.*"
10 Interview with Eyal Ben-Reuven, June 26, 2024.
11 "*Mivtza Rosh Ha'Dag—Ha'Tzi'h Le'Hisulo Shel Yasir Arafat,*" *Amutat Bogrei 8200*, April 9, 2024, https://www.8200.org.il/post/__440.
12 https://www.youtube.com/watch?v=OUcmxbhJ7Ik.
13 *Michemet Shlom Ha'Galil 5 L'yuni Ad Ha 29 Le'September—Mapot Ve'Mivtzaim* (Israel Ministry of Defense, Tel Aviv, 2022), p. 180.
14 Interview with Eyal Ben-Reuven, Tel Aviv, June 26, 2024.
15 May Ben-Zeev, "40 Years Since Yasir Arafat Left Beirut While Israel Had Him Targeted," i24 News, August 28, 2022.
16 Bassem Mroue, "Palestinians Commemorate Horrific 1982 Massacre in Beirut," Associated Press, September 16, 2022.
17 "*Ani Nishba Helek B.*"

CHAPTER THIRTEEN  The Land of Martyrs and Spies

1  Morteza Mutaharri, *"Jihad and Shahadat: Struggle and Martyrdom in Islam,"* ed. and trans. Mehdi Abdei and Gary Legenhausen (Houston: Institute for Research and Islamic Studies, 1986), p. 126, as referenced in Captain Daniel Helmer (U.S. Army), "Hezbollah's Employment of Suicide Bombing During the 1980s: The Theological, Political, and Operational Development of a New Tactic," *Military Review*, July-August 2006.
2  Dubi Eichnold, *"Tzor 1982, Hayiti Kavur Be'Gehenom,"* *Ynet/Yediot Aharonot*, October 26, 2012.
3  Robert Baer, "The Cult of the Suicide Bomber: Ex-CIA Agent Robert Bair Uncovers the Mystery of This Weapon of Terror," produced by the Disinformation Company Limited.
4  Ofer Aderet, "New Inquiry Refutes Original Israeli Probe: 1982 Tyre Disaster Was Terror, Not a Gas Explosion," *Haaretz*, July 4, 2024.
5  *"Shloshim Le'Moto Shel Meir Dagan."*
6  Sharon Rofa, *"Yechidat Ha'Kishur Le'Levanon,"* *Ynet/Yediot Aharonot*, June 11, 2000.
7  Interview with Eliezer Tzafrir, Tel Aviv, September 5, 2015 (for the book *Beirut Rules*).
8  *"Shloshim Le'Moto Shel Meir Dagan."*
9  *"Shloshim Le'Moto Shel Meir Dagan."*
10  Associated Press, "Ali Akbar Mohtashamipour, Shiite Cleric and a Founder of Hezbollah, Dies at 74," *Washington Post*, June 7, 2021.
11  Terry A. Anderson, "Bomb Kills at Least 28 at U.S. Embassy, Associated Press, April 18, 1983.
12  "Maj. Saad Haddad, 47, Christian Ally in Southern Lebanon," *New York Times*, January 15, 1984.
13  Interview with Dan Dagan, Israel, January 1, 2024.
14  Bergman, *Rise and Kill First*, p. 378.

CHAPTER FOURTEEN  The Sharif of Lebanon

1  Interview with Sami Mutzafi Barak, Ashdod, November 21, 2024.
2  Interview with Sami Mutzafi Barak, Ashdod, November 21, 2024.
3  Interview with Sami Mutzafi Barak, Ashdod, November 21, 2024.
4  "George Hawi Knew Who Killed Kamal Jumblatt," *Ya Liban*, June 22, 2005.

CHAPTER FIFTEEN  Major General

1  Oren, *"Ha'Outsider She'Balam."*
2  "Colonel Says Rabin Ordered Breaking of Palestinians' Bones," *Los Angeles Times*, June 22, 1990.
3  *"Ani Nishba Helek B."*
4  *"Shloshim Le'Moto Shel Meir Dagan."*
5  Interview, Tel Aviv, June 18, 2024.

6 *"Shloshim Le'Moto Shel Meir Dagan."*
7 Avi Kfiri, *Ha'Mivtza Ha'Anak Le'Hatzalat Yehdei Brit Ha'Mo'atzot,"* *Makor*, October 10, 2014.
8 Kifri, *"Yoter Me'Entebbe."*
9 Oren, *"Ha'Outsider She'Balam."*

CHAPTER SIXTEEN **Code Name Mango**

1 Amir Oren, "'The Queen's File': How the Mossad Got to King Hussein of Jordan's Mother," *Haaretz*, January 25, 2022.
2 Interview with Mansour Abu Rashid, Amman, November 6, 2024.
3 Interview with Baruch Spiegel, Haifa, June 25, 2024.
4 https://www.youtube.com/watch?v=iEmmKNzHLPQ&t=472s.
5 Electronic interview with Mansour Abu Rashid, November 6, 2024.
6 Electronic interview with Mansour Abu Rashid, November 6, 2024.
7 Paul R. Pillar, "Jack O'Connell's *King's Counsel: A Memoir of War, Espionage, and Diplomacy in the Middle East,"* *Washington Post*, July 14, 2011.
8 https://www.youtube.com/watch?v=iEmmKNzHLPQ&t=472s.
9 Ron Katri and Ophir Shoha *"Sicha Im Ephraim Halevy Al Lawrence of Arabia,"* *Mabat Malam*, Issue 91, March 2022.

CHAPTER EIGHTEEN **On-the-Job Training**

1 Marjorie Miller and Mary Curtius, "20 Killed, 10 Injured in Jerusalem Bus Explosion," *Los Angeles Times*, March 3, 1996.
2 Evelyn Gordon, "A Tale of Two Shootings," *Commentary*, April 13, 2016.
3 Brigadier General (Ret.) Dr. Yossi Ben Ari, *"Omanut Ha'Modi'in: Kal Me'od Le'Ha-tria, Kashe Yoter La'Hargiya . . . Al Katzin Mode'in Mushlam,"* *Mabat Ma'Lam*, Issue 91, March 2022.
4 Tim Weiner, "C.I.A. Officers, With Israel's Knowledge, Teach Palestinians the Tricks of the Trade," *New York Times*, March 5, 1998.
5 Yossi Melman and Dan Raviv, "Spies Like Us," *Tablet*, April 8, 2010.
6 "Former Palestinian Islamic Jihad Leader Ramadan Shalah Dies at 62," *Times of Israel*, June 7, 2020.
7 Joel Greenberg, "Islamic Group Vows Revenge for Slaying of Its Leader, *New York Times*, October 30, 1995.
8 Yossi Melman, *"Be'Hazara Le'Zirat He'Pesha'a,"* *Haaretz*, September 24, 2007.
9 Alan Cowell, "The Daring Attack That Blew Up in Israel's Face," *New York Times*, October 15, 1997.
10 Cowell, "The Daring Attack."
11 Amir Bar Shalom, "Begging Royal Mercy: How Israel Recovered from the Botched Mashaal Hit, 25 Years Ago," *Times of Israel*, August 24, 2022.
12 Bergman, *Rise and Kill First*, p. 485.
13 *"Intimi Im Rafi Reshef,"* N12 News, March 26, 2025.
14 Serge Schmemann, "Mossad Chief Quits but Defends His Role in Jordan Fiasco," *New York Times*, February 25, 1998.

15 Itamar Levin, *"Danny Yatom Hitpater Me'Roshit Ha'Mossad Be'Akavot Ha'Bikoret Ha'Kasha Be'Parashat Meshal,"* *Globus*, February 25, 1998.
16 Interview, Ari Harow, December 19, 2024.
17 Yossi Melman, *"Et Mi Nehasel Ha'Boker,"* *Haaretz*, February 16, 2005.

CHAPTER NINETEEN  The Architect

1 *"Zohar Palti: Mutrad Me'Ha'Hasha'a Shel Suria al Yarden. Im Yikre Ma'She'Hu Nehiyeh Be-Seret She Lo Hayinu Bo Be'Olam,"* Nadav Peri's Podcast, December 22, 2024.
2 "The Mount Dov Abductions," *Ynet*, March 12, 2009.
3 TOI Staff, "Bill Clinton: Young Americans Shocked to Learn Arafat Turned Down Palestinian State," *Times of Israel*, December 5, 2024.
4 Interview with Tamir Pardo, Israel, June 20, 2024.
5 Interview with Sami Mutzafi Barak, Ashdod, November 11, 2024.
6 *"Al Meir Dagan She'Halch Le'Olamo,"* interview with Danny Yatom, *Arutz Ha'Knesset*, March 16, 2016, https://www.youtube.com/watch?v=FFDdXLvGFdM&t=1s.
7 Yossi Melman, *"Rosh Ha'Mossad Ha'Yotze Be'Va'adat Bach: He'Edafti Minui Mi'Toch Ha'Irgun,"* *Haaretz*, September 19, 2002.
8 *"Zohar Palti: Mutrad Me'Ha'Hasha'a Shel Suria al Yarden."*
9 Ahiya Raved, *"Meir Dagan Nitman: 'Semel Ma'avar Me'Shoah Le'Tkuma,"* *Ynet*, March 20, 2016.
10 Interview with Sami Mutzafi Barak, Ashdod, November 11, 2024.

CHAPTER TWENTY  At the Head of the Table

1 Efrat Weiss, Diana Behor, Felix Frisch, and Dor Cohen, *"Harugim Ve'Ptzuim Be'Mitkafat Terror Al Yisraelim Be'Kenya,"* *Yediot Aharonot*, November 28, 2002.
2 Interview, New York City, November 27, 2023.
3 https://www.intelligence.org.il/?module=articles&item_id=17&article_id=54&art_category_id=23.
4 Gordon Thomas, "Mossad's License to Kill," *Telegraph*, February 17, 2010.
5 *"Divuach: Yechidat Kidon Shel Ha'Mossad Ehrait Le'Hisul,"* *Yediot Aharonot*, November 16, 2020.
6 Interview, Ramat HaHayl, January 3, 2024.
7 Interview, Tel Aviv, December 31, 2023.
8 Interview, Herzliya, January 1, 2024.
9 Interview, Udi Levi, Central Israel, December 29, 2023.
10 Shimon Shifer and Gad Lior, *"155 Anshei Mossad: Hichlatnu Lifrosh,"* *Yediot Aharonot*, April 7, 2003.
11 Interview with Hagai Hadas, Northern Israel, December 27, 2023.
12 *Dagan, Ha'Milhama Ha'Aharona*, Episode 4, Yes TV, December 2024.
13 *Dagan, Ha'Milhama Ha'Aharona*, Episode 4.
14 Ronen Bergman, *"Ba Le'Mossad Bahur Hadash,"* *Yediot Aharonot*, April 22, 2003.
15 "Bomb in Lebanon Kills Suspected Qaeda Figure," *New York Times*, March 2, 2003.
16 "Palestinian Militant Slain in Damascus," *Chicago Tribune*, September 27, 2004.

CHAPTER TWENTY-ONE Friends, Enemies, New Alliances

1  Yossi Melman, "'Herr Hezbollah': The German Spy Who Mediated Between Israel and Terror Groups Speaks for First Time," *Haaretz*, September 23, 2021.
2  Ronen Bergman, "Gilad Shalit and the Rising Price of an Israeli Life," *New York Times Magazine*, November 9, 2011.
3  Greg Myre, "Sharon Urges Trade of 400 Arabs for an Israeli and Remains of 3," *New York Times*, November 7, 2003.
4  Interview, Tel Aviv, November 23, 2024.
5  "Prisoners Swapped in Cologne and Israel," *DW*, January 29, 2004.
6  https://www.goldameir.org.il/index.php?dir=site&page=content&cs=5155&lang page=heb
7  David Ignatius, "Pasha of the Spies," *Oregonian*, December 14, 2009.
8  Ian Black, "Fear of a Shia Full Moon," *Guardian*, January 26, 2007.
9  Brian Murphy, "Shabtai Shavit, Mossad Chief Who Helped Open Jordan Peace Talks, Dead at 84," *Washington Post*, September 13, 2023.
10  Interview, Tel Aviv, June 24, 2024.
11  Patrick Devenny, "The List: The Middle East's Most Powerful Spooks," *Foreign Policy*, July 20, 2009.
12  https://catalog.archives.gov.il/site/chapter/mivtza-yachin/.
13  Yossi Melman, "Assassination, Bribes, and Smuggling Jews: Inside the Israeli Mossad's Long Secret Alliance with Morocco," *Haaretz*, December 17, 2020.
14  https://www.kan.org.il/content/kan-news/local/253458/.
15  "A Look at Israel's Decades-Long Covert Intelligence Ties with Morocco," *Times of Israel*, December 11, 2020.
16  "*Shalom Dan Be'Morocco al Hidush Ha'Yahasim Bein Ha'Medinot*," *Haaretz*, September 2, 2003.
17  "Sub-Saharan Africa: Growing Iranian Activity: A Research Paper," Central Intelligence Agency: Office of Africa and Latin America Analysis, December 1984.
18  Sheera Frankel, "Azerbaijan: Where East Meets West, a Den of Spies," NPR, February 17, 2012.
19  Interview, Tel Aviv, January 1, 2024.
20  Interview with Ram Ben Barak, Jerusalem, June 26, 2024.
21  https://www.youtube.com/watch?v=imM7i5oLce0.
22  Interview, Tel Aviv, June 24, 2024.
23  Interview, Herzliya, January 1, 2024.
24  https://www.youtube.com/watch?v=imM7i5oLce0.
25  Interview, Ramat Ha'Hayal, January 3, 2024.

CHAPTER TWENTY-TWO The Race to Stop the Bomb

1  "Israel's Illusion," *New York Times*, June 9, 1981.
2  Jonathan Steele, "The Bush Doctrine Makes Nonsense of the UN Charter," *Guardian*, June 6, 2002.
3  John F. Burns, "Nuclear Anxiety: The Overview; Pakistan Answers India, Carries Out Nuclear Test; Clinton's Appeals Rejected," *New York Times*, May 29, 1998.

4  Ian Traynor, "Pakistan Admits It Might Be the Source of Iran's Nuclear Expertise," *Guardian*, December 23, 2003.
5  "The Muammar Gaddafi Story," *BBC News*, October 21, 2011.
6  Carla Anne Robbins, "In Giving Up Arms, Libya Hopes to Gain New Economic Life," *Wall Street Journal*, February 12, 2004.
7  "Ex-SS Man Worked for Mossad Against Egyptian Rocket Project," *Jerusalem Post*, September 20, 1989.
8  Ronen Bergman, "The Secret History of Israel's War Against Hitler's Scientists," *Newsweek*, April 12, 2018.
9  Interview with David Meidan, Herzliya, January 1, 2024.
10 Interview with David Meidan, Herzliya, January 1, 2024.
11 Suzan Quitaz, "The Historic Ties Between Israel and the Kurds of Iraq Will Continue," *Jerusalem Center for Security and Foreign Affairs*, No. 663, June 2023.
12 Wolf Blitzer, "Mossad-CIA Ties Legacy of Casey and Angleton," *Wall Street Journal*, May 22, 1987.
13 Blitzer, "Mossad-CIA Ties Legacy."
14 Uri Dan, "Tenet Warned of Israeli Spy," *New York Post*, August 8, 2004.
15 David Horovitz, "How Israel's Leaders Use Targeted Killings to Try to 'Stop History,'" *Times of Israel*, January 26, 2018.
16 Interview, Tel Aviv, November 16, 2024.
17 Robert D. Hershey, Jr., "Senate Confirms Tenet as C.I.A.'s Director," *New York Times*, July 11, 1997.

CHAPTER TWENTY-THREE  The Disruptors

1  https://www.youtube.com/watch?v=imM7i5oLce0.
2  Interview, Tel Aviv, December 27, 2023.
3  Interview, Tel Aviv, December 31, 2023.
4  https://www.youtube.com/watch?v=imM7i5oLce0.
5  Chris McGreal, Conal Urquhart, and Richard Norton-Taylor, "The British Suicide Bombers," *Guardian*, April 30, 2003.
6  John Ward Anderson and Molly Moore, "Hamas Leader Killed in Gaza," *Washington Post*, March 21, 2004.
7  Interview, Ramat Gan, April 12, 2016.
8  Darshan-Leitner and Katz, *Harpoon*, p. 106.
9  Darshan-Leitner and Katz, *Harpoon*, p. 90.
10 Darshan-Leitner and Katz, *Harpoon*, p. 108.
11 https://www.fbi.gov/history/famous-cases/willie-sutton.
12 Stephanie Clifford, "Arab Bank Reaches Settlement in Suit Accusing It of Financing Terrorism," *New York Times*, August 14, 2015.
13 "Report: Sharon Brain Disease Caused Stroke," NBC News, January 10, 2006.

CHAPTER TWENTY-FOUR  Meirke

1  Interview with Ehud Olmert, Tel Aviv, January 2, 2024.
2  Interview with Ehud Olmert, Tel Aviv, January 2, 2024.

3 *"Bdidoto Shel Rams'ad: Avodato Shel Rosh Ha'Irgun Ha'Hashe'I Be'Yoter Be'Ysirael,"* *Forbes (Israel)*, April 9, 2017.
4 "Bush: U.S. Would Aid Israel if Attacked," CNN, May 23, 2006.
5 Interview with one of Dagan's division chiefs, Tel Aviv, September 18, 2016.
6 Interview with Ehud Olmert, January 2, 2024.
7 Chris O'Malley, "Information Warriors of the 609th," *Popular Science*, July 1997.
8 "Israel Army Chief Admits Failures," BBC News, August 24, 2006.
9 Interview, Washington D.C., December 22, 2023
10 Interview, New York, May 11, 2022.
11 Adam Ciralsky, Lisa Myers, and the NBC News Investigative Unit, "Hezbollah Banks Under Attack in Lebanon," NBC News, July 24, 2006.
12 Ciralsky, Myers, and NBC, "Hezbollah Banks Under Attack."
13 Rory McCarthy, "Hezbollah Leader: We Regret the Two Kidnappings That Led to War with Israel," *Guardian*, August 27, 2006.

CHAPTER TWENTY-FIVE  The Other Sons of Abraham

1 Guy Britzman, *"Bachir Ha'Mossad Le'Sha'avar: Kvar Be-2005 Hipasnu Kesher I'm Ihud Ha'Ameriot,"* Kan, August 27, 2020.
2 Interview with David Meidan, Herzliya, January 1, 2024.
3 Interview with David Meidan, Herzliya, January 1, 2024.
4 https://www.youtube.com/watch?v=imM7i5oLce0.
5 Roi Mandel, "WikiLeaks: Arab World According to Mossad Chief," *Ynet*, November 29, 2010.
6 Pazit Rabina, *"Be'Derech Le'Normalizatzia: Ha'Tango Ha'Hasha'I Aroch Shanim She'Hitnahel Bein Yisrael Le'Saudiya,"* *Makor Rishon*, September 29, 2023.
7 Rabina, *"Be'Derech Le'Normalizatzia."*
8 Tamara Nasser, "How Saudi Arabia Supported Israel's 2006 War on Lebanon," The Electronic Intifada, February 25, 2019.
9 Yonah Jeremy Bob and Ilan Evyatar, *Target Tehran: How Israel Is Using Sabotage, Cyberwarfare, Assassination—and Secret Diplomacy—to Stop a Nuclear Iran and Create a New Middle East* (New York: Simon and Schuster, 2023), p. 49.
10 Rabina, *"Be'Derech Le'Normalizatzia."*
11 Interview, Kfar Saba, November 23, 2024.

CHAPTER TWENTY-SIX  Alpha!

1 https://www.youtube.com/watch?v=8hQYjoas2H8.
2 Dagan, *"Ha'Milhama Ha'Achorna: Yad Ha'Mikre,"* Episode 4.
3 Dagan, *"Ha'Milhama Ha'Achorna: Yad Ha'Mikre,"* Episode 4.
4 Abdulah Alghadawi, "The Fourth Division: Syria's Parallel Army," Middle East Institute, September 24, 2021.
5 Erich Follath and Holgar Stark, "How Israel Destroyed Syria's Al Kibar Nuclear Reactor," *Spiegel International*, November 2, 2009.
6 Interview with Ram Ben Barak, Jerusalem, June 26, 2024.

7 Judah Ari Gross, "Ex-Mossad Chief: Only 'Luck' Corrected 'Intelligence Failure' on Syria," *Times of Israel*, March 21, 2018.

8 Yonah Jeremy Bob, "Analysis: Israel's Intelligence Battle Over 2007 Syrian Nuclear Operation," *Jerusalem Post*, March 21, 2018.

9 "Kebel Arizona: *Kach Hishmid Heyl Ha'Avir et Ha'Kur Ha'Suri*," Kan/Hadashot, March 20, 2018.

10 *Dagan, Ha'Milhama Ha'Aharona*," Episode 4.

11 Nicholas Blanford, "The Mystery Behind a Syrian Murder," *Time*, August 7, 2008.

12 *Ha'Milhama Ha'Achorna: Yad Ha'Mikre.* Episode 4.

13 Nak Thyer, "The Violent Consequences of the North Korea–Syria Arms Trade," *NK News*, June 20, 2013.

14 Michael V. Hayden, *Playing to the Edge: American Intelligence in the Age of Terror* (New York: Penguin Press, 2016), p. 265.

15 David Makovsky, "The Silent Strike," *New Yorker*, September 10, 2012.

16 Interview with Ehud Olmert, Tel Aviv, January 2, 2024.

17 https://www.youtube.com/watch?v=cpCqCNPHJBU.

18 Interview with Michael Hayden, December 8, 2023.

19 https://www.youtube.com/watch?v=imM7i5oLce0.

20 Dick Cheney with Liz Cheney, *In My Time: A Personal and Political Memoir* (New York: Threshold Editions, 2011), p. 466.

21 Interview, April 16, 2024.

22 Cheney with Cheney, *In My Time*, p. 468.

23 George W. Bush, *Decision Points* (New York: Crown Publishers, 2010), p. 414.

24 https://www.youtube.com/watch?v=cpCqCNPHJBU.

25 Interview with Ehud Olmert, Tel Aviv, January 2, 2024.

26 Uzi Mahnaimi, Sarah Baxter, and Michael Sheridan, "Snatched: Israel Commandos 'Nuclear' Raid," *Sunday Times*, September 23, 2007.

27 "Kebel Arizona: *Kach Hishmid Heyl Ha'Avir et Ha'Kur Ha'Suri*."

28 https://www.youtube.com/watch?v=cpCqCNPHJBU.

29 Interview with Ehud Olmert, Tel Aviv, January 2, 2024.

CHAPTER TWENTY-SEVEN **Code Name Wild Child**

1 Ronen Bergman, "Ex-CIA Director: I Was Sure If We Didn't Strike Syria's Nuclear Reactor, Israel Would," *Ynet*, December 30, 2016.

2 Interview, Tel Aviv, November 15, 2024.

3 https://www.youtube.com/watch?v=u4xvxyXu_PY.

4 https://www.youtube.com/watch?v=u4xvxyXu_PY.

5 "Iranian Cleric Who Helped Create Hezbollah Dies of COVID," *Iran International*, June 7, 2021.

6 https://www.youtube.com/watch?v=_tYEhhk8J_o.

7 Interview with Meir Dagan, Tel Aviv, September 8, 2015.

8 *Dagan: Ha'Milhama Ha'Aharona—Perek 3, Even Ha'Rosha.*

9 *Dagan: Ha'Milhama Ha'Aharona—Perek 3, Even Ha'Rosha.*

10 Ali Alfoneh, "Brigadier General Qassem Suleimani: A Biography," *American Enterprise Institute for Public Policy Research*, No. 1, January 2011.
11 https://x.com/ghadifrancis/status/1864959867011694645.
12 Bergman, *Rise and Kill First*, p. 159.
13 *Dagan: Ha'Milhama Ha'Aharona—Perek 3, Even Ha'Rosha.*
14 Adam Goldman and Ellen Nakashima, "CIA and Mossad Killed Senior Hezbollah Figure in Car Bombing," *Washington Post*, January 20, 2015.
15 https://www.archives.gov/federal-register/codification/executive-order/12333.html.
16 Matthew Levitt, "Why the CIA Killed Imad Mughniyeh," *Politico*, February 9, 2015.
17 TOI Staff, "In First, Olmert Confirms Israel Killed Hezbollah Chief Mughniyeh in Syria in 2008," *Times of Israel*, September 29, 2024.
18 Interview, Tel Aviv, November 21, 2024.
19 Interview with Ehud Olmert, Tel Aviv, January 2, 2024.
20 Interview, Tel Aviv, December 31, 2023.
21 Goldman and Nakashima, "CIA and Mossad Killed Senior Hezbollah Figure."
22 Ian Black, "WikiLeaks Cables: Syria Stunned by Hezbollah Assassination," *Guardian*, December 7, 2010.
23 "Gazans Celebrate at Sight of Coffins Turned Over by Hizbullah," *Jerusalem Post*, July 16, 2008.
24 *Dagan: Ha'Milhama Ha'Aharona—Perek 3, Even Ha'Rosha.*

CHAPTER TWENTY-EIGHT **New Bosses, Different World**

1 Interview with Ehud Lavi, Tel Aviv, June 20, 2024.
2 Uzi Mahnaimi, "Looking for Love: Livni the Lonely Spy," *Sunday Times*, February 15, 2009.
3 Scott Shane, "Blunt Words by Biden and Panetta at C.I.A.," *New York Times*, February 19, 2009.
4 Interview with Leon Panetta, United States, August 16, 2024.
5 Courtesy of CIA Public Affairs, February 24, 2025.
6 Interview with Leon Panetta, United States, August 16, 2024.
7 Stuart Winer, "Dutch Mole Planted Stuxnet Virus in Iran Nuclear Site on Behalf of CIA, Mossad," *Times of Israel*, September 3, 2019.
8 Interview with David Meidan, Israel, January 1, 2024.
9 Interview with Leon Panetta, United States, August 16, 2024.
10 Leon Panetta, *Worthy Fights: A Memoir of Leadership in War and Peace* (New York: Penguin Books, 2015), p. 273.
11 Interview, March 24, 2025.
12 Interview, January 3, 2024.
13 Interview with Ehud Olmert, Tel Aviv, January 2, 2025.
14 Ronen Bergman, "The Dubai Job," *GQ*, January 4, 2011.
15 "WikiLeaks: Arab World According to Dagan," *Ynet*, November 29, 2010.
16 Interview with Udi Levi, Modi'in, January 1, 2024.
17 Anshel Pfeffer, "Mossad Chief Reportedly Visited Saudi Arabia for Talks on Iran," *Haaretz*, July 26, 2010.

18  Yossi Melman, "Former Mossad Chief: Israel Air Strike on Iran 'Stupidest Thing I Have Ever Heard," *Haaretz*, May 7, 2011.

19  *Dagan: Ha'Milhama Ha'Aharona—Perek 5, Anashim Regilim.*

20  Interview with Ari Harow (former Netanyahu chief of staff), March 24, 2025.

21  Anshel Pfeffer, "The Israelis Who Prevented a War with Iran," *Foreign Policy*, May 11, 2018.

22  Ronen Bergman, "When Israel Hatched a Secret Plan to Assassinate Iranian Scientists," *Politico*, March 6, 2018.

CHAPTER TWENTY-NINE  **End of Term**

1  Bergman, "The Dubai Job."

2  *Time* Staff, "How Israel Foiled an Arms Convoy Bound for Hamas," *Time*, March 30, 2009.

3  "Report: Naval Commando Forces Involved in Sudan Strike," *Ynet*, August 4, 2009.

4  Ilan Evyatar, "Smoke, Mirrors, Cloaks, and Daggers," *Jerusalem Post*, September 24, 2010.

5  Ronen Bergman et al., "The Anatomy of Mossad's Dubai Operation," *Spiegel International*, January 17, 2011.

6  Siham Al Najami, "New Suspect in Al Mabhouh Murder in Dubai," *Gulf News*, September 15, 2018.

7  Danna Harman, "Dubai Assassination Spotlights Top Cop Skills in a Modern-Day Casablanca," *Christian Science Monitor*, March 19, 2010.

8  "'Mossad' Hit Snares Australians," *Sydney Morning Herald*, February 26, 2010.

9  Bergman, "The Dubai Job."

10  Interview with Ehud Lavi, Tel Aviv, June 20, 2024.

11  https://www.youtube.com/watch?v=-piIF-xHFw4.

CHAPTER THIRTY  **A Warrior's Epitaph**

1  Ben Hartman, "Ex-Mossad Chief at Anti-Netanyahu Rally: Our Leadership Scares Me More Than Our Enemies," *Jerusalem Post*, March 7, 2015.

2  Yuval Hirshorn, "Inside Black Cube—The 'Mossad' of the Business World," *Forbes Israel*, June 9, 2018.

3  Interview with Udi Levi, Tel Aviv, June 18, 2024.

4  Interview with Udi Levi, Modi'in, December 31, 2023.

5  Interview, Zohar Palti, Tel Aviv, November 18, 2024.

6  *"Dagan Yuva Ha'Yom Le'Kvura: Le'Bakashat Mishpachto Ha'Levaya Lo Te'Sukar,"* *Haaretz*, March 20, 2016.

7  https://www.youtube.com/watch?v=Z7s_mO_lXPo.

8  Yair Kraus, *"Ha'Nasi Rivlin Safad Le'Dagan: 'Dugma U'Mofet Le'Giburei Yisrael,"* *Makor Rishon*, March 20, 2016.

9  Judah Ari Gross, "From Friends and Enemies, Posthumous Praise for Meir Dagan," *Times of Israel*, March 17, 2016.

10  Ahiya Raved, *"Aba Shel Sof Shavu'a: Meir Dagan Nitman,"* *Ynet*, March 20, 2016.

11 "Prime Minister Benjamin Netanyahu's Remarks at the Funeral of the Former Director of the Mossad, Meir Dagan," March 23, 2016.
12 Interview with Leon Panetta, United States, August 16, 2024.

EPILOGUE **Never Again**

1 Emanuel Fabian, "Hamas Leaders Asked Iran for $500 Million in 2021 to Destroy Israel Within 2 Years, Documents Revealed by Katz Show," *Times of Israel*, April 6, 2025.
2 Ronen Bergman and Adam Goldman, "Israel Knew Hamas's Attack Plan More Than a Year Ago," *New York Times*, November 30, 2023.
3 TOI Staff, "Surveillance Soldiers Charge Sexism a Factor in Their Oct. 7 Warnings Being Ignored," *Times of Israel*, November 19, 2023.
4 https://youtu.be/Bh7Hm7gpXvA?si=b_tdH82lEigAM8ll.
5 Adam Goldman, Ronen Bergman, Julian Barnes, and Aaron Boxerman, "As Hezbollah Threat Loomed, Israel Built Up Its Spy Agencies," *New York Times*, September 28, 2024.
6 Mehul Srivastava, James Shotter, Charles Clover, and Raya Jalabi, "How Israel's Spies Penetrated Hezbollah," *Financial Times*, September 29, 2024.
7 Interview, Austin, Texas, December 11, 2024.
8 Mark Mazzetti, Sheera Frankel, and Ronen Bergman, "Behind the Dismantling of Hezbollah: Decades of Israeli Intelligence," *New York Times*, December 29, 2024.
9 Mazzetti, Frankel, and Bergman, "Behind the Dismantling of Hezbollah."
10 "Hezbollah Device Blasts: How Did Pagers and Walkie-Talkies Explode and What Do We Know About the Attacks?" *Guardian*, September 18, 2024.
11 Danielle Wallace, "Israeli Spy Network Uncovers Hezbollah Commander's Plans to Marry His 4 Mistresses," Fox News, December 30, 2024.
12 "Former CIA Director: Israel Pager Attack 'A Form of Terrorism,'" *Jerusalem Post*, September 23, 2024.

POSTSCRIPT **Rising Lions and Midnight Hammers**

1 Amos Yadlin, "Why Israel Had to Act," *New York Times*, June 21, 2025.
2 Naval Frieberg and Emanuel Fabian, "Mossad Hails Israel's 'Historic' Iran Offensive, Thanks CIA in Rare Public Message," *Times of Israel*, June 25, 2025.

**Glossary**

1 Alon Ben-David, "*Ha'Atid Shel Kesaria:cumb Kach Meshane Ha'Yechida Ha'Mivtzait Shel Ha'Mossad Et Pane'ha*," Maariv Online, February 4, 2022.
2 Ian Black, "Shadowy and Deadly—the Long Arm of the Mossad," *Guardian*, February 16, 2010.

# Image Credits

# Index

Baghdad, 108, 238, 249–50
Bahrain, 167
Baku, 230
Bandar bin Sultan al-Saud, Prince, 270–71
Bangkok, 232
Barak, Ehud, 25, 26, 91, 163–64, 166n, 174, 176, 179, 197, 229, 244, 283–84, 308, 312, 313
  Camp David Summit and, 200
  Dagan and, 163–64, 179, 197, 308
  elected prime minister, 198–99
  IDF forces withdrawn from Lebanon by, 199–200
  resignation of, 201
  second intifada and, 201
Barak, Sami Mutzafi, 49, 151–53, 189
Bar-Lev, Haim, 48
Barnea, David "Dadi," 242n, 337, 345
Barzani, Masoud, 243
Bat Yam, 15–17, 20, 22, 27, 31, 33, 52, 77, 78, 82, 99
Bedouins, 57–58, 71, 72, 169
Beersheba, 218
Begin, Menachem, 78, 97, 104, 107–10, 119, 128, 137, 257
  Adam appointed as Mossad head by, 126
  Iraqi reactor and, 236, 280
  Operation Olympia and, 110–11
Beirut, 44, 71, 74, 95, 101, 102, 107, 116–17, 137, 139, 141, 144, 153, 291, 295, 296, 339–41
  bombings in, 143–45, 262, 291–92, 295
  Dahya section of, 267
  in Operation Peace for Galilee, 119, 121, 122, 124–33
  Sabra and Shatila Massacres in, 133, 140
Beirut-Damascus Highway, 263
Beirut International Airport, 128–31, 133, 263, 266, 291–92
Beit al-Mal, 265
Belarus, 325
Ben Barak, Ram, 232, 278, 349

Ben Barka, Mehdi, 228
Ben-Gal, Avigdor, 99–100, 104, 105, 109, 111
Ben-Gurion, David, 18, 118, 188, 240
Ben Hanan, Yossi, 49–50, 98, 180–81
Ben-Reuven, Eyal, 114, 122, 125, 127, 131
Ben-Yishai, Ron, 71
Bergman, Ronen, 70n
Bibas family, 331, 332
Biden, Joe, 304–5, 339
Big Pines, 118
bin Laden, Osama, 202, 210, 217, 229, 253
  killing of, 307
Bird, Kai, 290n
Birds of Prey operation, 317
BKA, 221
Black Cube, 324
Black September civil war, 46, 97, 170, 193, 224
Black September Organization, 75, 101, 212, 290n, 291
BND, 206, 221, 224, 231
bombs, bombings
  airplane, 74–75, 129n, 220n, 238
  in Beersheba, 218
  in Beirut, 143–45, 262, 291–92, 295
  of buses, 74, 176, 179–80
  of Drakkar building, 144–45
  of embassies, 143–44, 291, 292, 295, 295n, 340
  in Jerusalem, 108, 187, 192, 193
  letter, 75
  Mughniyeh's involvement in, 291–92
  of Paradise Hotel, 209–10
  of Radisson Hotel, 225
  school bus, 74, 176
  subway, 192
  suicide, xxiii, 136–38, 144–45, 168, 175–76, 180, 185–87, 192, 193, 201–2, 218, 225n, 229, 251, 253, 291, 292, 317
  in Tel Aviv, 176, 202, 251
  in Tyre, 136–38, 144, 145, 291
  of U.S. Marine Corps barracks, 144, 262, 291–92, 295, 295n, 339, 340

World War II, xxii, xxxin, 3, 5, 9, 10, 55, 56, 87, 188, 244, 250

Ya'alon, Moshe, 327
Yaari, Ehud, 292
Yadlin, Amos, 259, 276, 284, 306–7, 345
Yamadayev, Sulim, 319n
Ya'ma'm, 96n
Yanai, Shlomo, 202–3
Yariv, Aharon, 55
Yaron, Amos, 124, 127
Yasin, Ahmed, 158, 195, 220, 251–52
Yassin, Mohammed (Abu Nimer), 62–64

Yatom, Danny, 26, 188, 193–96, 204, 244
Yatom, Ehud, 188
*Yediot Aharonot*, 70n
Yemen, 13, 344
Yiddish, 4, 6
Yishuv, 56n
Yom Kippur War (1973), 80–90, 98, 101, 111, 113, 125, 224–25, 229, 233, 241–42, 257, 333, 334
Yovell, Yoram, 19

Zaidan, Muhammed (Abu Abbas), 105n
al-Zarqawi, Abu Musab, 225

# About the Author

Samuel M. Katz is a *New York Times* bestselling author who has written over twenty books on the Arab Israeli conflict, military and law enforcement special operations, espionage, and counterterrorism. He has written hundreds of articles for magazines and journals around the world, as well as documentaries for television. He is also the former editor in chief of *Special Operations Report*, a trade publication for the world's commando and counterterrorist community. Katz lectures police agencies and military commands around the world on the history of terrorism, and he is a frequent guest on television and radio networks.